# Learning Microsoft® PowerPoint® 2010

**Chris Katsaropoulos**

**Katherine Murray**

**Christy Parrish**

**Faithe Wempen**

PEARSON

Prentice Hall

Boston • Columbus • Indianapolis • New York • San Francisco • Upper Saddle River
Amsterdam • Cape Town • Dubai • London • Madrid • Milan • Munich • Paris • Montreal • Toronto
Delhi • Mexico City • Sao Paulo • Sydney • Hong Kong • Seoul • Singapore • Taipei • Tokyo

**Editor in Chief:** Michael Payne
**Product Development Manager:**
 Eileen Bien Calabro
**Editorial Assistant:** Nicole Sam
**Director of Marketing:** Kate Valentine
**Marketing Manager:** Tori Olson Alves
**Marketing Coordinator:** Susan Osterlitz
**Marketing Assistant:** Darshika Vyas
**Senior Managing Editor:** Cynthia Zonneveld
**Associate Managing Editor:** Camille Trentacoste
**Production Project Manager:** Lynne Breitfeller
**Operations Director:** Alexis Heydt

**Senior Operations Specialist:** Natacha Moore
**Text and Cover Designer:** Vanessa Moore
**Media Development Manager:** Cathi Profitko
**VP, Director of Digital Development:** Zara Wanlass
**Media Project Manager, Editorial:** Alana Coles
**Media Project Manager, Production:** John Cassar
**Editorial and Product Development:** Emergent Learning, LLC
**Composition:** Vanessa Moore
**Printer/Binder:** R.R. Donnelly Menasha
**Cover Printer:** Lehigh-Pheonix Color
**Text:** 10/12 Helvetica

Credits and acknowledgements borrowed from other sources and reproduced, with permission, in this textbook are as follows: All photos courtesy of Shutterstock.com.

Microsoft® and Windows® are registered trademarks of the Microsoft Corporation in the U.S.A. and other countries. Screen shots and icons reprinted with permission from the Microsoft Corporation. This book is not sponsored or endorsed by or affiliated with the Microsoft Corporation.

Many of the designations by manufacturers and seller to distinguish their products are claimed as trademarks. Where those designations appear in this book, and the publisher was aware of a trademark claim, the designations have been printed in initial caps or all caps.

3 4 5 6 7 8 9 10  V064  16 15 14 13

Prentice Hall
is an imprint of

**www.pearsonhighered.com**

ISBN 10: 0-13-511209-5
ISBN 13: 978-0-13-511209-0

# Table of Contents

*Introduction* . . . . . . . . . . . . . . . . . . . . . . *vii*

## Chapter 1
## Getting Started with Microsoft PowerPoint 2010 . . . . . . . . . . 2

**Lesson 1** – Getting Started with PowerPoint . . . . . . . 4
**Lesson 2** – Working with Slides . . . . . . . . . . . . . . 12
**Lesson 3** – Working with Notes and Headers and Footers . . . . . . . . . . . . . . . . . 19
**Lesson 4** – Inserting and Formatting Pictures . . . . . 25
**Lesson 5** – Formatting Text . . . . . . . . . . . . . . . 30
**Lesson 6** – Aligning Text . . . . . . . . . . . . . . . 36
**Lesson 7** – Displaying the Presentation Outline . . . . 43
**Lesson 8** – Arranging Slides . . . . . . . . . . . . . . 47
**Lesson 9** – Adding Slide Transitions . . . . . . . . . . . 51
End-of-Chapter Assessments . . . . . . . . . . . . . . . . . 55

## Chapter 2
## Working with Lists and Graphics . . . . . . . . . . . . 58

**Lesson 10** – Working with Bulleted and Numbered Lists . . . . . . . . . . . . . . . 60
**Lesson 11** – Using Clip Art Pictures . . . . . . . . . . . 67
**Lesson 12** – Inserting Symbols and Text Boxes . . . . . 73
**Lesson 13** – Drawing and Formatting Shapes . . . . . . 79
**Lesson 14** – Positioning and Grouping Shapes . . . . . 88
**Lesson 15** – Creating WordArt . . . . . . . . . . . . . . 94
**Lesson 16** – Creating SmartArt Diagrams . . . . . . . 100
**Lesson 17** – Creating a Photo Album . . . . . . . . . . 108
End-of-Chapter Assessments . . . . . . . . . . . . . . . . . 111

## Chapter 3
## Enhancing a Presentation . . . 114

**Lesson 18** – Modifying a Theme . . . . . . . . . . . . . 116
**Lesson 19** – Modifying a Background . . . . . . . . . . 121
**Lesson 20** – Using Effects and Animations . . . . . . . 128
**Lesson 21** – Creating Multimedia Presentations . . . 133
**Lesson 22** – Working with Tables . . . . . . . . . . . . 141
**Lesson 23** – Working with Charts . . . . . . . . . . . . 147
End-of-Chapter Assessments . . . . . . . . . . . . . . . . . 153

## Chapter 4
## Finalizing a Presentation . . . 156

**Lesson 24** – Working with Slide Masters . . . . . . . 158
**Lesson 25** – Using Presentation Templates and Linked Objects . . . . . . . . . . . . . 166
**Lesson 26** – Customizing Themes and Templates . . . . . . . . . . . . . . . . . 173
**Lesson 27** – Enhancing a Slide Show . . . . . . . . . 180
**Lesson 28** – Preparing for a Slide Show . . . . . . . . 185
**Lesson 29** – Reviewing and Finalizing a Presentation . . . . . . . . . . . . . . . 193
**Lesson 30** – Distributing a Presentation . . . . . . . . 199
End-of-Chapter Assessments . . . . . . . . . . . . . . . . . 208

## Chapter 5
## Working with Masters, Comments, Handouts, and Pictures . . . . . . . . . . . . . 210

**Lesson 31** – Advanced Slide Master Features . . . .212
**Lesson 32** – Working with Notes and Handouts . . .218
**Lesson 33** – Working with Comments in a Presentation . . . . . . . . . . . . . . . . . . .225
**Lesson 34** – Exporting Slide Handouts to Word. . . .231
**Lesson 35** – Working with Presentation Properties. . . . . . . . . . . . . . . . . . . . .236
**Lesson 36** – Making a Presentation Accessible to Everyone . . . . . . . . . . . . . . . . . . .242
End-of-Chapter Assessments . . . . . . . . . . . . . . . . .247

## Chapter 6
## Applying Advanced Graphic and Media Techniques . . . . . 252

**Lesson 37** – Advanced Picture Formatting . . . . . . .254
**Lesson 38** – Advanced Multimedia Features. . . . . .261
**Lesson 39** – Working with Advanced Photo Album Features. . . . . . . . . . . . . . . . .267
**Lesson 40** – Advanced Animation Features . . . . . .273
**Lesson 41** – Finalizing Slide Shows . . . . . . . . . . . .284
**Lesson 42** – Working with Actions . . . . . . . . . . . . .290
End-of-Chapter Assessments . . . . . . . . . . . . . . . . .296

## Chapter 7
## Creating Presentations Using Tables and Charts . . . 300

**Lesson 43** – Drawing and Adjusting Tables. . . . . . .302
**Lesson 44** – Formatting Tables . . . . . . . . . . . . . . . .310
**Lesson 45** – Formatting Charts . . . . . . . . . . . . . . . .317
**Lesson 46** – Adding Objects to Your Presentation . . . . . . . . . . . . . . . . . . .322
End-of-Chapter Assessments . . . . . . . . . . . . . . . . .327

## Chapter 8
## Publishing a Presentation. . . 332

**Lesson 47** – Customizing Your Presentation . . . . . .334
**Lesson 48** – Fine-Tuning Content Placement . . . . .341
**Lesson 49** – Searching for and Researching Content . . . . . . . . . . . . . . . . . . . . .350
**Lesson 50** – Sharing a Presentation . . . . . . . . . . .355
**Lesson 51** – Presenting on the Web. . . . . . . . . . . .360
**Lesson 52** – Protecting and Finalizing a Presentation . . . . . . . . . . . . . . . . . . .364
End-of-Chapter Assessments . . . . . . . . . . . . . . . . .368

## Index . . . . . . . . . . . . . . . . . . . . . . . . 371

# Introduction

Microsoft Office PowerPoint 2010 is Microsoft's tool for creating dynamic on-screen presentations. Use PowerPoint to build the exciting, changing, and interactive presentations that today's information-driven world demands from businesses, governments, schools, and virtually every organization that needs to communicate.

## HOW THE BOOK IS ORGANIZED

Lessons are comprised of short exercises designed for using Microsoft PowerPoint 2010 in real-life business settings. Each lesson is made up of eight key elements:

- **What You Will Learn.** Each lesson starts with an overview of the learning objectives covered in the lesson.
- **Software Skills.** Next, a brief overview of the Microsoft Office tools that you'll be working with in the lesson is provided.
- **Application Skills.** The objectives are then put into context by setting a scenario.
- **Words to Know.** Key terms are included and defined at the start of each lesson, so you can quickly refer back to them. The terms are then highlighted in the text.
- **What You Can Do.** Concise notes for learning the computer concepts.

- **Try It.** Hands-on practice activities provide brief procedures to teach all necessary skills.
- **Create It.** These projects give students a chance to create presentations by entering information. Steps provide all the how-to information needed to complete a project.
- **Apply It.** Each lesson concludes with a project that challenges students to apply what they have learned through steps that tell them what to do, without all the how-to information. In the Apply It projects, students must show they have mastered each skill set.
- Each chapter ends with two assessment projects: **Make It Your Own** and **Master It**, which incorporate all the skills covered throughout the lesson.

## WORKING WITH DATA AND SOLUTION FILES

As you work through the projects in this book, you'll be creating, opening, and saving files. You should keep the following instructions in mind:

- For many of the projects you can use the data files provided on the CD-ROM that comes with this book. Other projects will ask you to create new documents and files, and then enter text and data into them, so you can master creating documents from scratch.

- The data files are used so that you can focus on the skills being introduced—not on keyboarding lengthy documents.
- When the project steps tell you to open a file name, you can open the data file provided on CD.
- All the projects instruct you to save the files created or to save the project files under a new name that includes your first and last name as part of the file name. This is to make the project file your own, and to avoid overwriting the data file in the storage location.

- Follow your instructor's directions for where to access and save the data files on a network, local computer hard drive, or portable storage device such as a USB drive.
- Many of the projects also provide instructions for including your name in a header or footer. Again, this is to identify the project work as your own for grading and assessment purposes.
- Unless the book instructs otherwise, use the default settings for creating a file. If someone has changed the default software settings for the computer you're using, your exercise files may not look the same as those shown in this book. In addition, the appearance of your files may look different if the system is set to a screen resolution other than 1024 × 768.
- Also note that if someone has opened an Office 2010 file in a previous version of Microsoft Office, such as Office 2007, the file may open in Compatibility Mode. This means that new features from Office 2010 may not be available for use. If this happens, simply save the file as an Office 2010 document and continue working with it in Office 2010.

## WHAT'S ON THE CD

The CD contains the following:

- Data Files for many of the projects.
- Glossary of key Microsoft Office terms.
- Bonus Microsoft Office Basics chapter, which introduces essential Microsoft Office 2010 skills—including starting Microsoft Office, using the mouse and keyboard, screen elements, and an overview of the applications.

## TO ACCESS THE FILES INCLUDED ON THE CD

1. Insert the Learning Microsoft PowerPoint 2010 CD in the CD-ROM drive.
2. Navigate to your CD-ROM drive; right-click and choose Explore from the shortcut menu.
3. Right-click the folder that you wish to copy.
4. Navigate to the location where you wish to place the folder.
5. Right-click and choose Paste from the Shortcut menu.

# Learning
# Microsoft®
# PowerPoint® 2010

## Chapter 1

# Getting Started with PowerPoint

## Lesson 1
## Getting Started with PowerPoint
## Projects 1-2

- About PowerPoint
- Starting PowerPoint
- Saving a Presentation
- Opening an Existing Presentation
- Closing a Presentation
- Exploring the PowerPoint Window
- Entering Text Using Placeholders
- Applying a Theme
- Checking Spelling in a Presentation

## Lesson 2
## Working with Slides
## Projects 3-4

- Inserting New Slides
- Selecting Slide Layout
- Moving from Slide to Slide
- Changing List Levels
- Printing a Presentation

## Lesson 3
## Working with Headers, Footers, and Speaker Notes
## Projects 5-6

- Reusing Slides from Other Presentations
- Adding Speaker Notes
- Changing Slide Size and Orientation
- Inserting Headers and Footers

## Lesson 4
## Inserting and Formatting Pictures
## Projects 7-8

- Inserting a Picture from a File
- Formatting Pictures Using Styles and Artistic Effects

## Lesson 5
## Formatting Text
## Projects 9-10

- Finding and Replacing Text in a Presentation
- Selecting Text and Placeholders
- Changing the Appearance of Text Using Fonts, Font Sizes, Styles, and Colors
- Using Undo and Redo
- Clearing Formatting

## Lesson 6
## Aligning Text
## Projects 11-12

- Aligning Text
- Adjusting Line Spacing
- Adjusting Paragraph Spacing
- Moving and Copying Text
- Using AutoFit Options
- Adjusting and Formatting Placeholders

## Lesson 7
## Displaying the Presentation Outline
## Projects 13-14

- Displaying and Editing the Presentation Outline
- Viewing and Editing a Presentation in Reading View

## Lesson 8
## Arranging Slides
## Projects 15-16

- Copying, Duplicating, and Deleting Slides
- Rearranging Slides in Slide Sorter View

## Lesson 9
## Adding Slide Transitions
## Projects 17-18

- Identifying Guidelines for Using Graphics, Fonts, and Special Effects in Presentations
- Evaluating and Selecting Appropriate Sources of Information
- Adding Slide Transitions
- Controlling Slide Advance

## End of Chapter Assessments
## Projects 19-20

# Lesson 1

# Getting Started with PowerPoint

## WORDS TO KNOW

**Presentation**
A set of slides or handouts that contains information you want to convey to an audience.

**Normal View**
PowerPoint's default view that displays the Slide pane, the Notes pane, and the Slides/Outline pane.

**Placeholders**
Designated areas in PowerPoint layouts that can be used to easily insert text, graphics, or multimedia objects.

**Slide Layout**
Prearranged sets of placeholders for various types of slide content.

**Theme**
Formatting feature that applies a background, colors, fonts, and effects to all slides in a presentation.

## ➤ What You Will Learn

**About PowerPoint**
**Starting PowerPoint**
**Saving a Presentation**
**Opening an Existing Presentation**
**Exploring the PowerPoint Window**
**Entering Text Using Placeholders**
**Applying a Theme**
**Checking Spelling in a Presentation**
**Closing a Presentation**

**Software Skills**   PowerPoint's many features make it easy to create both simple and sophisticated presentations. One way to create a new slide show is to start with the default blank presentation that displays when PowerPoint opens. Once a presentation is open, you can enter text and apply a theme to give it a consistent design.

**Application Skills**   Wynnedale Medical Center has contacted you about preparing a presentation announcing their new laser eye surgery unit. In this lesson, you start a new presentation and explore basic features such as placeholders and themes.

## What You Can Do

### About PowerPoint

■ PowerPoint is a presentation graphics program that lets you create slide shows you can present using a computer projection system or publish as interactive Web pages.

- A **presentation** can include handouts, outlines, and speaker notes as well as slides.

- PowerPoint slides may contain text and various other types of content, such as clip art, pictures, movies, tables, or charts.

- You can create all the slide content in PowerPoint or import data from other Microsoft Office programs such as Word and Excel to create slide content.

- You use Microsoft Windows to start PowerPoint.

- When PowerPoint starts, it displays a single blank slide you can use to start a new presentation. The default slide is intended to be the first slide of the presentation, so it is set up for you to add the presentation's title and subtitle.

- The title slide is only one of several different slide types you can use to create a new presentation. You will learn more about **slide layouts** in Lesson 2.

## Starting PowerPoint

- To use PowerPoint 2010 you must first start it so it is running on your computer.

### Try It!    Starting PowerPoint

**1** Click Start 🌐 >All Programs. If necessary, scroll down until you see the Microsoft Office folder icon.

**2** Click the Microsoft Office folder icon.

**3** Click Microsoft PowerPoint.

OR

**1** Click Start 🌐.

**2** Click PowerPoint in the list of recently used programs.

OR

**1** Double-click the PowerPoint shortcut icon 📄 on the desktop.

OR

**1** Click the PowerPoint 📄 icon on the Taskbar:

## Saving a Presentation

- PowerPoint supplies the default title *Presentation* and a number (for example, *Presentation1*) in the title bar of each new presentation. You should change this default title to a more descriptive title when you save a new presentation so that you can work on it again later.

- By default, a new presentation is saved in XML format, the standard for Office 2007 and Office 2010 applications, giving the file an extension of .pptx.

- If you wish to use a presentation with earlier versions of PowerPoint, you can save the file in PowerPoint 97-2003 Presentation format. You can also save the presentation in several other formats, such as PDF or XPS, or as a template or show.

    ✓ *You will save presentations as templates and shows in later lessons.*

### Try It!    Saving a Presentation

**1** If necessary, start PowerPoint.

**2** Click Save 💾 on the Quick Access Toolbar.

OR

   a.  Click File.

   b.  Click Save 💾.

**3** Select the File name text box if it is not selected already.

**4** Type **PTry01_studentfirstname_ studentlastname.**

    ✓ *Replace the text studentfirstname with your own first name, and studentlastname with your own last name. For example, if your name is Mary Jones, type PTry_Mary_ Jones.*

*(continued)*

**Try It!**    **Saving a Presentation** *(continued)*

**5** Use the Navigation pane to navigate to the location where your teacher tells you to store the files for this lesson.

✓ *Refer to Lesson 1 of the Basics section on the companion CD for information on navigating with Windows Explorer.*

**6** Click Save 🖫 or press ⌗ENTER⌗ .

**7** If a confirmation dialog box displays, click OK.

## Closing a Presentation

- Closing a PowerPoint presentation can be done in the same manner as closing other Microsoft Office documents and spreadsheets.

- Make sure to save your work before closing.

 **Try It!**    **Closing a Presentation**

**1** In the **PTry01_studentfirstname_ studentlastname** file, click File > Exit.

**OR**

Press ⌗CTRL⌗ + ⌗W⌗ to close the file.

**OR**

Click Close ▬✕▬ to close the file and PowerPoint.

## Opening an Existing Presentation

- Open an existing presentation to modify, add, or delete material.

- PowerPoint makes it easy to open presentations on which you have recently worked by listing them in Backstage view under Recent.

- If you do not see the presentation on this list, you can use the Open command and the Open dialog box to navigate to the presentation you want to open.

 **Try It!**    **Opening an Existing Presentation**

**1** Click File > Open.

**2** In the Open dialog box, use the Navigation pane to navigate to the location where your teacher tells you to store the files for this lesson.

**3** Select **PTry01_studentfirstname_ studentlastname** (the file you saved with your first and last name in the file name), then click Open 🗁 .

**4** Leave **PTry01_studentfirstname_ studentlastname** open for use in the next Try It.

## Exploring the PowerPoint Window

- PowerPoint, like other Microsoft Office 2010 applications, displays the Ribbon interface that groups commands on tabs across the top of the window below the title bar.

- The status bar displays information about the presentation, such as the slide number and theme name.

- A presentation opens by default in **Normal view**, which displays the Slide pane, the Notes pane, and the Slides/Outline pane. You will learn more about these views in a later lesson.

- Normal view, the default view, allows you to work with slides in several ways:
  - Use the Slide pane to insert and modify slide content.
  - Use the Notes pane to add text for personal reference, such as material you want to remember to cover during the presentation. Notes recorded in the Notes pane can also be printed along with the slide to use as audience handouts.

- The Slides tab in the Slides/Outline pane shows a small version of all slides in the presentation and can be used to quickly select slides or reorganize them.

- The Outline tab, behind the Slides tab in the Slides/Outline pane, lets you view all slide content in outline format.

## Try It!    Exploring the PowerPoint Window

**1** In the **PTry01_studentfirstname_studentlastname** file, move your mouse pointer over each window element shown in the figure.

**2** Save the **PTry01_studentfirstname_studentlastname** file and leave it open to use in the next Try It.

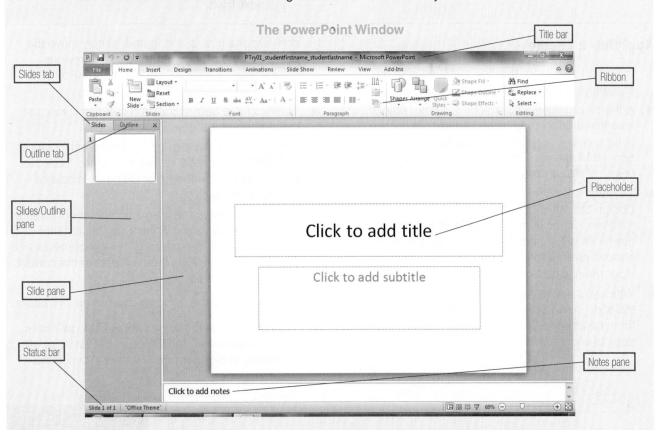

The PowerPoint Window

## Entering Text Using Placeholders

- PowerPoint displays **placeholders** to define the arrangement and location of text and other objects you can add to slides.

- The title slide you see when creating a new presentation has two placeholders: one for the title and one for the subtitle.

- To insert text in a placeholder, click inside the placeholder and begin typing. When you click the placeholder, PowerPoint selects the box with a dashed outline, displays sizing handles you can use to resize the placeholder, and displays a blinking insertion point that shows where text will appear when typed.

- Different types of slides in a presentation have different types of placeholders. In the illustration in the following Try It, the slide offers a title placeholder and a subtitle placeholder. Other types of slides offer content placeholders in which you can insert a bulleted list or other types of content such as a table, a chart, or a picture.

## Try It!     Entering Text Using Placeholders

**1** In the **PTry01_studentfirstname_studentlastname** file, click once in the Title placeholder to select it and position the insertion point.

**2** Type **Premier Soccer Club** in the Title placeholder.

**3** Click the Click to add subtitle placeholder. Type **Top Travel Soccer Competition for Boys and Girls**.

✓ *Note: The Subtitle text will appear in a lighter, grey font, compared to the Title.*

**4** Save the **PTry01_studentfirstname_studentlastname** file and leave it open to use in the next Try It.

## Applying a Theme

- In PowerPoint 2010, **themes** are used as a means of supplying graphical interest for a presentation.

- A theme provides a background, a color palette, a selection of fonts for titles and text, distinctive bullets, and a range of special effects that can be applied to shapes. The theme also controls the layout of placeholders on slides.

- Themes are located in the Themes group on the Design tab, as shown in Figure 1-1. The size of the PowerPoint window determines how many theme thumbnails display in the group. If you have created custom themes, they display along with PowerPoint's built-in themes.

- When you rest the pointer on a theme thumbnail, the slide in the Slide pane immediately displays the theme elements. This Live Preview feature makes it easy to choose a graphic look for slides—if you don't like the look of the theme, simply move the pointer off the theme to return to the previous appearance or point at a different theme to try another appearance.

- Themes have names that you can see if you rest the pointer on a theme thumbnail.

- By default, the Themes group shows only a few of the available themes. To see all themes, click the More button in the theme scroll bar to display a gallery of themes.

- The gallery shows the theme (or themes) currently used in a presentation in the This Presentation area. Options at the bottom of the gallery allow you to search for other themes or save the current theme for future use.

✓ *You will learn how to change and save a theme in Chapter 3.*

- Clicking a theme thumbnail applies it to all slides in the presentation. You can also choose to apply the theme to one or more selected slides in the presentation.

**Figure 1-1**

The Themes group on the Design tab

---

**Try It!** **Applying a Theme**

**1** In the **PTry01_studentfirstname_studentlastname** file, click the Design tab.

**2** Click the More button to display all themes.

**3** Point to several themes in the gallery to preview them in the presentation.

**4** Click the Perspective theme to apply it to the presentation.

**5** Save the **PTry01_studentfirstname_studentlastname** file and leave it open to use in the next Try It.

---

## Checking Spelling in a Presentation

- PowerPoint provides two methods of spell checking your presentation: automatic and manual.

- Automatic spell checking works while you're typing, displaying a wavy red line under words PowerPoint doesn't recognize. Right-click a wavy underline to see a list of possible correctly spelled replacements.

- To check spelling manually, use the Spelling button on the Review tab. The process of checking spelling in a presentation using the Spelling dialog box is similar to that in other Microsoft Office applications.

---

**Try It!** **Checking Spelling in a Presentation**

**1** In the **PTry01_studentfirstname_studentlastname** file, click the subtitle text and select the entire subtitle.

**2** Type **The Top Travil Soccer Clubb for Boys and Girls**.

✓ Note: "Travil" and "Clubb" should be typed incorrectly for purposes of the Try It.

**3** Right-click on **Travil** to see a list of suggested spellings. Click **Travel** to replace with the correct spelling.

**4** Click the Review tab, and then click Spelling ABC✓.

**5** Click Change in the Spelling dialog box to replace the misspelled word Clubb with Club.

**6** Click OK OK.

**7** Save the **PTry01_studentfirstname_studentlastname** file and leave it open to use in the next Try It.

# Project 1—Create It

## Laser Surgery Presentation

### DIRECTIONS

1. Click **Start** 🎯 > **Microsoft Office** > **Microsoft PowerPoint 2010**, if necessary.

2. Click **File** > **Save As** 🖫. The Save As dialog box opens. Navigate to the folder your teacher tells you to use when saving your work. Type **PProj01_studentfirstname_studentlastname** in the File Name text box, then click **Save**.

3. Click on the title placeholder and enter the text **Wynnedale Medical Center**.

4. Click on the subtitle placeholder and enter the text **Laser Eye Surgery Unit**.

5. Click the **Design** tab, then click the **More** button to see the gallery of themes.

6. Click the **Austin** theme to apply it, as shown in Figure 1-2.

7. Click **Review** > **Spelling** 🗸 to check spelling in the presentation.

8. Click Ignore All to skip changing the spelling of Wynnedale, then click OK.

9. Click **Save** 🖫 to save your work, then click **File** > **Exit** ▬ to close the file and close PowerPoint.

**Figure 1-2**

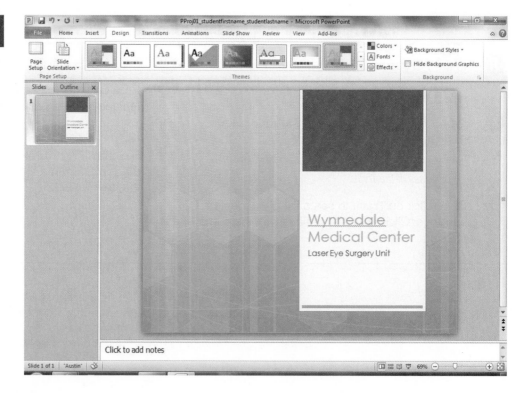

# Project 2—Apply It

## Laser Surgery Presentation

### DIRECTIONS

1. Start PowerPoint, if necessary.
2. Open **PProj02** from the data files for this lesson.
3. Save the presentation as **PProj02_ studentfirstname_studentlastname** in the location where your teacher instructs you to store the files for this lesson.
4. Enter the following text in the subtitle placeholder: **Find out if Laser Surgery is right for you.**
5. Apply the **Metro** theme to the presentation.
6. Check the spelling.
7. Close the presentation, saving all changes, and exit PowerPoint.

# Lesson 2

# Working with Slides

## ➤ What You Will Learn

**Inserting New Slides**
**Selecting Slide Layout**
**Moving from Slide to Slide**
**Changing List Levels**
**Printing a Presentation**

**Software Skills**    In PowerPoint, you can quickly and easily add new slides to a presentation. After adding new slides, you can change the slide layout and change the level of an item in a bulleted list. It's easy to move from one slide to the other, and you can also preview your slide show before printing it or presenting it.

**Application Skills**    In this lesson, you continue to work with the Wynnedale Medical Center presentation. You will add more content to the presentation using slides with different layouts.

## What You Can Do

### Inserting New Slides

- Most presentations consist of a number of slides. Use the New Slide button on the Home tab to add a slide to a presentation.

- If you simply click the New Slide button, PowerPoint adds the kind of slide you are most likely to need. With the default title slide displayed, for example, PowerPoint will assume the next slide should be a Title and Content slide.

- If the **active slide**—the currently displayed slide—uses a layout other than Title Slide, PowerPoint inserts a new slide with the same layout as the one currently displayed.

- A new slide is inserted immediately after the active slide.

**Try It!**     **Inserting New Slides**

**1**  Start PowerPoint and open **PTry02** from the data files for this lesson.

**2**  Save the file as **PTry02_studentfirstname_ studentlastname** in the location where your teacher instructs you to store the files for this lesson.

**3**  Click Home > New Slide 🖼.

**4**  Press CTRL + M to add another slide.

**5**  Save the **PTry02_studentfirstname_ studentlastname** file and leave it open to use in the next Try It.

## Selecting Slide Layout

- To specify a particular layout for a slide, click the down arrow on the New Slide button to display a gallery of slide layout choices.

- A slide layout arranges the standard objects of a presentation—titles, charts, text, clip art—on the slide to make it attractive. Each layout provides placeholders for specific types of content.

- PowerPoint 2010 has fewer layout choices than some previous versions of PowerPoint offered, but layouts are multifunctional. Rather than having a layout that offers side-by-side text and a layout that offers side-by-side content, for example, PowerPoint 2010 has one layout that allows you to insert side-by-side content of any type, including text, graphics, charts, or movies.

- The New Slide drop-down gallery also provides options to Duplicate Selected Slides, add new Slides from Outline, and Reuse Slides.

**Try It!**     **Selecting Slide Layout**

**1**  In the **PTry02_studentfirstname_ studentlastname** file, click the New Slide button 🖼 down arrow. A gallery of available slide types appears as shown in the figure.

**2**  Click the Two Content slide.

**3**  Click New Slide 🖼 > Duplicate Selected Slides.

**4**  Save the **PTry02_studentfirstname_ studentlastname** file and leave it open to use in the next Try It.

The New Slides gallery

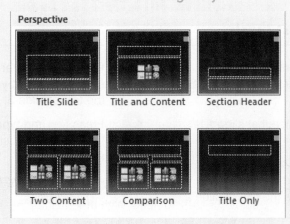

Perspective

Title Slide     Title and Content     Section Header

Two Content     Comparison     Title Only

## Moving from Slide to Slide

- Most presentations include multiple slides. You will need to move from slide to slide in Normal view to enter text and modify the presentation.

- PowerPoint offers a variety of ways to select and display slides. Click in the scroll bar or drag the scroll box to display slides, or use the Previous Slide and Next Slide buttons at the bottom of the scroll bar to move through the slides.

- You can also select slides by clicking them in the Slides tab.

### Try It!    Moving from Slide to Slide

**1** In the **PTry02_studentfirstname_studentlastname** file, click slide 3 in the Slides tab.

**2** Click the Next Slide button ⬇.

**3** Press ⟦PG UP⟧ twice.

**4** Click in the scroll bar three times. You should now be on slide 5, as shown by the highlighted slide in the Slides tab.

**5** Save the **PTry02_studentfirstname_studentlastname** file and leave it open to use in the next Try It.

## Changing List Levels

- You can enter or modify text in the Outline tab if desired. As you type the text in the Outline tab, it appears on the current slide in the Slide pane.

- Slide text content consists mostly of bulleted items. First-level bullets are supplied on content placeholders. PowerPoint supplies formatting for five levels of bullets. Each subordinate level uses a smaller font size than the previous level and a different bullet character.

- Create subordinate levels of bullets as you type by pressing Tab at the beginning of a line. You can also use the Increase List Level and Decrease List Level buttons in the Paragraph group on the Home tab to apply subordinate level formatting.

- Themes supply bullet characters for all levels of bullets in specific sizes and colors. If you change a theme, you will notice that the bullet characters change along with colors, fonts, backgrounds, and placeholder layout.

- You can change the bullets for a text placeholder using the Bullets and Numbering dialog box.

### Try It!    Changing List Levels

**1** In the **PTry02_studentfirstname_studentlastname** file, click slide 2 in the Slides tab.

**2** Click the Outline tab. Notice that slide 2 is highlighted as your current location within the presentation.

**3** Type **Tryouts Begin Next Week**. The text you entered should appear as the title of slide 2.

**4** Press the down arrow and type **All Age Groups Invited**. The text you entered should appear as the title of slide 3.

**5** Press ⟦ENTER⟧ and type **Directions to Fields**. The text you entered should appear as the title of slide 4.

✓ *Note that pressing Enter added a new slide to the presentation.*

*(continued)*

**Try It!**   **Changing List Levels** *(continued)*

**6** Click at the end of the text in Slide 2 in the Outline tab and press ENTER . A new slide is added after slide 2.

✓ *Make sure you don't click on the slide 2 icon at the left of the Outline tab. Pressing Enter if the entire slide is selected will delete the slide.*

**7** Click Home > Increase List Level ▧. This deletes the new slide and positions the cursor for new text to be entered into the body of Slide 2.

**8** Type **Club tryouts start Wednesday, June 8** and press ENTER .

**9** Press TAB . Type **4 p.m. for under-11** and press ENTER .

**10** Type **5 p.m. for all others**. Your presentation should look like the one shown in the figure below. Note the different levels of outline in the slide 2 bullet points.

**11** Save the **PTry02_studentfirstname_ studentlastname** file and leave it open to use in the next Try It.

Insert bullet text in the Outline tab

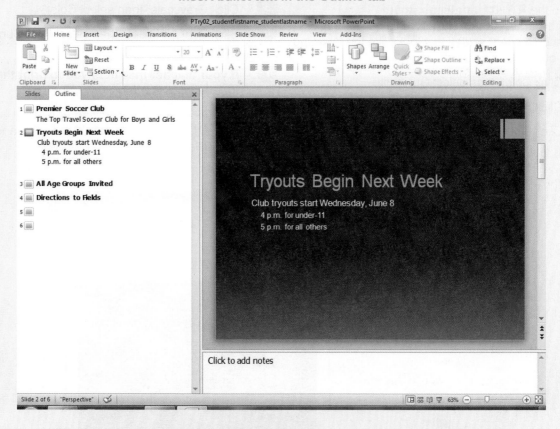

## Printing a Presentation

- Printing PowerPoint materials is similar to printing pages in other Microsoft Office programs, with a few exceptions.

- A presentation can be printed in various formats: as slides, notes pages, handouts, or as an outline. You choose the settings for these formats by clicking the File tab and then clicking the Print tab, shown in the illustration in the following Try It.

- Among the options you can choose are:
  - Which slides to print and number of copies to print.
  - What material (slides, notes pages, handouts, or outline) to print.
  - Whether to print in grayscale, color, or black and white.
  - If handouts are to be printed, how many slides per page and the order in which the slides display on the page.
  - Whether the material should be scaled (sized) to fit the page or framed by a box.
  - Whether comments and markup annotations should be printed.
  - Whether hidden slides should be printed.

---

**Try It!**    **Printing a Presentation**

**1** In the **PTry02_studentfirstname_ studentlastname** file, click File > Print. You should see a screen that looks like the following figure.

**2** Click Color, then select Grayscale.

**3** Click Full Page Slides, then select Outline.

**4** Click Outline, then select 3 Slides.

**5** Click Grayscale, then select Color.

**6** Click Print All Slides, then select Print Current Slide.

**7** **If your teacher instructs you to print the Try It activity,** click Print.

**8** Close **PTry02_studentfirstname_ studentlastname**, saving all changes, and exit PowerPoint.

The Print Tab

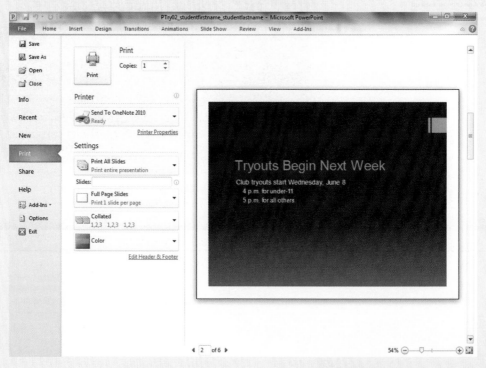

# Project 3—Create It

## Laser Surgery Presentation

### DIRECTIONS

1. Start PowerPoint if necessary and open **PProj03** from the data files for this lesson. Save the file as **PProj03_studentfirstname_studentlastname** in the location where your teacher instructs you to store files for this lesson.

2. Click on slide 3 to display it in the slide pane.

3. On the Home tab, click the New Slide ⬚ drop-down arrow, then click Two Content.

4. Click in the Title placeholder and type **Laser Eye Surgery Facts**.

5. Click in the left content placeholder and type the first bullet item, **LASIK is the most common refractive surgery**.

6. Click on the Outline tab, then click just to the right of the word surgery on the outline of the current slide.

7. Press [ENTER] and type the next bullet item, **Relative lack of pain**.

8. Click **Review** > **Spelling** ᴬᴮᶜ to check spelling in the presentation, then click OK.

9. **With your teacher's permission**, click **File** > **Print**. Select **Print All Slides**, then click **Print** 🖨 to print the presentation.

10. Click **Save** 💾 to save your work, then click **File** > **Exit** to close the file and close PowerPoint.

# Project 4—Apply It

## Laser Surgery Presentation

### DIRECTIONS

1. Start PowerPoint, if necessary.

2. Open **PProj04** from the data files for this lesson.

3. Save the presentation as **PProj04_studentfirstname_studentlastname** in the location where your teacher instructs you to store the files for this lesson.

4. Move to slide 4 and enter the two additional bullets in the left content placehholder:

    **Almost immediate results (within 24 hours)**

    **Both nearsighted and farsighted can benefit**

5. Apply the **Clarity** theme to the presentation, and then move through the slides to see how the new theme has changed the appearance of slides.

6. Change the layout of slide 4 to Title and Content. Your presentation should look like the one shown in Figure 2-1.

7. Check the spelling.

8. **With your teacher's permission**, print the presentation.

9. Close the presentation, saving all changes, and exit PowerPoint.

**Figure 2-1**

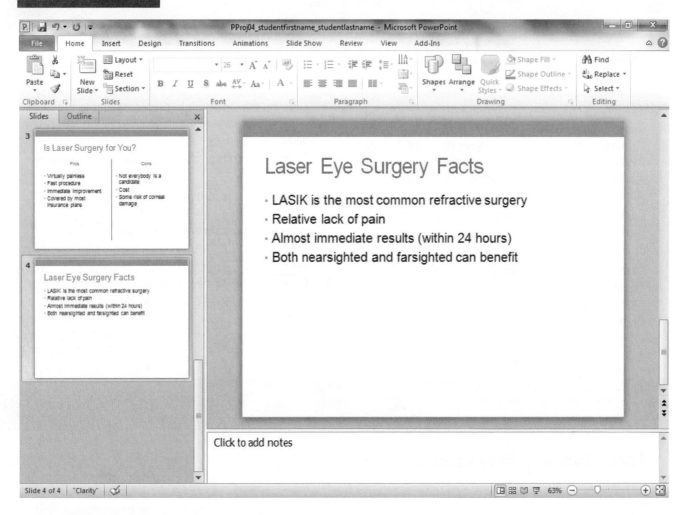

# Lesson 3

# Working with Headers, Footers, and Speaker Notes

## ➤ What You Will Learn

**Reusing Slides from Other Presentations**
**Adding Speaker Notes**
**Changing Slide Size and Orientation**
**Inserting Headers and Footers**

**Software Skills**    PowerPoint makes it easy to reuse slides from other presentations by inserting them into your presentation. Footers, dates, and numbers provide additional information on slides to help users navigate and work with presentations. Notes pages allow you to easily refer to slide notes during a presentation, while handouts can give the audience a helpful reference of what has been covered in the presentation.

**Application Skills**    You have a draft of the laser surgery presentation to show your client, Wynnedale Medical Center. In this lesson, you will prepare notes pages and handouts to present to the client. You'll also add information on each slide to help identify and organize the slides. You will also work with a new travel adventures presentation.

## WORDS TO KNOW

**Handouts**
Printed copies of the presentation for the audience to refer to during and after the slide show.

**Landscape orientation**
A slide or printout is wider than it is tall.

**Portrait orientation**
A slide or printout is taller than it is wide.

**Footer**
An area at the bottom of a slide in which you can enter a date, slide number, or other information that repeats on each slide.

**Header**
An area at the top of a slide in which you can enter a date or other information that repeats for each slide.

# What You Can Do

## Reusing Slides from Other Presentations

- You will find that preparing presentations can be a time-consuming process, especially as you venture into more complex formatting and content. It makes sense to reuse slides whenever you can to save time.

- Borrowing slides from other presentations can also help to ensure consistency among presentations, an important consideration when you are working with a number of presentations for a company or organization.

- You can find the Reuse Slides command on the New Slide drop-down list. This command opens the Reuse Slides task pane where you can specify the presentation file to open. The slides are then displayed in the task pane. To see the content more clearly, rest the pointer on a slide in the current presentation. To insert a slide, simply click it.

- By default, slides you insert this way take on the formatting of the presentation they're inserted into (the destination presentation).

- If you want to retain the original formatting of the inserted slides, click the Keep source formatting check box at the bottom of the Reuse Slides task pane.

✓ *This is also covered in Lesson 19.*

---

**Try It!**    **Reusing Slides from Other Presentations**

1. Start PowerPoint and open **PTry03a** from the data files for this lesson.

2. Save the file as **PTry03a_studentfirstname_ studentlastname** in the location where your teacher instructs you to store the files for this lesson.

3. Click slide 4 in the Slides tab to select it.

4. Click Home > New Slide [icon] drop-down arrow, then click Reuse Slides.

5. In the Reuse Slides pane, click Browse. Navigate to the location where the files for this lesson are stored and open **PTry03b**. The slides from this presentation appear in the Reuse Slides pane, as shown in the following figure.

6. Point to the first slide to view the slide content in a larger format. Point to each of the slides to see their content as well.

7. Click *June Calendar* to insert it into the destination presentation.

✓ *Note that the inserted slide takes on the theme and formatting of the destination presentation.*

8. Click on the remaining four slides in the Reuse Slides pane to insert them in the presentation.

9. Click the Close button on the Reuse Slides pane to close the pane.

10. Save the **PTry03a_studentfirstname_ studentlastname** file and leave it open to use in the next Try It.

The Reuse Slides pane

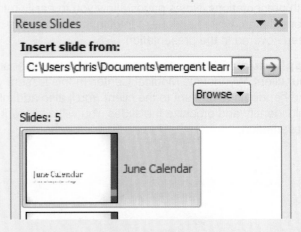

## Adding Speaker Notes

- You do not need to "create" either notes pages or **handouts** in PowerPoint. Notes pages and handouts are simply another way to view and print existing slides.

- To view notes pages before printing, you can use Notes Page view. To view handouts, you can go to Backstage view and click Full Page Slides to see the various Handout formats available. The 3 Slides handout configuration provides lines next to each slide for audience members to take notes.

- By default, notes pages display a page number and handouts display a date and a page number. You can add information such as date and time, header, page number, and footer to both notes pages and handouts by adding **headers** and **footers**, covered later in this lesson.

- You can use the Handout Master view and Notes Master view to see what handouts and Notes pages will look like and adjust settings before printing.

---

### Try It! Adding Speaker Notes

**1** In the **PTry03a_studentfirstname_ studentlastname** file, click slide 5 in the Slides tab.

**2** Click View > Notes Page 🔳.

**3** Click in the Notes placeholder and type **Tell them about what's coming up in June.**

**4** Press ⌨PG UP . Click in the Notes placeholder of slide 4 and type **Remind them that membership is free.**

**5** Click File > Print. Click Full Page Slides, then click 3 Slides.

**6** Click View > Handout Master 🔳. Click Close Master View ❌ .

**7** Save the **PTry03a_studentfirstname_ studentlastname** file and leave it open to use in the next Try It.

---

## Changing Slide Size and Orientation

- By default, slides are displayed in **landscape orientation**—they are wider than they are tall—and notes pages and handouts are displayed in **portrait orientation**—they are taller than they are wide.

- In some instances, you may want to reverse the usual orientation of slides to display them in portrait orientation. You can use the Slide Orientation button on the Design tab to quickly switch from one orientation to another.

  ✓ *If your presentation includes graphics, they may become distorted when orientation is changed.*

- For more control over orientation and slide size, use the Page Setup dialog box.

- Slides are initially sized for an on-screen show on a screen that uses a standard 4:3 aspect ratio. You can change slide sizes to better fit the type of output device, such as a wide-screen display with a 16:9 aspect ratio.

- You can also select a size that will work best for a particular paper size, for 35mm slides, for overheads, or even for a custom size that you specify in the Width and Height boxes.

---

**Try It!**    **Changing Slide Size and Orientation**

**1** In the **PTry03a_studentfirstname_ studentlastname** file, click View > Normal 🔲.

**2** Click Design > Slide Orientation 🔲 > Portrait.

**3** Click Design > Page Setup 🔲.

**4** Click Landscape, then click On-screen Show (16:10) from the Slides sized for drop-down list, then click OK.

**5** Save the **PTry03a_studentfirstname_ studentlastname** file and leave it open to use in the next Try It.

---

## Inserting Headers and Footers

- You can add several types of information that repeat for each slide to help organize or identify slides.
    - Use a slide **footer** to identify a presentation's topic, author, client, or other information.
    - Add the date and time to a slide footer so you can tell when the presentation was created or updated.
    - Include a slide number in the footer to identify the slide's position in the presentation.

- Use the Header and Footer dialog box to specify these options. Note that you can choose a fixed date or a date that updates each time the presentation is opened. You can also choose to not display the information on the title slide; apply the information only to the current slide, or apply it to all slides.

- If you are working with notes pages or handouts, you can use the options on the Notes and Handouts tab to add a **header** in addition to date and time, slide number, and footer.
    - ✓ You will work with notes pages and handouts in the next project.

---

**Try It!**    **Inserting Headers and Footers**

**1** In the **PTry03a_studentfirstname_ studentlastname** file, click Insert > Header & Footer 🔲.

The Header and Footer dialog box

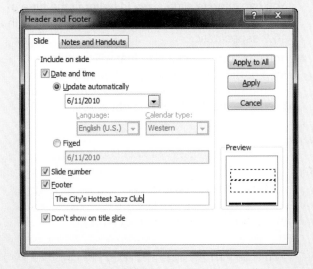

**2** Click the Slide tab in the Header and Footer dialog box, then click Date and time.

**3** Click Slide number and Don't show on title slide.

**4** Click Footer, and type **The City's Hottest Jazz Club**. The dialog box should look like the one shown in the following illustration.

**5** Click the Notes and Handouts tab, then click Header and type **The City's Hottest Jazz Club**.

**6** Click Apply to All. Click through the slides to view the footers.

**7** On slide 5, click View > Notes Page 🔲 to view the notes page headers and footers.

**8** Close **PTry03a_studentfirstname_ studentlastname**, saving all changes, and exit PowerPoint.

# Project 5—Create It

## Travel Adventures Presentation

### DIRECTIONS

1. Start PowerPoint if necessary and open **PProj05a** from the data files for this lesson. Save the file as **PProj05a_studentfirstname_studentlastname** in the location where your teacher instructs you to store files for this lesson.

2. Click on slide 3 to display it in the slide pane.

3. Click Home > New Slide 🖼 drop-down arrow. Then click Reuse Slides.

4. In the Reuse Slides pane, click Browse. Navigate to the location where the files for this lesson are stored and open **PProj05b**.

5. Point to the second slide to view the slide content in a larger format. Click **Adventure Travel Packages** to insert it into the destination presentation.

   ✓ Note that the inserted slide takes on the theme and formatting of the destination presentation.

6. Click the **Close** button on the Reuse Slides pane to close the pane.

7. Click slide 2, then click View > Notes Page 📄.

8. Click in the Notes placeholder and type **Be sure to mention special group rates.**

9. Press [PG DN]. Click in the Notes placeholder of slide 3 and type **Also tell them about special rates on the Web site.**

10. Click Insert > Header & Footer 📄.

11. Click the **Slide** tab in the **Header and Footer** dialog box, then click **Date and time**.

12. Click **Slide number** and **Don't show on title slide**.

13. Click **Footer** and type **Everywhere You Want to Go**. Click **Apply to All** 🖅.

14. Click **Design** > **Slide Orientation** 🖼 > **Portrait**.

15. Click View > **Normal** 🖳 and scroll through the slides to see the new layout.

   ✓ Note that the two headings on Slide 1 are overlapping.

16. Click **Design** > **Slide Orientation** 🖼 > **Landscape**.

17. Click **Review** > **Spelling** ᴬᴮᶜ to check spelling in the presentation, then click **OK**.

18. **With your teacher's permission**, click File > Print. Select **Print All Slides**, then click **Print** 🖨 to print the presentation.

19. Click **Save** 🖫 to save your work, then click **File** > **Exit** to close the file and close PowerPoint.

# Project 6—Apply It

## Laser Surgery Presentation

### DIRECTIONS

1. Start PowerPoint, if necessary.

2. Open **PProj06a** from the data files for this lesson.

3. Save the presentation as **PProj06a_studentfirstname_studentlastname** in the location where your teacher instructs you to store the files for this lesson.

4. Open **PProj06b** from the data files for this lesson, move to slide 4 and insert both slides from the presentation. Close the Reuse Slides pane.

5. In **PProj06a_studentfirstname_studentlastname**, move to slide 5 and note that the main heading overlaps the body content. Change the presentation theme to **Elemental**.

6. Add the following note to slide 5: **Compare surgery cost to the cost of glasses or contacts**. Add the following note to slide 6: **Make sure potential patients know that the surgery is painless**.

7. Add the following footers to all slides except for the title slide: **Date and time**, **Slide number**, and the following footer: **Clear Vision in a Day**.

8. Change the slide aspect ratio to **16:10**. Your presentation should look like the one in Figure 3-1.

9. Check the spelling.

10. **With your teacher's permission**, print the presentation.

11. Close the presentation, saving all changes, and exit PowerPoint.

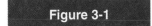

Figure 3-1

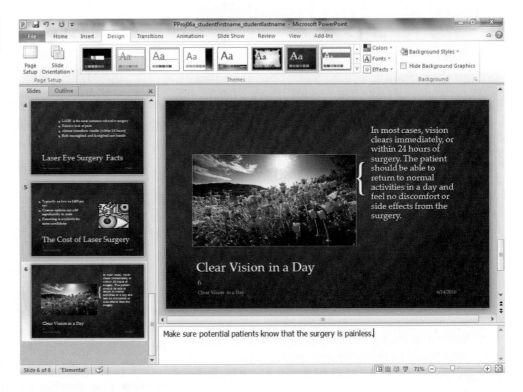

# Lesson 4

# Inserting and Formatting Pictures

➤ **What You Will Learn**

**Inserting a Picture from a File**
**Formatting Pictures Using Styles and Artistic Effects**

**Software Skills**   You can insert your own pictures in a presentation and then use the enhanced picture tools to adjust the picture's appearance and apply special effects.

**Application Skills**   A local environmental group, Planet Earth, has asked you to prepare a presentation they can show on Earth Day. In this lesson, you begin the presentation by inserting and formatting several pictures.

**WORDS TO KNOW**

**Crop**
Remove a portion of a picture that you don't want.

**Scaling**
Specifying an exact width and height for an object.

## What You Can Do

### Inserting a Picture from a File

■ You may be able to illustrate your presentations adequately using clip art graphics and photos. But in some instances, you may want to include your own pictures of specific locations, events, or people.

■ You can scan your own pictures into the computer using a scanner. Using the scanner and computer, you can save the scanned image to the folder where you store your photos.

■ Use the Insert Picture from File icon in any content placeholder or the Picture button on the Insert tab to place your own picture file on a slide. This command opens the Insert Picture dialog box so you can navigate to and select the picture you want to insert.

**Try It!**    **Inserting a Picture from a File**

**1**  Start PowerPoint and open **PTry04** from the data files for this lesson.

**2**  Save the file as **PTry04_studentfirstname_studentlastname** in the location where your teacher instructs you to store the files for this lesson.

**3**  Go to slide 2 and click the Insert Picture from File 🖼 icon in the content placeholder.

**4**  Open to the location where your teacher tells you to store files for this lesson, and select the **Skyline** image, then click Insert.

**5**  Press CTRL + M to add a new slide, and type **The Haystack at Cannon Beach** in the title placeholder.

**6**  Click in the content placeholder, then click Insert > Picture 🖼. Navigate to the location where your teacher tells you to store files for this lesson, and select the **Haystack** image, then click Insert.

**7**  Save the **PTry04_studentfirstname_studentlastname** file, and leave it open to use in the next Try It.

## Formatting Pictures Using Styles and Artistic Effects

■ Once you have inserted a picture, you can resize it by dragging a corner handle, or reposition it by dragging it to a new location.

■ For more control over the formatting process, use the tools on the Picture Tools Format tab to modify and enhance a picture. Options on this tab allow you to create interesting and unusual picture effects as well as specify a precise size.

■ Use the tools in the Adjust group to change brightness or contrast. You can also recolor a picture using the current theme colors.

■ The Picture Styles group lets you apply a number of interesting styles to your pictures. You can also choose a shape in which to enclose the picture, select border options, or apply standard effects such as shadows or reflections.

■ The Size group allows you to **crop** a picture to remove portions of the picture you don't need. You can restore the hidden portion of the picture by using the Crop tool again.

■ Once you are certain the picture has the right appearance, you can compress the picture to remove the hidden portions. This action reduces the presentation's file size and makes it more efficient.

■ The Size group also supplies width and height settings that allow you to precisely size a picture. Specifying an exact width and height is called **scaling**. You can scale any drawing object, including clip art graphics and shapes you draw yourself.

**Try It!**    **Formatting Pictures Using Styles and Artistic Effects**

**1**  In the **PTry04_studentfirstname_studentlastname** file, click slide 2 and click the picture.

**2**  Click the left corner handle and drag it up and to the left to enlarge the picture. Then click and drag the photograph to the right side of the slide, in line with the blue graphic above, as shown in the following illustration.

**3**  Click Picture Tools Format > Corrections ☼ and then click the far-right image in the Sharpen and Soften row.

**4**  Click Picture Tools Format > Color 🖼 and select Saturation: 200% in the Color Saturation row.

*(continued)*

**Try It!**    **Formatting Pictures Using Styles and Artistic Effects** *(continued)*

**5** Click Picture Tools Format and select Soft Edge Rectangle from the Picture Styles gallery.

**6** Click Picture Tools Format > Crop 🖼️ > Crop to activate the crop tool. Click the bottom middle handle and drag it up to remove most of the trees from the picture.

**7** Click Crop 🖼️ again to complete the crop.

**8** Click slide 3 and click the picture. Click Picture Tools > Picture Effects 🔵 > Soft Edges > 25 Point.

**9** Click Picture Tools Format > Artistic Effects ▪, then select Glow Diffused.

**10** Close **PTry04_studentfirstname_ studentlastname**, saving all changes, and exit PowerPoint.

Click and Drag to Change Picture Size and Position

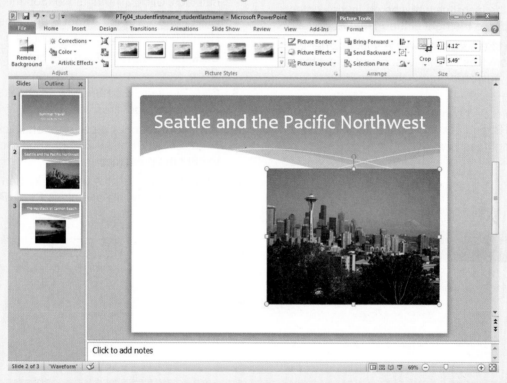

# Project 7—Create It

## Planet Earth Presentation

### DIRECTIONS

1. Start PowerPoint if necessary and open **PProj07** from the data files for this lesson. Save the file as **PProj07_studentfirstname_studentlastname** in the location where your teacher instructs you to store files for this lesson.

2. Click on the insert picture icon ▨ in the content placeholder to the right of the Planet Earth text.

3. Navigate to the location where your teacher tells you to store files for this lesson and select the **PProj07_earthpic** image, then click **Insert**.

4. Click **Picture Tools Format** > **Corrections** ☀ and then click the image to the right of the current image in Brightness and Contrast to increase the image brightness by 20%.

5. Right-click the image and click **Format Picture** to open the Format Picture dialog box. Click and drag to select the **0** in the Contrast box and type **25%**. Click **Close**.

6. Click **Picture Tools Format** > **Crop** ▥ > **Crop**, then click and drag the bottom middle handle up a half inch. Click **Crop** again to crop the picture.

7. Click **Picture Tools Format** > and type **3.9"** in the Height box ▥, as shown in Figure 4-1.

8. Click the **Compress Pictures** button ▣, then click **OK**.

9. Click **Review** > **Spelling** ABC to check spelling in the presentation, then click **OK**.

10. **With your teacher's permission**, click **File** > **Print**. Select **Print All Slides**, then click **Print** 🖶 to print the presentation.

11. Click **Save** 💾 to save your work, then click **File** > **Exit** to close the file and close PowerPoint.

**Figure 4-1**

The height box

# Project 8—Apply It

## Planet Earth Presentation

### DIRECTIONS

1. Start PowerPoint, if necessary.

2. Open **PProj08** from the data files for this lesson.

3. Save the presentation as **PProj08_ studentfirstname_studentlastname** in the location where your teacher instructs you to store the files for this lesson.

4. Insert the **Dolphin** image in slide 2.

5. Increase the image brightness by 20%.

6. Recolor the image to **Sky Blue, Accent color 3 Dark**.

7. Apply the **Pencil Sketch** Artistic Effect to the image. Your presentation should look like the one in Figure 4-2.

8. Compress the picture using document resolution.

9. Check the spelling.

**10.** **With your teacher's permission**, print the presentation.

**11.** Close the presentation, saving all changes, and exit PowerPoint.

**Figure 4-2**

# Lesson 5

# Formatting Text

## WORDS TO KNOW

**Font**
A complete set of characters in a specific design, style, and size.

**Font color**
The color of characters in a font set.

**Font effects**
Enhancements applied to font characters.

**Font size**
The height of an uppercase letter in a font set.

**Font style**
The slant and weight of characters in a font set.

**Format Painter**
A tool that lets you copy text formatting from one text selection and apply it to any other text in the presentation.

➤ **What You Will Learn**

**Finding and Replacing Text in a Presentation**
**Selecting Text and Placeholders**
**Changing the Appearance of Text Using Font Sizes, Styles, and Colors**
**Copying Text Formatting**
**Using Undo and Redo**
**Clearing Formatting**

**Software Skills**　　Although themes and theme fonts are designed to produce a pleasing appearance, you may sometimes wish to modify the appearance of text by changing font, font style, size, or color. Use the Format Painter to copy formatting from one slide to another.

**Application Skills**　　Great Grains Bakery, a company that sells fresh-baked breads and other bakery items at various locations around your area, wants you to help them create a presentation to display at a trade show. In this lesson, you explore ways to improve the appearance of text in the presentation. You will also modify a presentation about an Internet acceptable use policy.

## What You Can Do

### Finding and Replacing Text in a Presentation

■ As with other Microsoft Office 2010 applications, you can search for specific text in a PowerPoint presentation and replace it with new text. You can use the Find 🔍 and Replace ᵇᵃᵇ buttons in the Editing group of the Home tab to do this.

■ You can also use the Replace Fonts to find and replace text fonts throughout a presentation. Just indicate the font you want to replace, and the new font you want to use.

**Try It!**      **Finding and Replacing Text in a Presentation**

**1** Start PowerPoint and open **PTry05** from the data files for this lesson.

**2** Save the file as **PTry05_studentfirstname_ studentlastname** in the location where your teacher instructs you to store the files for this lesson.

**3** Click Home > Find 🔍 and type **walkathon** in the Find dialog box. Click Find Next.

**4** Click Replace and type **Walkathon** in the Replace dialog box. Click Find Next.

**5** Click OK and then click Close.

**6** Click Home > Replace ▧ > Replace Fonts. The font Book Antiqua, which is used throughout the presentation, should be highlighted in the Replace list box.

**7** Click to select Agency FB in the With list box, click Replace, then click Close.

**8** Save the **PTry05_studentfirstname_ studentlastname** file and leave it open to use in the next Try It.

## Selecting Text and Placeholders

■ Manipulating text in a presentation requires you to know some basics about selecting text and placeholders to ensure you are working efficiently.

■ You can select text by dragging the insertion point over it, highlighting the selected text. You can also double-click a single word to select it.

■ As you are working with text in a placeholder, the placeholder displays a dashed line, sizing handles, and a rotation handle.

■ You can also select the placeholder by clicking its outline with the four-headed pointer. The selected placeholder has a solid outline.

■ While a placeholder is selected, any change you make using text tools will apply to all text in the placeholder.

■ When you want to make a change to all text in a placeholder, it is speedier to select the placeholder rather than dragging over the text to select it.

**Try It!**      **Selecting Text and Placeholders**

**1** In the **PTry05_studentfirstname_ studentlastname** file, go to slide 2, then click and drag to select **Homeless** in the slide title. Note the dashed line, sizing handles and rotation handle shown in the following figure.

Placeholder Tools with Selected Text

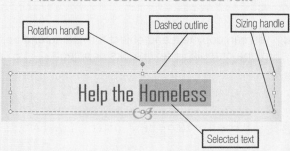

**2** Move the mouse arrow down below the rule until it changes to a four-headed pointer, then click to select the slide content placeholder.

**3** Double-click the word **homeless** in the second bullet to select it.

**4** Move the mouse arrow slightly over the selected word to make the Mini Toolbar appear. This toolbar can be used to change formatting of the selected text.

**5** Save the **PTry05_studentfirstname_ studentlastname** file and leave it open to use in the next Try It.

## Changing the Appearance of Text Using Font Sizes, Styles, and Colors

- PowerPoint's themes guarantee a presentation with a sophisticated design, and that includes the appearance of text. You can, however, easily customize text appearance to emphasize it or to make your presentation more readable, interesting, or unique.

- Text appearance attributes include **font family, size, color, style,** and **special effects**. You can also change the case of text to control use of uppercase and lowercase letters.

- You can change text attributes:
  - Select text or a placeholder and then use the options in the Font group on the Home tab of the Ribbon. Commands in this group allow you to change font, font size, font style, and font color. You can also increase or decrease font size by set increments and clear formatting to restore default appearance.

- You can use the Mini toolbar that appears near selected text (see the following illustration) to modify text appearance as well as adjust paragraph features such as alignment, indents, and bullet formatting.

- You can open the Font dialog box by clicking the Font group's dialog box launcher to change multiple attributes and apply them all at once.

- Note that effects such as superscript and subscript that are not available on Ribbon buttons are available in this dialog box.

- The Character Spacing option on the Home tab and in the Font dialog box allows you to control the amount of space between characters from very tight to very loose, or you can set a specific spacing amount.

---

### Try It!  Changing the Appearance of Text Using Font Sizes, Styles, and Colors

**1** In the **PTry05_studentfirstname_studentlastname** file, click slide 5 and click the content placeholder.

**2** Click Home > Font drop-down list, then click Book Antiqua in the Theme Fonts section of the Font drop-down list.

**3** Click and drag to select the title **How to Get Involved.** Click Home > Font Color A and then select Dark Red, Accent 5, Lighter 60% from the Theme Colors.

**4** Click Home > Text Shadow S .

**5** With the title still selected, Click Home > Character Spacing AV > Loose.

**6** With the title still selected, click Home > Font Size drop-down list > 66.

**7** Double-click **Walkathon** in the second bullet, then click the Font dialog box launcher. Click Equalize Character Height, then click OK.

**8** Save the **PTry05_studentfirstname_studentlastname** file and leave it open to use in the next Try It.

---

## Copying Text Formatting

- You can quickly copy and apply text formatting in PowerPoint by using the **Format Painter**.

- You can copy text and object formatting and apply it to one or multiple text blocks or objects.

---

**Try It!**    **Copying Text Formatting**

**1** In the **PTry05_studentfirstname_ studentlastname** file, click slide 5 and click the title placeholder.

**2** Click Home > Format Painter ✐.

**3** Click the title placeholder in slide 4 to apply the formatting.

**4** Save the **PTry05_studentfirstname_ studentlastname** file and leave it open to use in the next Try It.

---

## Using Undo and Redo

■ PowerPoint contains an Undo feature, as in other Microsoft Office applications, which reverses the most recent action or a whole series of previous actions.

■ The Redo button allows you to redo actions after you undo them, if you change your mind.

■ You can find the Undo and Redo buttons on the Quick Access Toolbar.

---

**Try It!**    **Using Undo and Redo**

**1** In the **PTry05_studentfirstname_ studentlastname** file, click slide 5 and click Undo ↺ in the Quick Access Toolbar.

**2** Now click Redo ↻ in the Quick Access Toolbar.

**3** Click the Undo drop-down list arrow to see a list of the most recent actions you can undo. Click Text Shadow. Notice that all the subsequent actions are also undone.

**4** Save the **PTry05_studentfirstname_ studentlastname** file and leave it open to use in the next Try It.

---

## Clearing Formatting

■ You can use the Reset 📄 button to clear formatting you have added to text and return the position, size, and formatting of the slide placeholders to the default settings.

---

**Try It!**    **Clearing Formatting**

**1** In the **PTry05_studentfirstname_ studentlastname** file, go to slide 5.

**2** Click Reset 📄. The placeholder formatting returns to the default settings.

**3** Close **PTry05_studentfirstname_ studentlastname**, saving all changes, and exit PowerPoint.

# Project 9—Create It

## Great Grains Bakery Presentation

### DIRECTIONS

1. Start PowerPoint if necessary and open **PProj09** from the data files for this lesson. Save the file as **PProj09_studentfirstname_studentlastname** in the location where your teacher instructs you to store files for this lesson.

2. Click **Home** > **Find** 🔍 and type **Breads, baguettes, and bagels** in the Find dialog box. Click **Find Next**.

3. Click **Replace** and type **Breads and baguettes** in the Replace with text box. Click **Replace All**.

4. Click **OK**. Click **Close**.

5. Click **Home** > **Replace** 🔤 > **Replace Fonts**. The font Arial, which is used throughout the presentation, should be highlighted in the Replace list box.

6. Click to select **Agency FB** in the With list box, click **Replace**, then click **Close**.

7. Click to select slide 3, then select the title placeholder.

8. Click **Home** > **Font** drop-down list, then click **Arial (headings)** in the Theme Fonts section of the Font drop-down list.

9. Click **Home** > **Font Color** drop-down list 🔺 and then select **Indigo, Accent 5** from the Theme Colors.

10. Click **Home** > **Character Spacing** 🔤 > **Loose** and then click **Home** > **Font Size drop-down list** > **54**.

11. Click **Home** > **Format Painter** 🖌. Click the title placeholder in slide 4. Use the format painter to apply the title placeholder formatting to all the remaining slides.

12. Click slide 5 and click **Undo** ↺ in the Quick Access Toolbar. Then click **Redo** ↻.

13. Click **Reset** 📋, then click **Undo** ↺. Your presentation should look like the one shown in Figure 5-1.

14. Click **Review** > **Spelling** 🔤 to check spelling in the presentation, then click **OK** ⬜.

15. **With your teacher's permission**, click **File** > **Print**. Select **Print All Slides**, then click **Print** 🖶 to print the presentation.

16. Click **Save** 💾 to save your work, then click **File** > **Exit** to close the file and close PowerPoint.

**Figure 5-1**

# Project 10—Apply It

## Acceptable Use Policy Presentation

### DIRECTIONS

1. Start PowerPoint, if necessary.

2. Open **PProj10** from the data files for this lesson.

3. Save the presentation as **PProj10_ studentfirstname_studentlastname** in the location where your teacher instructs you to store the files for this lesson.

4. Replace the word **teacher** with **instructor** throughout the presentation.

   ✓ *Be sure to check capitalization and punctuation throughout after replacing.*

5. On slide 2, change the title font to **Calibri, 40 point**. Change the font color to **Theme Color Blue, Accent 2**, and apply the **Shadow** effect.

6. Copy this text formatting to the titles of all the slides in the presentation, including the title slide.

7. On slide 2, change the bullet list font to **Calibri, 28 point**. Change the font color to **Theme Color Gray-50%, Accent 6**.

8. Copy this text formatting to the bullet lists of all the slides in the presentation.

9. On slide 6, use Undo or the Reset button to remove copied formatting from the sub-bullets.

10. On slide 6, format the sub-bullet font as **Calibri, 22 point, Gray-50%, Accent 6**. Your presentation should look like the one shown in Figure 5-2

11. Check the spelling.

12. **With your teacher's permission**, print the presentation.

13. Close the presentation, saving all changes, and exit PowerPoint.

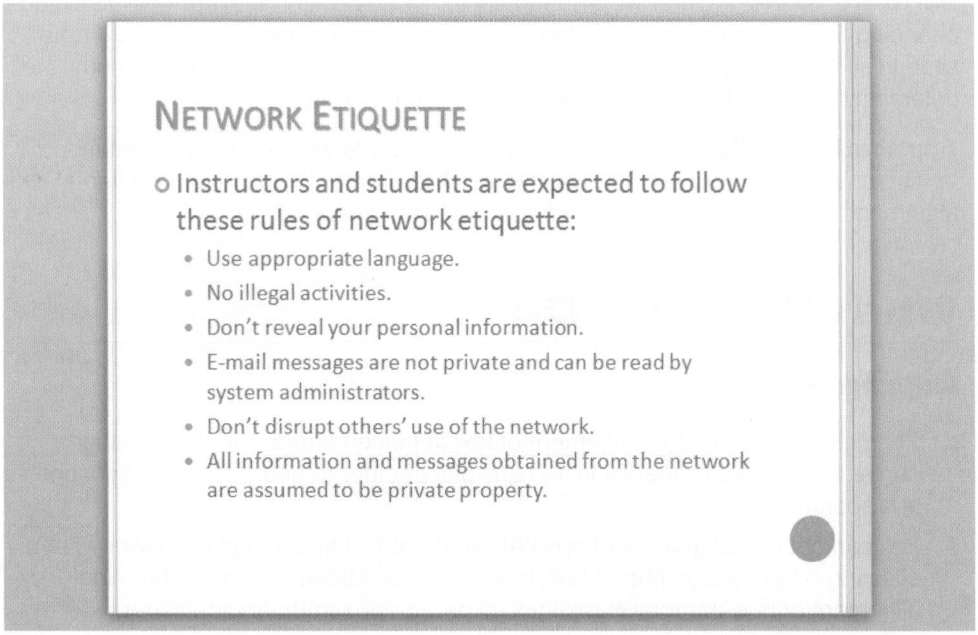

**Figure 5-2**

NETWORK ETIQUETTE

o Instructors and students are expected to follow these rules of network etiquette:

- Use appropriate language.
- No illegal activities.
- Don't reveal your personal information.
- E-mail messages are not private and can be read by system administrators.
- Don't disrupt others' use of the network.
- All information and messages obtained from the network are assumed to be private property.

# Lesson 6

# Aligning Text

## WORDS TO KNOW

**AutoFit**
PowerPoint feature designed to reduce font size to fit text in the current placeholder.

**Justify**
To align text flush with both the left and right margins of a column width or page width.

## ➤ What You Will Learn

**Aligning Text**
**Adjusting Line Spacing**
**Adjusting Paragraph Spacing**
**Moving and Copying Text**
**Using AutoFit Options**
**Adjusting and Formatting Placeholders**

**Software Skills**    Other ways to modify the appearance of text on a slide include changing text alignment and tweaking paragraph spacing. Move or copy text from slide to slide just as you would in a document. You can also move, resize, copy, or delete any placeholder on a slide or any object on a slide.

**Application Skills**    In this lesson, you continue to work on the presentations for Great Grains Bakery and the Holmes Medical Center by modifying list items, text alignment, text, and the position and size of placeholders.

## What You Can Do

### Aligning Text

- Themes also control the alignment of text in placeholders. You can left-align, center, right-align, or **justify** text in any placeholder to add interest or enhance text appearance.

- You can change alignment of any paragraph of text in a text placeholder without affecting other paragraphs of text. In a title placeholder, however, changing alignment of one paragraph realigns all paragraphs in that placeholder.

- Use buttons in the Paragraph group on the Home tab to align text. You can also use the Mini toolbar to apply left, center, or right alignment or use the Paragraph dialog box, discussed in the next section, to specify alignment.

- You can also click the Align Text button ▤ in the in the Paragraph group on the Home tab to adjust the vertical alignment of text within a placeholder. Settings include Top, Middle, and Bottom.

---

**Try It!**　**Aligning Text**

**1** Start PowerPoint and open **PTry06** from the data files for this lesson.

**2** Save the file as **PTry06_studentfirstname_ studentlastname** in the location where your teacher instructs you to store the files for this lesson.

**3** Go to slide 6 and click on the text placeholder underneath the slide title.

**4** Click Home > Align Text Left ▤.

**5** Click Home > Justify ▤.

**6** Double-click on any word in the text placeholder, then move the arrow over the Mini toolbar and click Align Text Right ▤.

**7** Click Home > Paragraph dialog box launcher. Click Centered in the Alignment drop-down list, then click OK.

**8** Go to slide 3 and click on the text placeholder. Click Home > Align Text ▤ > Middle.

**9** Save the **PTry06_studentfirstname_ studentlastname** file and leave it open to use in the next Try It.

## Adjusting Line Spacing

- You can also change the spacing between lines of text in a placeholder.
- Use the Line Spacing ▤ button to apply line spacing options: 1.5, 2.0, and so on. Line spacing affects all lines of a paragraph.
- With the insertion point in a single paragraph in a placeholder, the new line spacing option applies only to that paragraph. To adjust line spacing for all items in a placeholder, select them or select the placeholder.

- From the Line Spacing drop-down list, you can click Line Spacing Options to open the Paragraph dialog box for more customized line spacing options.
- In the Paragraph dialog box, you can specify Single, Double, Exact, Multiple, or 1.5 Lines of spacing.
- If you choose Exact or Multiple spacing, you can specify the exact amount of space you want between lines or the number of lines of space you want between lines by using the At text box in the Paragraph dialog box.

---

**Try It!**　**Adjusting Line Spacing**

**1** In the **PTry06_studentfirstname_ studentlastname** file, click slide 2 and click in the second bullet of text in the text placeholder.

**2** Click Home > Line Spacing ▤ > 2.0.

**3** This spacing is too large. Click Home > Line Spacing ▤ > 1.5.

**4** This spacing is still a bit too large. Click Home > Line Spacing ▤ > More Options.

**5** In the Paragraph dialog box, click Exactly in the Line Spacing drop-down list, then enter **32** in the At text box and click OK.

**6** Click in the third bullet of text in the text placeholder. Click Home > Line Spacing ▤, then roll the arrow over all the line spacing options to see the effect on the paragraph.

**7** Move the arrow away from the drop-down list without changing the spacing.

**8** Click to select the entire text placeholder. Click Home > Paragraph dialog box launcher.

**9** In the Paragraph dialog box, click Exactly in the Line Spacing drop-down list, then enter **32** in the At text box and click OK.

**10** Click Home > Align Text ▤ > Middle.

**11** Save the **PTry06_studentfirstname_ studentlastname** file and leave it open to use in the next Try It.

## Adjusting Paragraph Spacing

- Adjust paragraph spacing between bullets or other paragraphs to make text easier to read or to control space on a slide.

- For greater control over paragraph spacing, use the Paragraph dialog box. You can choose alignment and indention settings as well as specify a space before and/or after each paragraph and choose a line spacing option.

---

**Try It!**     **Adjusting Paragraph Spacing**

1. In the **PTry06_studentfirstname_studentlastname** file, click slide 2 and click the text placeholder to select it.

2. Click Home > Paragraph dialog box launcher.

3. In the Paragraph dialog box, click in the Before text text box and enter **0.5"** to change the indentation.

4. Click in the By text box and enter **0.5"** and click First Line in the Indentation drop-down list.

5. Click in the Before text box and enter **10 pt**. Click OK.

6. Save the **PTry06_studentfirstname_studentlastname** file and leave it open to use in the next Try It.

---

## Moving and Copying Text

- As you review a slide or presentation, you may rearrange the text to make it easier to follow.

- You can move text in PowerPoint using drag-and-drop or cut-and-paste methods.

- Use the drag-and-drop method to move text to a nearby location, such as within the same placeholder or on the same slide, or from the Outline pane to a slide.

- When you move text, a vertical line moves with the mouse to help you position the text.

- Use the cut-and-paste method to move text between two locations that are some distance apart, such as from one slide to another or from one presentation to another.

---

**Try It!**     **Moving and Copying Text**

1. In the **PTry06_studentfirstname_studentlastname** file, click slide 5 and select the text in the second bullet.

2. Click and drag the text in the second bullet down beneath the next bullet text, *Volunteer your services*.

3. Open the file **PTry06_support** from the location where the files for this lesson are stored.

4. In the **PTry06_studentfirstname_studentlastname** file, click slide 6, then click Home > New Slide 🖾 > Title and Content.

5. In the **PTry06_support** file, click slide 1 and select the text in the title placeholder. Press CTRL + C .

6. Go to slide 7 of the **PTry06_studentfirstname_studentlastname** file, click in the title placeholder, then press CTRL + V .

7. Save the **PTry06_studentfirstname_studentlastname** file and leave it open to use in the next Try It. Leave the **PTry06_support** file open to use in the next Try It as well.

## Using AutoFit Options

- If you enter more text than a placeholder can handle—such as a long slide title or a number of bullet entries—PowerPoint will by default use **AutoFit** to fit the text in the placeholder. AutoFit reduces font size or line spacing (or both) to fit the text into the placeholder.

- You can control AutoFit options using the AutoFit Options button ⊞ that displays near the bottom left corner of a placeholder.

---

**Try It!**    **Using AutoFit Options**

**1** In the **PTry06_support** file, click slide 1 and select all three bullets of text in the text placeholder. Press `CTRL` + `C`.

**2** In the **PTry06_studentfirstname_ studentlastname** file, go to slide 7 and click in the text placeholder, then press `CTRL` + `V`.

**3** In the **PTry06_support** file, click slide 2 and select all three bullets of text in the text placeholder. Press `CTRL` + `C`.

**4** In the **PTry06_studentfirstname_ studentlastname** file, go to slide 7 and click in the text placeholder after the three bullets of text you previously inserted, then press `CTRL` + `V`. Note that PowerPoint has used AutoFit to fit the text in the placeholder.

**5** Click AutoFit Options ⊞ > Change to Two Columns.

**AutoFit to Two Columns**

## The Power of Giving

- We are so grateful for the incredible support our organization has received from the community.
- We truly appreciate your investing in this outreach project, which, in turn, is an investment in the lives of those who come to us in need.
- One young homeless man entered our doors a little over a year ago. He was living on the streets of our city, and describes his former life as one filled with darkness and despair.

- With the help of your donations, he has completed our recovery program and now says he has hope.
- His future looks bright as opportunities have been presented to him which will bring further stability to his new life.
- Thanks for your part in his recovery.
- We truly appreciate your support!

● The Power of Giving                                      7/15/2010 ● 7

AutoFit Options button

**6** Click AutoFit Options ⊞ > Split Text Between Two Slides.

**7** Save the **PTry06_studentfirstname_ studentlastname** file and leave it open to use in the next Try It. Save the **PTry06_support** file and leave it open to use in the next Try It.

---

## Adjusting and Formatting Placeholders

- You can move or size any text or object placeholder to make room on the slide for other objects such as text boxes or images.

- You can also delete any placeholder to remove it from a slide, or copy a placeholder to use on another slide or in another presentation.

- To move, copy, size, or delete a placeholder and everything in it, select the placeholder so that its border becomes a solid line.

  - To move the placeholder, drag it by its border or use cut-and-paste to remove it from one slide and paste it on another.

  - To copy the placeholder, use copy-and-paste. A pasted placeholder appears in the same location on the new slide as on the original slide.

  - Delete a placeholder by simply pressing Delete while it is selected.

  - To resize a placeholder, drag one of the sizing handles at the corners and centers of the sides of the placeholder box.

- PowerPoint 2010 makes it easy to format a placeholder in interesting ways. Use a Quick Style, for example, to apply color and other effects to an entire placeholder.

- You can also apply a fill, outline, or other shape effect to a placeholder.

## Try It!   Adjusting and Formatting Placeholders

**1**   In the **PTry06_studentfirstname_studentlastname** file, go to slide 8, then click Home > New Slide 📄 > Title and Content.

**2**   In the **PTry06_support** file, go to slide 3 and click to select the title placeholder. Press CTRL + C.

**3**   In the **PTry06_studentfirstname_studentlastname** file, go to slide 8, then click to select the title placeholder. Press CTRL + V.

**4**   Click the bottom center sizing handle and drag it up to resize the title placeholder.

**5**   In the **PTry06_support** file, go to slide 3 and click to select the text placeholder. Press CTRL + C.

**6**   In the **PTry06_studentfirstname_studentlastname** file, go to slide 8, then click to select the text placeholder. Press CTRL + V.

**7**   Click the right center sizing handle of the text placeholder and drag it left to the center of the slide to resize the text placeholder.

**8**   Go to slide 4 and click to select the text placeholder. Click the center top sizing handle of the text placeholder and drag it down slightly to move the text away from the title.

**9**   Click Home > Quick Styles 🔽, then move the arrow over the various Quick Styles in the palette to see how they look in the text placeholder. Click on the Quick Style of your choice to apply it.

**10**   Save the **PTry06_studentfirstname_studentlastname** presentation and close the file. Close the **PTry06_support** file without saving and exit PowerPoint.

# Project 11—Create It

## Holmes Medical Center Presentation

### DIRECTIONS

1. Start PowerPoint if necessary and open **PProj11** from the data files for this lesson. Save the file as **PProj11_studentfirstname_studentlastname** in the location where your teacher instructs you to store files for this lesson.

2. Go to slide 5 and click the text placeholder. Click **Home > Align Text Left** 📄.

3. Go to slide 4 and click the text placeholder. Click **Home > Align Text** 📄 > **Middle**.

4. Now click **Home > Line Spacing** 📄 > 1.5.

5. Go to slide 2 and click the text placeholder. Click **Home > Line Spacing** 📄 > 1.5.

6. Go to slide 5 and click the text placeholder. Click **Home > Line Spacing** 📄 > 1.5.

7. Go to slide 3 and click the left text placeholder. Click **Home > Paragraph** dialog box launcher.

8. In the Paragraph dialog box, click in the **Before text** text box and enter **0.5"** to change the indentation.

9. Click in the **By** text box and enter **0.5"** and click First Line in the Indentation drop-down list. Click OK.

10. Click the right text placeholder. Click **Home > Paragraph** dialog box launcher.

11. In the Paragraph dialog box, click in the **Before text** text box and enter **0.5"** to change the indentation.

12. Click in the **By** text box and enter **0.5"** and click **First Line** in the Indentation drop-down list. Click OK.

13. Go to slide 6 and click the picture placeholder. Click and drag the picture to the align with the title placeholder at the left.

14. Click the center right sizing handle and drag it to the left to display the entire right text placeholder. Your slide should look similar to the one in Figure 6-1.

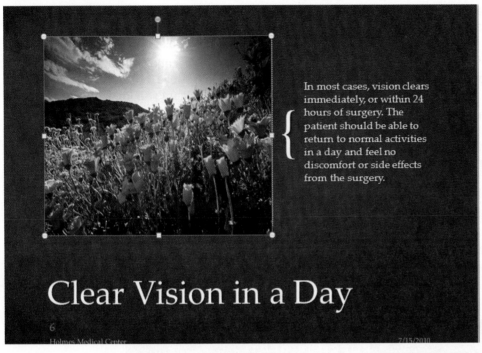

Figure 6-1

15. Click **File** > **Open** and navigate to the location where the files for this lesson are stored. Open **PProj11_integrated**.

16. Select the text in the text placeholder. Press CTRL + C.

17. Go to slide 5 in the **PProj11_studentfirstname_studentlastname** file, click after the last text bullet, then press CTRL + V.

18. Click to select the text placeholder, then click the bottom center sizing handle and drag it down to expand the text placeholder. PowerPoint AutoFits the text to the new placeholder size.

19. Select the text in the top three bullets, then Click **Home** > **Line Spacing** > **1**.

20. Click **Review** > **Spelling** to check spelling in the presentation. Click **Ignore All** for *Wynnedale* and *waveforming*, then click **OK**.

21. **With your teacher's permission**, click **File** > **Print**. Select **Print All Slides**, then click **Print** to print the presentation.

22. Click **Save** to save your work, then click **File** > **Exit** to close the file and close PowerPoint.

## Project 12—Apply It

## Great Grains Bread Presentation

### DIRECTIONS

1. Start PowerPoint, if necessary.

2. Open **PProj12** from the data files for this lesson.

3. Save the presentation as **PProj12_studentfirstname_studentlastname** in the location where your teacher instructs you to store the files for this lesson.

4. On slide 1, center the title and subtitle.

5. On slide 2, change the paragraph indent of the four bullet items under *Breads* and the three bullet items under *Sweet specialties* to: **0.5"** indentation before text and **Hanging indentation** by **0.5"**.

6. On slide 3, position the insertion point after the first bullet item, press ENTER, and type **Franchises available**. Move the last bullet item on the slide to be the first bullet item.

7. On slide 4, copy the first item and paste it at the end of the list. Add an exclamation point at the end of the word *Quality* in item 5. Then change the word *FOUR* in the slide title to **FIVE**.

8. Change the line spacing for all items in the text placeholder to **1.5**.

9. On slide 5, delete the *Turbinado sugar* and *Gourmet sea salt* items and then drag the bottom of the placeholder upwards to redistribute the items so the *Fair trade* item is positioned in the right column. Your slide should look like the one shown in Figure 6-2.

10. On slide 6, select the text placeholder on top of the photo and delete it.

11. Select the photo placeholder and drag it to the left, to the middle of the gray background.

12. Select the photo placeholder and drag it to the left, to the middle of the gray background. Right-align the text in the placeholder to the right of the photo.

13. Copy the subtitle placeholder from slide 1 and paste it on slide 6. Move it below the photo and resize the placeholder to be the same width as the photo.

14. Apply a Quick Style to the placeholder. You may need to change the text color to make it stand out against the Quick Style formatting.

15. Check the spelling.

16. **With your teacher's permission**, print the presentation.

17. Close the presentation, saving all changes, and exit PowerPoint.

| Figure 6-2 |
|------------|

### FRESH IS BEST!

- Locally grown herbs
- Whole grain flours
- Fresh creamery butter
- Free range eggs
- Locally produced honey
- Fair trade coffee and chocolate
- Certified organic fruits and vegetables
- Local and imported cheeses

# Lesson 7

# Displaying the Presentation Outline

## ➤ What You Will Learn

**Displaying the Presentation Outline**
**Viewing a Presentation in Reading View**

**Software Skills**    Use PowerPoint views to work with the outline when doing detailed editing work and to view a finished presentation.

**Application Skills**    In this lesson, you begin work on a presentation for a charity foundation, as well as the presentation for Voyager Travel Adventures by editing text in outline view and viewing the finished presentations in reading view.

## What You Can Do

### Displaying the Presentation Outline

- It is sometimes easier to edit a presentation that has lots of text using the presentation outline.
- To display the outline, click the Outline tab in the slide list pane at the left of the Normal view window.
- The outline of the presentation displays in the pane. You can cut, copy, and edit text here as you would within slide placeholders.

**Try It!**  **Displaying the Presentation Outline**

**1** Start PowerPoint and open **PTry07** from the data files for this lesson.

**2** Save the file as **PTry07_studentfirstname_ studentlastname** in the location where your teacher instructs you to store the files for this lesson.

**3** Click the outline tab of the slide pane in Normal view.

✓ *Note that the outline of the current slide is highlighted in the Outline tab.*

**4** Read the presentation by scrolling through the outline using the scroll bar at the right of the Outline tab of the slide pane.

**5** Click at the end of each bullet in the outline (not including the titles of the slides) and insert a period.

✓ *Note that the slide displayed in the center pane changes as you click on bullets of subsequent slides. The Outline tab is good for this kind of detailed editing work.*

**6** Save the **PTry07_studentfirstname_ studentlastname** file and leave it open to use in the next Try It.

## Viewing a Presentation in Reading View

■ Reading view can be used instead of full-screen Slide Show view to see how a presentation will appear when you deliver it to an audience.

■ Reading view includes a simple control menu you can use to copy slides and move around the presentation.

■ Reading view is also useful for someone who wants to display your presentation on a computer, rather than on a large screen with Slide Show view.

**Try It!**  **Viewing a Presentation in Reading View**

**1** In the **PTry07_studentfirstname_ studentlastname** file, click Reading View 📖 on the Status bar.

**2** Click Next ▷ and Previous ◁ to scroll through the presentation.

**3** Click Menu 📝 > Go to Slide > 4 Fair Use of Material.

**4** Click Menu 📝 > Full Screen.

**5** Click the left mouse button to advance to the next slide.

**6** Right-click to display the shortcut menu, then click End Show.

**7** Click Normal 🔲 on the Status bar to return to Normal view.

**8** Save the **PTry07_studentfirstname_ studentlastname** presentation and close the file.

# Project 13—Create It

## The Power of Giving Presentation

### DIRECTIONS

1. Start PowerPoint if necessary and open **PProj13** from the data files for this lesson. Save the file as **PProj13_studentfirstname_studentlastname** in the location where your teacher instructs you to store files for this lesson.

2. Go to slide 1 and click the outline tab of the slide pane in **Normal** view.

3. Click after *services* in the third bullet of slide 4, then press ENTER .

4. In the new fourth bullet, delete **or** and capitalize the word **every** to start the new bullet.

   ✓ *Note the changes as they appear in the slide displayed in the center pane.*

5. Delete the period at the end of the final bullet.

6. Click **Reading View** 📖 on the Status bar.

7. Click **Next** ▷ and **Previous** ◁ to scroll through the presentation.

8. Click **Menu** > **Go to Slide** [Go to Slide] > 3 **Giving Can Mean....**

9. Click **Menu** > **Full Screen**.

10. Click the left mouse button to advance to the next slide.

11. Right-click to display the shortcut menu, then click **End Show**.

12. If necessary, click **Normal** on the Status bar to return to Normal view.

13. Click **Review** > **Spelling** ABC to check spelling in the presentation. Click **OK**.

14. **With your teacher's permission**, click **File** > **Print**. Select **Print All Slides**, then click **Print** 🖶 to print the presentation.

15. Click **Save** 🖫 to save your work, then click **File** > **Exit** to close the file and close PowerPoint.

# Project 14—Apply It

## Adventure Travels Presentation

### DIRECTIONS

1. Start PowerPoint, if necessary.
2. Open **PProj14** from the data files for this lesson.
3. Save the presentation as **PProj14_ studentfirstname_studentlastname** in the location where your teacher instructs you to store the files for this lesson.
4. Display the presentation in the **Outline** tab.

5. On slide 2, add the text shown in Figure 7-2.

   ✓ *Remember, you can press* ⌷ENTER *in the Outline tab to enter a new bullet in the list, and press tab to decrease the level of an item within the outline.*

6. View the presentation in **Reading View**, then return to **Normal** view.
7. Check the spelling.
8. **With your teacher's permission**, print the presentation.
9. Close the presentation, saving all changes, and exit PowerPoint.

---

**Figure 7-2**

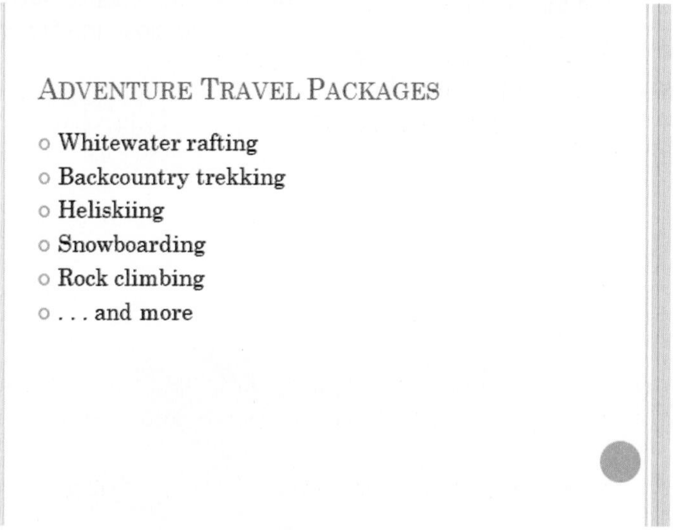

ADVENTURE TRAVEL PACKAGES

- Whitewater rafting
- Backcountry trekking
- Heliskiing
- Snowboarding
- Rock climbing
- . . . and more

# Lesson 8

# Arranging Slides

> ## What You Will Learn

**Copying, Duplicating, and Deleting Slides in Slide Sorter View**

**Rearranging Slides In Slide Sorter View**

**Software Skills**   As you work on a presentation, you often need to copy, delete, or rearrange slides. Slide Sorter view is the best view to use when arranging slides in a presentation.

**Application Skills**   In this lesson, you begin work on presentations for Restoration Architecture, a local architecture firm, as well as starting a presentation on strategic planning. You will modify these presentations by copying, moving, and deleting slides in slide sorter view.

## What You Can Do

### Copying, Duplicating, and Deleting Slides

■ In the course of working with a presentation, you may often need to create slides similar to one another. You can simplify this process by copying or duplicating slides.

- Copy a slide if you want to paste the copy some distance from the original or in another presentation.

- Duplicate a slide to create an identical version immediately after the original slide.

■ To remove a slide from the presentation, delete it using the Cut button on the Home tab, or press DEL . Note that PowerPoint does not ask you if you're sure you want to delete a slide—the slide is immediately deleted. If you change your mind about the deletion, use Undo to restore the slide.

## Try It!    Copying, Duplicating, and Deleting Slides

**1** Start PowerPoint and open **PTry08** from the data files for this lesson.

**2** Save the file as **PTry08_studentfirstname_ studentlastname** in the location where your teacher instructs you to store the files for this lesson.

**3** Click Slide Sorter ⊞, then click slide 3.

**4** Click Home > Copy 📋.

**5** Click in the space between slides 4 and 5, as shown in the following figure, then click Paste 📋.

✓ *Note that a large vertical blinking cursor appears in the space between two slides when you have clicked there or dragged a slide there.*

**6** Click slide 8, then click Home > Copy 📋 > Duplicate.

**7** With slide 8 selected, click Home > Cut ✂.

**8** Save the **PTry08_studentfirstname_ studentlastname** file and leave it open to use in the next Try It.

## Rearranging Slides in Slide Sorter View

- Another task you must frequently undertake when working with slides is to rearrange them. Slide Sorter view is your best option for moving slides from one place in a presentation to another.

- Rearrange slides in Slide Sorter view by simply dragging a slide to a new location.

- You can also rearrange slides in the Slides tab in Normal view, using the same dragging technique. This is an easy process in a presentation that has only a few slides, but for a large presentation, Slide Sorter view is the better choice because you can see more slides at a time without scrolling.

## Try It!    Rearranging Slides in Slide Sorter View

**1** In the **PTry08_studentfirstname_ studentlastname** file, click slide 5 and drag it to the end of the presentation, after slide 8.

**2** Select slide 8 and press DEL .

**3** Click slide 7 and drag it to the position between slides 5 and 6.

**4** Click slide 2 and drag it after slide 7.

**5** Again, click slide 2 and drag it after slide 7.

**6** Close **PTry08_studentfirstname_ studentlastname**, saving all changes, and exit PowerPoint.

# Project 15—Create It

## Restoration Architecture Presentation

### DIRECTIONS

1. Start PowerPoint if necessary and open **PProj15** from the data files for this lesson. Save the file as **PProj15_studentfirstname_studentlastname** in the location where your teacher instructs you to store files for this lesson.

2. Click **Slide Sorter** 🔠, then click slide 11.

3. Click **Home > Copy** 📋 **> Duplicate**.

4. Click and drag slide 12 to the space between slides 4 and 5.

5. Click and drag slide 11 to the space between slides 4 and 5.

6. Click **File > Open** 📂 and navigate to the location where the files for this lesson are stored. Open **PProj15_gallery**.

7. Click **Slide Sorter** 🔠, then hold the `CTRL` key down while you click to select slides 1, 2, and 3.

8. Click **Home > Copy** 📋.

9. In the **PProj15_studentfirstname_ studentlastname** presentation, click between slides 6 and 7, then click **Home > Paste** 📋.

10. Click slide 15, then press `DEL`. Your presentation should look like the one shown in Figure 8-1.

11. **With your teacher's permission**, click **File > Print**. Select **Full Page Slides > 6 Slides Horizontal**, then click **Print** 🖨 to print the presentation.

12. Click **Save** 💾 to save your work, then click **File > Exit** to close both the **PProj15_studentfirstname_ studentlastname** and **PProj15_gallery** files and close PowerPoint.

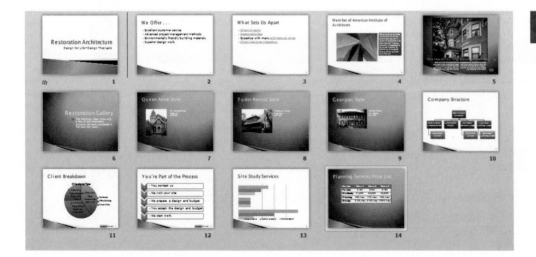

**Figure 8-1**

# Project 16—Apply It

## Recommending a Strategy Presentation

### DIRECTIONS

1. Start PowerPoint, if necessary.
2. Open **PProj16** from the data files for this lesson.
3. Save the presentation as **PProj16_ studentfirstname_studentlastname** in the location where your teacher instructs you to store the files for this lesson.
4. Change to **Slide Sorter** view.
5. Move slide 2 to follow slide 3.
6. Duplicate slide 4.
7. Double-click slide 5 to return to **Normal** view and change the title of slide 5 to **Additional Options**.
8. Open **PProj16_slide**.
9. Copy the slide and then paste it after slide 5 in **PProj16_studentfirstname_studentlastname**.
10. Change to **Slide Sorter** view again to view the sequence of the slides, which should look like that shown in Figure 8-2.
11. Check the spelling.
12. **With your teacher's permission**, print the presentation.
13. Close both presentations, saving all changes, and exit PowerPoint.

Figure 8-2

# Lesson 9

# Adding Slide Transitions

> ## What You Will Learn

**Identifying Guidelines for Using Graphics, Fonts, and Special Effects in Presentations**

**Evaluating and Selecting Appropriate Sources of Information**

**Adding Slide Transitions**

**Controlling Slide Advance**

**Software Skills**    PowerPoint allows you to add transitions to make your slides more visually interesting during a presentation. After you set up the transitions, you can rehearse the show to make sure you have allowed enough time for the audience to view slide content.

**Application Skills**    In this lesson, you continue to work on the presentation for the charity organization as well as the Holmes Medical Center laser surgery unit by adding appropriate slide transitions.

## WORDS TO KNOW

**Transitions**
The visual effects used when one slide moves off of the screen and another moves onto the screen.

**Advance slide timing**
A setting that controls the amount of time a slide displays on the screen.

## What You Can Do

### Identifying Guidelines for Using Graphics, Fonts, and Special Effects in Presentations

- When working with graphic information such as a PowerPoint presentation, keep in mind that you should avoid overloading a presentation with too many graphics, fonts, and special effects.

- Make sure all graphics you use, including photos, clip art, and custom shapes, fit with the color scheme of the slide or presentation, and serve a purpose for conveying your message.

- PowerPoint Themes make it easy to provide visual interest with color and fonts that are combined in a pleasing way. You can modify fonts to make key information stand out or provide additional visual appeal to a presentation.

■ Make sure that all text stands out against placeholder backgrounds and is large enough to be readable. Also, make sure you're using text effects such as bold, italic, and underline in an appropriate way. Don't get too carried away with special effects like drop shadows.

■ PowerPoint also provides a wide variety of slide transitions and special effects to provide interest and movement as you present a slide show. Again, make sure that the effects you use are appropriate to the visual theme and the message of the presentation.

■ In most cases, simpler, more subtle transition effects will prove to be most effective, and won't detract from the message you're delivering.

## Evaluating and Selecting Appropriate Sources of Information

■ When doing research for a project or presentation, it's important to evaluate and select appropriate sources of information, whether the source is print, electronic, video, or a person you interview.

■ Use Internet search engines and bookmarks to locate and access information. Basic and advanced search techniques will help you pinpoint exactly what you need to find using search engines, directories, biographical dictionaries, and other research tools.

■ Be sure to evaluate the accuracy and validity of the information you find by understanding the author's point of view, credentials, and any potential bias that might come as a result of his or her position.

■ Finding information on the Internet often gives a source more credibility than it may deserve. It's important to be able to decide what is someone's opinion, and what is a fact backed up by research and data.

■ As always, cite the sources of the information, and request permission to use if necessary.

## Adding Slide Transitions

■ PowerPoint provides **transitions** that you can use to make the slide show more interesting. You can apply transitions in either Normal view or Slide Sorter view using tools on the Transitions tab.

■ The Transition gallery offers almost 60 different transitions. If you are in Normal view, resting the pointer on a transition previews the transition on the current slide. In Slide Sorter view, select a transition from the gallery to apply it and see a preview of the effect.

■ The Transition gallery organizes transition effects by Subtle, Exciting, and Dynamic Content.

■ The Transitions tab offers several other important options. You can:

● Select a sound effect or sound clip to accompany the transition.

● Choose a speed for the transition: Slow, Medium, or Fast.

● Choose how to advance slides: by clicking the mouse or automatically based on a specific time lapse.

● Apply settings to all slides at the same time.

● After you have applied a transition, you can use the Preview button to review all effects you have applied to the slides.

---

**Try It!**    **Adding Slide Transitions**

**1** Start PowerPoint and open **PTry09** from the data files for this lesson.

**2** Save the file as **PTry09_studentfirstname_ studentlastname** in the location where your teacher instructs you to store the files for this lesson.

**3** With slide 1 selected, click Transitions, then double-click Reveal.

✓ *Note that a star with lines appears next to the slide thumbnail in the Slides pane at left to indicate a transition has been applied.*

**4** Go to slide 2 and then double-click Fade from the Transitions gallery.

**5** Go to slide 3, then double-click Flash from the Transitions gallery.

*(continued)*

## Try It!     Adding Slide Transitions *(continued)*

**6** Go to slide 4, then double-click Random Bars from the Transitions gallery.

**7** Go to slide 5, then double-click Ripple from the Transitions gallery.

**8** Go to slide 6, then double-click Fly Through from the Transitions gallery.

**9** Go to slide 1, then click Transitions > Preview. Click Slide Sorter, then click each slide and Preview the transition.

**10** Click Normal, go to slide 1, then click Sound > Drum Roll. Click Apply to All.

**11** Click Slide Show > From Beginning to view the transitions with the sound. Click to exit the slide show.

**12** Try experimenting with the different Effect Options by clicking Transition > Effect Options.

**13** You can also try changing the duration of transitions by entering times in the duration text box, or clicking the up or down arrows to increase or decrease the time.

**14** Save the **PTry09_studentfirstname_ studentlastname** file and leave it open to use in the next Try It.

## Controlling Slide Advance

- By default, you advance slides in a presentation manually by clicking the mouse button or a keyboard key. If you do not want to advance slides manually, you can have PowerPoint advance each slide automatically.

- **Advance slide timing** defines the amount of time a slide is on the screen before PowerPoint automatically advances to the next slide.

- You can set advance slide timing on the Transitions tab for individual slides or for all slides in a presentation. Set advance slide timing in seconds or minutes and seconds.

- Even if you set advance timings for your slides, you can also choose to advance a slide manually.

- The advance slide timing for each slide is indicated in Slide Sorter view by a number below the slide.

## Try It!     Controlling Slide Advance

**1** In the **PTry09_studentfirstname_ studentlastname** file, click Slide Sorter

**2** Click slide 1, then click Advance Slide After and type **5.**

**3** Click Apply To All.

**4** Click Sound > No Sound, then click Apply To All.

**5** Click Slide Show > From Beginning to view the transitions without the sound. Click to exit the slide show.

**6** Close **PTry09_studentfirstname_ studentlastname**, saving all changes, and exit PowerPoint.

# Project 17—Create It

## The Power of Giving Presentation

### DIRECTIONS

1. Start PowerPoint if necessary and open **PProj17** from the data files for this lesson. Save the file as **PProj17_studentfirstname_studentlastname** in the location where your teacher instructs you to store files for this lesson.
2. Go to slide 1 and click **Transitions**, then double-click **Wipe** from the Transitions gallery.
3. Go to slide 2 and double-click **Wipe** from the Transitions gallery.
4. Go to slide 3 and double-click **Cover** from the Transitions gallery.
5. Go to slide 4 and double-click **Flip** from the Transitions gallery.
6. Go to slide 5 and double-click **Doors** from the Transitions gallery.
7. Go to slide 6 and double-click **Conveyor** from the Transitions gallery.
8. Go to slide 7 and double-click **Shape** from the Transitions gallery.
9. Go to slide 1, then click **Slide Sorter** 🖽, then click each slide to preview the transition.
10. Click **Normal** 🖽, go to slide 1, then click **Sound** 🔊 > **Chime**.
11. Click **Transitions** > **Effect Options** 🖾 > **From Left**.
12. Click **Advance Slide After**, then enter **5** in the text box. Click **Apply To All** 🖾.
13. Click **Slide Show** > **From Beginning** 🖳 to view the transitions. Click to exit the slide show.
14. **With your teacher's permission**, click **File** > **Print**. Select **Full Page Slides** > **6 Slides Horizontal**, then click **Print** 🖨 to print the presentation.
15. Click **Save** 🖫 to save your work, then click **File** > **Exit** to close the **PProj17_studentfirstname_studentlastname** file and close PowerPoint.

# Project 18—Apply It

## Laser Surgery Unit Presentation

### DIRECTIONS

1. Start PowerPoint, if necessary.
2. Open **PProj18** from the data files for this lesson.
3. Save the presentation as **PProj18_studentfirstname_studentlastname** in the location where your teacher instructs you to store the files for this lesson.
4. Apply several different slide transitions to the slides using a medium speed. View the slides in Slide Show view to see the transitions.
5. Apply the **Laser** sound to the first slide and the last slide.
6. Choose to advance all slides after 5 seconds.
7. View the presentation as a slide show, without clicking the mouse to advance each slide.
8. Check the spelling.
9. **With your teacher's permission**, print the presentation.
10. Close the presentation, saving all changes, and exit PowerPoint.

# Chapter Assessment and Application

## Project 19—Make It Your Own

### Aquatic Center

The student athletics council has asked you to update a presentation about the benefits of the campus aquatics center. Follow the guidelines below to make a stronger case for all members of the local community to use the aquatics center.

## DIRECTIONS

1. Start PowerPoint. Save a new blank file as **PProj19_studentfirstname_studentlastname** in the location where your teacher tells you to save the files for this project.

2. Apply a theme from the themes available on the Design tab. Pick one that you think is appropriate for the audience. Apply a different color theme if the colors in the design you chose are not bright and cheerful.

3. On slide 1, type **Campus Recreation Center** in the Title placeholder. In the subtitle placeholder, type your full name.

4. Add two new **Title and Content** slides. On slide 2, type **CRC Introduces . . .** in the Title placeholder. In the text placeholder, type the following bullets:

   **The Bedard Aquatics Center**

   - **Lap pool—50 meters by 25 yards, with 1 meter and 3 meter diving boards**
   - **Leisure pool—features a current channel, vortex, and waterwall**
   - **Whirlpool—temperature ranges from 101 degrees to 104 degrees**

5. On slide 3, type **Why We're Talking** in the Title placeholder. In the subtitle placeholder, type the following bullets:

   - **The Aquatics Center is currently underused**
   - **Maintaining fitness is a lifelong goal for students, faculty, staff, and community members**
   - **Surveys suggest the university community is interested in regular visits to the CRC**
   - **Talking about the Center will increase that interest**

6. Open the file **PProj19_aquatics** from the data files for this chapter and reuse the slides from this presentation after slide 3 of **PProj19_studentfirstname_studentlastname**. Close the **PProj19_aquatics** file.

7. Move slide 3 to the end of the presentation.

8. Go to the new slide 3, titled **Specific Programs**, and select the text placeholder. Change the text formatting to **Calibri, 36 pt**. Change the font color to one of the Theme colors. Be sure to choose one that stands out enough to be readable.

9. Use the format painter to apply this text formatting to the level 1 bullets in slides 4 and 7.

10. If necessary, use text AutoFit options to resize the text on slide 7.

11. Display the presentation outline and promote the three bullets under *The Bedard Aquatics Center* to the same level as the first bullet.

12. Change the slide layout of slide 5 to **Two Content**. In the right placeholder, insert the picture **PProj19_youthswim** from the location where the data files for this chapter are stored.

13. Lengthen the picture to more closely match the size of the chart at left. Apply a picture style and artistic effect of your choice.

14. In slide sorter view, move slides 3 and 4 after slide 6.

15. Insert a header that includes the **Date and time** and the **Slide number**. Insert a footer that includes your full name. Don't show these on the title slide. Include the page number on notes and handouts pages.

16. Add speaker's notes to slide 5 that say **Don't forget to mention unlimited lap swimming hours!**

17. Find **university** and replace with **University.** Be sure to match case when you replace. Replace the **Calibri** font with **Agency FB** throughout the presentation.

18. On slide 5, adjust line spacing to **1.5.**

19. Add slide transitions, sounds, and timings of your choosing.

20. View the presentation in Reading View.

21. Check spelling, and, **with your teacher's permission**, print one copy of your presentation.

22. Close the presentation, saving changes, and exit PowerPoint.

# Project 20—Master It

## Franchise Sales Presentation

As a new sales manager for Great Grains Bakery, one of your sales representatives has asked if you can help him spruce up his presentation for customers and potential franchisees. Follow the guidelines below to add stronger introductory slides to the presentation, additional photos and text formatting, as well as a new theme and transitions.

### DIRECTIONS

1. Start PowerPoint, if necessary, and open **PProj20_ bakery** from the data files for this chapter. Save the file as **PProj20_studentfirstname_ studentlastname** in the location where your teacher tells you to save the files for this project.

2. Apply a theme from the themes available on the Design tab. Pick one that you think is appropriate for the audience.

3. Insert three new slides before slide 1. Make the first new slide a **Title** slide, the second new slide a **Two Content** slide, and the third new slide should be a **Title and Content** slide.

4. On slide 1, type **Great Grains Bakery** in the Title placeholder. In the subtitle placeholder, enter **Fresh to You Each Day**.

5. On slide 2, type **A Variety of Baked Goods** in the Title placeholder. In the left content placeholder, type the following bullets:

- Breads
- Croissants
- Bagels
- Muffins
- Rolls

6. On slide 2, in the right content placeholder, type the following bullets:

- Sweet specialties
- Pastries
- Cookies
- Cakes

7. On slide 3, type **Fresh Is Best!** in the Title placeholder. In the content placeholder, type the following bullets:

- **Locally grown herbs**
- **Whole grain flours**
- **Fresh creamery butter**
- **Free range eggs**
- **Locally produced honey**
- **Fair trade coffee and chocolate**
- **Certified organic fruits and vegetables**
- **Local and imported cheeses**

8. Change the title and text fonts throughout the presentation to a font, font size, and font color of your choice. Check all slides for text alignment and fit within placeholders after making the change.

9. Insert the **PProj20_bagel** picture on a slide of your choice. Check the sizing of the picture placeholder on slide 7. Add picture styles and formatting to both photos.

10. Change the header to show neither the **Date and time** nor the **Slide number**. Change the footer to show your full name.

11. Add speaker's notes to slide 6 that say **Remind seminar audiences that franchises are going fast!**

12. In slide sorter view, move slides 6 and 7 after slide 9. Copy slide 5 and add it to the end of the presentation.

13. Add slide transitions, sounds, and timings of your choosing.

14. View the presentation in Reading View.

15. Check spelling, and, **with your teacher's permission**, print one copy of your presentation.

16. Close the presentation, saving changes, and exit PowerPoint.

# Chapter 2

# Working with Lists and Graphics

## Lesson 10
## Working with Bulleted and Numbered Lists
## Projects 21-22

- Removing a Bullet Symbol from a Bullet Point
- Changing a Bullet List to a Numbered List
- Modifying the Bullet List Style

## Lesson 11
## Using Clip Art and Pictures
## Projects 23-24

- Inserting Clip Art
- Resizing and Positioning Clip Art
- Inserting a Picture from a File
- Inserting a Photo from the Clip Art Task Pane
- Removing the Background from a Picture

## Lesson 12
## Inserting Symbols and Text Boxes
## Projects 25-26

- Inserting Symbols
- Inserting and Formatting a Text Box
- Using Multiple Columns in a Text Box

## Lesson 13
## Drawing and Formatting Shapes
## Projects 27-28

- Using Rulers, Guides, and Gridlines
- Drawing Shapes
- Moving and Sizing Shapes
- Applying Fills and Outlines
- Applying Shape Styles
- Applying Shape Effects
- Adding Text to Shapes

## Lesson 14
## Positioning and Grouping Shapes
## Projects 29-30

- Stacking Objects
- Grouping Objects
- Duplicating Objects
- Aligning and Distributing Objects

## Lesson 15
## Creating WordArt
## Projects 31-32

- Understanding WordArt
- Applying WordArt Styles to Existing Text
- Inserting and Formatting WordArt

## Lesson 16
## Creating SmartArt Diagrams
## Projects 33-34

- Creating a SmartArt Diagram
- Adding, Removing, and Resizing Shapes in a Diagram
- Reordering Diagram Content
- Changing the Diagram Type
- Changing the Color and Style of a Diagram
- Creating Picture-Based SmartArt

## Lesson 17
## Creating a Photo Album
## Projects 35-36

- Creating a Photo Album

## End of Chapter Assessments
## Projects 37-38

## Lesson 10

# Working with Bulleted and Numbered Lists

**WORDS TO KNOW**

**Layout Master**
A template on which individual slides that use a certain layout are based.

**Picture bullet**
A graphic specifically designed to be used as a bullet character.

**Slide Master**
A template on which the individual slides in the presentation are based.

➤ **What You Will Learn**

> Removing a Bullet Symbol from a Bullet Point
> Changing a Bullet List to a Numbered List
> Modifying the Bullet List Style

**Software Skills**   Bullet points are the most common format for presenting data in a PowerPoint presentation. Sometimes, though, the default bulleted list needs a little uplift to keep it from being repetitive. This lesson shows you how to make some changes to a bulleted list, including how to convert it into a list that doesn't use bullets at all.

**Application Skills**   At Wynnedale Medical, the manager you have created a presentation for has commented that she does not like the bullet character in the draft presentation. You will change to a different bullet character, and demonstrate on a few slides how the presentation might look with numbered lists or with no bullets at all.

## What You Can Do

### Removing a Bullet Symbol from a Bullet Point

■  In some cases, you may not want bullets at all.  Sometimes a regular paragraph is more appropriate for a slide than a series of bulleted items.

- You can easily remove the bullets from paragraphs with the Bullets button on the Home tab. This button is an on/off toggle for the Bullets feature.

✓ *The Bullets button also has a drop-down list for selecting a different bullet character. You will learn how to switch characters later in this chapter.*

---

**Try It!**     **Removing a Bullet**

**1** Start PowerPoint and open **PTry10** from the data files for this lesson.

**2** Save the presentation as **PTry10_ studentfirstname_studentlastname** in the location where your teacher instructs you to store the files for this lesson.

**3** Click to move the insertion point into the first bulleted paragraph on the first slide.

**4** Click Home > Bullets ⊞▾. The bullet character is toggled off.

**5** Click Home > Bullets ⊞▾. The bullet character is toggled back on again.

**6** Save the changes to the **PTry10_ studentfirstname_studentlastname** file and leave open to use in the next Try It.

---

## Changing a Bulleted List to a Numbered List

- Numbered lists are almost identical to bulleted ones except they use consecutive numbers rather than using the same character for each paragraph.

- Use a numbered list whenever the order of the items is significant, such as in step-by-step instructions.

✓ *Avoid using numbered lists when the order is not significant, because the audience may erroneously read significance into it.*

---

**Try It!**     **Changing a Bulleted List to a Numbered List**

**1** In the **PTry10_studentfirstname_ studentlastname** file, click slide 2 to display it.

**2** In the Slides list, click slide 6 to display it.

**3** Drag across the entire bulleted list to select it.

**OR**

Click to move the insertion point into the bulleted list and press CTRL + A to select all.

**4** Click Home > Numbering ⊞▾. The list becomes numbered.

**5** Save the changes to the **PTry10_ studentfirstname_studentlastname** file and leave open to use in the next Try It.

---

## Modifying the Bulleted List Style

- There are two ways of modifying a bulleted list's style. You can manually edit the individual paragraphs or lists that you want to specifically affect, or you can change the overall style for bulleted lists on the Slide Master.

- A wide variety of bullet characters are available, including symbols and pictures. You can select a bullet character from any font installed on your PC, or from a large collection of **picture bullets**.

- Changes to the default bullet are made in the Bullets and Numbering dialog box.

| **Try It!** | **Modifying the Bulleted List Style** |

**1** In the **PTry10_studentfirstname_studentlastname** file, click slide 2 to display it.

**2** Click anywhere in the bulleted list and press CTRL + A to select all.

**3** On the Home tab, in the Paragraph group, click the down arrow on the Bullets button, opening its menu.

**4** Click the small round bullets on the menu. The bullets change.

**5** With the bulleted list still selected from the previous steps, click the down arrow on the Bullets button again.

**6** Click Bullets and Numbering to open the Bullets and Numbering dialog box.

**7** Click the Customize button. The Symbol dialog box opens.

**8** If the Wingdings font is not already selected in the Font list, open the Font list and click Wingdings.

✓ *You can choose any character from any font as a bullet symbol. Wingdings is a font designed specifically for this purpose, but you may have others available that have interesting bullet characters, too.*

**9** Click a fancy star symbol in Symbol dialog box. and click OK.

**10** Click the up increment arrow next to the Size text box 10 times, increasing the size of the bullet to 110%.

**11** Open the Color button's palette and click Dark Red, Accent 5 color from the theme colors.

**12** Click OK. The bullets on the slide change.

**13** Save the changes to the **PTry10_studentfirstname_studentlastname** file and leave open to use in the next Try It.

Select a symbol

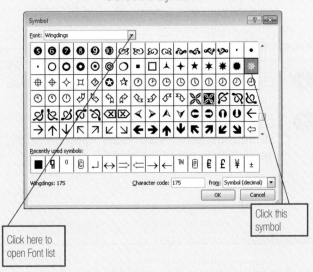

Click here to open Font list

Click this symbol

Select a color

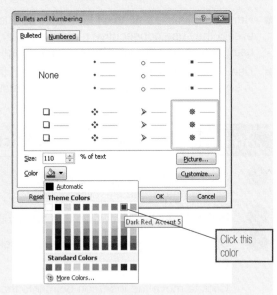

Click this color

## Try It!     Using a Picture as a Bullet Character

**1** In the **PTry10_studentfirstname_studentlastname** file, click slide 3 to select it.

**2** Click anywhere in the bulleted list and press `CTRL` + `A` to select all.

**3** On the Home tab, in the Paragraph group, click the down arrow on the Bullets button, opening its menu.

**4** Click Bullets and Numbering.

**5** Click Picture. The Picture Bullet dialog box opens.

**6** Scroll through the list and click on a green sphere graphic. Click OK. The bullet character changes.

**7** Save the changes to the **PTry10_studentfirstname_studentlastname** file, and leave it open to use in the next Try It.

## Changing Bullets on the Slide Master

■ The **Slide Master** is the template on which each slide is based. When you modify the Slide Master, all slides that use that template are affected. If you want to affect all the bullets in the presentation, regardless of the slide layout, make the changes here.

■ A slide master has one or more Layout Masters. Each **Layout Master** determines the placement of the text boxes and other placeholders for a certain slide layout. If you want to affect the bullets only on slides that use a certain layout, make the changes on that particular layout's Layout Master.

## Try It!     Changing the Bullets on a Slide Master

**1** In the **PTry10_studentfirstname_studentlastname** file, View > Slide Master .

**2** In the Slides pane at the left, click the top thumbnail image on the list (the Slide Master itself).

**3** On the Slide Master slide, click in the paragraph that reads *Click to edit Master text styles*.

**4** On the Home tab, click the down arrow on the Bullets button and click the white circles preset.

✓ *Only the bullet character for the first level of bullets changes. You can specify a different character for each of the preset levels here if desired.*

**5** On the Slide Master tab, click Close Master View to return to the presentation.

✓ *Notice that the slides you manually changed earlier in this lesson are not affected by the new bullet character selection. That's because manual settings override the automatic ones.*

**6** Click slide 2 in the Slides pane, click in the bulleted list, and press `CTRL` + `A` to select all.

Change the bullet on the Slide Master

**7** Click Home > Bullets , removing the old bullet character.

**8** Click Bullets again, applying the new default bullet character (the circle).

**9** Repeat steps 6-8 for slide 3.

**10** Save the changes to the **PTry10_studentfirstname_studentlastname** file and leave open to use in the next Try It.

**Try It!**    **Changing the Bullets on a Layout Master**

**1** In the **PTry10_studentfirstname_ studentlastname** file, click View > Slide Master ⬚ .

**2** In the Slides pane at the left, click the fifth thumbnail image from the top (the Two Content Layout).

**3** Click in the left placeholder box of the layout and press CTRL + A to select all levels of bullets in that box.

**4** On the Home tab, open the Bullets buttons list and click the filled square bullet character.

**5** Click Slide Master > Close Master View ⊠ .

**6** Save the **PTry10_studentfirstname_ studentlastname** file and close it.

Choose a filled square bullet for only one placeholder box, in only this one layout

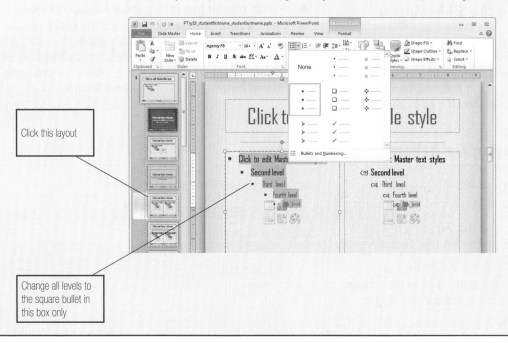

Click this layout

Change all levels to the square bullet in this box only

# Project 21—Create It

## Laser Surgery Presentation

### DIRECTIONS

1. Start PowerPoint if necessary, and open **PProj21** from the data files for this lesson.

2. Save the presentation as **PProj21_ studentfirstname_studentlastname** in the location where your teacher instructs you to store the files for this lesson.

3. Display slide 1, and click **Insert > Text Box** [icon] . Click at the bottom of the slide and type your full name.

   ✓ *Remember to replace the sample text studentfirstname with your own first name and studentlastname with your own last name.*

4. Click **View > Slide Master** [icon] .

5. Click the top slide in the Slides pane (the Slide Master).

6. Click in the bulleted list area, and press [CTRL] + [A] to select all.

7. On the **Home** tab, click the down arrow on the Bullets button, opening a menu.

8. Click **Bullets and Numbering**. The Bullets and Numbering dialog box opens.

9. Click **Customize**. The Symbol dialog box opens.

10. Open the Font drop-down list and click **ZapfDingbats**.

    ✓ *If you do not have this font, choose Wingdings.*

11. Click a check mark symbol.

12. Click **OK** to close the Symbol dialog box.

13. Click **OK** to close the Bullets and Numbering dialog box.

14. Click **Slide Master > Close Slide Master** [icon] .

15. Browse through the slides. Each slide should use the check mark bullet.

16. **With your teacher's permission**, print slide 2 of the presentation.

    ✓ *Refer to Lesson 2 of the Basics section on the companion CD for information on printing a file.*

17. Close the presentation, saving changes, and exit PowerPoint.

# Project 22—Apply It

## Laser Surgery Presentation

### DIRECTIONS

1. Start PowerPoint if necessary, and open **PProj22** from the data files for this lesson.

2. Save the presentation as **PProj22_ studentfirstname_studentlastname** in the location where your teacher instructs you to store the files for this lesson.

3. Display slide 1, and place a text box at the bottom of the slide containing your full name.

4. Open Slide Master view, and change the bullet character for all slides (all layouts) to a picture bullet. Choose any yellow sphere from the Picture Bullet dialog box.

5. On the Title and Content Layout Master, change only the first-level bullet character to any red sphere picture bullet. Set the bullet size to 100% of Text.

6. Close Master view.

7. Remove the bullet from the paragraph on slide 7.

8. Convert the bullet points on slide 6 to a numbered list.

9. Browse the presentation in Slide Sorter view, looking at the bullets on the slides. See Figure 10-1.

   ✓ *Notice that slides 3 and 5 use the yellow bullet because they do not use the Title and Content layout. The slides that use Title and Content as their layout appear with red bullets.*

10. **With your teacher's permission**, print the presentation as handouts (6 slides per page).

11. Close the presentation, saving changes, and exit PowerPoint.

**Figure 10-1**

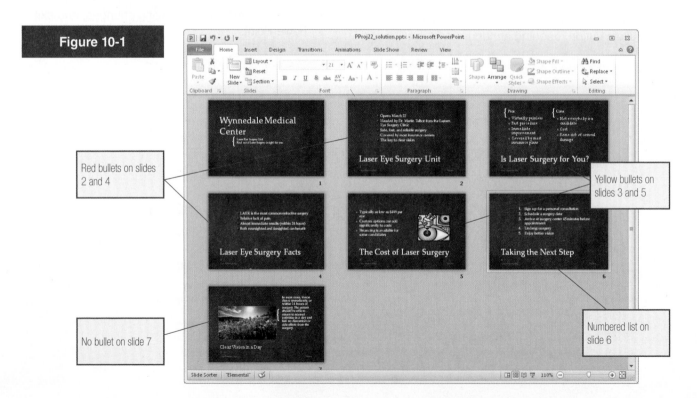

Red bullets on slides 2 and 4

Yellow bullets on slides 3 and 5

No bullet on slide 7

Numbered list on slide 6

# Lesson 11

# Using Clip Art and Pictures

## ➤ What You Will Learn

**Inserting Clip Art**
**Resizing and Positioning Clip Art**
**Inserting a Picture from a File**
**Inserting a Photo from the Clip Art Task Pane**
**Removing the Background from a Picture**

**WORDS TO KNOW**

Clip art
Generic, reusable drawings of common people, places, things, and concepts.

Keyword
A descriptive word attached to an image, used for searching and indexing the image library.

**Software Skills**   Clip art can be a tremendous asset to you as you create presentations. Your copy of PowerPoint includes free access to a huge library of ready-made drawings on Microsoft's Web site. You can access them through the Clip Art feature in PowerPoint.

**Application Skills**   In this lesson, you continue to work with the Wynnedale Medical Center presentation. You will select appropriate clip art images and insert them in the presentation to enhance its appearance.

## What You Can Do

### Inserting Clip Art

- **Clip art** can be used in any Office application, but is especially suitable for PowerPoint because of the graphical focus of most slides.

- If you are connected to the Internet when you search for clips, PowerPoint automatically searches the large Office.com collection of clips. Otherwise, fewer clips are returned when you search, from the much smaller collection stored on your hard disk.

- You can find clip art by searching for specific **keywords**. Each clip art image has one or more keywords assigned to it that describe it. For example, a picture of a dog might include the keywords *dog, pup, canine, animal,* and *pet*.

- If the slide contains an open Content placeholder, you can place the clip art using that. You can also insert clip art on any slide without using a placeholder.

## Try It!    Inserting Clip Art

**1** Start PowerPoint and open **PTry11** from the data files for this lesson.

**2** Save the presentation as **PTry11_ studentfirstname_studentlastname** in the location where your teacher instructs you to store the files for this lesson.

**3** Click slide 8 in the Slides pane.

**4** In the empty placeholder on slide 8, click the Clip Art icon 🔲 . The Clip Art task pane opens.

**5** In the Search For box in the Clip Art task pane, type **Donation** and press ⌷ENTER⌷ .

**6** Click a clip that shows people making a donation (any kind). The clip appears in the placeholder.

**7** Click slide 4 in the Slides pane.

**8** In the search results in the Clip Art task pane, locate another suitable donation clip and click it. It appears in the center of slide 4.

**9** Save the changes to the **PTry11_ studentfirstname_studentlastname** file, and leave it open to use in the next Try It

## Resizing and Positioning Clip Art

- When you insert a clip art image in a placeholder, the placeholder determines the starting size and position.

- When you insert a clip art image without a placeholder, the clip appears in the center of the slide, at a default size.

- You can resize a clip by dragging one of the selection handles (circles) on its border.

- You can move a clip by dragging the clip itself. Position the mouse pointer inside the clip's frame, away from any selection handles, and drag.

- Another way to size and position a clip is with the Size tab in the Format Picture dialog box. Right-click the clip, click Size and Position on the shortcut menu, and then enter exact settings in the dialog box.

## Try It!    Inserting, Sizing, and Positioning Clip Art

**1** In the **PTry11_studentfirstname_ studentlastname** file, on slide 4, click the clip to select it (if not already selected). Selection handles appear around it.

**2** Drag the clip so its upper left corner is at the 4" mark on the horizontal ruler (right of center) and at the 1" mark on the vertical ruler (above center).

✓ *If the ruler is not displayed, click View > Ruler to turn it on.*

**3** Drag the bottom left selection handle on the clip so the bottom left corner is at the 1" mark on the horizontal ruler (right of center).

**4** Click slide 8 in the Slides pane.

*(continued)*

**Try It!**        **Inserting, Sizing, and Positioning Clip Art** *(continued)*

**5** Right-click the clip art and click Size and Position. The Format Picture dialog box opens with the Size tab displayed.

**6** Enter 4" in the Height box.

✓ *The value in the Width box will change automatically in proportion.*

**7** Click the Position tab.

**8** Enter 1.5" for both the Vertical and Horizontal positions. (Measurements are from the top left corner.)

**9** Click Close.

**10** Save the changes to the **PTry11_studentfirstname_studentlastname** file, and leave it open to use in the next Try It.

Reposition the clip art on the slide

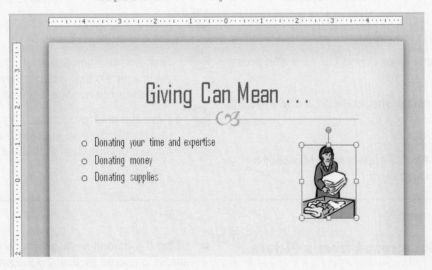

## Inserting a Picture from a File

■ You can insert your own pictures on slides with the Insert > Picture command.

**Try It!**        **Inserting a Picture from a File**

**1** In the **PTry11_studentfirstname_studentlastname** file, display slide 3.

**2** Click Insert > Picture 🖼. The Insert Picture dialog box opens.

**3** Navigate to the folder containing the data files for this lesson, and click **PTry11a.jpg**.

**4** Click Insert. The picture appears on the slide.

**5** Resize and reposition the picture so that it is attractive and does not overlap any text.

**6** Save the changes to the **PTry11_studentfirstname_studentlastname** file, and leave it open to use in the next Try It.

## Inserting a Photo from the Clip Art Task Pane

■ Through the Clip Art task pane, you can insert more types of content than just clip art. Microsoft's online library of images also includes photographs, sounds, and video clips.

■ To search the online library of photos, perform a search in which the file type is set to Photographs.

  ✓ *You can also insert your own pictures with the Insert > Picture command.*

### Try It!          Inserting a Photo Using the Clip Art Task Pane

1   In the **PTry11_studentfirstname_ studentlastname** file, display slide 5.

2   Click Insert > Clip Art ▦ to open the Clip Art task pane.

3   In the Search For box, type **Careers** and press ENTER .

4   Open the Results Should Be drop-down list and mark the check box for Photographs. Clear all other check boxes.

5   Press ENTER . Photos appear from Microsoft's library of stock photography.

6   Click a career-related photo, such as a classified ad job search. The photo is placed on the slide.

7   Click the Close button ☒ on the Clip Art task pane to close it.

8   Size and position the photo, just as with a clip art image, so that it looks attractive on the slide and does not overlap any text.

9   Save the changes to the **PTry11_ studentfirstname_studentlastname** file, and leave it open to use in the next Try It.

## Removing the Background from a Picture

■ In some photos, the background detracts from the main image. Using a graphics program, you can cut out the part of the image you want to use.

■ PowerPoint 2010 also provides this capability, so you can remove a photo's background without leaving PowerPoint.

■ Using the default settings may produce strange effects on some pictures; you can fine-tune where the dividing lines are between the foreground and background of the image if PowerPoint does not guess them correctly.

### Try It!          Removing a Picture Background

1   In the **PTry11_studentfirstname_ studentlastname** file, display slide 3. It already has a photo on it, inserted earlier.

2   Select the photo and click Picture Tools Format > Remove Background ⬈ . Purple shading appears on the areas of the image that will be cropped, and a Background Removal tab appears.

3   Click Keep Changes.

4   Save the **PTry11_studentfirstname_ studentlastname** file and close it.

## Project 23—Create It

### Laser Surgery Presentation

**DIRECTIONS**

1. Start PowerPoint, if necessary, and open **PProj23** from the data files for this lesson.

2. Save the presentation as **PProj23_studentfirstname_studentlastname** in the location where your teacher instructs you to store the files for this lesson.

3. Display slide 1, and click **Insert > Text Box** ⒶⒹ. Click at the bottom of the slide and type your full name.

4. Click slide 2, and click **Insert > Picture** 🖾.

5. Navigate to the folder containing the data files for this lesson, click **PProj23a.jpg**, and click **Insert**.

6. Drag the picture to place it to the left of the bulleted list.

7. Click slide 5 to display it.

8. Click the **Clip Art** placeholder icon.

9. In the Clip Art task pane, open the **Results Should Be** drop-down list.

10. Mark the **Illustrations** check box, and clear all other check boxes. Click away from the list to close it.

11. Click in the Search For box and type **dollar bill**. Click **Go** or press ⏎ .

12. Click any of the found clips to insert it on the slide.

   ✓ *Try to find a clip that fits the content of the list as well as possible.*

13. **With your teacher's permission**, click **File > Print**. Select **Print All Slides**, and then click **Print** 🖨 to print the presentation.

14. Close the presentation, saving changes, and exit PowerPoint.

## Project 24—Apply It

### Laser Surgery Presentation

**DIRECTIONS**

1. Start PowerPoint, if necessary, and open **PProj24** from the data files for this lesson.

2. Save the presentation as **PProj24_studentfirstname_studentlastname** in the location where your teacher instructs you to store the files for this lesson.

3. Display slide 1, and insert a text box at the bottom of the slide and type your full name.

4. On slide 2, position the clip art to the left of the bulleted list.

5. Size the clip art so it is the same height as the list.

6. On slide 4, insert **PProj24a.jpg** from the data files for this lesson.

7. Size the picture to be exactly **2"** high.

8. Position the picture to be **0.5"** horizontally and **1"** vertically from the upper left corner of the slide.

9. On slide 7, in the placeholder, insert **PProj24b.jpg** from the data files for this lesson.

10. Remove the background from the picture.

   ✓ *Notice that PowerPoint does not include all of the person's body by default. You can fix this by dragging the bottom left corner of the dotted outline inside the picture frame out to the edge of the picture. See Figure 11-1.*

11. Enlarge the picture to about **4"** in height. Use the vertical ruler to gauge size.

12. **With your teacher's permission**, print the presentation as handouts, 6 slides per page.

13. Close the presentation, saving changes, and exit PowerPoint.

**Figure 11-1**

Drag the inner selection handle outward

# Lesson 12

# Inserting Symbols and Text Boxes

> ## What You Will Learn

**Inserting Symbols**
**Inserting and Formatting a Text Box**
**Using Multiple Columns in a Text Box**

## WORDS TO KNOW

**Symbol**
A typographical character that is not a letter or a number. Some symbols can be typed on a keyboard, and others must be inserted.

**Text box**
A non-placeholder container for text that you can position anywhere on a slide.

**Software Skills**   Not all characters are available for insertion by typing on the keyboard. Some characters such as ® and © are available only as symbols.  In this lesson you will learn how to insert symbols in a presentation. You will also learn how to manually create text boxes that are not a part of a slide layout, and to format the text in multiple columns in a single text box.

**Application Skills**   In the Wynnedale Medical Center presentation, you will add a page containing customer testimonials. This page will contain a manually placed, multicolumn text box, as well as some typographical symbols.

## What You Can Do

### Inserting Symbols

■ **Symbols** are characters that are neither alphabetic nor numeric. Most of them cannot be typed from the keyboard. Symbols can include decorative characters, foreign language characters, and mathematical or punctuation characters.

- You can insert symbols from the Symbols dialog box. You have a choice of fonts there. You can choose Normal Text, which uses the same font as the default used for bullet paragraphs in the presentation, or another font.

    ✓ *If you want decorative characters instead, you can choose a font such as Zapf Dingbats or Wingdings, both of which are specifically designed for symbol use.*

## Try It!    Inserting Symbols

**1** Start PowerPoint and open **PTry12** from the data files for this lesson.

**2** Save the presentation as **PTry12_studentfirstname_studentlastname** in the location where your teacher instructs you to store the files for this lesson.

**3** Display slide 1, and click to place the insertion point immediately after the word *Giving* in the title.

**4** Click Insert > Symbol Ω . The Symbol dialog box opens.

**5** If (normal text) does not appear in the Font box, open its drop-down list and select (normal text).

**6** Scroll through the symbols, and click the TM (trademark) symbol. It is in the next-to-the-bottom row.

**7** Click Insert.

**8** Click Close. The symbol appears in the title.

**9** Save the changes to the **PTry12_studentfirstname_studentlastname** file, and leave it open to use in the next Try It.

The Insert Symbol dialog box

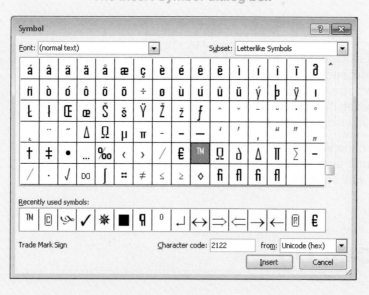

## Inserting and Formatting a Text Box

- A **text box** is a container for text that you can position anywhere on a slide. It is not a placeholder, and not part of a slide layout. Like other slide objects, text boxes are inserted from the Insert tab.

- There are two ways to use the Text Box tool. After selecting Insert > Text Box ⌐A⌐ , you can:

  - Click on the slide and start typing. This creates a text box in which the text does not wrap; the text box just keeps getting wider to accommodate your text.

  - Drag on the slide to define the size and shape of the text box, and then click inside it and start typing. This creates a text box in which text wraps to multiple lines automatically.

- You can resize a text box as you would any other object, by dragging the selection handles.

- You can format a text box as you would any other object. This includes adding a border, shading, and special effects. Use the tools in the Drawing group on the Home tab, or use the Drawing Tools Format contextual tab. You can also right-click the border of the text box and click Format Shape.

  ✓ *Lesson 14 covers object formatting in detail. The same basic formatting commands work for all types of objects, including drawn shapes and text boxes.*

- In the Format Shape dialog box, you can use the Text Box tab to control how the text appears in the text box (alignment, margins, and so on.)

---

**Try It!**     **Inserting a Text Box**

**1** In the **PTry12_studentfirstname_studentlastname** file, in the Slides pane, click between slides 6 and 7, and press ⌐ENTER⌐ , creating a new slide there.

**2** With the new slide displayed, click Home > Layout ▦ > Title Only.

**3** In the title placeholder, type **What People are Saying**.

**4** Click Insert > Text Box ⌐A⌐ .

**5** On the slide, drag the mouse pointer to create a box that is at least 4" wide and 3" high. Use the rulers to gauge size.

  ✓ *Notice that PowerPoint accepts the width you dragged, but the height snaps back to a much smaller size—the size of a single line of text at the default size. This is normal. The text box will expand vertically as you type.*

**6** Type the text shown below. To manually insert a line break between the end of the quotation and the person's name, press ⌐SHIFT⌐ + ⌐ENTER⌐ .

**7** Save the changes to the **PTry12_studentfirstname_studentlastname** file, and leave it open to use in the next Try It.

Type this text in the text box

"Without the support of good people in our community who want to make a difference, our family would not have been able to stay together last year when I was unable to find work."
--Trisha K.

## Try It!    Formatting a Text Box

**1** In the **PTry12_studentfirstname_ studentlastname** file, click the outer border of the text box. This selects the box itself, and not the text inside.

**2** On the Drawing Tools Format tab, click the More button ⏷ in the Shape Styles group to open the Shape Styles gallery.

**3** Click the second style in the bottom row.

**4** Click Drawing Tools Format > Edit Shape ⌕ > Change Shape and click a rounded rectangle.

**5** Click Drawing Tools Format > Shape Effects ⬭ > Reflection and click the first reflection type in the Reflection Variations section.

**6** Click Drawing Tools Format > Shape Effects ⬭ > 3D Rotation and click the second sample in the first row of the Perspective section. When you are finished, the text box should look like that shown in the figure on the right.

**7** Save the changes to the **PTry12_ studentfirstname_studentlastname** file, and leave it open to use in the next Try It.

The formatted text box

"Without the support of good people in our community who want to make a difference, our family would not have been able to stay together last year when I was unable to find work."
—Trisha K.

## Using Multiple Columns in a Text Box

■ You can place text in multiple columns in a single text box. This gives a different look than placing two text boxes side-by-side, and makes it easier to move text between columns after making edits.

■ Use the Columns dialog box, accessed from the Format Shape dialog box, to select the number of columns and space between them.

## Try It!    Creating a Multiple Column Text Box

**1** In the **PTry12_studentfirstname_ studentlastname** file, in the Slides pane, click between slides 7 and 8, and press ENTER , creating a new slide there.

**2** With the new slide displayed, click Home > Layout ▦ > Title Only.

**3** In the title placeholder, type **In the News**.

**4** Click Insert > Text Box ᴀ⃞ .

**5** On the slide, drag the mouse pointer to create a box that runs from the 4" mark on the ruler at the left to the 4" mark on the right.

✓ The height you drag does not matter because PowerPoint will make the box as tall as needed for the content.

*continued*

**Try It!**     **Creating a Multiple Column Text Box** *(continued)*

**6**   Type the following paragraphs into the new text box:

**In a recent study at Purdue University, it was shown that the return on investment (ROI) for investing in job skills training programs for people living below the poverty line is approximately 5:1.**

**How is this money generated? When you train people who are currently receiving government assistance, they can get jobs and stop needing those payments. In addition, they begin paying income taxes, sales taxes, and property taxes as income rises and property is purchased.**

**7**   Click **Home > Columns** ▦ **> Two Columns**.

**8**   Click **Home > Columns** ▦ **> More Columns**. The Columns dialog box opens.

**9**   In the Spacing text box, type **0.2"**.

**10**   Click **OK**.

**11**   Position the insertion point at the end of the first paragraph and press ENTER once, forcing the second paragraph to begin at the top of the second column.

  ✓ *Unfortunately PowerPoint lacks a Column Break command.*

**12**   Save the **PTry12_studentfirstname_studentlastname** file and close it.

The Columns dialog box

# Project 25—Create It

## Laser Surgery Presentation

### DIRECTIONS

1. Start PowerPoint, if necessary, and open **PProj25** from the data files for this lesson.

2. Save the presentation as **PProj25_studentfirstname_studentlastname** in the location where your teacher instructs you to store the files for this lesson.

3. Click slide 1 to display it.

4. Click **Insert > Text Box** ▦ . Click at the bottom of the slide and type your full name.

5. Click **Insert > Text Box** ▦ .

6. Drag to create a 7" wide text box at the bottom of the slide. Center it horizontally.

7. In the text box, type **Copyright** and press SPACEBAR once.

8. Click **Insert > Symbol** Ω .

9. Click the Copyright symbol © and click **Insert**. Then click **Close**.

10. Press SPACEBAR again.

11. Type **2011 Wynnedale Medical Group, LLC**.

12. Press CTRL + A to select all the text in the text box.

13. Press CTRL + E to center the text.

14. On the **Home** tab, in the Font group, open the **Size** drop-down list and click **10**.

15. Close the presentation, saving changes, and exit PowerPoint.

# Project 26—Apply It

## Laser Surgery Presentation

### DIRECTIONS

1. Start PowerPoint, if necessary, and open **PProj26** from the data files for this lesson.

2. Save the presentation as **PProj26_ studentfirstname_studentlastname** in the location where your teacher instructs you to store the files for this lesson.

3. On slide 1, insert a text box at the top of the slide, and type your full name.

4. Move to slide 6 and create the text boxes shown in Figure 12-1.

   a. Create the other three text boxes.

   b. Italicize the names of the people.

c. On the **Drawing Tools Format** tab, use four different colors of presets from the bottom row of the palette of Shape Styles.

5. Move to slide 7 and set the text box that contains the numbered list to **Two Columns**.

6. Decrease the height of the text box so that items 1 and 2 appear in the first column and the other items appear in the second column. See Figure 12-2.

7. Check the spelling.

8. **With your teacher's permission**, print the presentation as handouts, six slides per page.

9. Close the presentation, saving changes, and exit PowerPoint.

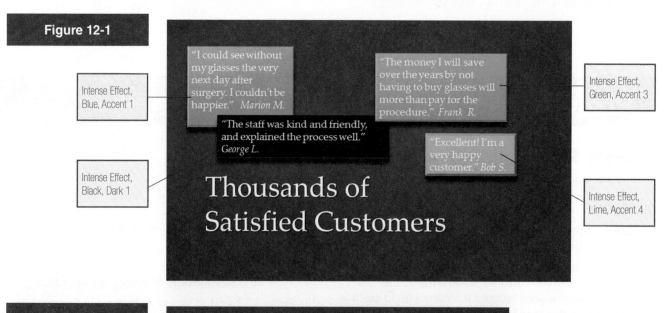

**Figure 12-1**

**Figure 12-2**

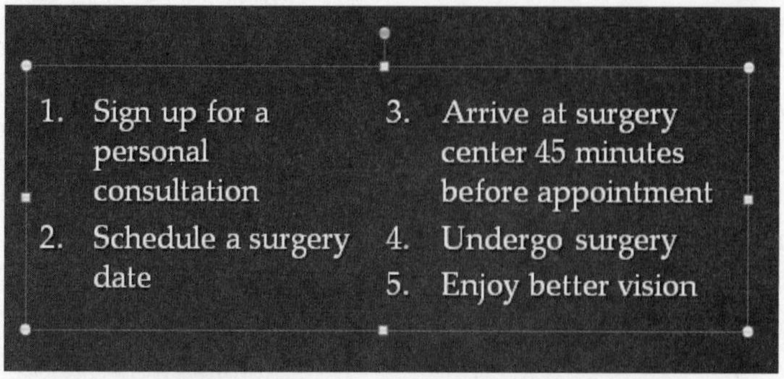

# Lesson 13

# Drawing and Formatting Shapes

## ➤ What You Will Learn

**Using Rulers, Guides, and Gridlines**
**Drawing Shapes**
**Moving and Sizing Shapes**
**Applying Fills and Outlines**
**Applying Shape Styles**
**Applying Shape Effects**
**Adding Text to Shapes**

**WORDS TO KNOW**

**Aspect ratio**
The proportion of width to height for an object.

**Gridlines**
A regular grid of dotted lines displayed on a slide to help arrange objects.

**Guides**
Nonprinting vertical and horizontal lines you can use to align objects on a slide.

**Shape Effects**
Special effects such as glow, shadow, 3D rotation, and soft edges applied to drawn shapes.

**Shape Styles**
Preset combinations of shape effects that can be applied as a single formatting action.

**Snap**
To change position to align precisely with a gridline.

**Software Skills**   Use PowerPoint's many drawing tools to help enhance a presentation. You might use rulers and guides or the grid to line up text or drawing objects, for example. Use shape tools to draw logos, illustrations, or other objects to add to slides.

**Application Skills**   A friend who works for Kelly Greenery, a landscaping company, has asked you to create a simple logo that he can use in his marketing presentations. You will use PowerPoint's Shapes tools to construct a logo.

# What You Can Do

## Using Rulers, Guides, and Gridlines

■ PowerPoint provides a vertical and horizontal ruler that you can show or hide at any time. You can use these rulers to adjust indents or add tabs to text. You can also use rulers to align objects on the slide.

■ The ruler's origins (0 measurement on the ruler) change depending on whether you're using text or an object. The origin appears on the edge of the ruler when you're working with text and in the center point of the ruler when you're working with an object.

■ As you move the mouse pointer, an indicator moves on each ruler showing your horizontal and vertical locations.

■ **Guides** are alignment tools that help you line up objects and text. PowerPoint supplies one vertical and one horizontal guide that you can move and copy, as shown in Figure 13-1.

■ PowerPoint's **gridlines** display as a grid of dotted lines over the entire slide. Like guides, they can help you line up objects or position them attractively on the slide.

■ By default, objects **snap** to the grid as they are drawn or positioned on the slide, even if the gridlines are not currently displayed. Generally this is an advantage, but if you find you want to position an object more exactly, you can turn off the snapping feature or hold down Alt while dragging to temporarily disable the snapping feature.

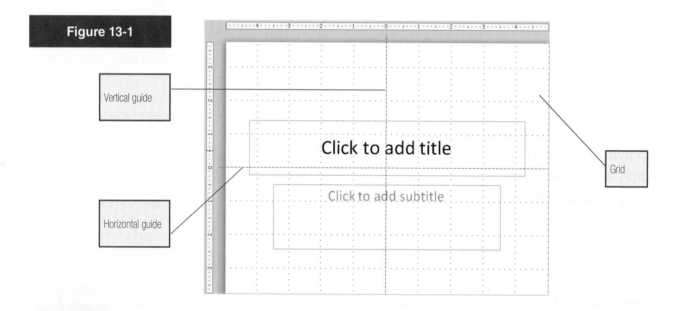

**Figure 13-1**

Vertical guide

Horizontal guide

Grid

Click to add title

Click to add subtitle

## Try It! Turning On Rulers, Gridlines, and Guides

**1** Start PowerPoint and open **PTry13** from the data files for this lesson.

**2** Save the presentation as **PTry13_ studentfirstname_studentlastname** in the location where your teacher instructs you to store the files for this lesson.

**3** Click the View tab.

**4** If the Ruler check box is not already marked, click to mark it.

**5** If the Gridlines check box is not already marked, click to mark it.

**6** If the Guides check box is not already marked, click to mark it.

**7** Save the changes to the **PTry13_ studentfirstname_studentlastname** file, and leave it open to use in the next Try It.

## Try It!     Adjusting Grid and Guide Settings

**1** In the **PTry13_studentfirstname_studentlastname** file, position the mouse pointer over the dotted vertical guide and click and hold the left mouse button.

✓ *The mouse pointer changes to show 0.00.*

**2** Drag to the right until the mouse pointer shows 1.50, and then release the mouse button.

**3** On the View tab, click the dialog box launcher ▤ for the Show group. The Grid and Guides dialog box opens.

**4** Click the Snap Objects to Grid check box if it is not already marked.

**5** Open the Spacing drop-down list and click 1/16".

✓ *PowerPoint converts the measurement to decimal automatically in the Spacing text box: 0.063".*

**6** Click OK.

**7** Leave the changes to the **PTry13_studentfirstname_studentlastname** file, and leave it open to use in the next Try It.

The Grid and Guides dialog box

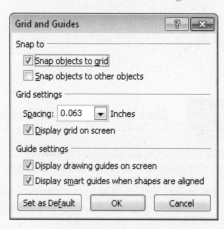

## Drawing Shapes

- Use the shapes on the Home tab or Drawing Tools tab to draw basic objects such as lines, rectangles, and circles as well as more complex shapes such as stars, banners, and block arrows.

- The Shapes gallery is divided into several sections that organize shapes of various kinds. Click a shape and then drag on the slide to draw it. You control the size as you draw.

- If you click on the slide instead of dragging, you get a default-sized shape.

- You can hold down SHIFT as you drag to constrain the shape to its original **aspect ratio**. For example, if you draw an oval while holding down SHIFT, it's a perfect circle; if you draw a rectangle, it's a perfect square.

## Try It!     Drawing Shapes

**1** In the **PTry13_studentfirstname_studentlastname** file, click Home > Layout ▦ > Blank to switch to a blank layout with no placeholders.

**2** Click Insert > Shapes 🗊 . In the Stars and Banners section, click the five-pointed star.

**3** Hold down SHIFT and draw a star in the center of the slide, approximately 4" x 4".

✓ *Each square in the grid is 1".*

**4** Click Insert > Shapes 🗊 . In the Basic Shapes section, click the oval.

**5** Hold down SHIFT and draw a circle to the left of the star, approximately 3" in diameter.

**6** Leave the changes to the **PTry13_studentfirstname_studentlastname** file, and leave it open to use in the next Try It.

## Moving and Sizing Shapes

■ You can move, size, copy, and delete drawing
objects just like any other PowerPoint object.

- To move a shape, drag it.

   ✓ *You can also display the Format Shape dialog box and*
   *enter precise position measurements on the Position*
   *tab there.*

- To size a shape, drag one of its selection
  handles.

   ✓ *You can also display the Format Shape dialog box and*
   *enter precise size measurements on the Size tab there.*
   *You can also enter a precise height and width on the*
   *Drawing Tools Format tab, in the Size group.*

- To delete a shape, select it and press DEL .
- To nudge an object (move it in small increments),
  hold down CTRL while pressing an arrow key in
  the direction you want it to move.

■ Some shapes also have one or more yellow
diamond resize handles that you can use to adjust
the appearance of the shape.

---

**Try It!**     **Moving and Sizing Shapes**

**1** In the **PTry13_studentfirstname_**
**studentlastname** file, click the circle to select it.

**2** Hold down SHIFT and drag the shape's bottom
right corner selection handle, to shrink the circle
to approximately 3" in diameter.

**3** On the Drawing Tools Format tab, click in the
Shape Height box 🔲 and type 2.5".

**4** Click in the Shape Width box 🔲 and type 2.5".

**5** Drag the circle to the upper right corner of the
slide.

**6** Right-click the circle and click Format Shape.
The Format Shape dialog box opens.

**7** Click the Position tab.

**8** In the Horizontal box, type **0.5"**.

**9** In the Verical box, type **0.5"**.

**10** Click Close.

**11** Click Insert > Shape 🔲 and in the Block Arrows
section, click the up arrow.

**12** Drag on the slide to place a block arrow to the
right of the star, approximately 4" high and 2" wide.

   ✓ *Two yellow diamonds appear on it: one on the*
   *arrowhead and one on the arrow shaft.*

**13** Drag the diamond on the arrowhead to change
the shape of the arrowhead.

**14** Drag the diamond on the arrow shaft to change
the width of the shaft.

**15** Save the changes to the **PTry13_**
**studentfirstname_studentlastname** file, and
leave it open to use in the next Try It.

Modify the arrow by dragging the yellow diamonds

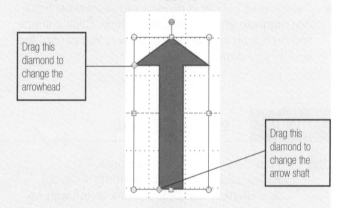

Drag this
diamond to
change the
arrowhead

Drag this
diamond to
change the
arrow shaft

## Applying Fills and Outlines

- By default, shapes are formatted with the current theme colors. The fill is the Accent 1 color in the theme (the fifth color) and the outline is the Text 2 color (the fourth color).

- On the Drawing Tools Format tab, you can use the Shape Fill and Shape Outline drop-down lists to format a shape differently from the default.

- You can also right-click the shape and choose Format Shape for access to the Format Shape dialog box, where a wider variety of formatting options are available.

---

**Try It!**     **Applying Fills and Outlines**

**1**   In the **PTry13_studentfirstname_ studentlastname** file, click the star to select it.

**2**   Click the Drawing Tools Format tab.

**3**   Click the Shape Fill ⬙ drop-down arrow, opening its menu.

**4**   Click the yellow square under Standard Colors.

**5**   Click the Shape Outline ⬙ drop-down arrow, opening its menu.

**6**   Click More Outline Colors.

**7**   In the Colors dialog box, click the Standard tab.

**8**   Click an orange hexagon.

**9**   Click OK.

**10**   Right-click the triangle and click Format Shape.

**11**   In the Format Shape dialog box, click the Line Style tab.

**12**   In the Width box, type **1 pt**.

**13**   Click the Dash Type button, openings its menu, and choose the Square Dot dash style (the third style on the list).

**14**   Click Close to close the dialog box.

**15**   Save the changes to the **PTry13_ studentfirstname_studentlastname** file, and leave it open to use in the next Try It.

Select an outline color

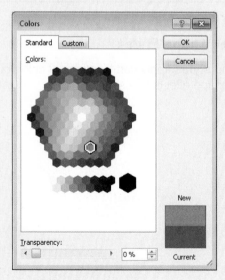

Select a fill color

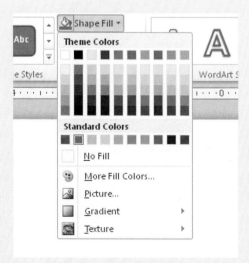

## Applying Shape Effects

- **Shape effects** are special formatting options you can apply to objects in PowerPoint 2007/2010 presentations. They are not available in backward-compatible presentations (97-2003).

- The available effects include shadows, reflections, soft edges, bevels, and 3D rotation. After opening the Shape Effects menu, you point to a submenu name and then click one of the presets from the submenu that appears.

✓ The shape effect you choose does not affect the color or border of the object. However, some effects hide the shape's outline.

- Each of the effect submenus has an Options command at the bottom that opens the Format Shape dialog box with the corresponding tab selected. For example, the Shadow Options command opens it to the Shadow tab.

---

**Try It!**    **Applying Shape Effects**

**1** In the **PTry13_studentfirstname_ studentlastname** file, click the circle to select it.

**2** Click Drawing Tools Format > Shape Effects ⬙ > Preset and click the second preset in the first row of the Presets section.

**3** Click Shape Fill ⬙ , and click the light green square in the Standard section.

✓ Notice that the effect remains, even though you have changed the color.

**4** Click Shape Effects ⬙ > Bevel > Riblet (the second effect in the third row of the Bevel section).

**5** Save the changes to the **PTry13_ studentfirstname_studentlastname** file, and leave it open to use in the next Try It.

---

## Applying Shape Styles

- **Shape styles** apply combinations of color, outline, and shape effects in a single action.

- Each shape style is available in any of the current theme's colors. You can also apply a shape style and then manually change the color.

**Try It!**   **Applying Shape Styles**

**1** In the **PTry13_studentfirstname_ studentlastname** file, click the star to select it.

**2** On the Drawing Tools Format tab, in the Shape Styles group, click the More button ⊡ to open the Shape Styles gallery.

**3** Click the style in the lower right corner of the gallery.

**4** Click the block arrow shape.

**5** Click the More button ⊡ to open the Shape Styles gallery again.

**6** Click the first style in the fourth row of the gallery.

**7** Save the changes to the **PTry13_ studentfirstname_studentlastname** file, and leave it open to use in the next Try It.

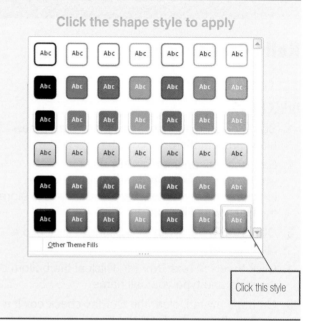

Click the shape style to apply

Other Theme Fills

Click this style

## Adding Text to Shapes

■ You can add text to any filled shape. Simply click on the shape and start typing. PowerPoint handles line length and text wrap. This allows you, in effect, to have any shape of text box you want, not just rectangular.

■ You can edit and format text in a shape just as you would edit text in a text box. For a special effect, you can change text direction so that text reads from top to bottom or bottom to top.

**Try It!**   **Adding Text to a Shape and Rotating the Text**

**1** In the **PTry13_studentfirstname_ studentlastname** file, click the block arrow to select it.

**2** Type **Check out our specials**. The text appears in the shaft of the arrow, with only a few characters per line.

**3** Right-click the block arrow and click Format Shape.

**4** In the Format Shape dialog box, click the Text Box tab.

**5** Open the Text Direction drop-down list and click Rotate All Text 270°.

**6** Click Close to close the dialog box. The text now runs vertically in the shape.

**7** Save the **PTry13_studentfirstname_ studentlastname** file and close it.

# Project 27—Create It

## Kelly Greenery Logo

### DIRECTIONS

1. Start PowerPoint, if necessary, and start a new blank presentation.

2. Save the presentation as **PProj27_ studentfirstname_studentlastname** in the location where your teacher instructs you to store the files for this lesson.

3. Click **Home > Layout** 📧 > Blank to switch to a blank layout.

4. Click **Insert > Text Box** 🄰 . Click at the bottom of the slide and type your full name.

5. On the View tab, clear the **Guides** check box if it is marked. Leave the Gridlines check box marked.

6. Click **Insert > Shapes** 🔷 . Click the oval in the Basic Shapes section.

7. Drag on the slide to create an oval in the center of the slide that is approximately 8" wide and 4" tall.

8. On the **Drawing Tools Format tab,** in the Shape Styles group, click the **More** button 🔽 to open the Shape Styles gallery.

9. Click the light green style in the next-to-last row.

10. With the oval selected, type **Kelly Greenery**.

11. Press CTRL + A to select all the text you just typed.

12. On the Home tab, open the **Font** drop-down list and click **Algerian**.

13. Open the Size drop-down list and click **44**.

14. Click the arrow on the **Font Color** button and click the black square in the theme colors (second square in the top row).

15. On the **Drawing Tools Format** tab, click **Shape Effects** ◔ > **Preset** and click the rightmost preset in the first row of the Presets section.

   ✓ *The finished logo is shown in Figure 13-3.*

16. Close the presentation, saving changes, and exit PowerPoint.

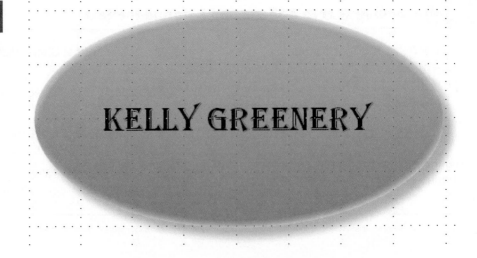

**Figure 13-3**

# Project 28—Apply It

## Kelly Greenery Logo

### DIRECTIONS

1. Start PowerPointand open **PProj28** from the data files for this lesson.

2. Save the presentation as **PProj28_ studentfirstname_studentlastname** in the location where your teacher instructs you to store the files for this lesson.

3. Create a text box at the bottom of the slide and type your name in it.

4. Set the height and width of the oval to exactly **4"** high and **8"** wide.

5. Remove the Bevel effect from the oval.

6. Apply an **Offset Diagonal Bottom Right** shadow using Shape Effects.

7. Change the shape fill to the Orange standard color.

8. Apply a 3-point dark green outline to the oval.

9. Apply that same shade of green to the text in the oval.

10. If gridlines are displayed, turn them off. The finished logo is shown in Figure 13-4.

11. **With your teacher's permission**, print the presentation.

12. Close the presentation, saving changes, and exit PowerPoint.

**Figure 13-4**

# Lesson 14

# Positioning and Grouping Shapes

## WORDS TO KNOW

**Group**
To combine multiple shapes or other objects into a collective unit that can be controlled as a single object.

**Stack**
To overlap objects, and control the order in which overlapping objects appear.

## ➤ What You Will Learn

**Stacking Objects**
**Grouping Objects**
**Duplicating Objects**
**Aligning and Distributing Objects**

**Software Skills**   Many of the drawings you create with the Shapes tools in PowerPoint will consist of multiple shapes that overlap each other. When a graphic consists of several pieces, you need to know how to combine and position them to make a cohesive whole.

**Application Skills**   The Kelly Greenery logo you have been working on currently consists of several separate drawn shapes. You will stack the pieces in the correct order, and then group them into a single object that the customer can use as his business's logo. You will also fix the problem of the yellow background showing through part of the clip art image.

## What You Can Do

### Stacking Objects

■ As you create objects on a slide, they **stack** from the "back" (the first object created) to the "front" (the last object created). You can think of this process as a series of layers stacked on top of each other with an object on each layer.

- Use the Drawing Tools Format tab's arrangement tools to change an object's stack order:
  - Bring to Front and Send to Back move the object all the way to the top or bottom of the stack, respectively.
  - Bring Forward and Send Backward move an object back or forward one layer at a time.
- To make it easy to select objects for arranging or other manipulation, use the Selection and Visibility pane. Access it from the Drawing Tools Format tab.

- The Selection and Visibility pane shows all objects currently displayed on the slide. To select any object, click it in the Selection and Visibility pane. You can also click on the visibility symbol (the open eye) to hide an object.
  - ✓ You can click on an object name to open the default name for editing and supply your own names for objects. Meaningful names for objects can also help you when you are creating animations for slide objects.

## Try It!    Stacking Drawn Objects

**1** Start PowerPoint and open **PTry14** from the data files for this lesson.

**2** Save the presentation as **PTry14_ studentfirstname_studentlastname** in the location where your teacher instructs you to store the files for this lesson.

**3** Click any of the shapes, and then click Drawing Tools Format > Selection Pane. The Selection and Visibility pane opens.

**4** In the Selection and Visibility pane, click the eye symbol 👁 next to Oval 4. The circle disappears and the button changes to a blank. Click the blank button to make the circle reappear.

**5** Click the circle to select it. Then hold down [SHIFT] and drag a corner selection handle on the circle to expand it so it is large enough to completely cover the star. Drag it to reposition it so it is directly over the star.

**6** With the circle still selected, on the Drawing Tools Format tab, click the arrow to the right of the Send Backward button and click Send to Back.

**7** Adjust the size and position of the circle so that the tips of the star barely touch the edges of the circle.

**8** Click the pentagon, either on the slide or in the Selection and Visibility pane.

**9** Click the arrow to the right of the Bring Forward button and click Bring to Front.

**10** Position the pentagon on top of the star, at its center.

**11** Click Drawing Tools Format > Selection Pane to turn off the Selection and Visibility pane.

**12** Click View > Gridlines to turn off the gridlines. The design should look like that shown in the following figure.

**13** Save the changes to the **PTry14_ studentfirstname_studentlastname** file, and leave it open to use in the next Try It.

Select any object easily in this pane

Arrange and stack the pieces of the design

## Grouping Objects

- You can **group** the objects within a drawing so that they can be treated as a single object. Grouping objects makes them easier to copy, move, or resize.

- You can ungroup objects when you want to work with the objects individually again.

- Some changes can be made to the individual elements of a grouped object without ungrouping it, such as changing the colors.

- To select the objects to be grouped, you can hold down CTRL as you click on each one, or you can drag a lasso around all the objects to be included. To lasso a group, drag to draw an imaginary box around them.

### Try It!    Grouping Objects

1. In the **PTry14_studentfirstname_ studentlastname** file, drag to lasso all the drawn shapes. To lasso, use the mouse pointer to drag an imaginary box around everything you want to select, and then release the mouse button. Each one appears with its own selection handles.

2. Click Drawing Tools Format > Group ▦ > Group. The group now has a single set of selection handles.

3. Hold down SHIFT and drag the bottom right corner of the shape inward to shrink it in size by 1".

✓ All shapes are resized together because they are all part of the group.

4. Click to select the grouped object if it is not already selected.

5. Click Drawing Tools Format > Group ▦ > Ungroup. The shapes become ungrouped.

6. Click Drawing Tools Format > Group ▦ > Group again, because you will need the objects grouped for the next steps.

7. Save the changes to the **PTry14_ studentfirstname_studentlastname** file, and leave it open to use in the next Try It.

## Duplicating Objects

- After drawing an object, you may want to duplicate it rather than drawing additional objects from scratch. For example, if you need three circles that are all exactly the same size, duplicating the first one twice ensures that they are identical.

- You can duplicate either with drag-and-drop, or with copy-and-paste.

### Try It!    Duplicating an Object

1. In the **PTry14_studentfirstname_ studentlastname** file, select the object, and on the Drawing Tools Format tab, enter a Height and Width of 2" each.

✓ This makes the shape small enough that multiple copies of it will fit on the slide.

2. Select the object and press CTRL + C. It is copied to the Clipboard.

3. Press CTRL + V. A copy is pasted on the slide.

4. Drag the copy to move it so it does not overlap the original.

5. Click the original object.

6. Hold down the CTRL key and drag the original to a different spot on the slide. It is copied there.

✓ Now you have three copies of the shape, which you will use in the next Try It.

7. Save the changes to the **PTry14_ studentfirstname_studentlastname** file, and leave it open to use in the next Try It.

## Aligning and Distributing Objects

- Sometimes it is important that the objects on a slide be precisely aligned, either with one another or with the slide itself. PowerPoint has several commands to help you accomplish this.

- The Align command aligns objects by their top, bottom, right side, left side, or center. It can also be used to place one or more objects in relation to the slide itself. In Figure 14-1, the shapes are top-aligned.

- The Distribute command equalizes the spacing among objects.

- On the Align button's menu is an Align to Slide command that is a toggle. When it is turned on, a check mark appears by it.

- When this command is on, the Align and Distribute commands apply to the object in relation to the slide, as well as in relation to the other selected objects.

- When this command is on, you can use Align or Distribute on a single object. When this command is off, the minimum number of selected objects to use Align is 2, and the minimum to use Distribute is 3.

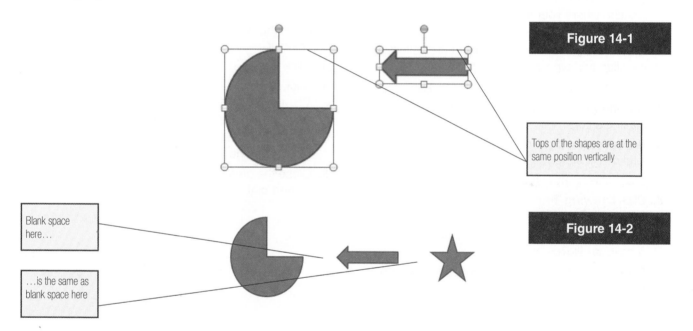

**Figure 14-1**

Tops of the shapes are at the same position vertically

Blank space here…

…is the same as blank space here

**Figure 14-2**

### Try It!    Aligning and Distributing Objects

**1** In the **PTry14_studentfirstname_studentlastname** file, manually drag the three copies of the object so that they are in a single horizontal row in the center of the slide.

   ✓ *The placement does not have to be precise. In fact, the results will be more obvious if one of them is slightly higher than the others.*

**2** Click one copy, hold down CTRL, and click the other two copies to also select them.

**3** Click Drawing Tools Format > Align ⊩ > Align Top.

**4** Click Drawing Tools Format > Align ⊩ Distribute Horizontally.

**5** To confirm that they are aligned, click View > Gridlines to turn on the gridlines. Click the Gridlines check box to turn off gridlines again when finished.

**6** Save the **PTry14_studentfirstname_studentlastname** file and close it.

# Project 29—Create It

## Kelly Greenery Logo

### DIRECTIONS

1. Start PowerPoint, if necessary, and open **PProj29** from the data files for this lesson.

2. Save the presentation as **PProj29_ studentfirstname_studentlastname** in the location where your teacher instructs you to store the files for this lesson.

3. Click **Insert** > **Text Box** ⊞. Click at the bottom of the slide and type your full name.

4. Select the star.

5. Hold down CTRL and drag the star to the right, making a copy of it.

6. Repeat step 4 three more times, so you have a total of five stars.

7. Drag a lasso around all five stars to select them.

8. Click **Drawing Tools Format** > **Align** ⊫ > **Align Selected Objects**.

9. Click **Drawing Tools Format** > **Align** ⊫ > **Distribute Horizontally**.

10. Click **Drawing Tools Format** > **Align** ⊫ > **Align Middle**.

11. Click **Drawing Tools Format** > **Group** ⊞ > **Group**. The stars are now a single object.

12. Select the clip art image.

13. Click **Drawing Tools Format** > **Bring Forward** ⊫ .

14. Select the oval, the stars, and the banner. Hold down the Shift key as you click each shape to select it.

15. Click **Drawing Tools Format** > **Align Center**.

16. Click **Drawing Tools Format** > **Group** ⊞ > **Group**. The finished logo is shown in Figure 14-3.

17. **With your teacher's permission**, click **File** > **Print**. Select **Print All Slides**, and then click **Print** 🖨 to print the presentation.

18. Close the presentation, saving changes, and exit PowerPoint.

**Figure 14-3**

# Project 30—Apply It

## Kelly Greenery Logo

### DIRECTIONS

1. Start PowerPoint, if necessary, and open **PProj30** from the data files for this lesson.

2. Save the presentation as **PProj30_ studentfirstname_studentlastname** in the location where your teacher instructs you to store the files for this lesson.

3. Insert a text box at the bottom of the slide, and type your full name in it.

4. Draw an oval that covers up as much of the clip art graphic as possible, while not overrunning its border. See Figure 14-4.

5. Remove the outline (border) from the oval and change its fill color to white.

6. Use the **Send Backward** command to send the oval behind the clip art.

✓ Now the part of the clip art that overlaps the yellow oval does not show yellow.

7. Group the clip art, the white oval, and the yellow oval into a single object.

8. Apply an orange outline to the stars.

9. Select everything on the slide, and group all the pieces into a single object.

10. Center the logo on the slide vertically and horizontally.

✓ Here's one way: On the Align button's menu, make sure Align to Slide is marked. Then use the Distribute Vertically and Distribute Horizontally commands.

11. **With your teacher's permission**, print one copy of the slide. The finished logo is shown in Figure 14-5.

12. Close the presentation, saving changes, and exit PowerPoint.

**Figure 14-4**

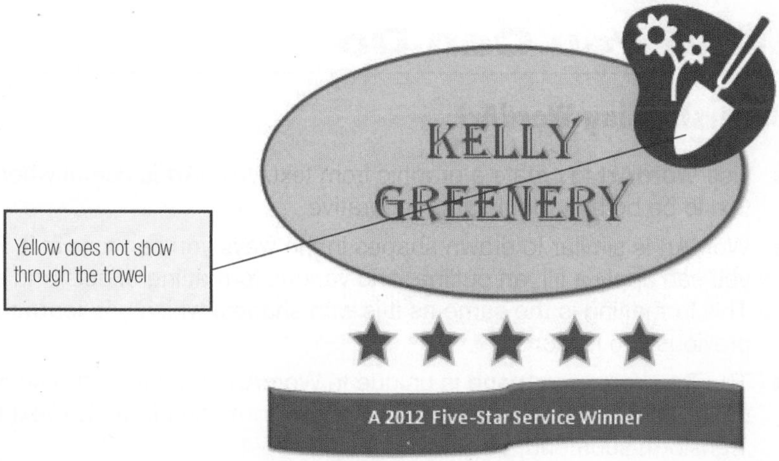

**Figure 14-5**

Yellow does not show through the trowel

KELLY GREENERY

★ ★ ★ ★ ★

A 2012 Five-Star Service Winner

# Lesson 15

# Creating WordArt

**WORDS TO KNOW**

WordArt
Text that is formatted with
graphical effects.

## ➤ What You Will Learn

**Understanding WordArt**
**Applying WordArt Styles to Existing Text**
**Inserting and Formatting WordArt**

**Software Skills**   WordArt enables you to apply special effects to text to make it
appear more graphical. Using WordArt you can create logos and decorative text.

**Application Skills**   Your friend at Kelly Greenery likes the logo you created for
him, but would like some alternatives to choose from. You will create two alternate
company logos using a combination of shapes and WordArt.

## What You Can Do

### Understanding WordArt

■  Use **WordArt** to create a graphic from text. WordArt is useful whenever you want
  text to be both readable and decorative.

■  WordArt is similar to drawn shapes in the ways you can format it. For example,
  you can apply a fill, an outline, and various formatting effects and styles to it.
  This formatting is the same as it is with shapes, which you learned about in the
  previous two lessons.

■  The Transform command is unique to WordArt. It modifies the shape of the text to
  make it conform to a path. Choose a transformation from the Text Effects button's
  Transform submenu, as shown in Figure 15-1.

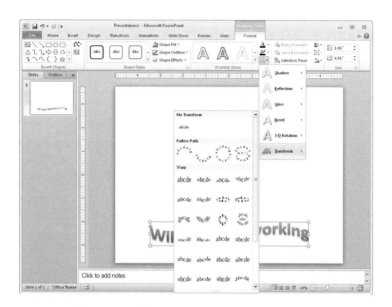

**Figure 15-1**

## Applying WordArt Styles to Existing Text

■ Any text can be easily turned into WordArt. Select any existing text, and then on the Drawing Tools Format tab, use the WordArt Styles group's commands and lists to select the effects that you want.

■ When applying WordArt presets from the WordArt Styles gallery, there are two sections in the gallery:

● Applies to Selected Text: These effects can be applied to individual characters and words in a text box without affecting the entire text box.

● Applies to All Text in the Shape: These effects apply to the entire text box.

---

**Try It!**    **Applying WordArt Styles to Existing Text**

**1** Start a new blank presentation and save it as **PTry15_studentfirstname_studentlastname** in the location where your teacher instructs you to store the files for this lesson.

**2** Click Home > Layout ▦ > Blank to change to a blank layout.

**3** Click Insert > Text Box ▣ .

**4** Click on the slide, and type **Lowe Insurance**.

**5** Press CTRL + A to select all the text.

**6** Click the Drawing Tools Format tab.

**7** Click the More button ▾ in the WordArt Styles group to open the WordArt Styles gallery.

**8** Click the bottom right style in the Applies to Selected Text section of the gallery.

**9** Click the text box containing the WordArt.

**10** Click the More button ▾ in the WordArt Styles group to open the WordArt Styles gallery.

**11** Click Clear WordArt.

**12** Save the changes to the **PTry15_studentfirstname_studentlastname** file, and leave it open to use in the next Try It.

---

*(continued)*

**Try It!**     **Applying WordArt Styles to Existing Text** *(continued)*

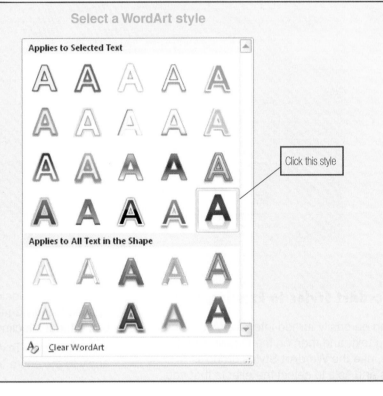

Select a WordArt style

Click this style

## Inserting and Formatting WordArt

■ You can also insert WordArt from scratch. This creates a text box and applies a WordArt style to it in a single step.

**Try It!**     **Inserting WordArt**

**1** In the **PTry15_studentfirstname_ studentlastname** file, click Insert > WordArt ◢. A palette of WordArt samples appears.

　✓ *These samples are the same as the ones that appeared in the WordArt Styles list you saw in the preceding steps.*

**2** Click the second sample in the fourth row.

　✓ *A WordArt object appears, with generic text. The text is highlighted, so if you type something, it will be replaced.*

**3** Type **Apex Industries.** Your text replaces the generic text.

**4** Save the changes to the **PTry15_ studentfirstname_studentlastname** file, and leave it open to use in the next Try It.

## Try It!    Formatting WordArt

**1** In the **PTry15_studentfirstname_studentlastname** file, with the WordArt object selected, click Drawing Tools Format > Text Effects Ⓐ > Transform. A gallery of transformation options appears, as you saw in Figure 15-1.

**2** In the Warp section, click the first sample in the second row (Chevron Up).

**3** Drag the pink diamond at the left edge of the WordArt down as far as it will go.

    ✓ *The WordArt shape is further transformed.*

**4** With the insertion point in the WordArt, press `CTRL` + `A` to select all the text.

    ✓ *If you do not select all the text, the formatting applies only to the word where the insertion point was.*

**5** Click Drawing Tools Format > Text Fill 🔽. A palette of colors appears.

**6** Click the light blue square in the Standard Colors section.

**7** Click Drawing Tools Format > Text Outline ✎. A palette of colors appears.

**8** Click the medium blue square in the Standard Colors section.

**9** Click Drawing Tools Format > Text Outline ✎.

**10** Point to the Weight command. A submenu appears.

**11** Click the solid 1½ point line.

**12** With the insertion point in the WordArt, press `CTRL` + `A` to select all the text.

**13** Click Drawing Tools Format > Text Effects Ⓐ > Shadow.

**14** Click the first shadow in the Perspective section.

**15** Click Drawing Tools Format > Text Effects Ⓐ > Bevel.

**16** Click the fourth sample in the third row of the Bevel section (Art Deco).

**17** Click Drawing Tools Format > Text Effects Ⓐ > 3-D Rotation.

**18** Click the fourth sample in the second row of the Parallel section (Off Axis 2 Left).

**19** Click away from the WordArt object to deselect it. It should look like the following figure.

**20** Save the **PTry15_studentfirstname_studentlastname** file and close it.

The finished WordArt object

The transformed WordArt object

# Project 31—Create It

## Kelly Greenery Logo

### DIRECTIONS

1. Start PowerPoint, if necessary, and open **PProj31** from the data files for this lesson.

2. Save the presentation as **PProj31_ studentfirstname_studentlastname** in the location where your teacher instructs you to store the files for this lesson.

3. Click **Insert** > **Text Box** 🄰. Click at the bottom of the slide and type your full name.

4. Click **Insert** > **WordArt** ⊿ and click the fourth sample in the third row.

5. Type **Kelly Greenery**.

6. Drag the WordArt so that the last letter overlaps the trunk of the tree graphic.

7. Press CTRL + A to select all the text.

8. Click **Drawing Tools Format** > **Text Fill** ♨ and click the light green square in the Standard section.

9. Click **Drawing Tools Format** > **Text Outline** ⊿ and click **No Outline**.

10. Click **Drawing Tools Format** > **Text Effects** 🄰 > **Transform** and click the first sample in the fifth row of the Warp section (Wave 1).

11. Click the WordArt, hold down CTRL, and click the clip art.

12. Click **Drawing Tools Format** > **Group** 🄴 > **Group**.

    Your slide should look like Figure 15-2.

13. **With your teacher's permission**, click **File** > **Print**. Select **Print All Slides**, and then click **Print** 🖶 to print the presentation.

14. Close the presentation, saving changes, and exit PowerPoint.

**Figure 15-2**

## Project 32—Apply It

### Kelly Greenery Logo

**DIRECTIONS**

1. Start PowerPoint, if necessary, and open **PProj32** from the data files for this lesson.

2. Save the presentation as **PProj32_ studentfirstname_studentlastname** in the location where your teacher instructs you to store the files for this lesson.

3. Insert a text box at the bottom of the slide, and type your full name in it.

4. Insert WordArt that uses the second sample in the sixth row of the WordArt gallery. (It is the shiny orange sample.)

5. Replace the placeholder text with **Kelly Greenery**.

6. Apply the **Arch Up** transformation from the Follow Path section of the **Text Effects** Ⓐ > **Transform** menu.

7. Apply a bright green fill to the text, matching the bright green in the clip art image as closely as possible.

8. Apply a dark green outline to the WordArt text.

9. Apply a green **Glow** effect to the WordArt. (Use the green sample from the top row.)

10. Increase the height of the WordArt frame to **3"** and position the WordArt so it is arched over the clip art.

11. **With your teacher's permission**, print one copy of the slide. The finished logo is shown in Figure 15-3.

12. Close the presentation, saving changes, and exit PowerPoint.

Figure 15-3

# Lesson 16

# Creating SmartArt Diagrams

## WORDS TO KNOW

**SmartArt**
Professionally designed graphics that organize and display information in various graphic types such as lists, processes, or hierarchical displays.

**SmartArt style**
The shading and texture effects on the shapes used in the diagram. Some of the styles make the shapes looked raised or shiny, for example.

## ➤ What You Will Learn

**Creating a SmartArt Diagram**
**Adding, Removing, and Resizing Shapes in a Diagram**
**Reordering Diagram Content**
**Changing the Diagram Type**
**Changing the Color and Style of a Diagram**
**Creating Picture-Based SmartArt**

**Software Skills**   SmartArt enables you to combine graphics with text to present information in a much more interesting and attractive layout than a plain bulleted list provides.

**Application Skills**   In the Wynnedale Medical Center presentation, most of the information is presented in bulleted lists. In this lesson, you will switch over some of those lists to SmartArt, for a more interesting and graphical presentation.

## What You Can Do

### Creating a SmartArt Diagram

- **SmartArt** is a tool that enables you to place text in graphical containers that make it more interesting to read. These container graphics are specially designed to arrange items in conceptually relevant ways, such as in an organization chart, cycle diagram, or pyramid.

- You can insert a SmartArt graphic in a content slide layout, or you can add it without a placeholder using the SmartArt button on the Insert tab. You can also, if desired, convert a bulleted list to a SmartArt graphic.

- Each SmartArt diagram has a fly-out text pane where you can edit its content. Click the arrow button to the left of the diagram to open the text pane. You can also make text edits directly in the shapes.

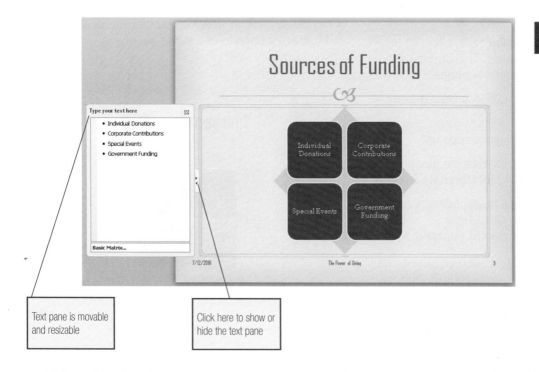

**Figure 16-1**

Text pane is movable and resizable

Click here to show or hide the text pane

---

**Try It!**     **Converting a Bulleted List to SmartArt**

**1** Start PowerPoint and open **PTry16** from the data files for this lesson.

**2** Save the presentation as **PTry16_ studentfirstname_studentlastname** in the location where your teacher instructs you to store the files for this lesson.

**3** Display slide 6. Click in the numbered list and press CTRL + A to select all the text.

**4** Right-click the selected list and click Convert to SmartArt. A palette of samples appears.

**5** Point to the Basic Timeline design (second design in the fourth row). The design is previewed behind the list.

**6** Click the Continuous Block Process design (first design in the fourth row). The design is applied to the list.

**7** Display slide 9. Click in the content area and press CTRL + A to select all the text.

**8** Right-click the selected text and click Convert to SmartArt.

**9** Click the Horizontal Bulleted List (the first sample in the second row). The design is applied to the list.

✓ *Because this slide contained a multilevel bulleted list, the subordinate levels appear as mini lists within the main shapes.*

**10** Save the changes to the **PTry16_ studentfirstname_studentlastname** file, and leave it open to use in the next Try It.

**Try It!**    **Inserting a New SmartArt Object**

**1** In the **PTry16_studentfirstname_ studentlastname** file, in the Slides pane, click between slides 2 and 3 and press ENTER , inserting a new blank slide.

**2** In the content area on the slide, click the Insert SmartArt Graphic icon ▣ . The Choose a SmartArt Graphic dialog box opens.

**3** Click Matrix, and then click the Basic Matrix design (the first design).

**4** Click OK. An empty diagram appears.

**5** In the upper right box, replace the [text] placeholder with **Individual Donations**.

**6** Replace the other three [text] placeholders (going clockwise) with **Corporate Contributions**, **Government Funding**, and **Special Events**.

✓ *Notice that the text resizes automatically to fit.*

**7** In the title placeholder at the top of the slide, type **Sources of Funding**.

**8** Save the changes to the **PTry16_ studentfirstname_studentlastname** file, and leave it open to use in the next Try It.

Fill in the placeholders on the new diagram

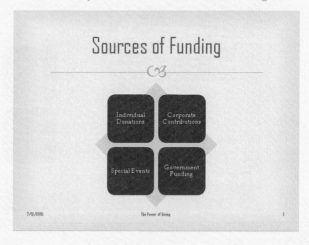

## Adding, Removing, and Resizing Shapes in a Diagram

■ Each diagram begins with a default number of shapes, but you can add or remove them as needed. Use the commands on the SmartArt Tools Design tab.

✓ *There are some exceptions; some diagram types require a certain number of shapes in them. For such diagrams the Add Shape command is unavailable.*

■ You can also resize each shape individually. Drag its selection handles to do so, just as you would any drawn shape. Instead of dragging, you can also use the Smaller or Larger buttons on the SmartArt Tools Format tab.

## Try It!    Removing, Adding, and Resizing a Shape

**1** In the **PTry16_studentfirstname_studentlastname** file, on slide 7, select the last shape ("Follow up to assess progress").

**2** Press [DEL]. The shape is removed and the other shapes resize to fill the space.

**3** With the rightmost shape selected on the diagram on slide 7, click SmartArt Tools Design > Add Shape 🗗 . A new shape appears.

✓ *The Add Shape button has a down arrow you can click to choose where the new shape will be added, but you don't need it in these steps because you want the new shape in the default position, to the right of the selected shape.*

**4** Click in the new shape and type the text that appeared in the deleted shape before ("Follow up to assess progress").

**5** On slide 7, click the first rounded rectangle in the diagram to select it.

**6** Hold down [CTRL] and click on each of the other rounded rectangles.

**7** Position the mouse pointer on a top selection handle on any of the selected shapes and drag upward 1/2". The height of each of the rectangles changes equally.

**8** Click SmartArt Tools Format > Smaller 🖳 . Then, click it again to make the shapes one more step smaller.

**9** Save the changes to the **PTry16_studentfirstname_studentlastname** file, and leave it open to use in the next Try It.

## Reordering Diagram Content

■ Even though each shape in a SmartArt diagram is individually movable, you should not drag shapes to reorder them in a SmartArt diagram, because it interrupts the automatic flow of the layout. Instead you should use the reordering commands on the SmartArt Tools Design tab.

■ The Promote and Demote commands change the level of the text within the diagram hierarchy. This is like promoting and demoting bulleted list levels on a text-based layout.

## Try It!    Reordering Diagram Content

**1** In the **PTry16_studentfirstname_studentlastname** file, file, on slide 3, click the top left rounded rectangle to select it.

**2** Click SmartArt Tools Design > Reorder Down ● . The content of that shape is moved one position in the layout.

✓ *Notice that it moved to the right, and not literally down. In this case, down means to move it down in the flow one position, regardless of the direction of the flow. If the diagram's flow was top-to-bottom, moving "down" would be up in the diagram.*

**3** On slide 10, click in the *Get friends involved* bullet point in the second column.

**4** Click SmartArt Tools Design > Promote ◆ . That bullet point becomes its own separate column.

**5** Click SmartArt Tools Design > Demote ➡ . The text goes back to being a bullet point in the center column.

**6** Click SmartArt Tools Design > Right to Left ⇄ . The diagram changes its flow direction, so that the right and left columns switch places.

**7** Save the changes to the **PTry16_studentfirstname_studentlastname** file, and leave it open to use in the next Try It.

## Changing the Diagram Type

- There are many diagram types to choose from. If you don't like the original diagram type you started with, you can switch to another.

- The diagram types are arranged in categories, but there is some overlap; some designs appear in more than one category.

- On the SmartArt Tools Design tab, you can open a gallery of layouts and choose the one you want to apply to the diagram.

---

**Try It!**    **Changing the Diagram Type**

**1** In the **PTry16_studentfirstname_ studentlastname**, click slide 10 to display it.

**2** Click the SmartArt to make the SmartArt tabs available.

**3** On the SmartArt Tools Design tab, in the Layouts group, click the More button ⊡ to open the gallery of design samples.

**4** Point at several different samples, and see previews of them on the slide, behind the open menu.

**5** Click the Vertical Bracket List (first sample in the second row). The diagram changes to that layout.

**6** Save the changes to the **PTry16_ studentfirstname_studentlastname** file, and leave it open to use in the next Try It.

---

## Changing the Color and Style of a Diagram

- A SmartArt diagram's colors are determined by the color theme in use in the presentation. You can choose different combinations of those theme colors.

- **SmartArt style** refers to the shading and texture effects on the shapes used in the diagram. Some of the styles make the shapes look raised or shiny, for example.

---

**Try It!**    **Changing the Style and Color of a Diagram**

**1** In the **PTry16_studentfirstname_ studentlastname**, click slide 10 to display it if it is not already displayed.

**2** Select the SmartArt object's frame if it is not already selected.

**3** On the SmartArt Tools Design tab, click the More button ⊡ in the SmartArt Styles group to open a gallery of style choices.

**4** Click Polished (the first sample in the first row of the 3D section). It is applied to the diagram.

**5** On slide 10, with the diagram still selected, click SmartArt Tools Design > Change Colors ⁙ . A palette of color presets appears.

**6** Point to several of the presets, and see them previewed on the slide behind the open menu.

**7** Click the fourth sample in the Colorful section. It is applied to the diagram.

✓ *The Colorful section's presets use a different color from the theme for each of the major shapes. Most of the other preset types use a single color.*

**8** Save the changes to the **PTry16_ studentfirstname_studentlastname** file, and leave it open to use in the next Try It.

## Creating Picture-Based SmartArt

- Some of the SmartArt layouts include picture placeholders. These are useful for providing small pieces of artwork, either to illustrate points being made in the text or as decoration.

- The main difference with this type of layout is that you have an extra step after inserting the SmartArt and typing the text—you must click each picture placeholder and select a picture to insert into it.

---

**Try It!**     **Creating Picture-Based SmartArt**

1. In the **PTry16_studentfirstname_studentlastname** file, on slide 5, select the clip art and press DEL to remove.

2. Select the bulleted list.

3. Right-click the bulleted list and click Convert to SmartArt > More SmartArt Graphics. The Choose a SmartArt Graphic dialog box opens.

4. Click the Picture category.

5. Click Captioned Pictures (the second sample in the second row.)

6. Click OK.

7. On the SmartArt diagram, double-click the Insert Picture from File 🖼 icon in the leftmost picture placeholder. The Insert Picture dialog box opens.

8. Navigate to the folder containing the files for this lesson.

9. Click **PTry16a.jpg** and click Insert. The picture appears in the placeholder.

10. Using this same process, insert **PTry16b.jpg** and **PTry16c.jpg** in the other two placeholders on the slide.

11. Save the **PTry16_studentfirstname_studentlastname** file and close it.

---

# Project 33—Create It

## Laser Surgery Presentation

### DIRECTIONS

1. Start PowerPoint, if necessary, and open **PProj33** from the data files for this lesson.

2. Save the presentation as **PProj33_studentfirstname_studentlastname** in the location where your teacher instructs you to store the files for this lesson.

3. Display slide 1, and click **Insert** > **Text Box** 🔳. Click at the top of the slide and type your full name.

4. On slide 3, click in the content area and press CTRL + A to select all.

5. Right-click the selection and point to **Convert to SmartArt**.

6. Click the Radial List (first sample in the third row). The list changes to a diagram.

7. Click the picture placeholder in the large circle on the SmartArt diagram.

8. In the Insert Picture dialog box, navigate to the data files for this lesson and click **PProj33a.jpg**.

9. Click **Insert**.

10. On the **SmartArt Tools Design** tab, click the **More** button 🔽 in the SmartArt Styles group to open the SmartArt Styles gallery.

11. Click **Polished** (the first sample in the 3D section).

12. **With your teacher's permission**, print one copy of the presentation as handouts, 6 slides per page.

13. Close the presentation, saving changes, and exit PowerPoint.

# Project 34—Apply It

## Laser Surgery Presentation

### DIRECTIONS

1. Start PowerPoint, if necessary, and open **PProj34** from the data files for this lesson.

2. Save the presentation as **PProj34_ studentfirstname_studentlastname** in the location where your teacher instructs you to store the files for this lesson.

3. Place a text box containing your full name at the top of slide 1.

4. On slide 4, convert the bulleted list to the Vertical Block List SmartArt design.

   ✓ *You can determine a sample's name by hovering the mouse over it.*

5. Change the SmartArt Style to **Moderate Effect**.

6. Change the colors to the first sample in the Colorful section of the color list. Figure 16-2 shows the finished slide.

7. On slide 5, change the colors for the SmartArt to the **Colored Fill** colors in the Accent 3 section of the color list.

8. On slide 8, convert the numbered list to the **Staggered Process** SmartArt.

   ✓ *You will need to open the Choose a SmartArt Graphic dialog box to find this design. After right-clicking the list, choose More SmartArt Graphics, and then look in the Process category.*

9. Drag the bottom of the SmartArt frame down **1"** on the slide, enlarging the diagram.

10. Change the colors for the diagram to the third sample in the Colorful section of the color list.

11. Change the SmartArt Style to **Polished** (the first sample in the 3D section of the SmartArt Styles gallery). Figure 16-3 shows the finished slide.

12. Close the presentation, saving changes, and exit PowerPoint.

**Figure 16-2**

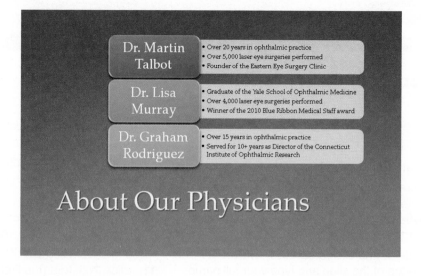

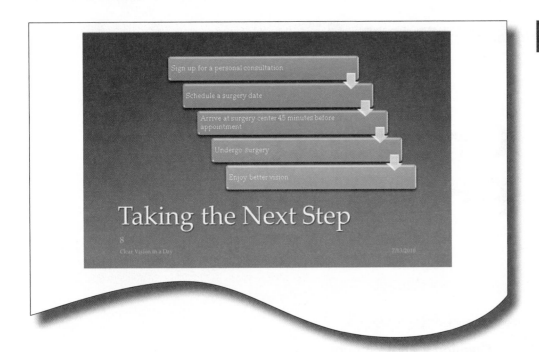

Figure 16-3

# Lesson 17

# Creating a Photo Album

**WORDS TO KNOW**

Photo album
A special type of
presentation in which the
main point is to display
photos.

> **What You Will Learn**

**Creating a Photo Album**

**Software Skills**   A photo album presentation enables you to display multiple photographs with very little text, to let the pictures tell their own stories. PowerPoint has a special Photo Album feature that makes it easy to create and modify photo albums in PowerPoint.

**Application Skills**   Orchard School, a small private school in your area, has asked you to help create a photo album of pictures to help market the school to local families. You will create a photo album with the pictures they have given you so far, as an example of what can be done in PowerPoint.

## What You Can Do

### Creating a Photo Album

- A photo album presentation doesn't have placeholders for bulleted lists or other text; it is designed to efficiently display and organize photos.
- In a photo album presentation you can easily import and arrange many photo files. You can change the order of the photos at any time.
- You can also choose from a variety of picture frame styles.
- You should edit a photo album presentation via the Photo Album dialog box as much as possible, rather than manually editing it. This allows PowerPoint's photo album management features to remain in operation, such as automatically reordering the pictures across multiple slides when you rearrange picture order in the dialog box.

## Try It!    Creating a Photo Album

**1**   Start PowerPoint.

> ✓ You do not need to save the presentation file yet because the Photo Album feature creates a brand-new presentation file.

**2**   Click Insert > Photo Album 🖼 . The Photo Album dialog box opens.

**3**   Click the File/Disk button. The Insert New Pictures dialog box opens.

**4**   Navigate to the location where data files for this lesson are stored and click **PTry17a.jpg**.

**5**   Hold down the `CTRL` key and click **PTry17b**, **PTry17c**, **PTry17d**, and **PTry17e**.

**6**   Click Insert. The file names appear on the Pictures In Album list.

**7**   Click **PTry17b** on the list, and then click the Decrease Brightness button 🔅 .

**8**   Open the Picture Layout drop-down list and click Two Pictures.

**9**   Open the Frame Shape drop-down list and click Rounded Rectangle.

**10**   Click Create. The photo album is created in a new presentation file.

**11**   Save the presentation as **PTry17_ studentfirstname_studentlastname** in the location where your teacher instructs you to store the files for this lesson, and leave it open to use in the next Try It.

## Try It!    Editing a Photo Album

**1**   In the **PTry17_studentfirstname_ studentlastname** file, on the Insert tab, click the arrow below the Photo Album button to open its menu. Then, click Edit Photo Album.

**2**   Open the Picture Layout drop-down list and click Fit to Slide.

**3**   Click **PTry17e** on the list, and click the Move Up button 🔼 four times, to move it to the top of the list.

**4**   Click **PTry17a** on the list, and click Remove.

**5**   Click Update.

**6**   Save the changes to the **PTry17_ studentfirstname_studentlastname** file, and leave it open to use in the next Try It.

## Try It!    Applying a Theme to a Photo Album

**1**   In the **PTry17_studentfirstname_ studentlastname** file, on the Insert tab, click the arrow below the Photo Album button to open its menu. Then, click Edit Photo Album.

**2**   Click the Browse button next to the Theme text box.

**3**   Click the Civic theme.

**4**   Click Select.

**5**   Click Update.

**6**   Save the **PTry17_studentfirstname_ studentlastname** file and then close it.

# Project 35—Create It

## Orchard School Photo Album

### DIRECTIONS

1. Start PowerPoint if necessary.
2. Click **Insert** > **Photo Album** 📷 . The Photo Album dialog box opens.
3. Click the **File/Disk** button. The Insert New Pictures dialog box opens.
4. Navigate to the location where data files for this lesson are stored and click **PProj35a.jpg**.
5. Hold down the `CTRL` key and click **PProj35b.jpg**.
6. Click **Insert**.
7. Open the **Picture Layout** drop-down list and click **1 Picture**.
8. Click the **Browse** button next to the Theme text box.
9. Click the **Pushpin** theme, and click **Select**.
10. Click **Create**. A new presentation is created.
11. Display slide 1, and click **Insert** > **Text Box** 🔤 . Click at the bottom of the slide and type your full name.
12. Save the presentation as **PProj35_ studentfirstname_studentlastname** in the location where your teacher instructs you to store the files for this lesson.
13. **With your teacher's permission**, print one copy of the presentation as handouts, 6 slides per page.
14. Close the presentation and exit PowerPoint.

# Project 36—Apply It

## Planet Earth Presentation

### DIRECTIONS

1. Start PowerPoint if necessary, and open **PProj36** from the data files for this lesson.
2. Save the presentation as **PProj36_ studentfirstname_studentlastname** in the location where your teacher instructs you to store the files for this lesson.
3. At the bottom of slide 1, insert a text box and type your full name.
4. Open the Edit Photo Album dialog box, navigate to the location where data files for this lesson are stored, and add **PProj36a.jpg** through **PProj36f. jpg** to the photo album.
5. Move the **PProj36a** photo to the bottom of the list.
6. Choose **Soft Edge Rectangle** as the frame shape.
7. Remove **PProj36e**.
8. Update the photo album.
9. Click the **Pushpin** theme, and click **Select**.
10. **With your teacher's permission**, print one copy of the presentation as handouts, 6 slides per page.
11. Close the presentation, saving changes, and exit PowerPoint.

## Chapter Assessment and Application

## Project 37—Make It Your Own

### MyPyramid Presentation

Childhood obesity has become a serious problem in the United States, and one way to combat it is to educate children about nutrition at an early age. The United States Department of Agriculture has created MyPyramid, a way of thinking about nutrition using a pyramid graphic. The MyPyramid system is a very popular tool for educating young people about nutrition today. Information about it is available at www.MyPyramid.gov.

Using the information you find at that site, create an educational presentation for children ages 9 to 12 that explains the importance of eating a healthy balance of foods every day. On the first slide of your presentation, include an original logo that you design yourself using the shapes in PowerPoint.

### DIRECTIONS

**Create the Logo**

1. Start PowerPoint. Save a new blank file as **PProj37_studentfirstname_studentlastname** in the location where your teacher tells you to save the files for this project.

2. Apply a theme from the themes available on the Design tab. Pick one that you think is appropriate for the audience. Apply a different color theme if the colors in the design you chose are not bright and cheerful.

3. On slide 1, type **Nutrition and You** in the Title placeholder. In the subtitle placeholder, type your full name.

4. On slide 1, use the Shapes tools to create a logo that consists of at least two shapes, stacked and grouped together, with two different fill colors chosen from the current color theme.

**Assemble the Information**

1. On the www.MyPyramid.gov Web site, read about the food pyramid and the recommendations for daily nutrition for children ages 9 to 12.

2. Visit the News & Media section of the site and download the jpeg version of the full-color MyPyramid graphic. Save it to your hard disk as **MyPyramid.jpg** in the location where your teacher tells you to save files for this project.

✓ *If you cannot download the logo from the Web site, use* **PProj37a.jpg** *from the data files for this chapter.*

**Create the Information**

1. Create a presentation of at least 9 slides (including the title slide) that explains how children ages 9 to 12 can use MyPyramid guidelines to choose what to eat each day. Include one slide explaining each of the colored stripes in the pyramid, plus whatever additional slides you think are necessary.

The presentation should include:

- At least one usage of the MyPyramid graphic.
- At least one piece of clip art.
- At least one symbol.
- At least one SmartArt graphic.
- At least one text box that is not a placeholder.

2. **With your instructor's permission**, print one copy of your presentation.

3. Close the presentation, saving changes, and exit PowerPoint.

# Project 38—Master It

## White River Restoration Project

The White River Restoration Society is recruiting new members to help with the cleanup and reforestation of some land they recently received as a donation. They have a basic presentation with all the text in it, but they need some graphics to make it more interesting. You will help them out by adding clip art, photos, SmartArt, and WordArt.

### DIRECTIONS

1. Start PowerPoint, if necessary, and open **PProj38** from the data files for this chapter.

2. Save the presentation as **PProj38_ studentfirstname_studentlastname** in the location where your teacher instructs you to store the files for this chapter.

3. At the bottom of slide 1, create a new text box and type the following:

   **Copyright 2012 Friends of the White River – Student Name.**

4. Insert a copyright symbol © after the word *Copyright*.

5. Format the text box as follows:
   - Format the text in the text box as 14-point and italic.

- Apply a background fill to the text box that uses the palest shade of the light green theme color (the third color in the theme).

6. On slide 1, create a piece of WordArt with the text **White River Restoration Project**:
   - Start with the orange gradient fill sample (second sample in the fifth row).
   - Press ⌷ENTER⌷ after the word River, so the text appears on two lines.
   - Apply the **Arch Up** transformation (the first sample in the Follow Path section).
   - Size the WordArt to exactly **3"** high and **9"** wide.
   - Change the text fill color to the darkest shade of light green (the third color) in the theme color set.

Illustration A

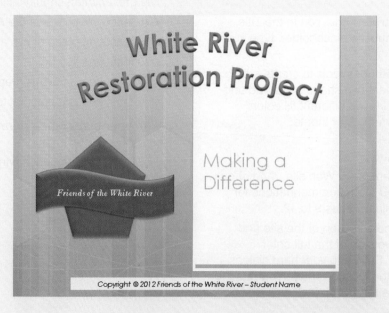

7. On slide 1, create the logo shown in Illustration A:

   - Both shapes were drawn with the Shapes feature.
   - The pentagon is gray, and the banner is brown.
   - Both have the **Preset 2** shape effect applied.
   - Type the text directly into the banner shape.

8. On the Slide Master, change the bullet character for all layouts to a picture bullet that looks like a light green square. Then, close Slide Master view.

   ✓ *Any light green square is acceptable; try to choose one that looks similar to the green background image on the slides.*

9. On slide 2, convert the bulleted list to the **Vertical Bulleted List** SmartArt layout.

10. Apply the **Moderate Effect** SmartArt style to the SmartArt.

11. Change the color of the SmartArt to Outline Effect – Accent 1. Illustration B shows the finished slide.

12. On slide 4, in the empty content placeholder, insert a clip art image of people canoeing on a river.

13. From the **Picture Tools** Format tab's **Picture Effects** menu, apply the Preset 5 settings to the clip art image.

14. On slide 5, in the empty content placeholder, insert **PProj38a.jpg** from the data files for this chapter.

15. On slide 6, convert the bulleted list to a **Target** type of SmartArt layout.

16. On slide 7, remove the bullet characters from both paragraphs.

17. **With your instructor's permission**, print the presentation (6 slides per page).

18. Close the presentation, saving changes, and exit PowerPoint.

Illustration B

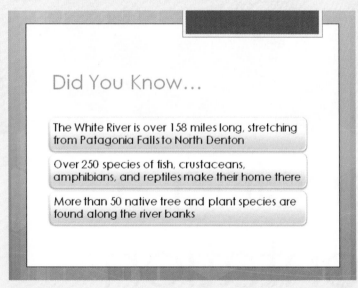

Did You Know...

The White River is over 158 miles long, stretching from Patagonia Falls to North Denton

Over 250 species of fish, crustaceans, amphibians, and reptiles make their home there

More than 50 native tree and plant species are found along the river banks

# Chapter 3

# Enhancing a
# Presentation

## Lesson 18
## Modifying a Theme
## Projects 39-40

- Changing Background Style
- Changing Theme Colors
- Changing Theme Fonts
- Creating New Theme Fonts

## Lesson 19
## Modifying a Background
## Projects 41-42

- Creating Slides from an Outline
- Hiding Background Graphics
- Formatting a Slide Background with a Picture
- Applying a Background Fill Color
- Resetting the Slide Background
- Reusing Slides from Other Presentations

## Lesson 20
## Using Effects and Animations
## Projects 43-44

- Applying Entrance Effects
- Setting Effect Options
- Applying Animation Effects with Animation Painter
- Apply Animations to Objects and SmartArt Graphics

## Lesson 21
## Creating Multimedia Presentations
## Projects 45-46

- Analyzing the Effectiveness of Multimedia Presentations
- Inserting a Video
- Editing a Video
- Applying Video Styles
- Adjusting Video Color
- Controlling a Video in a Presentation
- Inserting Sounds and Music

## Lesson 22
## Working with Tables
## Projects 47-48

- Inserting a Table
- Formatting and Modifying a Table

## Lesson 23
## Working with Charts
## Projects 49-50

- Inserting a Column Chart
- Formatting and Modifying a Chart
- Animating a Chart

## End of Chapter Assessments
## Projects 51-52

# Lesson 18

# Modifying a Theme

## WORDS TO KNOW

Font
A set of characters with a specific size and style.

## ➤ What You Will Learn

**Changing Background Style**
**Changing Theme Colors**
**Changing Theme Fonts**
**Creating New Theme Fonts**

**Software Skills**   You can change theme colors, fonts, and backgrounds to customize a presentation. You can also create new theme font combinations to easily apply in later presentations.

**Application Skills**   In this lesson, you continue work on presentations for Integrated Health Systems' new laser eye surgery centers. You want to explore how changing theme elements might improve the appearance of a presentation you have prepared for the company's Holmes Medical Center facility.

## What You Can Do

### Changing Background Style

- Each theme has a specific background color, and some have background graphics or other effects such as gradients—gradations from one color to another.

- To customize a theme, you can change the background style to one of the choices offered by the current theme, such as those shown in the Background Styles gallery on the Design tab.

- Background styles use the current theme colors. You can apply a new style to all slides or to selected slides.

■ As you rest your pointer on different background styles, the current slide shows what that background style will look like.

■ If you want to make a more radical change to the background, click the Background dialog box launcher on the Design tab to open the Format Background dialog box where you can create a new background using a solid color, a gradient, a texture, or a picture file.

---

**Try It!**  **Changing Background Style**

**1** Start PowerPoint and open **PTry18** from the data files for this lesson.

**2** Save the presentation as **PTry18_ studentfirstname_studentlastname** in the location where your teacher instructs you to store the files for this lesson.

**3** Select the words Student Name in the subtitle placeholder on slide 1 and type your first name and last name.

**4** On the Design tab, click the Background Styles button ⬛.

**5** Click the Style 6 to apply it to all the slides in the presentation.

**6** Display slide 1.

**7** On the Design tab, click the Background Styles button ⬛.

**8** Right-click Style 10 in the gallery.

**9** Click Apply to Selected Slides.

**10** Save the changes to the **PTry18_ studentfirstname_studentlastname** file, and leave it open to use in the next Try It.

---

## Changing Theme Colors

■ Each PowerPoint theme uses a palette of colors selected to work well together. These colors are automatically applied to various elements in the presentation, such as the slide background, text, shape fills, and hyperlink text.

■ You can see the color palettes for each theme by clicking the Colors button on the Design tab.

■ PowerPoint offers several ways to adjust theme colors:

  ✔ *If you like the layout and fonts of a particular theme but not its colors, you can choose to use the color palette of a different theme.*

  ✔ *You can change one or more colors in the current theme to customize the theme.*

■ You modify theme colors in the Create New Theme Colors dialog box.

■ Change a color by clicking the down arrow for a particular color to display a palette. Select a different tint or hue of a theme color, choose one of ten standard colors, or click More Colors to open the Colors dialog box and pick from all available colors.

■ As soon as you change a theme color, the preview in the Create New Theme Colors dialog box also changes to show how your new color coordinates with the others in the theme.

■ You can name a new color scheme and save it. It then displays in the Custom area at the top of the Theme Colors gallery. Custom colors are available to use with any theme.

  ✔ *You can delete custom theme colors by right-clicking the color palette set and selecting Delete.*

---

**Try It!**  **Changing Theme Colors**

**1** In the **PTry18_studentfirstname_ studentlastname** file, select slide 2.

**2** Hover over several color themes. Live Preview shows you how the color theme will look on your slide.

**3** Click Design > Colors ⬛.

**4** Select the Oriel theme.

**5** Click Design > Colors ⬛.

**6** Click Create New Theme Colors.

*(continued)*

**Try It!** **Changing Theme Colors** (continued)

**7** In the Name box, type your first name and last name.

**8** Click the down arrow for Accent 1.

**9** Select Ice Blue, Accent 5, Darker 50% from the palette.

**10** Click Save.

**11** Save the changes to the **PTry18_ studentfirstname_studentlastname** file, and leave it open to use in the next Try It.

## Changing Theme Fonts

- Themes also offer a set of two specific **fonts**, one font for all titles and the other for body text such as the text in bullet lists.

- You can apply the fonts of another theme by choosing a set from the Theme Fonts gallery.

- You can create your own theme fonts if desired, or you can change the font of text in any placeholder using the tools in the Font group on the Home tab.

**Try It!** **Changing Theme Fonts**

**1** In the **PTry18_studentfirstname_ studentlastname** file, select slide 2.

**2** Click Design > Fonts Ⓐ.

**3** Scroll through the available themes.

**4** Select Apex.

**5** Save the changes to the **PTry18_ studentfirstname_studentlastname** file, and leave it open to use in the next Try It.

## Creating New Theme Fonts

- PowerPoint makes it easy to change text appearance on one or more slides.

- If you know you want to change the font for each slide, you can create your own set of theme fonts and then apply them to change text on all slides at once.

- Create a new set of theme fonts in the Create New Theme Fonts dialog box. The Sample Preview window shows you the heading and body font as you select them.

- After you name your set of theme fonts, the set appears at the top of the Theme Fonts gallery in the Custom section.

✔ You can delete custom theme fonts by right-clicking the font set and selecting Delete.

- If you want to change only one font throughout a presentation, you can click Home > Replace ᵃᵇ꜀ > Replace Fonts. The Replace Font dialog box opens to allow you to select one of the presentation's fonts and replace it with any other installed font.

- If you want to make a number of changes to a presentation's fonts, you should change text on the slide master, which controls text appearance throughout the presentation.

**Try It!** **Creating New Theme Fonts**

**1** In the **PTry18_studentfirstname_ studentlastname** file, click Design > Fonts Ⓐ.

**2** Click Create New Theme Fonts.

**3** Click the Heading font down arrow and select Tahoma.

**4** Click the Body font down arrow and select Bookman Old Style.

**5** Click Save.

**6** Save the changes to the **PTry18_ studentfirstname_studentlastname** file and close it.

# Project 39—Create It

## Customizing a Presentation

### DIRECTIONS

1. Start PowerPoint, if necessary, and open **PProj39** from the data files for this lesson.

2. Save the presentation as **PProj39_ studentfirstname_studentlastname** in the location where your teacher instructs you to store the files for this lesson.

3. Click at the end of the subtitle text. The placeholder becomes active.

4. Press ENTER and type **Presented by** and then add your first name and last name.

5. Move to slide 4 and click **Home** > **New Slide** > **Content with Captions**.

6. In the caption placeholder, type the text shown in Figure 18-1.

7. Click **Design** > **Fonts** A > **Create New Theme Fonts**. The Create New Theme Fonts dialog box opens.

8. In the Heading font box, select **Arial** and in the Body font box, select **Corbel**. The Preview window shows you how the fonts look together.

9. Type your first name and last name in the Name box and click **Save**. The newly created Theme Font will appear at the top of the Theme Fonts gallery.

10. Click **Design** > **Colors** and select **Origin**. The new theme color is applied to all slides.

11. Click **Design** > **Background Styles** . The Background Styles gallery opens.

12. Select **Style 2** to apply the light blue color to all slides.

13. **With your teacher's permission**, print slide 4.

14. Close the workbook, saving changes, and exit PowerPoint.

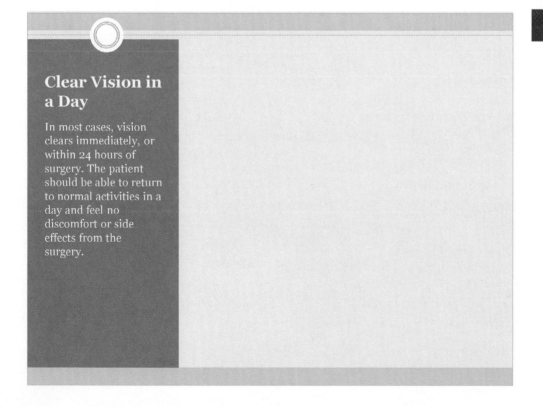

**Figure 18-1**

### Clear Vision in a Day

In most cases, vision clears immediately, or within 24 hours of surgery. The patient should be able to return to normal activities in a day and feel no discomfort or side effects from the surgery.

# Project 40—Apply It

## Customizing a Presentation

### DIRECTIONS

1. Start PowerPoint, if necessary, and open **PProj40** from the data files for this lesson.

2. Save the presentation as **PProj40_ studentfirstname_studentlastname** in the location where your teacher instructs you to store the files for this lesson.

3. Add an image to slide 5 to add interest.

   a. Search for an appropriate clip art photograph.

   b. Resize the image as necessary to fit in the placeholder.

4. Change the theme font to **Trek** (Franklin Gothic Medium and Franklin Gothic Book).

5. Change the background style to **Style 6**.

6. Using the Notes and Handouts tab in the Header and Footer dialog box, add your first name and last name to the footer.

7. **With your teacher's permission**, print a handout of slide 5.

8. Close the presentation, saving changes, and exit PowerPoint.

## Lesson 19

# Modifying a Background

➤ **What You Will Learn**

**Creating Slides from an Outline**
**Hiding Background Graphics**
**Formatting a Slide Background with a Picture**
**Applying a Background Fill Color**
**Resetting the Slide Background**
**Reusing Slides from Other Presentations**

**Software Skills**　Word outlines can be readily imported to create slides. In some instances, you may want to hide the background graphics created as part of a theme.

**Application Skills**　Your client, Voyager Travel Adventures, has supplied you with files they want you to use in the presentation you're creating for them. You'll also add information on each slide to help identify and organize the presentation.

## What You Can Do

### Creating Slides from an Outline

- You can save time by reusing text created in other programs, such as Word, in your PowerPoint presentation.
- You can use Word to help you organize the contents of a presentation and then transfer that outline to PowerPoint.
- If you want to use a Word outline to create slides, you must format the text using Word styles that clearly indicate text levels.

  ✔ *For instance, text formatted with the Word Heading 1 style become slide titles. Text styled as Heading 2 or Heading 3 becomes bulleted items.*

- You have two options for using a Word outline to create slides:
  - You can simply open the Word document in PowerPoint to create the slides. Use this option to create a new presentation directly from outline content.
  - You can use the Slides from Outline command on the New Slide drop-down list to add slides to an existing presentation.

    ✔ *You cannot use this command unless a presentation is already open.*

- When a Word document is used to create a new presentation, the slides will display the same fonts and styles used in the document. These will not change even if a new theme or theme fonts are applied.
- If you want to change the fonts in a presentation created from an outline, you need to click the Reset button on the Home tab.

  ✔ *You can also use this command to reverse changes made to slide layouts or themes.*

- The Reset function will delete the Word styles and apply the theme defaults for colors, fonts, and effects.

---

**Figure 19-1**

This text...

Heading 1 Text

Heading 2 Text

Heading 3 Text

*Heading 4 Text*

Heading 5 Text

# Heading 1 Text

- **Heading 2 Text**
  - **Heading 3 Text**
    - *Heading 4 Text*
      - Heading 5 Text

...Becomes slide content

---

**Try It!**    **Creating Slides from an Outline**

1. Start PowerPoint, click File > Open, and navigate to the location where the data files for this lesson are stored.

2. In the Open dialog box, click All PowerPoint Presentations and select All Files.

3. Select the Word document **PTry19_Giving** and click Open.

4. Scroll through the presentation to see how the Word styles are applied to the slides.

5. Save the presentation as **PTry19_Giving_ studentfirstname_studentlastname** in the location where your teacher instructs you to store the files for this lesson.

6. Close the file.

---

**Try It!**    **Adding Slides from an Outline to an Existing Presentation**

1. In PowerPoint, open **PTry19** from the data files for this lesson.

2. Save the presentation as **PTry19_ studentfirstname_studentlastname** in the location where your teacher instructs you to store the files for this lesson.

3. Select slide 1 (the new slides will appear after this slide).

4. Click Home > New Slide drop-down arrow  .

5. Click Slides from Outline.

*(continued)*

---

**Try It!**    **Adding Slides from an Outline to an Existing Presentation** *(continued)*

---

**6** In the Insert Outline dialog box, navigate to the location where the data files for this lesson are stored and select **PTry19_Outline**.

**7** Click Insert.

**8** Save the changes to the **PTry19_ studentfirstname_studentlastname** file, and leave it open to use in the next Try It.

---

**Try It!**    **Resetting a Slide**

---

**1** In the **PTry19_studentfirstname_ studentlastname** file, select slides 2-4 in the Slides pane.

**2** Click Home > Reset 🗒 .

**3** Save the changes to the **PTry19_ studentfirstname_studentlastname** file, and leave it open to use in the next Try It.

---

## Reusing Slides from Other Presentations

- Borrowing slides from other presentations is a good way to ensure consistency among presentations, which is important when you are working for a larger company.

- You can find the Reuse Slides command on the New Slide drop-down list. This command opens the Reuse Slides task pane.

- To display the slides available to reuse, specify a presentation in the Reuse Slides task pane.

✔ To see the content more clearly, rest the pointer on a slide in the current presentation.

✔ To insert a slide, simply click it.

- By default, slides you reuse take on the formatting of the presentation they're inserted into (the destination presentation).

✔ If you want to retain the original formatting of the inserted slides, click the Keep source formatting check box at the bottom of the Reuse Slides task pane.

---

**Try It!**    **Reusing Slides from Other Presentations**

---

**1** In the PTry19_**studentfirstname_ studentlastname** file, click Home> New Slide 🗒 > Reuse Slides.

**2** In the Reuse Slides task pane, click Browse and then click Browse File.

**3** Navigate to the location where you are storing the files for this lesson and select **PTry19_ Giving_ studentfirstname_studentlastname**.

**4** Click slide 4 in the Slides pane.

**5** Point to each of the slides in the Reuse Slides task pane to view their contents.

**6** Click slide 2 in the Reuse Slides task pane.

**7** Close the task pane.

**8** Save the changes to the **PTry19_ studentfirstname_studentlastname** file, and leave it open to use in the next Try It.

---

*(continued)*

**Try It!**    **Reusing Slides from Other Presentations** *(continued)*

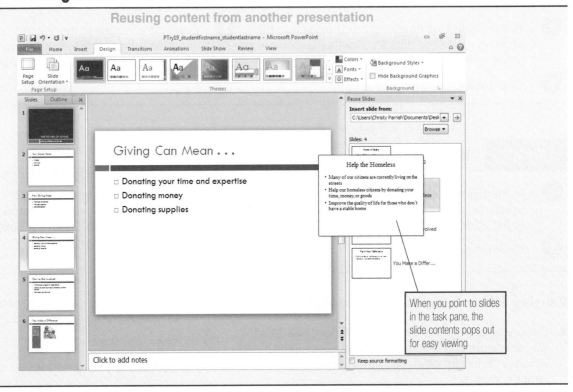

Reusing content from another presentation

When you point to slides in the task pane, the slide contents pops out for easy viewing

## Hiding Background Graphics

■ Many themes include some type of graphics such as lines or shapes that form a part of the slide background.

■ You can only select and modify theme background graphics in Slide Master view.

■ If you don't like these background graphics, you can simply remove them from a slide by clicking Design > Hide Background Graphics.

■ Remember that text colors are often chosen to contrast with the graphic background. If you hide the background graphic, the text colors might need to be changed so that they don't blend into the background.

**Try It!**    **Hiding Background Graphics**

**1** In the **PTry19_studentfirstname_ studentlastname** file, select slide 1.

**2** Click Design > Hide Background Graphics.

**3** Save the changes to the **PTry19_ studentfirstname_studentlastname** file, and leave it open to use in the next Try It.

## Applying a Background Fill Color

■ Instead of changing the entire color theme in a presentation, you can change just the background color.

■ You can apply a background fill color to one slide or to the entire presentation using the Format Background dialog box.

■ To open the Format Background dialog box, click the Background Styles button on the Design tab and then click Format Background.

## Try It!    Applying a Background Fill Color

**1** In the **PTry19_studentfirstname_studentlastname** file, click the Design tab.

**2** Click the Background group dialog box launcher ⬜.

**3** On the Fill page, click the Color button.

**4** Select Blue-Gray, Accent 6.

**5** Click Apply to All.

**6** Save the changes to the **PTry19_studentfirstname_studentlastname** file, and leave it open to use in the next Try It.

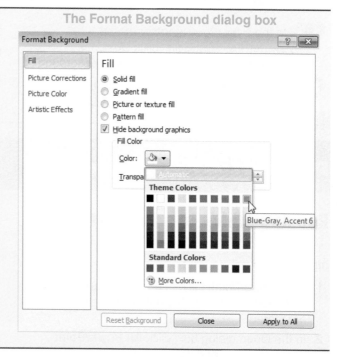

The Format Background dialog box

## Formatting a Slide Background with a Picture

- Adding a picture to your slide background adds interest and helps convey your message.

- You can format the background with a picture using the Format Background dialog box.

- You can use clip art or image files to add graphics to the slide background.

## Try It!    Formatting a Slide Background with a Picture

**1** In the **PTry19_studentfirstname_studentlastname** file, click the Design tab and then click the Background group dialog box launcher ⬜.

**2** In the Format Background dialog box, click Picture or texture fill.

✔ *Note that the background of the slide automatically changes to the first texture option.*

**3** Click the File button and navigate to the location where the data files for this lesson are stored.

**4** Select **PTry19_Soup.jpg** and click Insert.

**5** Click Close to apply the graphic to the title slide.

**6** Save the changes to the **PTry19_studentfirstname_studentlastname** file, and leave it open to use in the next Try It.

## Resetting the Slide Background

- Remember that only changes made to individual slide backgrounds can be reset. If you apply a change to all the slides in a presentation, you cannot reverse the change using the Reset Background option.

✔ *You can, however, use the Undo button to reverse global changes.*

**Try It!**     **Resetting the Slide Background**

**1** In the **PTry19_studentfirstname_ studentlastname** file, click Design > Background Styles 🖾 > Format Background.

**2** Click Reset Slide Background. Notice that the slide background changes immediately.

**3** Click Close.

**4** Save the changes to the **PTry19_ studentfirstname_studentlastname** file and close it.

# Project 41—Create It

## Reusing Slides in a Presentation

### DIRECTIONS

1. Start PowerPoint, click **File** > **Open**, and navigate to the location where the data files for this lesson are stored.

2. In the Open dialog box, click **All PowerPoint Presentations** and select **All Files**.

3. Select the Word document **PProj41** and click Open.

4. Save the presentation as **PProj41_ studentfirstname_studentlastname** in the location where your teacher instructs you to store the files for this lesson.

5. Click **View** > **Slide Sorter** 🖽 to display all the slides in the main window.

6. Click `CTRL` + `A` to select all the slides.

7. Click **Home** > **Reset** 🖺. Each slide will revert to the default formatting and placeholders.

8. Double-click slide 1. The presentation will change to Normal view.

9. Click **Home** > **Layout** 🖾 > **Title Slide**. Slide 1 changes to a Title Slide layout.

10. On the **Design** tab, click the **More** button to display the Themes gallery, and then click **Thatch**. The entire presentation changes to reflect the new Thatch theme.

11. Click **Design** > **Hide Background Graphics**. The stripes on the Title slide disappear.

12. Click **Insert** > **Header & Footer** 🖺. The Header and Footer dialog box opens.

13. Select **Footer** and type your first name and last name. Click **Apply** to apply the footer to the title slide only.

14. **With your teacher's permission**, print slide 1.

15. Close the presentation, saving changes, and exit PowerPoint.

# Project 42—Apply It

## Reusing Slides in a Presentation

### DIRECTIONS

1. Start PowerPoint, if necessary, and open **PProj42** from the data files for this lesson.

2. Save the presentation as **PProj42_studentfirst- name_studentlastname** in the location where your teacher instructs you to store the files for this lesson.

3. Use the Format Background dialog box to change the background styles as follows:

   a. Change the gradient fill color to **Aqua, Accent 5**. Apply the change to all the slides.

   b. Use the file **PProj42_Travel.jpg** located in the data files for this lesson as a picture fill on the title slide.

4. Choose to reuse slides from the presentation **PProj42_Slides**, located in the data files for this lesson.
   a. Point to each slide in the task pane to see its content.
   b. Click slide 2 in the task pane to insert the slide as slide 3 in the presentation. Note that the inserted slide takes on the theme of the current presentation.
   c. Display slide 5 in the current presentation and then insert the third slide in the task pane to become slide 6. Close the task pane.

5. Insert a date that updates automatically, slide numbers, and a footer that includes your first name and last name. Do not show this information on the title slide, but apply it to all other slides. Your presentation should look like Figure 19-2.

6. Spell check the presentation.

7. **With your teacher's permission,** print the presentation as a 6 slides per page handout.

8. Close the presentation, saving changes, and exit PowerPoint.

**Figure 19-2**

7/24/2010

1

# Lesson 20

# Using Effects and Animations

## WORDS TO KNOW

**Advance slide timing**

A setting that controls the amount of time a slide displays on the screen.

**Animate**

To apply movement to text or an object to control its display during the presentation.

**Transitions**

The visual effects used when one slide moves off of the screen and another moves onto the screen.

## ➤ What You Will Learn

**Applying Entrance Effects**
**Setting Effect Options**
**Applying Animation Effects with Animation Painter**
**Applying Animations to Objects and SmartArt Graphics**

**Software Skills**    PowerPoint allows you to add transitions and animations to make your slides more visually interesting during a presentation.

**Application Skills**    The public relations director at Holmes Medical Center has informed you that she will present the laser surgery unit slide show to a large audience. She wants to advance slides automatically but also wants to be able to control slides manually. She also wants transitions and animations. In this lesson, you will add transitions and animate both text and objects. Then, you will rehearse the presentation to check your timings.

## What You Can Do

### Applying Entrance Effects

■ You can **animate** text and objects in a presentation to add interest or emphasize special points.

■ Use the Animation gallery on the Animation tab to apply one of PowerPoint's preset animation effects. This gallery provides several animation effects from which to choose.

■ Because you must select a placeholder or object before the Animation gallery becomes active, you must be in Normal view to apply these animations.

**Try It!**   **Applying Entrance Effects Using the Animation Gallery**

**1** Start PowerPoint and open **PTry20** from the data files for this lesson.

**2** Save the presentation as **PTry20_ studentfirstname_studentlastname** in the location where your teacher instructs you to store the files for this lesson.

**3** On slide 2, click the content placeholder.

**4** On the Animations tab, click the More button ⏷, and click the Fly In animation from the gallery.

**5** Save the changes to the **PTry20_ studentfirstname_studentlastname** file, and leave it open to use in the next Try It.

## Setting Effect Options

- If you want more control over animation effects, use the Animation Pane. Using the Animation Pane, you can control how the effect is applied.

- For each animation effect you use, you can modify the direction the animation takes, along with its timing.

- When you add an effect, the object name and an effect symbol display in the Animation Pane. This list represents the order in which the effects take place when the slide is viewed.

- You can adjust the order in which effects take place using the Re-Order arrows at the bottom of the task pane.

- The Play button allows you to preview the animations to make sure they display as you want them to.

- To see more options for controlling an effect, click the drop-down arrow to the right of the effect item.

- The Effect Options button on the Animations tab offers options for controlling the direction and sequence of the selected animation.

**Try It!**   **Setting Effect Options**

**1** In the **PTry20_studentfirstname_ studentlastname** file, click the content placeholder on slide 4.

**2** Click Animations > Effect Options ⬈.

**3** Click From Left ⇒ From Left .

**4** Click Animations > Effect Options ⬈.

**5** Click By Paragraph.

**6** Save the changes to the **PTry20_ studentfirstname_studentlastname** file, and leave it open to use in the next Try It.

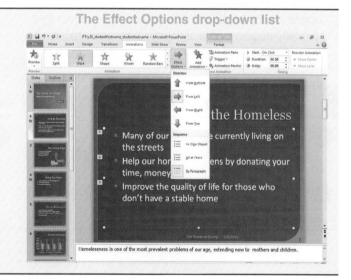

The Effect Options drop-down list

## Applying Animation Effects with Animation Painter

- Creating just the right animation effect can be time-consuming. When you want to use the same animation effect on more than one slide, the best choice is to use the Animation Painter.

- Like the Format Painter, the Animation Painter duplicates the animation formatting from one placeholder to another.

- To copy the animation to another placeholder, select a placeholder that has the animation you want to use and click the Animation Painter button. Then, click the placeholder to which you want to apply it.

- To apply the animation to multiple placeholders, double-click the Animation Painter button after selecting your animation placeholder.

---

**Try It!**    **Applying Animation Effects with Animation Painter**

① In the **PTry20_studentfirstname_ studentlastname** file, select the text placeholder on slide 2.

② Double-click Animations > Animation Painter ⚡.

③ Click slide 4 in the Slides pane. Click the text placeholder.

④ Click slide 5 in the Slides pane. Click the text placeholder.

⑤ Press ESC .

⑥ Save the changes to the **PTry20_ studentfirstname_studentlastname** file, and leave it open to use in the next Try It.

---

## Applying Animations to Objects and SmartArt Graphics

- Effects can be used to create an interesting entrance for an object, to emphasize an object that already appears on a slide, or to accompany an object's exit from a slide.

- Objects and SmartArt graphics can be animated using the same tools that you use to animate text.

---

**Try It!**    **Applying Animations to Objects and SmartArt Graphics**

① In the **PTry20_studentfirstname_ studentlastname** file, click the SmartArt graphic on slide 3.

② In the Animations gallery, click the More button and click Teeter.

③ Save the changes to the **PTry20_ studentfirstname_studentlastname** file and close it.

# Project 43—Create It

## Adding Animations

### DIRECTIONS

1. Start PowerPoint, if necessary, and open **PProj43** from the data files for this lesson.

2. Save the presentation as **PProj43_ studentfirstname_studentlastname** in the location where your teacher instructs you to store the files for this lesson.

3. Click the title placeholder on slide 1 and on the **Animations** tab, in the Animation gallery, click **Fade**. A preview of the fade animation displays.

4. Press [ENTER] and type **Presented** by and then add your first name and last name.

5. Click the border of the subtitle placeholder, click the **More** button on the Animation gallery, and click **Wipe**. A preview of the Wipe animation displays.

6. Select the content placeholder on slide 2 and on the **Animations** tab, in the Animation gallery, click **Fly In**. A preview of the Fly In animation displays. Your presentation should look like Figure 20-1.

7. Close the presentation, saving changes, and exit PowerPoint.

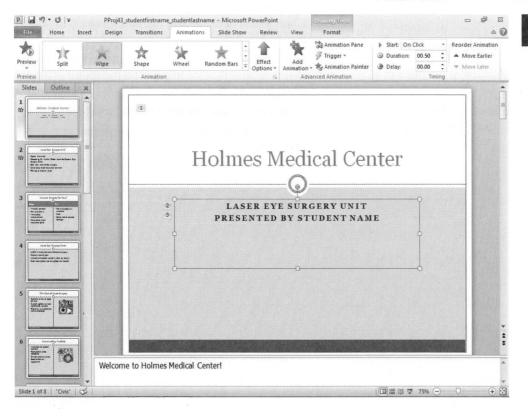

**Figure 20-1**

# Project 44—Apply It

## Adding Animations

### DIRECTIONS

1. Start PowerPoint, if necessary, and open **PProj44** from the data files for this lesson.
2. Save the presentation as **PProj44_studentfirstname_studentlastname** in the location where your teacher instructs you to store the files for this lesson.
3. Use the Animation Painter to copy the animation from the presentation title to the title placeholders on slides 2 through 6.
4. Apply custom animations to each slide as follows:
    a. On slide 1, apply a **Zoom** animation effect to the subtitle.
    b. On slide 2, apply a **Fly In** entrance effect for the text placeholder. Change the direction of the effect to  **From Left**.
    c. On slide 3, apply the **Grow & Turn** effect to the Pros text box.
    d. On slide 3, use the **Animation Painter** to apply the same effect to the Cons text box.
    e. On slide 4, apply the **Split** effect to the text placeholder. Use the Effect Options list to change the effect to **Vertical Out**.
    f. On slide 5, apply **Random Bars Entrance** effect to the text placeholder and the **Swivel** effect to the graphic. Modify the effects so that the text in the left-hand placeholder displays **All at Once** and then the clip art graphic displays.
    g. On slide 6, apply the same effects as slide 5.
    h. On slide 7, animate the title, text, and photo so that that all fly in from separate directions.
    i. On slide 8, apply the **Float In** effect to the WordArt graphic.
5. Change the text *Student Name* on slide 8 to your first name and last name.
6. Add an automatically updating date to the slide footer. Notice that for this theme the footer is along the right side of the slide.
7. Watch the slideshow from start to finish.
8. Close the presentation, saving changes, and exit PowerPoint.

# Lesson 21

# Creating Multimedia Presentations

> ## What You Will Learn

**Analyzing the Effectiveness of Multimedia Presentations**
**Inserting a Video**
**Editing a Video**
**Applying Video Styles**
**Adjusting Video Color**
**Controlling a Video in a Presentation**
**Inserting Sounds and Music**

**Software Skills**    PowerPoint has many tools and features, but selecting the options that make your presentation effective depends on many factors, including the topic, the audience, and the purpose. For example, a marketing presentation may be more effective if it uses lots of multimedia and animation effects, while a tutorial or training presentation may be more effective if it uses straightforward bullet text without distracting sounds and actions.

You can insert your own pictures in a presentation and then use the enhanced picture tools to adjust the picture's appearance and apply special effects. For a really dynamic presentation, add media clips such as movies and sounds.

**Application Skills**    A local environmental group, Planet Earth, has asked you to prepare a presentation they can show on Earth Day. In this lesson, you begin the presentation by inserting and formatting a picture and several multimedia files.

# What You Can Do

## Analyzing the Effectiveness of Multimedia Presentations

■ Always consider your audience when creating a presentation. Research the audience's needs and knowledge level, and tailor the presentation to it.

■ Also consider how the presentation will be delivered. Not all presentations are delivered by a live narrator to a live audience.

  ● Will it be printed? Select a light background and dark text for readability.

  ● Will it be standalone? Include navigation tools for the viewer.

  ● Will it run automatically in a loop? Keep it short so a viewer does not have to wait a long time for the presentation to begin anew.

  ● Will it be delivered over the Internet? Make sure the audio is high quality.

■ Follow general design guidelines when preparing a presentation. For example:

  ● Apply a consistent theme to all slides. That means using the same font and color scheme throughout, and repeating elements such as bullets and backgrounds.

  ● Limit bullet points to no more than five per slide.

  ● Limit the number of fonts to two per slide.

  ● Use contrasting colors when necessary to make text stand out. For example, use a dark background color such as dark green or blue and a light contrasting text color, such as yellow.

  ● Avoid the use of pastels, which can be hard to read.

  ● Make sure text is large enough so that even someone at the back of the room can read it. No smaller than 18 points and no larger than 48 points is usually effective.

  ● Use graphics such as tables, charts, and pictures to convey key points.

  ● Make sure graphics are sized to fill the slide.

  ● Use consistent transitions, sounds, and animations that enhance the presentation and do not distract from the content.

■ Be clear about the message you are trying to convey. For example, if you are creating a marketing presentation, be clear about what you are trying to sell. If you are creating a training presentation, be clear about what you are teaching.

■ Know your time limit based on your audience. Most people will lose interest if the presentation goes on too long.

■ An effective presentation has a logical progression:

  ● Introduction in which you tell your audience what you are going to present.

  ● Body in which you present the information.

  ● Summary in which you tell your audience what you presented.

■ Do not use slang, incorrect grammar, jargon, or abbreviations that your audience might not understand.

■ Your role in the delivery of a live presentation is key. Dress appropriately, speak loud and clear, and make eye contact with your audience.

■ You can assess a presentation's effectiveness by testing it on a practice audience. Ask for constructive criticism to help you improve.

## Inserting a Video

■ Insert a movie file using the Insert Media Clip button in a content placeholder or the Video button on the Insert tab.

■ When you insert animated clip art, the Picture Tools tab becomes available. It provides the same formatting tools available for other graphics.

■ By default, when you use a video clip on a slide, you will have access to the same sort of playback tools you would see with a Web video.

■ You have three options for adding a video to your presentation:

  ● Insert an animated clip art graphic.

  ● Insert a movie file saved in a format such as AVI or MPEG.

  ● Insert a movie from the Web.

■ When you insert a video file or a video from the Web, the Video Tools Format and Video Tools Playback tabs open.

■ Locate animated clip art graphics by searching for movies in the Clip Art task pane. These graphics tend to be small and usually cannot be enlarged without a loss of quality.

## Try It!     Inserting a Movie from a File

**1** Start PowerPoint and open **PTry21** from the data files for this lesson.

**2** Save the presentation as **PTry21_studentfirstname_studentlastname** in the location where your teacher instructs you to store the files for this lesson.

**3** Select slide 4 and click the Insert Media Clip icon 🎞 in the content placeholder.

**OR**

Click Insert > Video 🎞 and then click Video from File.

**4** Navigate to the location where the data files for this lesson are stored and select **PTry21_video**.

**5** Click Insert.

**6** Save the changes to the **PTry21_studentfirstname_studentlastname** file, and leave it open to use in the next Try It.

Insert a video from a file

## Editing a Video

- The Video Tools Format tab is very similar to the Picture Tools tab. It contains tools for changing the way the video clip looks within the slide.

- When video files are inserted into presentations, you'll see a black box effect. Rather than leaving the black margins on a video object, crop the object the way you would with a picture.

## Try It!     Editing a Video

**1** In the **PTry21_studentfirstname_studentlastname** file, select the video on slide 4.

**2** On the Video Tools Format tab, click the Crop button ⯆.

**3** Drag the left cropping handle to the right to remove the black.

**4** Drag the right cropping handle to the left to remove the black.

**5** On the Video Tools Format tab, click the Crop button ⯆ again to save the changes to video object.

**6** Save the changes to the **PTry21_studentfirstname_studentlastname** file, and leave it open to use in the next Try It.

Cropping a video

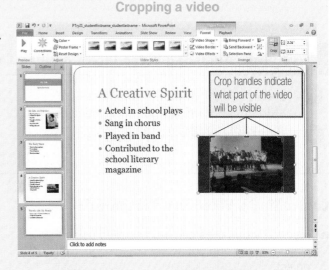

Crop handles indicate what part of the video will be visible

## Apply Video Styles

- When you insert a video into a slide, you can format it using the same tools that you would any graphic.

- Applying a video style to video gives it a more finished look.

- Before you settle on a video style, try several. Not all video styles are suited to every video.

- Depending on the video style you choose, you can add or change the video effects, change the color of the border, or the shape of the video screen.

### Try It!    Applying Video Styles

① In the **PTry21_studentfirstname_studentlastname** file, select the video on slide 4.

② On the Video Tools Format tab, click the More button ☑ to open the Video Styles gallery.

③ Move your mouse over several styles to see the live preview and then choose Drop Shadow Rectangle.

④ Save the changes to the **PTry21_studentfirstname_studentlastname** file, and leave it open to use in the next Try It.

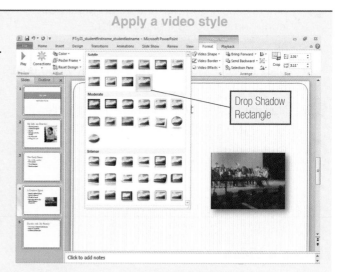

Apply a video style

## Adjusting Video Color

- You can use the same tools that you would use to change the color of a photo image in PowerPoint to change the color of a video.

- In addition to the most popular video color options: Black and White, Grayscale, Sepia, and Washout, you can also choose to tint the video in 14 different variations.

- If you don't see a color you like, you can choose More Variations to open the color pallet and choose from all Windows colors.

### Try It!    Adjusting Video Insert a Video Color

① In the **PTry21_ studentfirstname_studentlastname** file, select the video on slide 4.

② Click Video Tools Format > Color ▣.

③ Choose Grayscale.

④ Save the changes to the **PTry21_studentfirstname_studentlastname** file, and leave it open to use in the next Try It.

## Controlling a Video in a Presentation

- Inserted Video clips can be controlled using the standard play and pause controls on the video object.

- PowerPoint allows you to hide the movie during the presentation, play it full screen, loop it continuously, rewind it, change its arrangement relative to other objects, or scale it.

## Try It!   Previewing a Movie in Normal View

**1** In the **PTry21 _studentfirstname_ studentlastname** file, select the video on slide 4.

**2** Click Video Tools Playback > Play ▶ .

**OR**

Click the play button ▶ on the video itself.

**3** Watch for a few seconds and click Video Tools Playback > Pause ‖ .

**OR**

Click the pause button ‖ on the video itself.

**4** Save the changes to the **PTry21_ studentfirstname_studentlastname** file, and leave it open to use in the next Try It.

## Try It!   Viewing Videos in a Slide Show

**1** In the **PTry21_studentfirstname_ studentlastname** file, select slide 4, if necessary.

**2** Click Slide Show > From Current Slide 🖳 .

**3** Hover your mouse over the video to display the play button.

**4** Click the Play button ▶ .

**5** Watch the video for a few seconds and then click the slide to progress to the next slide.

**6** Press ESC .

**7** Select the video on slide 4, if necessary, and click Video Tools Playback > Start 🖳 Start: , and click Automatically.

**8** Click Slide Show > From Current Slide 🖳 . Notice that the video starts immediately.

**9** Press ESC .

**10** Save the changes to the **PTry21_ studentfirstname_studentlastname** file, and leave it open to use in the next Try It.

## Inserting Sounds and Music

■ You can add sound and music clips to your presentation to make it more interesting or to emphasize a slide. Your computer must have speakers and a sound card to play music or sounds during a presentation.

■ Use the Audio button on the Insert tab to choose what kind of sound to insert: a sound file, a sound from the clip art files, or record your own sounds.

■ When you insert an audio clip, a sound icon displays on the slide. You can move this icon to a new location (or even off the slide) or resize it to make it less obtrusive.

   ✔ *The sound icon must appear on the slide if you intend to control a sound by clicking it during the presentation.*

■ You can choose whether to play the sound automatically or when clicked.

■ Use the Audio Tools Playback tab to control sound options.

## Try It!   Inserting Sounds or Music from a File

**1** In the **PTry21_studentfirstname_ studentlastname** file, select slide 5.

**2** Click Insert > Audio 🔊 .

**3** Click Audio from File.

**4** In the Insert Audio dialog box, navigate to the location where the data files for this lesson are stored and select **PTry21_audio.mid**.

**5** Click Insert and drag the audio icon to the lower right of the slide.

*(continued)*

**Try It!**    **Inserting Sounds or Music from a File** *(continued)*

**6**  On the Audio Tools Playback tab, click the Start down arrow 🔊 Start: , and click Automatically.

**7**  Save the changes to the **PTry21_ studentfirstname_studentlastname** file, and leave it open to use in the next Try It.

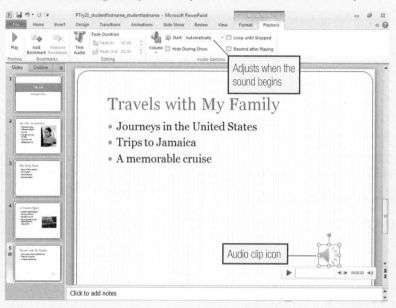

PowerPoint gives you complete control over audio clips

**Try It!**    **Inserting a Sound from the Clip Organizer**

**1**  In the **PTry21_Grades_studentfirstname_ studentlastname** file, select slide 1.

**2**  Click Insert > Audio 🔊 .

**3**  Select Clip Art Audio.

**4**  In the Clip Art task pane, scroll through the audio clips to see what's available.

   ✔ *To listen to a clip, hover over the clip. When the down arrow appears, click it and select Preview/Properties. Use the play button to hear the clip. Click Close when you're done.*

**5**  Double click Starter Music to insert the clip.

**6**  Close the task pane.

**7**  On the Audio Tools Playback tab, click the Start down arrow 🔊 Start: and click Automatically.

**8**  Click Slide Show > From Beginning and watch the presentation.

**9**  Close the **PTry21_Grades_studentfirstname_ studentlastname** file, saving changes, and exit PowerPoint.

# Project 45—Create It

## Creating a Multimedia Presentation

### DIRECTIONS

1. Start PowerPoint, if necessary, and open **PProj45** from the data files for this lesson.

2. Save the presentation as **PProj45_studentfirst name_studentlastname** in the location where your teacher instructs you to store the files for this lesson.

3. Select slide 1, click inside the subtitle placeholder, and type your first name and last name.

4. Select slide 2 and then click the **Insert Media Clip** icon in the right placeholder. The Insert Video dialog box opens.

5. Navigate to the location where the data files for this lesson are stored and select **PProj45_Earthmovie.mpeg**.

6. Click **Insert**. The video appears in the placeholder.

7. Select slide 3 and in the placeholder, click the **Insert Picture from File** icon. The Insert Picture dialog box opens.

8. Navigate to the location where the data files for this lesson are stored and select **PProj45_Earthpic.jpg**.

9. Click **Insert**. The picture appears in the placeholder, as shown in Figure 21-1.

10. Close the presentation, saving changes, and exit PowerPoint.

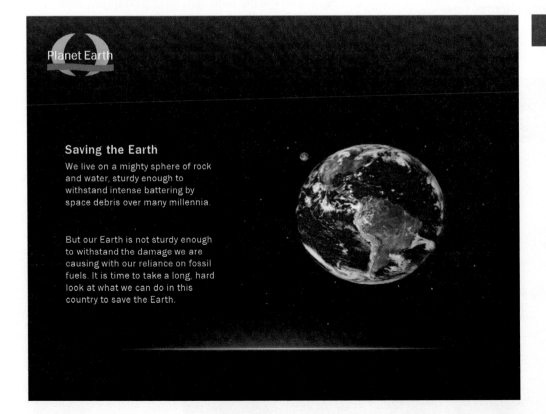

**Figure 21-1**

# Project 46—Apply It

## Creating a Multimedia Presentation

### DIRECTIONS

1. Start PowerPoint, if necessary, and open **PProj46** from the data files for this lesson.

2. Save the presentation as **PProj46_ studentfirstname_studentlastname** in the location where your teacher instructs you to store the files for this lesson.

3. Replace the text Student Name on the title slide with your first name and last name:

4. Modify the video clip on slide 2 as follows:

   a. Drag the movie down so that the top of it is more or less aligned with the top of the text in the placeholder to the left of the movie.

   b. Apply the **Simple Frame, White** video style to the movie.

   c. Set the movie to start automatically.

   d. Preview the movie in Normal view.

5. Format the picture on slide 3 as shown in Figure 21-2. Be sure to include the following:

   a. Adjust the brightness to make the picture 20% brighter.

   b. Adjust the contrast to 20%.

   c. Crop about a half an inch from the bottom of the picture.

   d. Apply the **Reflected Rounded Rectangle** picture style.

6. Locate a thunder sound using the Clip Art task pane. Insert the sound and choose to have it play automatically. Move the sound icon off the slide so it will not display when you show the slides.

7. View the slides in Slide Show view to see the movie and hear the sound.

8. **With your teacher's permission**, print slide 3.

9. Close the presentation, saving changes, and exit PowerPoint.

Figure 21-2

THE GATHERING STORM

# Lesson 22

# Working with Tables

> ## ➤ What You Will Learn

**Inserting a Table**

**Formatting and Modifying a Table**

**Software Skills**    Use tables to organize data in a format that is easy to read and understand. Table formats enhance visual interest and also contribute to readability.

**Application Skills**    In this lesson, you work on a presentation for Restoration Architecture. You'll insert and format a table that lists planning services.

## What You Can Do

### Inserting a Table

■ Use a table on a slide to organize information into rows and columns so it is easy for your audience to read and understand.

■ You have two options for inserting a table on a slide:

- Click the Insert Table icon in any content placeholder to display the Insert Table dialog box. After you select the number of columns and rows, the table structure appears on the slide in the content placeholder.

- Click the Table button on the Insert tab to display a grid that you can use to select rows and columns. As you drag the pointer, the table columns and rows appear on the slide.

  ✔ *If you use this option on a slide that does not have a content layout, you may have to move the table to position it properly on the slide.*

■ Note that the Table menu also allows you to access the Insert Table dialog box, draw a table using the Draw Table tool, or insert an Excel worksheet to organize data.

  ✔ *You'll learn more about using Excel worksheets later in this lesson.*

## Try It!    Inserting a Table

**1** Start PowerPoint and open **PTry22** from the data files for this lesson.

**2** Save the presentation as **PTry22_ studentfirstname_studentlastname** in the location where your teacher instructs you to store the files for this lesson.

**3** Select slide 2 and click the Insert Table icon in the content placeholder.

**4** Type 2 in the Number of Columns scroll box.

**5** Type 5 in the Number of Rows scroll box.

**6** Click OK.

**7** Select slide 4.

**8** Click Insert > Table .

**9** Drag the pointer over the grid or use arrow keys to select 5 columns and 3 rows.

**10** Click or press ENTER to insert the table on the slide.

**11** Save the changes to the **PTry22_ studentfirstname_studentlastname** file, and leave it open to use in the next Try It.

**Using the Insert Table icon to insert a table**

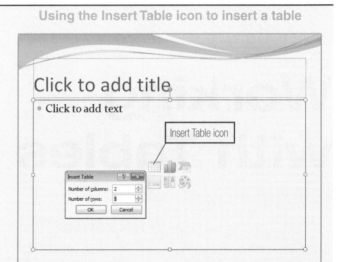

**Using the Table Grid to insert a table**

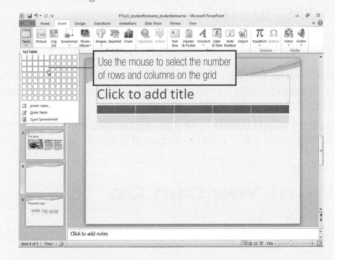

## Formatting and Modifying a Table

■ When a table appears on a slide, the Table Tools contextual tabs become active on the Ribbon.

■ Use the Table Tools Design tab to control formatting options, such as styles, shading, borders, and effects. You can also choose to emphasize specific parts of a table.

■ Use the Table Tools Layout tab to control the table structure, such as inserting or deleting rows and columns, merging or splitting cells, distributing rows or columns evenly, adjusting both horizontal and vertical alignment, changing text direction, and adjusting cell margins and table size.

■ If you do not want to enter specific measurements for cells and table size, you can adjust rows, columns, or the table itself by dragging borders. You can also drag the entire table to reposition it on the slide if necessary.

## Try It! Applying Table Formats

**1** In the **PTry22_studentfirstname_studentlastname** file, click slide 2.

**2** Click the table to select it.

**3** Click the Table Styles More button ⬇ to open the Table Styles gallery.

**4** Click Medium Style 2 – Accent 3.

**5** Select the entire table and click Table Tools Design > Borders ⊞.

**6** Select All Borders.

**OR**

Click the Shading button 🪣 and select a color, picture, gradient, or texture to fill table cells.

**7** Click the Effects button ◡ and select from bevel, shadow, or reflection effects for the table.

**8** Save the changes to the **PTry22_studentfirstname_studentlastname** file, and leave it open to use in the next Try It.

## Try It! Inserting a Row or Column

**1** In the **PTry22_studentfirstname_studentlastname** file, select slide 2.

**2** Click one of the rows in the table to select it.

**3** Click Table Tools Layout > Insert Above ⬛.

**OR**

Click the Insert Below button ⬛ to insert a row below the selected cell.

**OR**

Click the Insert Left button ⬛ to insert a column to the left of the selected cell.

**OR**

Click the Insert Right button ⬛ to insert a column to the right of the selected cell.

**4** Save the changes to the **PTry22_studentfirstname_studentlastname** file, and leave it open to use in the next Try It.

## Try It! Deleting Part of the Table

**1** In the **PTry22_studentfirstname_studentlastname** file, select slide 2.

**2** Click one of the rows in the table to select it.

**3** Click Table Tools Layout > Delete ⊠.

**4** Click Delete Rows.

**OR**

Click Delete Columns to delete the selected column instead.

**5** Save the changes to the **PTry22_studentfirstname_studentlastname** file, and leave it open to use in the next Try It.

**Try It!**     **Merging Table Cells**

① In the **PTry22_studentfirstname_ studentlastname** file, type **Table Heading** in the first row of the table on slide 2.

② Select the heading row and click Table Tools Layout > Merge Cells ▦.

③ Click Table Tools Layout > Center ▤.

④ Save the changes to the **PTry22_ studentfirstname_studentlastname** file, and leave it open to use in the next Try It.

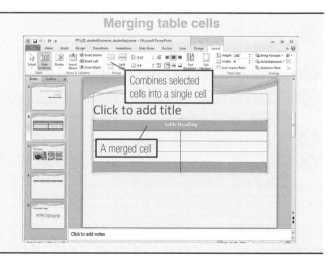

Merging table cells

**Try It!**     **Distributing Columns Evenly**

① In the **PTry22_studentfirstname_ studentlastname** file, select the third row in the table on slide 4.

② In the Cell Size group, type 1 in the Height box ▯.

③ Select the entire table, and click Table Tools Layout > Distribute Rows ▤.

④ Save the changes to the **PTry22_ studentfirstname_studentlastname** file and close it.

# Project 47—Create It

## Creating a Table

### DIRECTIONS

1. Start PowerPoint, if necessary, and open **PProj47** from the data files for this lesson.

2. Save the presentation as **PProj47_studentfirst name_studentlastname** in the location where your teacher instructs you to store the files for this lesson.

3. Click the subtitle placeholder and move to the end of the text. Press [ENTER] three times and then type your first name and last name.

4. Click on slide 3 and then click **Home > New Slide** 🖼 **> Title Only**. A new slide appears at the end of the presentation.

5. Click the title placeholder and type **Planning Services** as the slide title.

6. Click outside the placeholder and click **Insert > Table** ▦.

7. Drag to create a table that is five rows down and five columns wide.

8. Fill in the table with the text shown in Figure 22-1.

9. On the **Table Tools Layout** tab, type **3** in the **Height** ▯ box. The table height is adjusted and the row heights adjust evenly.

10. Click in the **Width** ▭ box and type **7.5**. The table width is adjusted and the text now all fits on a single row.

11. **With your teacher's permission**, print the presentation.

12. Close the presentation, saving changes, and exit PowerPoint.

Figure 22-1

# Planning Services

| Price List | | | | |
|---|---|---|---|---|
| Service | Zone 1 | Zone 2 | Zone 3 | Zone 4 |
| Site Study | $2,000 | $2,500 | $5,000 | $3,000 |
| Planning | $75/hour | $85/hour | $90/hour | $80/hour |
| Design | $150/hour | $250/hour | $400/hour | $200/hour |

## Project 48—Apply It

### Creating a Table

**DIRECTIONS**

1. Start PowerPoint, if necessary, and open **PProj48** from the data files for this lesson.

2. Save the presentation as **PProj48_ studentfirstname_studentlastname** in the location where your teacher instructs you to store the files for this lesson.

3. You have decided to stop offering services for Zone 4. On slide 4, delete the *Zone 4* column in the table on slide 4.

4. Use the Table Tools tabs to change the table style to **Medium Style 1 – Accent 2**. Apply All Borders to the table.

5. Center the entries in the last three columns, and position the table attractively on the slide.

6. Insert a row above the second row. Type the following:

   | | | | |
   |---|---|---|---|
   | **Permits** | $200 | $350 | $500 |

7. Merge the second, third, and fourth cell in the first row. Center the text in the cell.

8. Remove the shading in the first cell of the first row. Your slide should look like Figure 22-2.

9. Replace the text Student Name on the title slide with your first name and last name.

10. **With your teacher's permission**, print slide 4.

11. Close the presentation, saving changes, and exit PowerPoint.

**Figure 22-2**

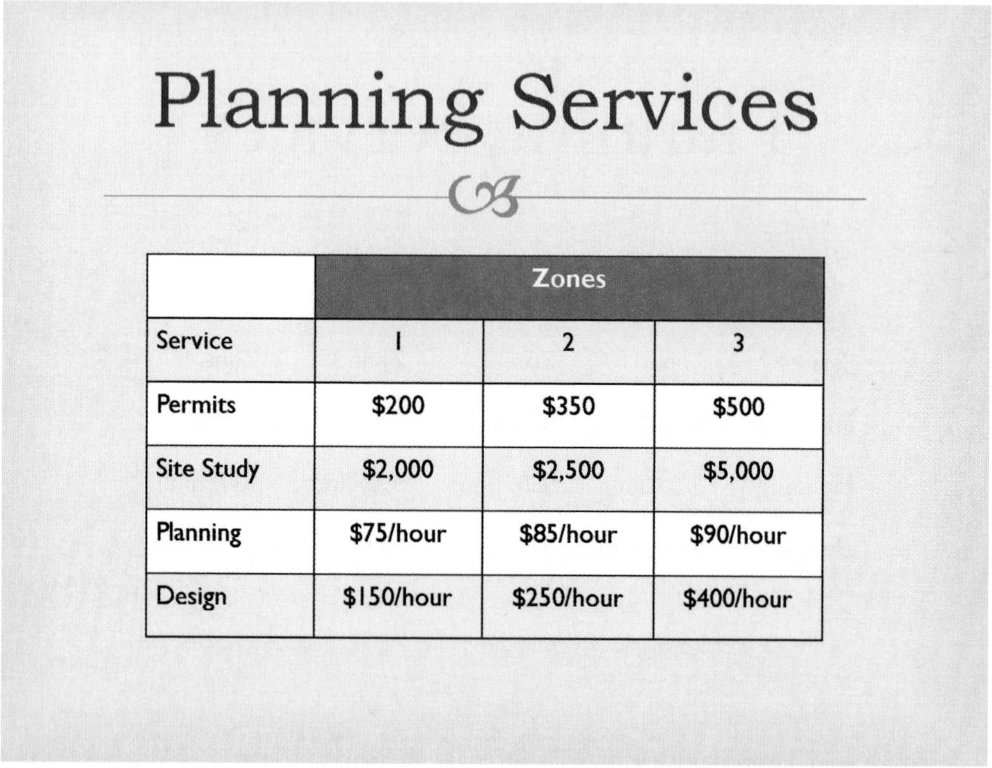

# Planning Services

|  | Zones | | |
|---|---|---|---|
| Service | 1 | 2 | 3 |
| Permits | $200 | $350 | $500 |
| Site Study | $2,000 | $2,500 | $5,000 |
| Planning | $75/hour | $85/hour | $90/hour |
| Design | $150/hour | $250/hour | $400/hour |

# Lesson 23

# Working with Charts

## ➤ What You Will Learn

**Inserting a Chart**
**Formatting and Modifying a Chart**
**Animating a Chart**

**Software Skills**    Add charts and diagrams to a presentation to illustrate data and other concepts in a graphical way that is easy to understand. Charts and diagrams can be formatted or modified as needed to improve the display.

**Application Skills**    In this lesson, you continue working on the presentation for the Campus Recreation Center. You insert a chart to show results of a usage survey and add a SmartArt diagram that shows the process of the marketing campaign.

## What You Can Do

### Inserting a Chart

- You can add a chart to your presentation to illustrate data in an easy-to-understand format or to compare and contrast sets of data.

- In PowerPoint 2010, you create a chart using Excel 2010 if Excel is installed on your system.

    ✔ *If you do not have Excel, charts are created using Microsoft Graph as in past versions of PowerPoint. However, you won't be able to use the advanced charting tools.*

- Excel charts are embedded in PowerPoint—an embedded object becomes part of the destination file and can be edited using the source application's tools. So, when you insert a chart in PowerPoint, you work with Excel's charting tools.

- You can insert a chart into a content slide layout or add it without a placeholder using the Chart button on the Insert tab.

- When you insert a new chart, Excel opens in a split window with sample data. The chart associated with that sample data displays on the PowerPoint slide.

- You can type replacement data in the worksheet. As you change the data, the chart adjusts on the slide. You can save the Excel worksheet data for the chart and then close the worksheet to work further with the chart on the slide.

## Try It!    Inserting a Chart

**1** Start PowerPoint and open **PTry23** from the data files for this lesson.

**2** Save the presentation as **PTry23_ studentfirstname_studentlastname** in the location where your teacher instructs you to store the files for this lesson.

**3** Select slide 3 and click the Insert Chart icon in the content placeholder.

**OR**

Click Insert > Insert Chart.

**4** Select the Clustered Column chart type and click OK.

**5** The chart is inserted on the slide and Excel opens with sample data displayed in the worksheet.

**6** Close the Excel data file.

**7** Save the changes to the **PTry23_ studentfirstname_studentlastname** file, and leave it open to use in the next Try It.

### Creating an Embedded Excel Chart in PowerPoint

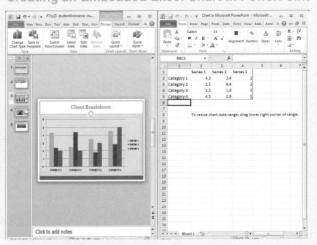

## Formatting and Modifying a Chart

- When you click on a chart in PowerPoint, three content-specific tabs open on the Ribbon: Chart Tools Format, Chart Tools Design, and Chart Tools Layout.

- Use the tools on the Chart Tools Design tab to modify the chart type and edit data.

- With PowerPoint, you can choose from several chart types, including line, pie, bar, area, scatter, stock, surface, doughnut, bubble, and radar.

- Tools on the Chart Tools Layout tab help you to customize a chart by choosing what chart elements to display.

- Use the tools on the Chart Tools Format tab to select a layout or chart style, or apply special effects to the chart elements.

- You can move, copy, size, and delete a chart just like any other slide object.

## Try It!    Formatting and Modifying a Chart

**1** In the **PTry23_studentfirstname_ studentlastname** file, click the chart to select it, if necessary.

**2** Click Chart Tools Design > Change Chart Type.

**3** Click Clustered Bar in 3D and click OK.

**4** Click the chart to select it, if necessary.

*(continued)*

**Try It!**        **Formatting and Modifying a Chart** (continued)

**5** On the Chart Tools Design tab, click the Chart Styles More button ⏷.

**6** Select Style 34.

**7** Save the changes to the **PTry23_ studentfirstname_studentlastname** file, and leave it open to use in the next Try It.

The Change Chart Type dialog box

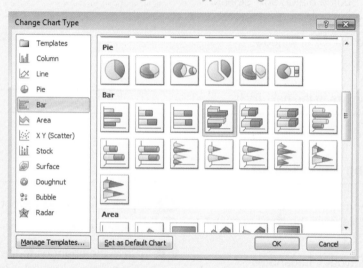

---

**Try It!**        **Editing the Excel Data**

**1** In the **PTry23_studentfirstname_ studentlastname** file, click the chart to select it, if necessary.

**2** Click Chart Tools Design > Edit Data 🖼.

**3** In the Excel data file, click cell R2C1.

**4** Type **Project 1**, and press ⌷ENTER⌷.

**5** Save the changes to the **PTry23_ studentfirstname_studentlastname** file, and leave it open to use in the next Try It.

---

**Try It!**        **Switching Rows and Columns**

**1** Both the Excel data file and the **PTry23_ studentfirstname_studentlastname** file should be open.

**2** On the chart slide in PowerPoint, click Chart Tools Design >Switch Row/Column 🗗.

**3** Close the Excel data file.

**4** Save the changes to the **PTry23_ studentfirstname_studentlastname** file, and leave it open to use in the next Try It.

**Try It!**    **Selecting Data to Chart**

1. In the **PTry23_studentfirstname_studentlastname** file, click the chart to select it, if necessary.

2. Click Chart Tools Design > Select Data.

3. In the Select Data Source dialog box, select Project 1 in the Legend Entries (Series) box.

4. Click OK and close the Excel window.

5. Save the changes to the **PTry23_studentfirstname_studentlastname** file, and leave it open to use in the next Try It.

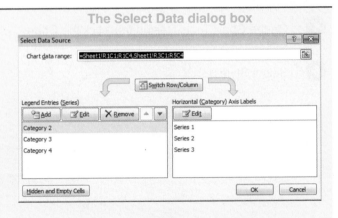

The Select Data dialog box

---

**Try It!**    **Changing Chart Layout**

1. In the **PTry23_studentfirstname_studentlastname** file, click the chart to select it, if necessary.

2. Click Chart Tools Layout > Legend.

3. Select Show Legend at Bottom.

4. Click Chart Tools Layout > Chart Wall.

5. Select None.

6. Save the changes to the **PTry23_student firstname_studentlastname** file, and leave it open to use in the next Try It.

---

## Animating a Chart

- You can animate charts on slides using the Animations tab.

- When you animate a chart, the entire chart is affected.

---

**Try It!**    **Animating a Chart**

1. In the **PTry23_studentfirstname_studentlastname** file, click the chart to select it, if necessary.

2. On the Animations tab, click Fade in the Animation gallery.

3. In the Timing group, type **01:00** in the Duration scroll box.

4. In the Timing group, type **0:75** in the Delay scroll box.

5. Save the changes to the **PTry23_student firstname_studentlastname** file and close it.

# Project 49—Create It

## Adding Charts to a Presentation

### DIRECTIONS

1. Start PowerPoint, if necessary, and open **PProj49** from the data files for this lesson.

2. Save the presentation as **PProj49_ studentfirstname_studentlastname** in the location where your teacher instructs you to store the files for this lesson.

3. Click the subtitle placeholder and move to the end of the text. Press ENTER three times and then type your first name and last name.

4. Click on slide 5 and then click **Home** > **New Slide** > **Title and Content**. A new slide appears.

5. Click the title placeholder and type **Survey Results** as the slide title.

6. Click outside the placeholder and click **Insert** > **Chart**. The Insert Chart dialog box opens.

7. Select **3-D Clustered Column** and click **OK**. An Excel data file appears.

8. Replace the sample data with the data shown in Figure 23-1. Remember, you'll need to drag the lower-right corner of the range indicator to include all the data.

9. In PowerPoint, on the **Chart Tools Design** tab, click the **Chart Layouts More** button and click **Layout 3**. The layout of the chart changes and a chart title appears.

10. On the **Chart Tools Design** tab, click the **Chart Styles More** button and click **Style 26**. The chart style changes using thinner and darker columns.

11. Select the chart title and type **Visits per Week**.

12. **With your teacher's permission**, print slide 6. It should look like that shown in Figure 23-2.

13. Close the Excel data file.

14. Close the presentation, saving changes, and exit PowerPoint.

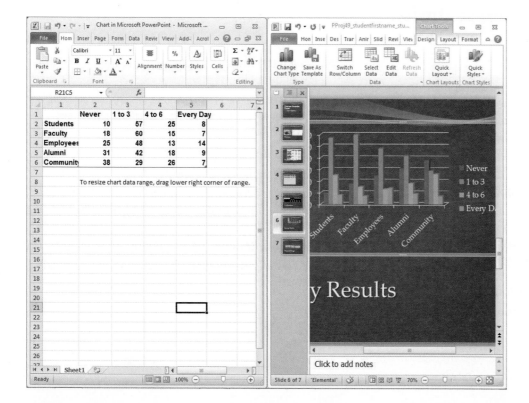

**Figure 23-1**

Figure 23-2

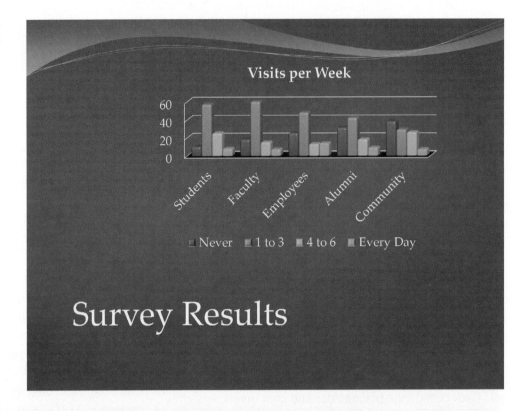

# Project 50—Apply It

## Adding Charts to a Presentation

### DIRECTIONS

1. Start PowerPoint, if necessary, and open **PProj50** from the data files for this lesson.

2. Save the presentation as **PProj50_ studentfirstname_studentlastname** in the location where your teacher instructs you to store the files for this lesson.

3. On slide 6, change the appearance of the chart as follows:

    a. Change the chart type to **Clustered Cylinder**.

    b. On the Layout tab, select the primary vertical gridlines option and then choose to display major gridlines.

4. Edit the Excel data as follows:

    a. Change the Student value for 1 to 3 to **47**.

    b. Change the Every Day value to **18**.

5. Switch the rows and columns, and then close the Excel data file.

    ✔ *If you find the Every Day data is missing from the chart, use the Select Data button to specify the correct rows and columns.*

6. Apply a **Zoom** animation to the chart.

7. Set the timing duration to **1:50**.

8. Add a slide footer to the presentation that includes your first name and last name and an automatically updating date.

9. **With your teacher's permission**, print slide 6.

10. Close the presentation, saving changes, and exit PowerPoint.

# Chapter Assessment and Application

## Project 51—Master It

### Enhancing a Presentation

The Marketing Manager of Restoration Hardware has asked you to take a recent presentation and improve its appearance to help get it ready for an upcoming event. You'll take advantage of your new skills to change the background, theme, colors, and fonts. You'll also add animations to the slides and change the chart and table.

### DIRECTIONS

1. Start PowerPoint and open **PProj51** from the data files for this chapter.

2. Save the presentation as **PProj51_studentfirstname_studentlastname** in the location where your teacher instructs you to store the files for this chapter.

3. Change the theme of the presentation to **Paper**. Note that the title doesn't change because it is a WordArt graphic.

4. Change the color theme to **Concourse**.

5. Change the background style to **Style 8**.

6. Change the font theme to **Verve**.

7. Select the chart on slide 3 and change the chart type to **Pie**.

8. Change the chart layout to **Layout 4**.

9. Change the chart style to **Style 30**.

10. Select the table object on slide 5 and change its height to **3.5"** and the width to **7"**.

11. Center-align the table on the slide.

12. Change the table style to **Themed Style 1-Accent 4**.

13. Select the WordArt graphic on slide 1 and change the WordArt style to **Fill – Gray 80%, Text 2, Outline – Background 2**.

14. Add a handout footer that includes a date that updates automatically and your first name and last name. Apply the footer to all.

15. **With your teacher's permission**, print a horizontal handouts page containing all the slides.

16. Close the presentation, saving changes, and exit PowerPoint.

# Project 52—Make It Your Own

## Creating an Effective Presentation

As the office manager at the Michigan Avenue Athletic Club, you have found that many staff members deliver ineffective presentations. You decide to research techniques to make presentations more effective, and create a presentation about it to deliver at the next staff meeting.

### DIRECTIONS

1. Use the Internet to research the topic "Creating an effective presentation in PowerPoint."
2. Start PowerPoint and create a new presentation.
3. Save the presentation as **PProj52_studentfirst name_studentlastname** in the location where your teacher instructs you to store the files for this chapter.
4. Apply the **Flow** theme to the presentation.
5. On slide 1, the title slide, enter the title **Effective Presentations** and the subtitle **Common Sense Rules for Delivering Your Message**.
6. Insert a footer that displays today's date and your first name and last name on all slides.
7. Add at least five slides to the presentation.
   a. Slide 2 should be an introduction.
   b. slide 3 should be bullet points.
   c. slide 4 should include a graphic.
   d. slide 5 should be a conclusion or summary.
   e. slide 6 should list your sources.
   f. You may choose to include additional slides between slide 4 and slide 5 to expand the topic, if necessary.
8. Apply transitions and animations to enhance the presentation's effectiveness.

9. If you have access to multimedia objects, insert them if they can enhance the presentation's effectiveness.
10. Save the presentation.
11. Review the presentation to identify errors and problems, and assess how you might improve its effectiveness. For example, you might add slides so you can have fewer bullets per slide. You might adjust the font size or color to make it more readable. Save all changes.
12. Add notes to help you deliver the presentation.
13. Practice delivering the presentation, and then make changes to the presentation if necessary to improve its effectiveness. For example, you might want to make it longer or shorter, or change the timing for advancing between slides. Save all changes.
14. Practice delivering the presentation again, until you are comfortable with it.
15. Deliver the presentation to your class.
16. **With your teacher's permission**, print the presentation.
17. Close the presentation, saving changes, and exit PowerPoint.

## Chapter 4

# Finalizing a Presentation

## Lesson 24
## Working with Slide Masters
## Projects 53-54

- Understanding the Slide Master
- Customizing Slide Master Elements
- Creating a Custom Layout
- Working with Notes and Handouts Masters

## Lesson 25
## Using Presentation Templates and Linked Objects
## Projects 55-56

- Creating a Presentation from a Template
- Inserting and Linking Excel Worksheet Data

## Lesson 26
## Customizing Themes and Templates
## Projects 57-58

- Creating a Theme
- Creating a Template
- Applying Custom Themes and Templates

## Lesson 27
## Enhancing a Slide Show
## Projects 59-60

- Creating a Custom Show
- Inserting Links on Slides
- Inserting an Action Button

## Lesson 28
## Preparing for a Slide Show
## Projects 61-62

- Hiding Slides
- Setting Slide Show Options
- Creating a Looping Presentation that Runs Automatically
- Controlling Slides During a Presentation
- Annotating Slides During a Presentation
- Rehearsing Timings

## Lesson 29
## Reviewing and Finalizing a Presentation
## Projects 63-64

- Sending a Presentation for Review
- Finalizing a Presentation

## Lesson 30
## Distributing a Presentation
## Projects 65-66

- Packaging a Presentation for CD
- Broadcasting a Slide Show
- Creating a Video of a Presentation
- Publishing Slides

## End-of-Chapter Projects
## Projects 67-68

# Lesson 24

# Working with Slide Masters

## ➤ What You Will Learn

**Understanding the Slide Master**

**Customizing Slide Master Elements**

**Creating a Custom Layout**

**Working with Notes and Handouts Masters**

**WORDS TO KNOW**

**Slide master**
A slide that controls the appearance of all slides in a presentation. If you make a change to the master, all slides based on that master will display those changes.

**Software Skills**    A presentation's slide master controls the appearance and layout of all slides in the presentation. Use the master to easily adjust elements for an entire presentation. Create a new layout to further customize a presentation. The notes and handouts masters allow you to change the layout of all notes pages or handouts.

**Application Skills**    Natural Light has asked you to fine-tune a presentation they are preparing for a home décor trade show. They have asked you to make some changes that will apply to a number of slides, so you will customize the slide master by changing bullets, colors, and the background, and by adding a new layout for a specific kind of content.

# What You Can Do

## Understanding the Slide Master

- A **slide master** controls the appearance of slides in a presentation. PowerPoint supplies a slide master for each theme.

- The slide master stores information about background, fonts, colors, and the placement of placeholders on a slide.

- The easiest way to make global changes throughout a presentation—for example, specifying a new font for all titles or adding a logo to all slides—is to make the change once on the slide master.

- There is a slide master for each of the layouts you choose among when you add a new slide or change a slide layout.

- You can use the Slide Master button on the View menu to display the slide master and the Slide Master tab.

- The slide master displays at the top of the left pane, and a master for each of the layouts display below the slide master.

**Try It!**    **Opening the Slide Master**

1. Start PowerPoint and open the **PTry24** presentation from the data files for this lesson.

2. Save the file as **PTry24_studentfirstname_studentlastname** in the location where your teacher instructs you to save the files for this lesson.

3. On the View tab, in the Master Views group, click the Slide Master button.

4. Click the Close Master View button.

   **OR**

   Click the Normal button on the Status bar.

5. Save the **PTry24_studentfirstname_studentlastname** file and leave it open to use in the next Try It.

Slide master and the Slide Master tab box

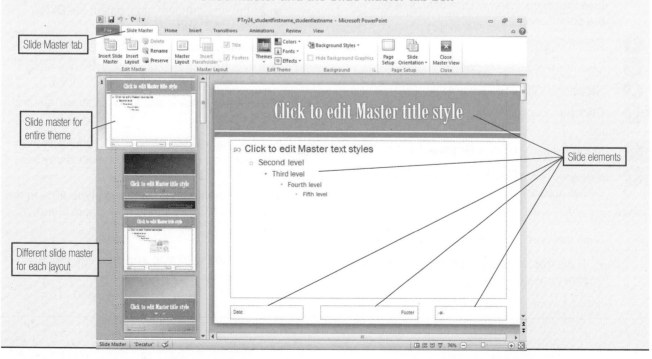

Slide Master tab

Slide master for entire theme

Different slide master for each layout

Slide elements

## Customizing Slide Master Elements

■ You can make changes to the slide master just as you would make changes in Normal view.

■ The Slide Master tab offers basic options for making changes to the slide master, such as applying a new theme, colors, fonts, effects, or background.

■ You can modify text formats, such as font, font style, font size, color, alignment, and so on, by clicking on the slide master in the Slide pane and then applying the desired text formats.

■ Modify the bullet symbols and colors by clicking in a bullet level and then selecting new formats in the Bullets and Numbering dialog box.

■ Regardless of which theme or template you use, you can change the colors used in the presentation.

■ You can also adjust the position of any placeholder or even delete any of the placeholders, including the title, content, date, footer, and slide number placeholders.

■ Some changes you make to the slide master will also appear on the other layouts. For example, if you change the title font on the slide master, the same change will be made to the title font on other layouts.

■ To adjust the elements of one of the other layouts, click it in the list below the slide master. Any changes you make to that layout will apply to all slides based on that layout.

■ You can add one or more slide masters from any theme to an existing presentation. Using more than one slide master gives you the freedom to pick and choose among layouts when creating slides.

■ If you have added slide masters to a presentation, you can delete them if you decide not to use them.

---

**Try It!**    **Customizing Slide Master Elements**

**1** In the **PTry24_studentfirstname_ studentlastname** file, click Design > Colors  .

**2** Click on various color schemes and notice how Live Preview shows you the effects of each of the color schemes.

**3** Select Origin.

**4** Click View > Slide Master 🗏 .

**5** Select the Title Slide Layout.

**6** Click the  Background group dialog box launcher 🖼 .

**7** In the Fill section, click Gradient fill.

**8** If desired, click Preset colors and choose a preset gradient.

   **OR**

   Click the Type list arrow and select Radial.

   ✔ *As you select different gradient types, Live Preview will show you what to expect.*

**9** Click Direction and select From Center to indicate the direction that the gradient will flow.

**10** Adjust the gradient stops and colors:

■ At the first gradient stop, select Ice Blue, Accent 2, Darker 25%.

■ Click the second gradient stop and then click the Remove gradient stop button 🔧 to delete the stop.

   ✔ *Click the Add gradient stop button 🔧 to add additional color stops.*

■ Click the middle gradient stop and click the Color drop button 🎨 and select Blue-Gray, Accent 1, Darker 25%.

■ Select the third stop and then type 90% in the Position box to change how colors blend.

   **OR**

■ Select the third stop and drag it to the left until the screen tip says 90%.

**Try It!**     **Customizing Slide Master Elements** *(continued)*

**11** Click Close to apply the background to only the title slide.

**12** In Slide Master view, select the Decatur Slide Master.

**13** Select *Click to edit Master text styles* in the bulleted text on the master slide.

   ✔ *You can use the same technique to modify each different level of bullet in the slide master.*

**14** Click Home > Bullets drop-down arrow.

**15** Select a different bullet character.

**OR**

Click the Bullets drop-down arrow and select Bullets and Numbering at the bottom of the menu. Use the following options to create a new bullet style.

- Click a standard bullet character or choose Picture to use art or Customize to create your own bullet character.

- Click Size and type the desired percentage of text size.

- Click Color and select a new color for the bullet from the palette.

**16** Click OK to apply the new bullet format.

**17** Save the **PTry24_studentfirstname_ studentlastname** file and leave it open to use in the next Try It.

The Bullets Gallery

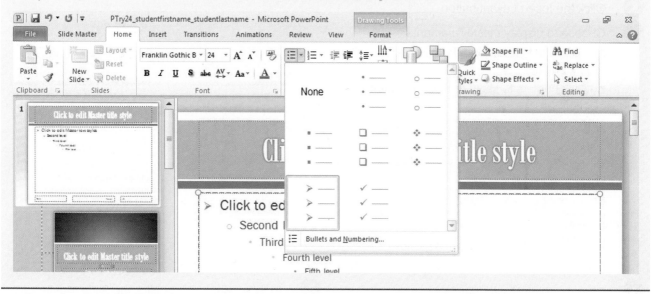

## Creating a Custom Layout

- You can create your own slide layout for a specific type of content.

- If you need several slides with this layout, creating a custom layout slide master can save time.

- Use the Insert Layout button to add a new slide master layout to the list in the left pane.

- You can then use the Insert Placeholder list to add any of the typical placeholders to the slide: Content, Text, Picture, Chart, Table, SmartArt, Media, or Clip Art.

- You draw and position the placeholders just as if they were shapes. If you insert a Text placeholder, you can format the text as desired so it will always display those formats on slides created from the layout.

- Once you've created your custom layout, click Rename to make it easy to find.

- Custom layouts display on the layout gallery along with the other default layouts.

---

**Try It!**          **Creating a Custom Layout in Slide Master View**

**1** In the **PTry24_studentfirstname_ studentlastname** file, in Slide Master view click the Slide Master tab.

**2** Click the Insert Layout button.

**3** Choose to display master elements.
- Click Title to show or hide the Title placeholder.
- Click Footers to show or hide the footer placeholders.

**The Edit Master and Master Layout Groups**

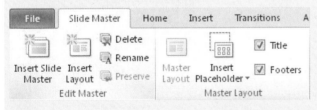

**4** Click the Slide Master tab.

**5** Click the Insert Placeholder button.

**6** Click the name of the placeholder you want to insert.

**7** Draw the placeholder on the slide.

**8** Format the placeholder as desired.

**9** Repeat steps 2–6 as necessary to complete the layout.

**Add Placeholders to Complete Master Layout**

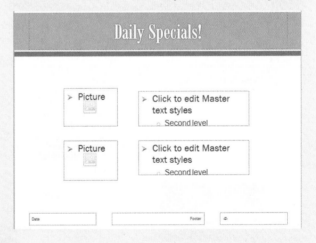

**10** In Slide Master view, click the Slide Master tab.

**11** Click the Rename button.

**12** In the Rename Layout dialog box, type **Specials** as the new name for the layout.

**13** Click Rename.

**14** Save the **PTry24_studentfirstname_ studentlastname** file and leave it open to use in the next Try It.

## Working with Notes and Handouts Masters

- The appearance of notes pages and handouts are controlled by their own masters, just like the appearance of slides is controlled by the slide master.

- You can use the notes master to adjust the size or position of the slide graphic or any of the text placeholders.

- You can use the notes masters to modify the text formats in any of the text placeholders.

- You can add content to the notes and handout masters, such as a new text box or a graphic that will then display on all notes pages.

- You can use the handout master to adjust the size, position, and text formats for any of the text placeholders on any of the handout options.

- You cannot move or resize the placeholders for the slides on the handout master.

| **Try It!** | **Working with the Notes and Handouts Masters** |

1. In the **PTry24_studentfirstname_ studentlastname** file, click View > Notes Master button.

2. Resize or modify the formatting of any of the placeholders you wish.

3. Click View > Normal to return to Normal view.

4. Click View > Handouts Master button.

5. Resize or modify the formatting of any of the placeholders you wish.

6. Click View > Normal to return to Normal view.

7. Save the **PTry24_studentfirstname_ studentlastname** file and exit PowerPoint.

The handout master

Header                                              6/20/2011

**Click to edit Master title style**

> Click to edit Master text styles
  ○ Second level
    · Third level
      · Fourth level
        · Fifth level

Click to edit Master text styles
  Second level
    Third level
      Fourth level
        Fifth level

Footer

# Project 53—Create It

## Trade Show Presentation

### DIRECTIONS

1. Start PowerPoint and open the **PProj53** presentation from the data files for this lesson.

2. Save the presentation as **PProj53_ studentfirstname_studentlastname** in the location where your teacher instructs you to store the files for this lesson.

3. Click **Design > Colors > Flow.** Your presentation should look like the one shown in Figure 24-1.

### Figure 24-1

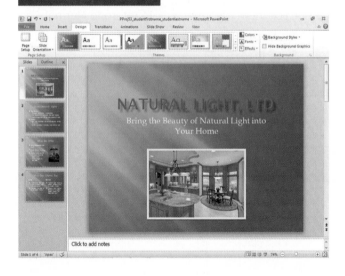

4. Click **View > Slide Master.**

5. Select the Apex Slide Master at the top of the left pane, if necessary.

6. Click the Background group dialog box launcher. In the Fill section, select **Gradient fill.**

7. Choose the Daybreak preset and the Linear type. Do not change direction.

8. Click on **Stop 1** and click the **Remove gradient stop** button ⬆. The gradient now has only three stops, rather than four.

9. For the new Stop 1, click the **Color** drop-down arrow and select **Blue, Accent 1, Lighter 60%** under Theme Colors. The gradient is now a more subtle blend of blues. Apply the background to all layouts and close the dialog box.

10. Click **View > Normal** to return to Normal view. Your presentation should look like the one shown in Figure 24-2.

### Figure 24-2

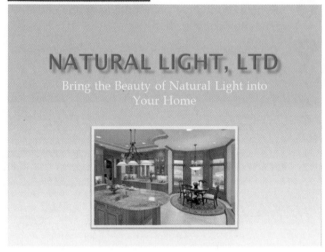

11. **With your teacher's permission**, print the title page of your presentation.

    ✔ When you print PowerPoint presentations, you'll notice that some graphic details, such as the drop shadows on the title font, do not print.

12. Save your changes, close the presentation, and exit PowerPoint.

# Project 54—Apply It

## Travel Brochure

### DIRECTIONS

1. Start PowerPoint and open the **PProj54** presentation from the data files for this lesson.

2. Save the presentation as **PProj54_ studentfirstname_studentlastname** in the location where your teacher instructs you to store the files for this lesson.

3. On the slide master, modify the bullet symbols and colors as shown in Figure 24-3.

   a. Change the first-level bullet as marked. (Choose Customize in the Bullets and Numbering dialog box to locate the star among the displayed symbols.)

   b. Change the second-level bullet as marked.

**Figure 24-3**

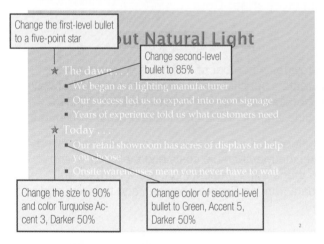

4. Create a custom layout to display featured products as shown in Figure 24-4.

   a. Change the title placeholder as marked.

   b. Create a Clip Art placeholder as marked.

   c. Create a Text placeholder as marked.

   d. Rename the custom layout as **Featured Item.**

5. Add a new slide at the end of the presentation with the new Featured Item layout. Add content as follows:

   a. Insert the title Featured Item.

   b. Insert a clip art image of a chandelier.

   c. Type the following text in the text box: **Chandeliers are in! We have an amazing variety, from rustic wrought iron to brass to glittering crystal.**

   d. Add the following note text: **Pictured chandelier is item #JT265 for $2,500.**

6. Modify the notes master as follows:

   a. Change the size of the text in the notes placeholder to 20 point and center the text.

   b. Increase the size of the slide placeholder.

   c. Decrease the size of the text placeholder.

7. In the Header and Footer dialog box, create a header for the Notes and Handouts pages as follows:

   a. Add an automatically updating date.

   b. Add your name to the header.

8. Preview the notes page for slide 5 to see your changes to the masters.

**Figure 24-4**

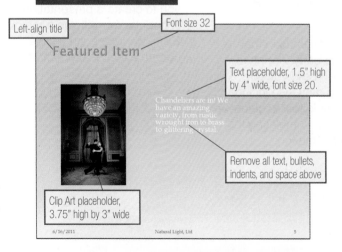

**Pictured chandelier is item #JT265 for $2,500.**

# Lesson 25

# Creating a Linked Presentation from a Template

## WORDS TO KNOW

**Cell address or cell reference**
The location of a cell in a worksheet as identified by its column letter and row number. Also known as the cell's address.

**Embed**
Insert data in a destination application from a source application so that you can edit it using the source application's tools.

**Link**
Insert data in a destination application from a source application so that a link exists between the source and the destination data.

**Template**
A presentation that is already formatted with a slide design and may also include sample text to guide you in completing the presentation.

> **What You Will Learn**

**Creating a Presentation from a Template**
**Inserting and Linking Excel Worksheet Data**

**Software Skills**     PowerPoint provides a number of templates you can use to format a presentation or help you create a specific kind of presentation. Another way to organize data on a slide is to embed or link worksheet data from Excel. Linked data automatically updates on the slide when it is changed in the original worksheet.

**Application Skills**     The manager of the Campus Recreation Center has asked you to create a presentation outlining the membership costs and the swim lesson schedule. You will use a template to prepare the presentation. You will create an Excel worksheet on a slide, insert data from an Excel worksheet, and then link and update Excel data on another slide.

# What You Can Do

## Creating a Presentation from a Template

- The easiest way to create a presentation is to use one of PowerPoint's many **templates**.

- Some templates provide a number of slides with sample text and graphics as well as slide layouts specifically designed for the template. Others provide only a single slide design.

- You can find PowerPoint templates in PowerPoint's Backstage view under New.

- Using Backstage view, the first six template categories are the templates installed on your system.

- The rest of the categories are templates that are available from Office.com.

- You must have an active Internet connection to download one of the templates from Office.com.

- When you select a template, PowerPoint displays a preview of the template design in the right pane.

- Once you choose your template, click Create (for templates on your PC) or Download (for templates from Office.com). PowerPoint opens the template with a default title such as Presentation1.

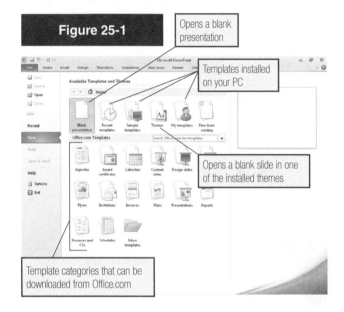

**Figure 25-1**

Opens a blank presentation

Templates installed on your PC

Opens a blank slide in one of the installed themes

Template categories that can be downloaded from Office.com

---

## Try It! — Creating a Presentation from a Template

Preview the template designs

1. Start PowerPoint and click File > New.
2. Click Sample templates, or one of the other template categories stored on your computer.
3. Select the desired template.
4. Click Create.
5. Press CTRL + W to close the file without saving changes.

Shows a preview of the selected template design

---

## Try It! — Downloading a Presentation from Office.com

1. Click File > New.
2. Under Office.com, click Presentations, or one of the other Office.com template categories.

   ✔ *You must be connected to the Internet to view and download Office.com templates.*

3. Select the desired template.
4. Click Download.
5. Press CTRL + W to close the file without saving changes.

## Inserting Excel Worksheet Data

■ The easiest way to show data that may need to be recalculated or otherwise manipulated is by inserting an Excel worksheet directly on a slide.

■ You can use the Excel Spreadsheet option in the Tables group of the Insert tab to create a blank Excel worksheet directly on a slide so that you can insert the data yourself.

   ● This option displays a blank Excel worksheet that you can resize as necessary.

   ● When you use this kind of worksheet, you can use all of Excel's features to calculate and manipulate data.

■ You can show data that already exists in an Excel worksheet by embedding the worksheet data on the slide.

   ● To **embed** data on a slide, copy the data in Excel and use the Embed button on the Paste Options shortcut menu.

   ● Unlike a PowerPoint table, this option allows you to work with the data using Excel tools.

■ To enter data in a worksheet, you must open it for editing by double-clicking it.

   ✔ *A worksheet ready for editing has a diagonal line border.*

■ You may need to adjust the size of embedded worksheet data (and increase or decrease the size of text in the object) by dragging a corner of the object container.

■ To eliminate blank columns and rows from the view, you crop the worksheet using the bottom or right handle while in editing mode.

---

### Try It!     Inserting a Blank Worksheet

**1** In PowerPoint, open the **PTry25** presentation from the data files for this lesson.

**2** Save the file as **PTry25_studentfirstname_ studentlastname** in the location where your teacher instructs you to save the files for this lesson.

**3** Select slide 4.

**4** On the Insert tab, click the Table button , and then click Excel Spreadsheet.

**5** Click on the lower right corner of the spreadsheet object and drag to add columns and rows as necessary.

**6** Click outside the worksheet.

   ■ Select slide 3.

   ■ On the Insert tab, click the Object button .

   ■ In the Insert Object dialog box, click Create from file and then click Browse.

   ■ Navigate to the location of the data files for this lesson and select **PTry25 Spring Cruise Specials.xlsx**.

   ■ Click Open and then click OK.

**7** Save the **PTry25_studentfirstname_ studentlastname** file and leave it open to use in the next Try It.

The Insert Object dialog box

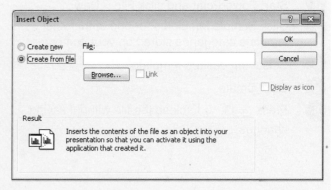

**Try It!**  **Resizing a Worksheet Object**

**1** In the **PTry25_studentfirstname_ studentlastname** file, select slide 3.

**2** Double-click the worksheet object if necessary to display a diagonal line border.

**3** Click the center handle in the bottom border and drag upward to crop any blank cells below the data.

**4** Click on the center handle in the right border and drag to the left to crop any blank cells to the right of the data.

**5** Click outside the worksheet.

**6** Select slide 4.

**7** Click once on the worksheet object to display the thick light grey container border.

**8** Click on the lower-right corner and drag to resize the entire object without distorting text in the worksheet.

**9** Click on the top-left corner and drag to resize the entire object without distorting text in the worksheet.

**10** Save the **PTry25_studentfirstname_ studentlastname** file and leave it open to use in the next Try It.

Resizing the worksheet object

---

**Try It!**  **Inserting and Editing Data in a Worksheet**

**1** In the **PTry25_studentfirstname_ studentlastname** file, select slide 4.

**2** Double-click the worksheet object to display the diagonal line border and the Excel Ribbon.

**3** Type **This is an Excel worksheet** in cell A1 as you would in Excel.

**4** Save the **PTry25_studentfirstname_ studentlastname** file and leave it open to use in the next Try It.

---

## Linking Excel Worksheet Data

■ If the data you need to show might change over time, the best option is to maintain a **link** between worksheet data in Excel and the data displayed on a slide.

■ To insert linked data on a slide, copy it in Excel and then use the Paste Special option on PowerPoint's Paste button.

■ When you modify the worksheet in Excel, the slide data updates to show the same modifications as long as neither file has been moved or renamed.

## Try It!          Linking Excel Worksheet Data

**1** Start Excel and open **PTry25 Adventure Travel Packages.xlsx** from the data files for this lesson.

**2** Save the file as **PTry25_Travel_ studentfirstname_studentlastname** in the location where your teacher instructs you to save the files for this lesson.

**3** Select cells A4-E10, which contain the data to link.

**4** Click **Home** > **Copy**.

**5** In the **PTry25** presentation, select slide 5.

**6** Click Home > Paste drop-down arrow 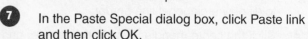, and then click Paste Special.

**7** In the Paste Special dialog box, click Paste link and then click OK.

**8** Close the workbook without saving changes and exit Excel.

**9** Save the **PTry25_studentfirstname_ studentlastname** file and leave it open to use in the next Try It.

Paste Special dialog box

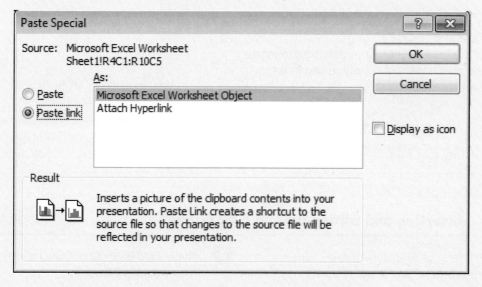

## Try It!          Editing Data in a Linked Worksheet

**1** In the **PTry25_studentfirstname_ studentlastname** file, select slide 5.

**2** Double-click the worksheet object to display the diagonal line border and open the linked file in Excel.

**3** In cell A4, type **Destination** and save the file using the same name. Close Excel.

**4** In the **PTry25_studentfirstname_ studentlastname** presentation, check that the changes you made to the Excel data are reflected in the worksheet object on slide 5.

**5** Save the **PTry25_studentfirstname_ studentlastname** file and exit PowerPoint.

# Project 55—Create It

## Aquatics Program Presentation

### DIRECTIONS

1. Start PowerPoint and click **File > New.**
2. Under Office.com Templates, click **Presentations** to open the list of template categories available.
3. Click **Business presentations** and select **Project Overview Presentation.** A preview of the first page of the presentation appears in the Preview pane.
4. Click **Download** to open a copy of the presentation template in PowerPoint 2010.

   ✔ *If you do not have an Internet connection or do not have the Business category, choose New from existing, browse to the location where your data files are located, and select* **PProj55.**

5. If the Help window displays, close it.
6. Save the presentation as **PProj55_ studentfirstname_studentlastname** in the location where your teacher instructs you to store the files for this lesson.
7. On slide 1, select the title *Project Overview* and type **Campus Recreation Center.**
8. Select the subtitle text and type **Aquatics Program Planning.**
9. Select **View > Slide Sorter** ⊞. Press CTRL and then click slides **2, 4, 5, 7, 8, 10,** and **11.** Once these slides are selected, press DEL.
10. Click the **Normal View** icon on the status bar. On slide 3, select the title text and type **Proposed Programs.** Delete the body text placeholder.
11. Click **Insert > Table** ⊞ **> Excel spreadsheet.**
12. Drag the bottom-right sizing handle as necessary to create a worksheet that is 4 columns wide by 8 rows.
13. Double click the spreadsheet to open the Excel tools in the ribbon.
14. On the Home tab, click the **Borders** down arrow and select **All Borders.** Click outside the object. Your slide should look like Figure 25-2
15. **With your teacher's permission,** print slide 3.
16. Save your changes, close the presentation, and exit PowerPoint.

**Figure 25-2**

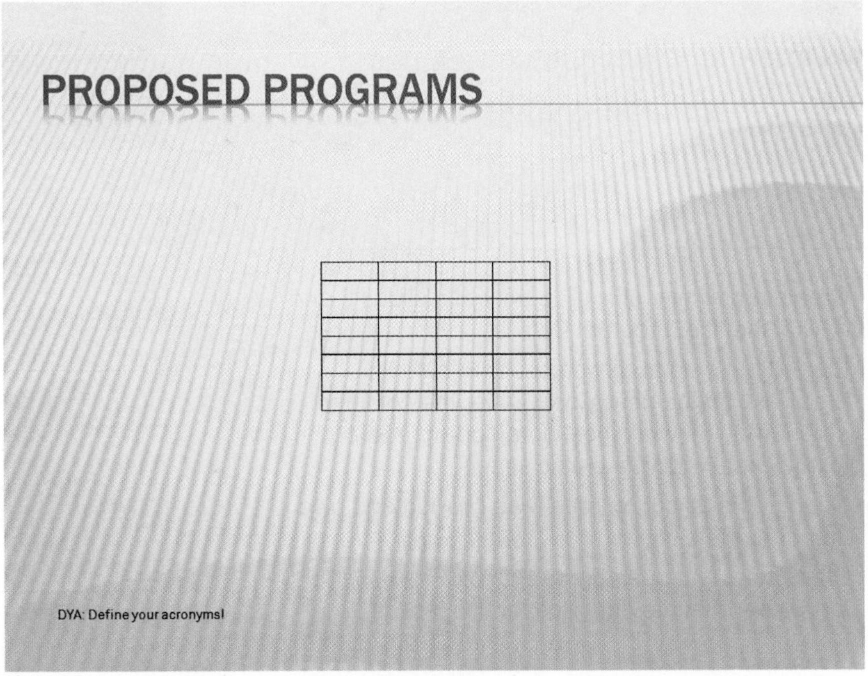

PROPOSED PROGRAMS

DYA: Define your acronyms!

# Project 56—Apply It

## Aquatics Program Presentation

### DIRECTIONS

1. Start PowerPoint and open the **PProj56** presentation from the data files for this lesson.

2. Save the presentation as **PProj56_ studentfirstname_studentlastname** in the location where your teacher instructs you to store the files for this lesson.

3. Insert an appropriate clip art graphic or photo on slide 2.

4. On slide 3, insert the text shown in Figure 25-3 in the Excel worksheet. Adjust the column widths as needed to create an attractive table.

### Figure 25-3

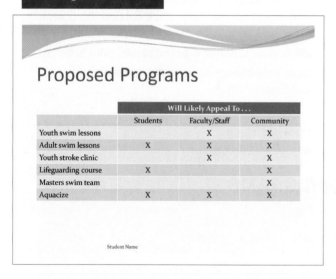

5. Create a new title-only slide between slides 3 and 4, with the title, Program Details.

6. Embed the data from worksheet **PProj56_ LinkData** on the new slide. Center the columns and format the worksheet data appropriately. Position it attractively on the slide.

7. Change the layout on slide 5 as needed and give it an appropriate title.

8. Start Excel and open the workbook **PProj56_ LinkData** from the data files for this lesson.

9. Copy cells A1:F6 and Paste link to slide 5. (Hint: Use Paste Special.) Position the data attractively on the slide.

10. Double-click the linked data to add the following parking fees data to the Excel worksheet:

    | | |
    |---|---|
    | **Part-time/Graduate Students** | 10 |
    | **Faculty/Employees** | 15 |
    | **Alumni** | 18 |
    | **Community** | 24 |

11. Save and close the Excel workbook. Your presentation should look like the one in Figure 25-4.

12. **With your teacher's permission**, print handouts of the entire presentation using a format with six slides to a page.

13. Save your changes, close the presentation, and exit PowerPoint.

### Figure 25-4

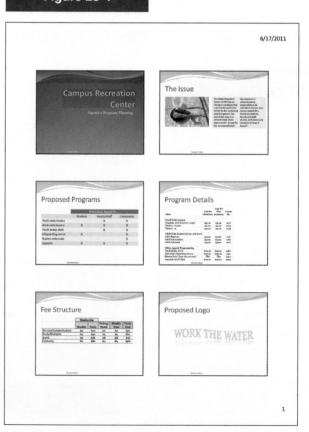

# Lesson 26

# Customizing Themes and Templates

➤ **What You Will Learn**

**Creating a Custom Theme**
**Creating a Custom Template**
**Applying Custom Themes and Templates**

**Software Skills**    Create custom themes and templates to develop your own unique presentations. You can apply a custom theme to any presentation. Custom templates display in Backstage view for easy access.

**Application Skills**    Michigan Avenue Athletic Club wants you to create a custom template that can be used for several presentations as part of a special public relations campaign. In this exercise, you will create a theme you can use for future presentations and then save the presentation as a template.

**WORDS TO KNOW**

Theme
Formatting feature that applies a background, colors, fonts, and effects to all slides in a presentation.

# What You Can Do

## Creating a Theme

- In PowerPoint, **themes** are applied to existing presentations to change formatting elements, such as colors, fonts, images, and effects, to a predefined coordinated set.

- Each PowerPoint theme has a unique background, slide layouts, and graphic elements in some instances.

- You can create your own custom theme by saving your changes to colors, fonts, layouts, and background in an existing theme.

- If you no longer want to use a custom theme, you can delete it from the Themes gallery.

---

**Try It!**    **Creating Custom Color Themes**

**1** Click File > New, then click Blank presentation.

**2** On the Design tab, in the Themes group, click the Colors button ■, and then click Create New Theme Colors.

**3** In the Theme Colors section, click the down arrow of the category item whose color you want to change.

**4** Select one of the following:
- A color from the Theme Colors palette
- A color from the Standard Colors palette
- Click More Colors, select a color from the Colors dialog box, and then click OK.

**5** Repeat as necessary for each category.

**6** In the Name text box, type your name, and then click Save.

**7** Save the **PTry26_studentfirstname_ studentlastname** file in the location where your teacher instructs you to save files for this lesson.

**OR**

In the newly created presentation, click Design > Colors ■.

**8** Select one of the built-in theme font combinations to apply it.

**9** Save the **PTry26_studentfirstname_ studentlastname** file and leave it open to use in the next Try It.

The Edit Theme Colors dialog box

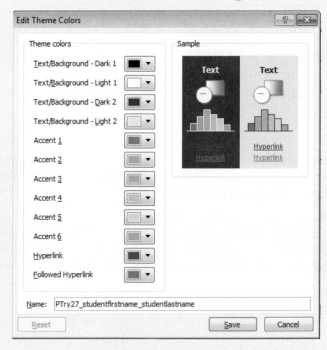

## Try It!    Create Custom Theme Fonts and Effects

**1** In the **PTry26_studentfirstname_ studentlastname** file, click Design > Fonts [A], and then click Create New Theme Fonts.

**2** In the Heading font drop-down menu, select Cambria.

**3** In the Body font drop-down menu, select Calibri.

**4** In the Name text box, type **Spring Light** and click Save.

**OR**

In the newly created presentation, click Design > Fonts [A].

**5** Select one of the built-in theme font combinations to apply it.

**6** In the presentation, click Design > Effects [○].

**7** Select one of the built-in theme effects options.

**8** In the presentation, click Design, then click the More button for the Themes gallery, and click Save Current Theme.

**9** In the Save Current Theme dialog box, type **PTry26_studentfristname_studentlastname** and click Save.

✔ *When you are using classroom computers, it is a good idea to delete custom themes when you are finished using them. To delete a theme, click Design > Themes > Themes, and then right-click the custom theme and select Delete.*

**10** Save the **PTry26_studentfirstname_student lastname** file and leave it open to use in the next Try It.

## Creating a Template

■ Like themes, PowerPoint templates contain a unique combination of formatting elements, such as colors, fonts, images, and effects, to a predefined coordinated set.

■ You can save a presentation that you have customized as a template. Then, you can use the template to create new presentations.

■ To create a template, you can customize an existing theme or template and then save your version with a new name.

■ You can also create a template from scratch. Use Slide Master view to format the background, fonts, colors, and layouts as desired.

## Try It!    Saving a Template

**1** In the **PTry26_studentfirstname_ studentlastname** file, click File > Save As.

**2** Type **PTry26_studentfirstname_ studentlastname** in the File name box.

**3** Click the Save as type drop-down arrow and click PowerPoint Template.

**4** Save the template in the location where your teacher instructs you to save the files for this lesson.

✔ *Because you are not saving your template to the default location, you'll need to look for the template in the New from existing template category in Backstage view.*

**5** Press [CTRL] + [W] to close the file, leaving PowerPoint open.

## Applying Custom Themes and Templates

- Custom templates are displayed in the My Templates area of the New page in Backstage view. Select the custom template to create a new presentation based on it.

- When you create a theme with a new name, it displays in the Themes gallery along with the built-in PowerPoint themes.

- To apply a custom theme, select it from the Themes gallery.

---

**Try It!**    **Applying a Custom Template Saved in the Default Location**

1. In PowerPoint, click File > New.

2. Click My templates.3. In the New Presentation dialog box, select the desired template and click OK.

3. Close the file without saving changes.

Select the custom template in the New Presentation dialog box

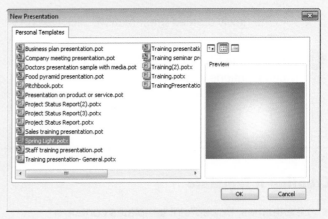

---

**Try It!**    **Applying a Custom Template Saved in the Custom Location**

1. In PowerPoint, click File > New.

2. Click New from existing.

3. In the New from Existing Presentation dialog box, navigate to the location you saved your custom template and select the **PTry26_studentfirstname_studentlastname** template and click Create New.

4. Close the file without saving changes and exit PowerPoint.

Creating a Presentation from an existing template

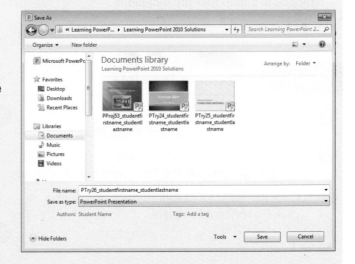

# Project 57—Create It

## Custom Presentation

### DIRECTIONS

1. Start PowerPoint and click **File > New**.
2. Click the **Blank presentation** template and then click **Create.**
3. Click **Design > Colors** ▨ **> Create New Theme Colors**. The Create New Theme Colors dialog box opens.
4. In the Name box, type **Michigan.**
5. Click the **Text/Background – Dark 2** drop-down arrow to open the palette.
6. Select **Dark Blue, Background 2, Lighter 80%.** The color in the drop-down box and the Sample box changes to reflect the new color as shown in Figure 26-1.

**Figure 26-1**

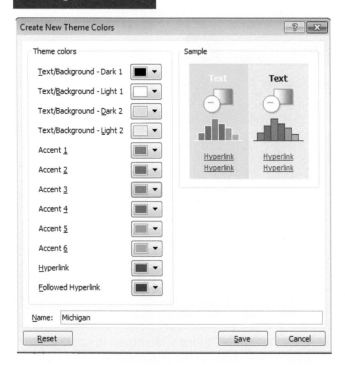

7. Click the **Accent 3** drop-down arrow to open the palette.
8. Click **More Colors.** The Colors dialog box opens.
9. Select the number in the Red box, and type **0.** The New color swatch changes to a shade of green.
10. Select the number in the Green box, and type **153.** The New color swatch changes to a darker shade of green.
11. Select the number in the Blue box, and type **153.** The New color swatch changes to a bright teal.
12. Click OK. Click **Save** to save your custom color theme.
13. Click **Design > Colors** ▨. Notice the new color theme in the Custom colors list as shown in Figure 26-2.

**Figure 26-2**

14. Click **Design > Fonts** Ⓐ **> Create New Theme Fonts.** The Create New Theme Fonts dialog box opens.
15. In the Heading font box, select **Bookman Old Style.** The heading text in the preview changes accordingly.
16. In the Body font box, select **Tahoma.** The body text in the preview changes accordingly.
17. In the Name box, type **Michigan.** Click **Save** to add the new theme fonts to the Fonts gallery.
18. Insert your name in the subtitle.
19. Save the theme with the name **PProj57_ studentfirstname_studentlastname.**

# Project 58—Apply It

## Custom Presentation

### DIRECTIONS

1. Start PowerPoint and click **File** > **New**.

2. Click the **Blank presentation** template and then click Create.

3. On the slide master, create a custom background fill:

   a. Click the dialog box launcher in the Background group of the Design tab.

   b. On the Fill page of the Format Background dialog box. Select Picture or texture fill.

   c. Click **File** and locate **PProj58_Background** in location where the data files for this lesson are stored.

4. Modify the background image as shown in Figure 26-3. Apply the changes to all slides:

   a. Offset the image to Left 39%, Right 2%, Top -6%, and Bottom 8%.

   b. Set the background image to 20% transparency.

   c. Use the Picture Color option in the Format Background dialog box to recolor the picture using the Dark Teal, Accent 3 Light present.

5. On the slide master, modify the background by inserting a Right Triangle shape as shown in Figure 26-3:

   a. Remove the shape outline.

   b. Apply the Aqua, Accent 5 fill color to the shape.

c. Modify the transparency to Lighter 80%, Transparency 10%.

d. Send the shape to the back, behind the text.

6. On the title master only, add an additional triangle that intersects in some way with the right triangle and make it a darker shade of aqua.

7. On the title master only, left-align the subtitle and change its color to match the footer text.

8. On the slide master, customize the text and layout options as shown in Figure 26-4:

   a. Left Align the title.

   b. Reduce the title font size to 40 pt.

   c. Modify the transparency as marked.

   d. Change the color of the date, footer, and slide number to Dark Teal, Accent 3, Darker 50%.

   e. Modify the shape and color of the first two bullet levels as shown in Figure 26-4.

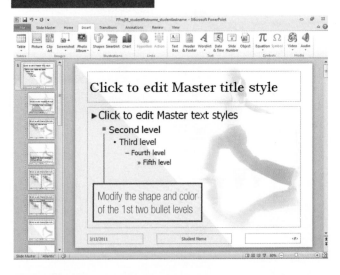

**Figure 26-4**

9. Click **Design** > **Colors** > **Michigan** to apply your new custom color to the presentation.

10. Click **Design** > **Fonts** > **Michigan** to apply your new custom fonts to the presentation.

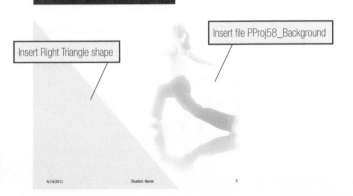

**Figure 26-3**

Insert Right Triangle shape

Insert file PProj58_Background

11. Save the theme with the name **Michigan_ studentfirstname_studentlastname**. Then, save the presentation in the location where your teacher instructs you to save as a template with the name **PProj58_Template_studentfirstname_ studentlastname**.

12. Create a new presentation based on your new template.

13. Insert the title **Michigan Avenue Athletic Club** and the subtitle **Fitness First!** Adjust the font size to make the title fit on one line.

14. Add a Text and Content slide and insert the text as shown in Figure 26-5.

15. Add another slide and add appropriate content.

16. Add a slide footer to the presentation:

    a. Display the date and slide numbers on all slides except the title slide.

    b. Use your name for the footer.

17. **With your teacher's permission**, print the presentation as handouts with 4 slides per page.

18. Save the presentation as **PProj58_ studentfirstname_studentlastname** in the location where your teacher instructs you to store the files for this lesson.

19. Save your changes, close the presentation, and exit PowerPoint.

**Figure 26-5**

Experience the Finest

- State-of-the-art equipment
- Attractive facilities
- Experienced staff
- Personalized training
  - Individual coaching
  - Group classes also available

4/20/2011                    Student Name                    2

# Lesson 27

# Running a Slide Show

## ➤ What You Will Learn

**Creating a Custom Show**
**Inserting Links on Slides**
**Inserting an Action Button**

**Software Skills**     Create a custom show to organize related slides that you can then show separately from the rest of the presentation. Links and action buttons allow you to move quickly from one slide to a distant one, connect to the Internet, or open other documents or applications.

**Application Skills**     You are working on the Aquatics Center campaign for the Campus Recreation Center. In this exercise, you will organize some of the slides into a custom show and add a link and an action button so that the presenter can move to specific slides while showing them.

# What You Can Do

## Creating a Custom Show

- You can create **custom shows** to organize groups of slides that you want to be able to show separately from the other slides in the presentation.

- Creating custom shows allows you to show only a portion of the slides to a specific audience. For example, although you would show the board of directors a show containing all the information about the status of a project, you might only want to show the sales staff the slides that contain sales data.

- Use the Custom Slide Show button in the Start Slide Show group on the Slide Show tab to define a new custom show. Use the Define Custom Show dialog box to name the show and select the slides that will be part of the custom show

- Once you have created a custom show, you can specify it when running a presentation unattended, link to it, or jump to it during the presentation.

---

**Try It!**     **Creating a Custom Show**

1. Start PowerPoint and open the **PTry27** presentation from the data files for this lesson.

2. Save the file as **PTry27_studentfirstname_studentlastname** in the location where your teacher instructs you to save the files for this lesson.

3. On the Slide Show tab, click the Custom Slide Show button 🖥 and then click Custom Shows.

4. In the Custom Shows dialog box, click New.

5. In the Define Custom Show dialog box, type **Gallery** in the Slide show name box.

6. Select slide 11 in the Slides in presentation box.

7. Click Add to add the slide to the custom show.

8. Add slides 12, 13, and 14.

9. Click OK.

10. Click Close.

11. Save the **PTry27_studentfirstname_studentlastname** file and leave it open to use in the next Try It.

Select the slides for a custom show

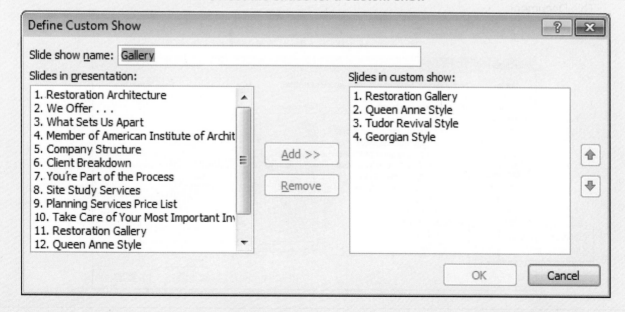

## Inserting Links on Slides

- Use the Hyperlink button in the Links group on the Insert tab to set up links from a slide to another slide, a custom show in the same presentation, a different presentation or document, or a Web site.

- The Insert Hyperlink dialog box allows you to select the target of the link—the slide that will display or the page that will open when the link is clicked.

- Links are displayed in a different color with an underline, as on a Web page. Links are active only in Slide Show view.

- You can also use an object such as a shape, picture, or other graphic as the link object.

- When you create a hyperlinks in a slide show, you can use the Show and return option to display the target slide and then resume the slide show where you left off.

### Try It!     Inserting Links on Slides

1  In the **PTry27_studentfirstname_studentlastname** file, switch to slide 3.

2  Select the text *Reasonable fees.*

3  On the Insert tab, click the Hyperlink button .

4  Click Place in this document from the Link to pane.

5  Select slide 9 from the list.

6  Click OK.

7  Save the **PTry27_studentfirstname_studentlastname** file and leave it open to use in the next Try It.

### Try It!     Showing a Custom Show and Returning to the Presentation

1  In the **PTry27_studentfirstname_studentlastname** file,  click slide 3.

2  Select the text *Expertise with many architectural styles.*

3  Click Insert > Hyperlink .

4  In the Insert Hyperlink dialog box, click Place in This Document.

5  From the Custom Shows list, select Gallery.

6  Click Show and return and then click OK.

7  Save the **PTry27_studentfirstname_studentlastname** file and leave it open to use in the next Try It.

Choose the target of the link

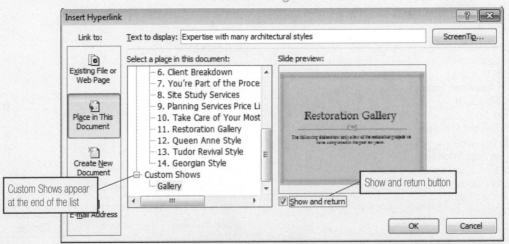

## Inserting an Action Button

- You can use **action buttons** to jump quickly from one slide to another.

- Action buttons are programmed to perform specific tasks, such as jump to the previous slide, play a sound, or run a program or a macro.

- Action buttons appear at the bottom of the Shapes gallery. Select the action button and then draw the button on the slide to open the Action Settings dialog box.

- Use the Action Settings dialog box to specify the button's action.

- By default, the action will occur when you click the mouse button; however, you can use the Action Settings dialog box to modify when the action occurs.

- Action buttons can be formatted like any other shapes. You can apply fills, outlines, and effects. They can also be resized or moved anywhere on the slide.

- You can turn any object, such as a picture or placeholder, into an action button by using the Action button on the Insert tab to give it an action to perform.

### Try It! Inserting an Action Button

1. In the **PTry27_studentfirstname_ studentlastname** file, click slide 6.

2. On the Home tab, click the Shapes More button.

3. Select the Action Button: Back or Previous ◁ from the Action Buttons group at bottom of gallery.

4. Draw the button shape (.5 x .5) on the lower-left side of the slide.

5. In the Action Settings dialog box, click the arrow on the Hyperlink to box.

6. Select Slide… to specify a slide.

7. In the Hyperlink to Slide dialog box, select slide 3.

8. Click OK and then click OK again.

9. Click Slide Show > From Current Slide 🖥 to view your action button.

10. When the slide show begins, click the action button to return to slide 3.

11. Save the **PTry27_studentfirstname_ studentlastname** file and exit PowerPoint.

# Project 59—Create It

## Aquatics Center Custom Show

### DIRECTIONS

1. Start PowerPoint and open the **PProj59** presentation from the data files for this lesson.

2. Save the presentation as **PProj59_studentfirst name_studentlastname** in the location where your teacher instructs you to store the files for this lesson.

3. Click **Slide Show > Custom Slide Show > Custom Shows**.

4. In the Custom Shows dialog box, click **New** to open the Define Custom Show dialog box, as shown in Figure 27-1.

5. Type **Family** in the Slide show name box.

6. Click slide 8 in the Slides in presentation box.

7. Press ⬚SHIFT and click slide 11 to select all the slides from 8 through 11.

8. Click the **Add** button, click **OK**, and then click **Close** to complete the custom show.

9. Click **Insert > Header & Footer** 📄 to open the Header and Footer dialog box.

10. Click **Footer**, type your name and click **Apply to All**.

11. **With your teacher's permission**, print slide 3.

12. Save your changes, close the presentation, and exit PowerPoint.

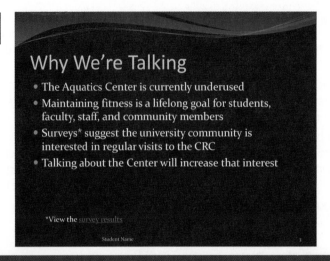

Figure 27-1

# Project 60—Apply It

## Aquatics Center Custom Show

### DIRECTIONS

1. Start PowerPoint and open the **PProj60** presentation from the data files for this lesson.
2. Save the presentation as **PProj60_studentfirst name_studentlastname** in the location where your teacher instructs you to store the files for this lesson.
3. On slide 3, convert the text *survey results* in the text box at the bottom of the slide into a link to slide 6.
4. On slide 4, make the second bullet item a show and return link to the custom show *Family*.
5. On slide 6, insert an action button that will return to slide 3. Place the action button in the lower-left of the slide.

6. Change the shape style to one that suits the presentation and place text next to the box that says Return to slide 3, as shown in Figure 27-2.
7. Play the Slide Show and work your way through each of the links and action buttons to ensure that everything moves as it should.
8. **With your teacher's permission**, print handouts of the entire presentation using a format with six slides to a page, as shown in Figure 27-3.
9. Save your changes, close the presentation, and exit PowerPoint.

Figure 27-3

Figure 27-2

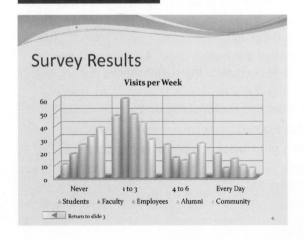

# Lesson 28

# Preparing a Slide Show

➤ **What You Will Learn**

**Hiding Slides**
**Controlling Slides During a Presentation**
**Annotating Slides During a Presentation**
**Rehearsing Timings**
**Setting Slide Show Options**
**Creating a Looping Presentation that Runs Automatically**

**Software Skills**     Hide slides that you don't want to show during a particular presentation. You can specify how a slide show runs for different kinds of presentations. When presenting slides, you have a number of options for controlling slide display. You can annotate slides during the presentation and save annotations if desired. After you set up animations, you can rehearse the show to make sure you have allowed enough time for the audience to view slide content.

**Application Skills**     Integrated Health Systems, Inc. would like you to work on a presentation for its Holmes Medical Center facility. You should run through it a final time before handing it over to the client. The client wants two versions of the show: one for the Vice President to present and one to run unattended at a kiosk in the Medical Center lobby. You will rehearse the presentation to check your timings.

# What You Can Do

## Hiding Slides

■ You can hide slides in your presentation so they do not show when you run the slide show. For example, you might hide certain slides to shorten the presentation, or hide slides that don't apply to a specific audience.

■ Hidden slides remain in the file and appear in all views except Slide Show view. PowerPoint indicates a slide is hidden by positioning a diagonal line across the slide number.

■ You can print hidden slides if desired.

■ You can go to a hidden slide while in Slide Show view by using the Go to Slide command on the Slide Show shortcut menu.

## **Try It!**          **Hiding Slides**

① Start PowerPoint and open the **PTry28** presentation from the data files for this lesson.

② Save the file as **PTry28_studentfirstname_ studentlastname** in the location where your teacher instructs you to save the files for this lesson.

③ Click the Slide Sorter View icon ⊞ and select slide 3.

④ On the Slide Show tab, click the Hide Slide button ⬛ .

⑤ Select slide 3.

⑥ Click Slide Show > Hide Slide ⬛ to unhide the slide.

⑦ Save the **PTry28_studentfirstname_ studentlastname** file and leave it open to use in the next Try It.

Hidden slide

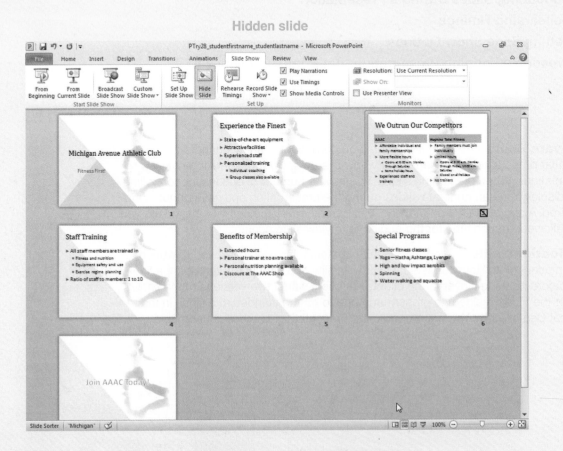

## Control Slides During a Presentation

- There are a number of other ways to control slide advance using keys or onscreen prompts.

- The Slide Show view shortcut menu also provides a number of ways to control slides.

- You can use this shortcut menu to navigate from slide to slide, go to the last-viewed slide or a specific slide (even a hidden slide), or go to a custom show.

- If you are using slide timings, you can use the Pause command to stop the automatic advance and then Resume to continue.

---

**Try It!**   **Controlling Slides During a Presentation**

**1** In the **PTry28_studentfirstname_ studentlastname** file, click Slide Show, and then click the From Beginning button 🖵 .

**2** Right-click the screen.

**3** Click Next.

*Slide Show shortcut menu*

## Michigan Avenue Athletic Club

Fitness First!

Next
Previous
Last Viewed
Go to Slide       ▸
Go to Section     ▸
Custom Show       ▸
Screen            ▸
Pointer Options   ▸
Help
Pause
End Show

**OR**

Use any of the following keyboard shortcuts to move through the slide show.
- Press N
- Press →
- Press ↓
- Press PG DN
- Press ENTER
- Press SPACE .

**OR**

Click the Right Presentation Arrow ⇨ at lower-left corner of screen.

**4** Click Slide Show > From Beginning 🖵 .

**5** Click the screen to advance the presentation.

**6** Right-click the screen.

**7** Click Previous.

**OR**

Click Last Viewed.

**OR**

Use any of the following keyboard shortcuts to move through the slide show:
- Press P
- Press ←
- Press ↑
- Press PG UP
- Press BACKSPACE .

**OR**

Click the Left Presentation Arrow ⇦ at lower-left corner of screen.

**8** Click Slide Show > From Beginning 🖵 .

**9** Right-click the screen.

**10** Click Go to Slide.

**11** Select slide to view.

**OR**

Type the slide number and press ENTER .

**12** Click Slide Show > From Beginning 🖵 .

**13** Right-click the screen.

**14** Click Pause.

**15** Click Slide Show > From Beginning 🖵 .

**16** Right-click the screen.

**17** Click Resume.

**18** Save the **PTry28_studentfirstname_ studentlastname** file and leave it open to use in the next Try It.

## Annotating Slides During a Presentation

- You can add annotations, such as writing or drawing, to a slide during a slide show to emphasize a specific point on a slide or add a comment to the slide.

- When you use the annotation feature, the mouse pointer becomes a pen.

- You can choose how you want the annotations to appear by selecting different pen colors and pen styles, such as ballpoint or highlighter.

- PowerPoint suspends automatic timings while you use the annotation feature.

- When you have finished annotating a slide, press [ESC] to change the pen pointer back to the mouse pointer.

- PowerPoint offers you the option of saving your annotations or discarding them. If you save them, you will see them in Normal view and they can be printed.

---

**Try It!**        **Annotating Slides During a Presentation**

1. In the **PTry28_studentfirstname_studentlastname** file, click Slide Show > From Beginning 🖳.

2. Right-click the screen.

3. Click Pointer Options.

4. Select a pen style:
   - Ballpoint Pen
   - Felt Tip Pen
   - Highlighter

5. Hold down the mouse button and drag to write annotations.

6. Click the Slide Show > From Beginning 🖳 .

7. Right-click the screen.

8. Click Pointer Options.

9. Click Ink Color.

10. Select a color from the color palette.

11. Right-click the screen.

12. Click Pointer Options.

13. Click Eraser.

14. Move the eraser over an annotation to erase.

**OR**

Press [E] to erase all annotations on the slide.

15. End the slide show.

16. Click Keep to save your annotations.

**OR**

Click Discard to remove the annotations.

17. Save the **PTry28_studentfirstname_studentlastname** file and leave it open to use in the next Try It.

---

## Rehearsing Timings

- To make sure you have allowed enough time for your audience to view your slides, you can rehearse the presentation.

- Use the Rehearse Timings command in the Set Up group on the Slide Show tab to start the presentation and display the Recording toolbar. As you view each slide, the timers show how much time you have spent on that slide as well as the total time elapsed for the show.

- You can use buttons on the Recording toolbar to pause and restart the show, and you can also repeat a slide if you find you need to start again.

- After you have finished viewing all slides, PowerPoint asks if you want to keep the slide timings. If you click Yes, these timings replace any other advance timings you have set.

## Try It!    Rehearsing Timings

**1** In the **PTry28_studentfirstname_studentlastname** file, click Slide Show, and then click the Rehearse Timings button .

**2** Advance from slide to slide, reading slide contents and any comments you intend to make in the presentation.

**3** At the end of the show, click Yes to keep slide timings.

**OR**

Click No to discard slide timings.

**4** Save the **PTry28_studentfirstname_studentlastname** file and leave it open to use in the next Try It.

The Recording toolbar

Recording  0:00:06  0:00:11

# Experience the Finest

▶ State-of-the-art equipment

▶ Attractive facilities

▶ Experienced staff

▶ Personalized training

 ■ Individual coaching

 ■ Group classes also available

## Setting Slide Show Options

■ Before finalizing a presentation, you must decide how it will be presented and set the slide show options accordingly.

■ Use the Set Up Show dialog box to specify options for the slide show, such as the following:

  • Specify how the slides will be shown—presented by a speaker, browsed by an individual reviewing the presentation onscreen, or viewed at a kiosk.

  • Specify how to show the presentation—looping continuously until ESC is pressed, without recorded narration, or without animation, and the color of the pen or laser pointer used.

  ✔ *You can use a built-in laser pointer during your presentation by pressing CTRL while pressing the left mouse button.*

  • Choose a range of slides to present or choose a custom show if the presentation has one.

  • Specify how to advance slides—manually or using timings.

  • Specify whether to display the presentation on multiple monitors.

  ✔ *Remember, not every projection system can handle multiple monitors.*

  • Hidden text is not displayed on-screen or printed unless you select to display it.

■ Using Presenter view, you can use a second monitor to show your presentation notes and other computer resources that can help with your presentation while your audience views the main presentation.

## Try It!  Setting Slide Show Options

**1** In the **PTry28_studentfirstname_studentlastname** file, click Slide Show, and then click the Set Up Slide Show button.

**2** In the Set Up Show dialog box, you can choose one of the following show types:
- Presented by a speaker
- Browsed by an individual
- Browsed at a kiosk

**3** You can choose any of the following show options:
- Loop continuously until 'Esc'
- Show without narration
- Show without animation

**4** You can choose how to advance slides:
- Manually
- Using timings, if present

**5** Click OK.

**6** Save the **PTry28_studentfirstname_studentlastname** file and leave it open to use in the next Try It.

Set Up Show dialog box

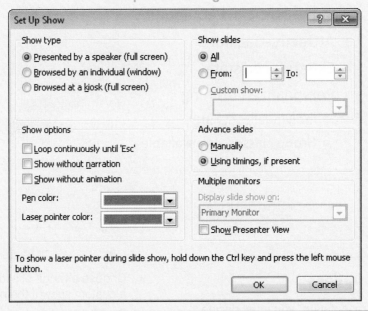

## Creating a Looping Presentation that Runs Automatically

- If you plan to run the presentation unattended, without a speaker to control the slides, you need to set up the show to loop continuously. For example, you might want a looping presentation if you want to run the presentation at a trade show booth where the audience can view but not interact with the slides.

- Use the Set Up Show dialog box to create a looping presentation, by specifying the following options:
  - In the Show type area, specify Browsed at a kiosk so that it will run unattended.
  - In the Show options area, specify Loop continuously until 'Esc'.
  - In the Advance slides area, select Using timings, if present.

  ✔ *Remember that you will need to create timings for the presentation in order for it to advance appropriately.*

**Try It!** **Creating a Looping Presentation that Runs Automatically**

1. In the **PTry28_studentfirstname_ studentlastname** file, click Slide Show > Set Up Slide Show .

2. Click Loop continuously until 'Esc'.

3. Click Browsed at a kiosk.

4. Click Using timings, if present.

5. Click OK.

6. Save the **PTry28_studentfirstname_ studentlastname** file and exit PowerPoint.

# Project 61—Create It

## Eye Surgery Promotion

### DIRECTIONS

1. Start PowerPoint and open the **PProj61** presentation from the data files for this lesson.

2. Save the presentation as **PProj61_ studentfirstname_studentlastname** in the location where your teacher instructs you to store the files for this lesson.

3. Select slide 7 and click the **Insert Picture from File** icon in the empty placeholder. The Insert Picture dialog box opens.

4. Browse to the data files for this lesson and select **PProj61_Flowers** to insert.

5. Click **Slide Show > From Beginning** to run the slide show. Let the automatic timings display the first two slides.

6. Right-click the screen and select **Go to Slide**. A shortcut menu appears listing all the slides in the presentation.

7. Select slide 6. Once you've read slide 6, right-click the screen again and select **Next** to view your changes to slide 7.

8. Click the **View** tab and select **Slide Sorter** in the Presentation Views group.

9. Unhide slide 8.

10. Click **Insert > Header & Footer** to open the Header and Footer dialog box.

11. On the Notes and Handouts tab, click **Footer**, type your name and click Apply to All, as shown in Figure 28-1.

12. **With your teacher's permission**, print a handout of slide 7.

13. Save your changes, close the presentation, and exit PowerPoint.

**Figure 28-1**

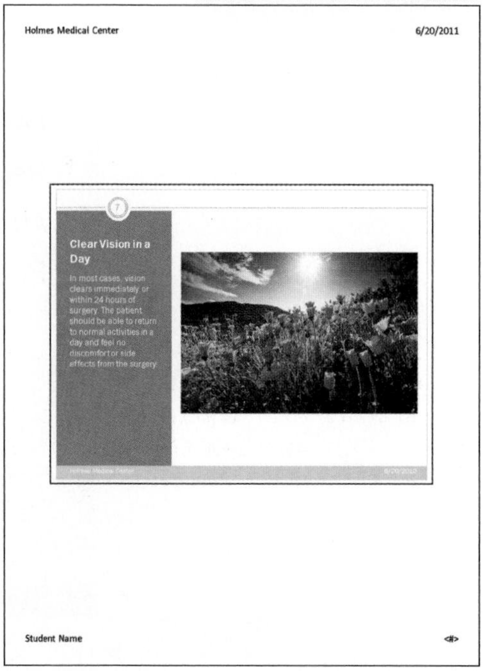

# Project 62—Apply It

## Laser Surgery Promotion

### DIRECTIONS

1. Start PowerPoint and open the **PProj62** presentation from the data files for this lesson.

2. Save the presentation as **PProj62_ studentfirstname_studentlastname** in the location where your teacher instructs you to store the files for this lesson.

3. Click **Insert  > Header & Footer** to open the Header and Footer dialog box.

4. On the Slides tab, click **Footer,** type your name and click **Apply to All**.

5. Start the slide show from the beginning and progress to slide 2.

6. Choose the felt tip pen option and draw an arrow to point to *Opens March 22.* Erase the annotation you just created.

7. Advance to slide 4 and annotate it as shown in Figure 28-2. Then finish viewing the slides by advancing them manually. Save the annotation at the end of the show.

8. Set the slide show up to run unattended.

   a. Click **Slide Show > Set Up Slide Show** to open Set Up Show dialog box.

   b. Click **Browsed at a kiosk** in the Show type section.

   c. Click **Using timings, if present** in the Advance slides section and click OK.

9. Restart the show and allow it to run all the way through once. When you reach slide 2 again, stop the show.

10. **With your teacher's permission,** print slide 4.

11. Save your changes, close the presentation, and exit PowerPoint.

---

**Figure 28-2**

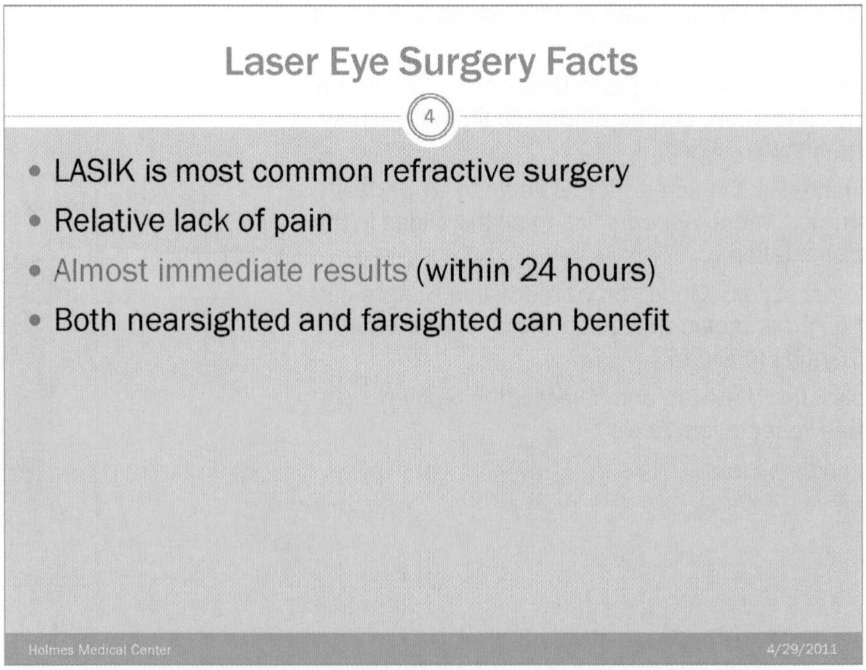

### Laser Eye Surgery Facts

④

- LASIK is most common refractive surgery
- Relative lack of pain
- Almost immediate results (within 24 hours)
- Both nearsighted and farsighted can benefit

Holmes Medical Center                                    4/29/2011

# Lesson 29

# Reviewing a Presentation

➤ **What You Will Learn**

**Sending a Presentation for Review**
**Finalizing a Presentation**

**WORDS TO KNOW**

**Comment**
A note you add to a slide
to provide corrections or
input to the slide content.

**Software Skills**   Send a presentation out for review so clients or colleagues can add comments. Use the options on the Prepare submenu to clean up and finalize the presentation.

**Application Skills**   In this exercise, you will send the Aquatics Center presentation out for review and then finalize it.

# What You Can Do

## Sending a Presentation for Review

■ PowerPoint makes it easy to send a presentation to colleagues to get their feedback, which is particularly useful in collaborative environments, such as companies and organizations.

■ Use the Save and Send command to send your presentation in many different forms.

- Send as Attachment. You can e-mail individual copies of the presentation.

- Send a Link. You can e-mail a link to a presentation that is stored on the same server as the e-mail recipients. This allows everyone to work on the same copy of the presentation.

- Send as PDF. Sends a PDF image of the presentation slides to recipients. PDFs preserve the fonts and formatting on most computers.

- Send as XPS. Sends the presentation in a format that can be viewed on most computers. XPS files maintain the fonts and formatting on most computers.

- Sends as Internet Fax. If you have a fax service provider, you can send a printed version of the presentation to a recipients fax machine.

    ✔ *You must have an active Internet connection a fax service to fax the file.*

■ Your reviewers can provide input to you using comments. You can add a comment to an entire slide, selected text, or other selected object. If you do not select any object, the comment displays in the upper-left corner of the slide.

■ The name and initials that display on each comment are those of the user who created the comment.

■ You can insert comments as reminders of changes you want to make.

---

## Try It!    Inserting a Comment

**1** Start PowerPoint and open the **PTry29** presentation from the data files for this lesson. Save the file as **PTry29_studentfirstname_ studentlastname** in the location where your teacher tells you to store files for this lesson.

**2** Select slide 9.

**3** Click Review > New Comment 🗨.

**4** Type **Consider adding a note to explain the three zones** in the comment box.

**5** Click outside the box to close the comment box.

**6** Click Review > Previous Comment 🗨 to jump to the comment on slide 6.

  ✔ *To make changes to the comment, click Review > Comments > Edit Comment.*

**7** Click Review > Next Comment 🗨.

**8** When PowerPoint opens the comment on slide 9, click Review > Delete Comment 🗨.

**9** Save the **PTry29_studentfirstname_ studentlastname** file and leave it open to use in the next Try It.

Comment inserted on a slide

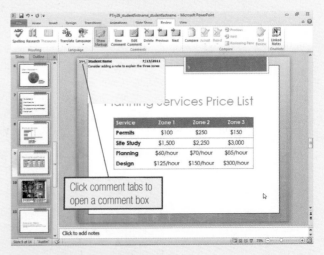

## Try It!    Sending a Presentation for Review

**1**   In the **PTry29_studentfirstname_ studentlastname** file, click **File > Save & Send**.

**2**   Select option for sending:

- Send as Attachment
- Send a Link
- Send as PDF
- Send as XPS
- Send as Internet Fax

**3**   Save the **PTry29_studentfirstname_ studentlastname** file and leave it open to use in the next Try It.

Save & Send tab

## Try It!    Sending a Presentation as a PDF Via E-mail

**1**   In the **PTry29_studentfirstname_ studentlastname** file, click **File > Save & Send**.

**2**   Select Send as PDF.

    ✔ *You will need an active Internet connection, Outlook installed and configured, and an e-mail address to send this e-mail. If you don't have one, your teacher will instruct you as to what to submit.*

**3**   When the e-mail message window opens, type your teacher's e-mail address.

    ✔ *Notice that the subject is filled in with the name of the presentation.*

**4**   In the message window, type **Here is a copy of the Restoration Hardware presentation.**

**5**   Press E and then type **Student Name.**

**6**   Click Send.

**7**   Save the **PTry29_studentfirstname_ studentlastname** file and leave it open to use in the next Try It.

## Finalizing a Presentation

- PowerPoint provides a number of tools and options you can use to finalize a presentation.

- Modify the presentation's properties to supply information such as the author and subject, which can help to identify the presentation.

- The Inspect Document option searches for personal information you may not want to accompany a presentation when you send it to someone else.

- Using the Protect Presentation option, you can Encrypt Document, Restrict Permission, and Add a Digital Signature to safeguard the data, prevent unauthorized changes, and verify authenticity. The Mark as Final option also prevents changes by making a presentation read-only.

- If you must often save presentations for use in earlier versions of PowerPoint, use the Compatibility Checker to make sure all slide content will display correctly in other versions.

---

### Try It!    Check a Presentation for Issues

**1** In the **PTry29_studentfirstname_studentlastname** file, click File > Info.

**2** Review and edit the presentation's properties in the Properties pane.

**3** Click Check for Issues.

**4** Select Inspect Document to check presentation for private information.

**5** Select all the boxes and click Inspect.

> ✔ *The Document Inspector should find at least one comment in the presentation as well as the document properties.*

**6** On the Comments and Annotations line, click Remove All.

**7** On the Document Properties and Personal Information line, click Remove All.

**8** Click Close.

**OR**

Click Reinspect to ensure that there is nothing left to be removed. Repeat steps 5 through 8.

**9** Save the **PTry29_studentfirstname_studentlastname** file and leave it open to use in the next Try It.

---

### Try It!    Finalizing a Presentation

**1** In the **PTry29_studentfirstname_studentlastname** file, click File > Info.

**2** Click Protect Presentation.

**3** Select Add a Digital Signature.

**4** At the message window that opens, click OK.

> ✔ *Bear in mind that the Microsoft Office digital signature is not a legally binding signature. For that you will need to select a third-party option by clicking Signature Services from the Office Marketplace.*

**5** Select Create your own digital ID and click OK.

**6** Complete the Create a Digital ID dialog box, with your name and e-mail address. In the Location box, type your class period.

**7** Click Create.

**8** At the Sign dialog box, type **lesson 29** in the

Purpose for signing this document box and click Sign.

**9** Click OK and then save the **PTry29_studentfirstname_studentlastname** file and exit PowerPoint.

Finalize the presentation using the Info page

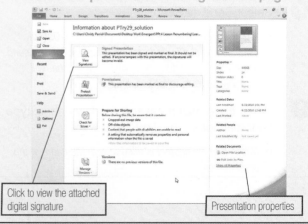

Click to view the attached digital signature

Presentation properties

# Project 63—Create It

## Aquatics Center Presentation

### DIRECTIONS

1. Start PowerPoint and open the **PProj63** presentation from the data files for this lesson.

2. Save the presentation as **PProj63_ studentfirstname_studentlastname** in the location where your teacher instructs you to store the files for this lesson.

3. On slide 1, click **Review > New Comment** . A comment box opens in the upper-left corner of the slide.

4. Type the following note for yourself: **Be sure to check every link before finalizing the presentation,** as shown in Figure 29-2.

5. Click **File > Info** to review the presentation's properties.

6. Click **Check for Issues** and then click **Inspect Document** to open the Document Inspector. Leave the default selections and click Inspect.

7. In the Document Inspector dialog box, click **Remove All** to remove all Document Properties and Personal Information. Then, click **Close**.

8. Click **Insert > Header & Footer** to open the Header and Footer dialog box.

9. On the Notes and Handouts tab, click **Footer,** type your full name and click **Apply to All**.

10. **With your teacher's permission**, print a handout of slide 1. Notice that the comment prints out on a second page.

11. Save your changes, close the presentation, and exit PowerPoint.

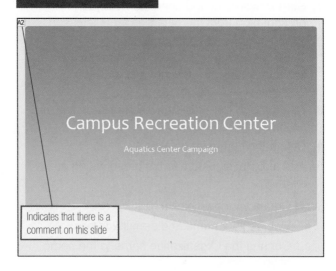

**Figure 29-1**

Campus Recreation Center

Aquatics Center Campaign

Indicates that there is a comment on this slide

**Figure 29-2**

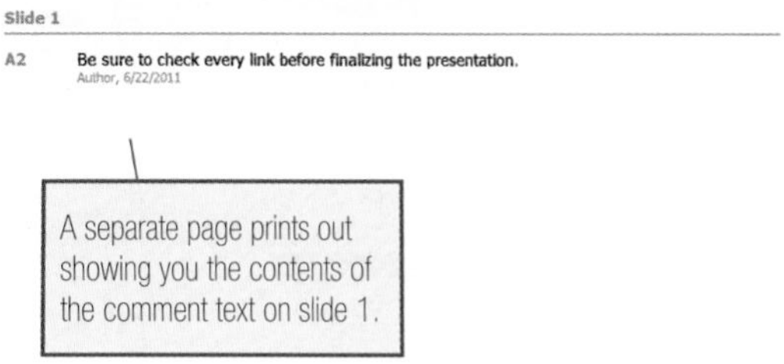

Slide 1

A2    Be sure to check every link before finalizing the presentation.
      Author, 6/22/2011

A separate page prints out showing you the contents of the comment text on slide 1.

# Project 64—Apply It

## Aquatics Center Presentation

### DIRECTIONS

1. Start PowerPoint and open the **PProj64** presentation from the data files for this lesson.

2. Save the presentation as **PProj64_studentfirstname_studentlastname** in the location where your teacher instructs you to store the files for this lesson.

3. Run through the slide show testing each link and action button to ensure they work.

4. Delete the comment on slide 1.

5. Add a digital signature to the presentation as follows:

   a. Create your own digital ID.

   b. Include your name and e-mail address.

   c. Change the Organization name to the name of your class.

d. Change the Location to your class period.

e. For the Purpose for signing this document, type **PowerPoint Project 64.**

6. Using the **Save & Send** options, send your presentation to your teacher as shown in Figure 29-3.

   a. Send the e-mail as a PDF attachment.

   b. Include an appropriate e-mail message that includes your name.

   ✔ *You will need an active Internet connection, Outlook installed and configured, and an e-mail address to send this e-mail. If you don't have one, your teacher will instruct you as to what to submit.*

7. **With your teacher's permission**, print the first three slides.

8. Save your changes, close the presentation, and exit PowerPoint.

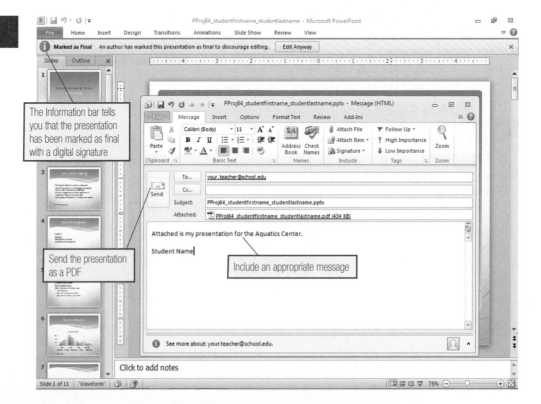

**Figure 29-3**

# Lesson 30

# Distributing a Presentation

> **What You Will Learn**

**Packaging a Presentation for CD**
**Broadcasting a Slide Show**
**Creating a Video of a Presentation**
**Publishing Slides**

**Software Skills**    You can easily package the presentation materials on a CD or video or use other output options, such as saving the presentation as a Web page or PowerPoint Show.

**Application Skills**    In this exercise, you will create a video of the Aquatics Center presentation and package it for distribution.

# What You Can Do

## Packaging for CD

- Use the Package Presentation for CD feature when you want to run a slide show on another computer.

- When you package a presentation show, it automatically includes a link to download the PowerPoint Viewer, which allows the presentation to be viewed on a PC or Mac even if PowerPoint is not installed.

✔ *The recipient must be able to connect to the Internet to download the PowerPoint Viewer.*

- The Package Presentation for CD dialog box lets you control the process of packaging the presentation files and copying them to a folder, CD, or iPod.

---

**Try It!**     **Packaging for CD**

1. Insert a recordable CD in the computer.

2. Start PowerPoint and open the **PTry30** presentation from the data files for this lesson.

3. Click File > Save & Send > Package Presentation for CD.

4. Click Package for CD 💿 .

5. In the Package for CD dialog box, type **PresentationCD** in the Name the CD box.

6. Click Options. Change what items the PowerPoint Viewer includes on the CD and click OK.

7. Click Copy to CD.

8. When asked if you want to use linked files, click Yes.

9. Click Close.

---

**Try It!**     **Copying to a Folder**

1. In the **PTry30** presentation, click File > Save & Send > Package Presentation for CD > Package for CD 💿 .

2. Type **PTry30** in the Name the CD box.

3. Click Copy to Folder.

4. Type **PTry30_studentfirstname_ studentlastname** in the folder name box.

5. Navigate to the folder where your teacher instructs you to store the files for this lesson.

6. Click OK and click Yes when prompted to copy linked files to the folder.

7. Click Close.

**Try It!**     **Unpacking and Running a Presentation**

**1** Insert the packaged CD in the computer.

**2** When the AutoPlay dialog box appears, choose PresentationPackage.html.

**3** Click Download Viewer.

**4** Click Download to download the PowerPoint 2010 Viewer.

**OR**

Click Start > Computer.
Click the CD drive to see files on CD.

**OR**

Navigate to the location of the folder in which you saved files.

**5** Double-click PowerPointViewer.exe.

**6** Accept the terms of use for the PowerPoint Viewer, if necessary, and click Continue.

**7** Click Next as necessary throughout the installation. When the installation completes, click OK.

**8** Go back to the browser window and click name of show.

**9** Click Open to start the show.

**10** Close the show when you are done viewing it.

Unpack a presentation using the PowerPoint Viewer

## Broadcasting a Slide Show

■ PowerPoint includes the new Broadcast a Slide Show feature that packages the presentation for broadcasting via the Internet.

■ You can broadcast the slide show from either the Slide Show tab or from the Save & Send tab on the File tab.

✔ *You will need a Windows Live ID to broadcast your slide show. If you do not already have one, you can sign up for one for free.*

■ Anyone who can access the Internet will be able to follow the provided link and view the presentation, even if they don't have PowerPoint 2010 installed on their computer.

■ The PowerPoint Broadcast Service will provide you with an URL that you can give to up to 50 people so they can watch the broadcast.

■ You will still control the broadcast by starting and pausing the presentation as desired.

✔ *Viewers of a broadcast slide show will not hear any accompanying audio or see any videos that might play in your slide show. You will need to provide any audio through conference calling.*

## Try It!     Broadcasting a Presentation Via the Internet

**1** In the **PTry30_studentfirstname_ studentlastname** file, click Slide Show > Broadcast Slide Show [icon].

**OR**

Click File > Save & Send > Broadcast Slide Show > Broadcast Slide Show [icon].

The Broadcast Slide Show dialog box

**2** Click Start Broadcast.

**OR**

Click Change Broadcast Service if you want to use an internal company broadcast service.

**3** Click Send in Email, if you want to send the provided URL to your attendees using Outlook.

**OR**

Click Copy Link to send the URL to your attendees in a memo or any other format. When you open the document you plan to send to the attendees, press CTRL + V to paste the link.

The Broadcast Slide Show URL

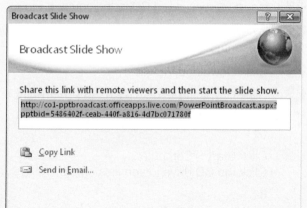

**4** Click Start Slide Show when you and your attendees are ready to begin the presentation.

**5** Advance through the presentation as you normally would. Your attendees will view the slide show through their browser window.

**6** Click  End Broadcast when the slide show ends and returns to the PowerPoint 2010 window.

**7** Click End Broadcast again when warned that the remote viewers will be disconnected.

The broadcasted slide show through a browser window

## Creating a Video

■ You can now save your PowerPoint presentations as video that can be shared with others to be viewed on a computer or uploaded to the Internet.

■ PowerPoint will save the presentation as a .wmv file, which can be uploaded to YouTube, Facebook, or other Web sites.

■ When you save your presentation as a video it can be played on any computer or DVD player.

■ Your presentation video can include unique timings and narration, or you can set a specific number of seconds that each slide will be paused.

---

**Try It!**     **Saving a Presentation as a Video**

**1** In the **PTry30_studentfirstname_studentlastname** file, click File > Save & Send > Create a Video.

**2** In the Create a Video pane, click Computer & HD Displays and then select the resolution you want to use.

**3** Change the number of seconds that you want to spend on each slide to 6:00.

✔ *If you're unsure about the number of seconds to use, you can set the number of seconds and then click the second button (Don't Use Recorded Timings and Narrations) to see what it will look like.*

**OR**

Click Don't Use Recorded Timings and Narrations to see the options available.

✔ *This second button says Don't Use Recording Timings and Narrations because these items haven't been set yet. If you had already recorded timings and narrations the button would say Use Recorded Timings and Narrations.*

**4** Select Record Timings and Narration.

**5** In the Record Slide Show dialog box, select one or both of the following:

■ Slide and animation timings

■ Narrations and laser pointer

**6** Click Start Recording.

✔ *At this point, you would begin the process of recording your presentation. For more information review the Rehearsing Slide Timings section in Lesson 28.*

**7** Click Create Video.

**8** Navigate to the location where your teacher instructs you to store the files for this lesson.

✔ *The file name box will have the same name that your PowerPoint presentation has. If you want to use a different name, select the name in the box and type a new name.*

**9** Click Save.

**10** Save the **PTry30_studentfirstname_studentlastname** file and leave it open to use in the next Try It.

Saving a presentation as a video

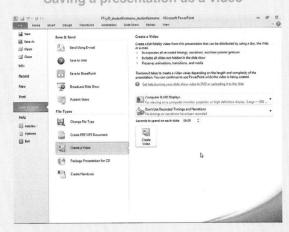

## Publishing Slides

- You have other output options for a PowerPoint presentation.

- You can publish it to your Windows Live SkyDrive site, where it can be viewed or edited online.

- You can save the presentation as a PowerPoint Show, which will open automatically in Slide Show view to save time.

- You can save the presentation to SharePoint, so that it is ready for collaboration.

- You can also set up a presentation to print on overhead transparencies, various paper sizes, or 35mm slides.

---

**Try It!**    **Save a Presentation to a Windows Live SkyDrive**

**1** In the **PTry30_studentfirstname_ studentlastname** file, click File > Save & Send > Save to Web.

**2** Click Sign In.

**3** Type your Windows Live E-mail address and Password.

**OR**

Sign up for a free Windows Live account.

**4** Click to select the Public or another SkyDrive folder.

**5** Click Save As.

**6** From the Save as type list, select the format you wish to use.

**7** Change the name of the presentation, if necessary.

**8** Click Save.

**9** Save the **PTry30_studentfirstname_ studentlastname** file and leave it open to use in the next Try It.

Sending a presentation to a Windows Live SkyDrive

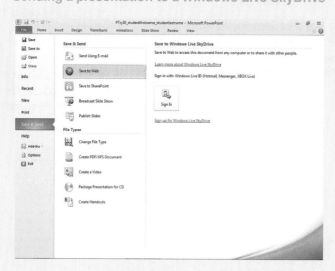

**Try It!**     **Save a Presentation as a Show**

**1**   In the **PTry30_studentfirstname_ studentlastname** file, click File > Save As.

**2**   Navigate to the location where your teacher instructs you to store the files for this lesson.

**3**   Click the Save as type arrow and click PowerPoint Show.

**4**   Type a different name for the file, if desired.

**5**   Click Save.

**6**   Exit PowerPoint.

Save as PowerPoint Show

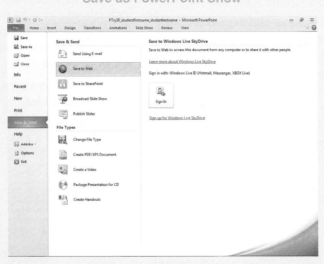

# Project 65—Create It

## Publishing the Aquatics Center Presentation

### DIRECTIONS

1. Start PowerPoint and open the **PProj65** presentation from the data files for this lesson.

2. Click **File** > **Save & Send** > **Create a Video**.

3. Click **Computers & HD Displays** and then click **Internet & DVD**. The presentation video will have good clarity, but keep the file size small.

4. Click **Don't Use Recorded Timings and Narrations** and then click **Preview Timings & Narration** to see how the presentation will look with the default 5:00 seconds spent on each slide.

5. Click the screen at the end of the slide show to return to the Create a Video options.

6. Type **6:00** in the Seconds to spend on each slide box.

7. Click **Create Video**. The Save As dialog box opens.

8. Navigate to the location where your teacher instructs you to store the files for this lesson. Type **PProj65_studentfirstname_studentlastname** in the File name text box, and then click **Save**, as shown in Figure 30-1.

    ✔ *Keep in mind that the it will take several minutes for the video file to be completed.*

9. Close the presentation and exit PowerPoint.

**Figure 30-1**

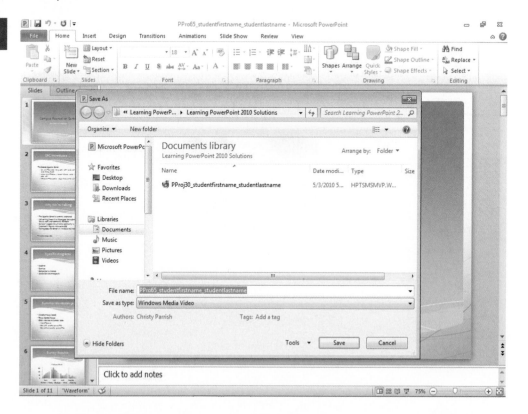

# Project 66—Apply It

## Publishing the Aquatics Center Presentation

### DIRECTIONS

1. Start PowerPoint and open the **PProj66** presentation from the data files for this lesson.
2. Save the file as **PProj66_studentfirstname_ studentlastname** in the location where your teacher instructs you to store the files for this lesson.
3. Go to slide 4. Insert the file **PProj66_Swimmer** from your data files. Place it attractively on the slide and modify it, if desired, using the Picture Formatting tools. Your slide should look similar to Figure 30-2.
4. Package the presentation as follows:
   a. Name the CD folder in which to store the files **PProj66_Aquatics**.
   b. Display Options and choose to embed TrueType fonts.

   c. If you have the ability to copy to a CD, do so.
   d. If you cannot create a CD, then copy the CD Folder to the folder where your teacher instructs you to store the files for this lesson.
5. Save the presentation as a PowerPoint Show.
6. Send the presentation to your teacher as an e-mail attachment. Be sure to include an appropriate message.
7. **With your teacher's permission**, print slide 4.
8. Save your changes, close the presentation, and exit PowerPoint.

**Figure 30-2**

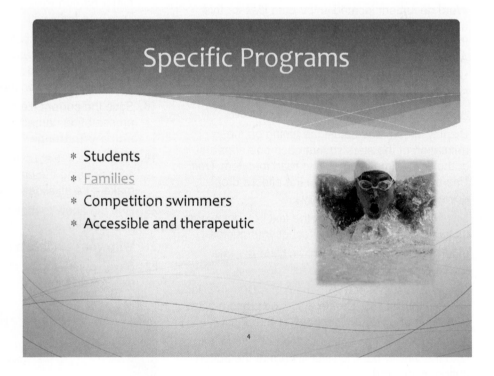

# Chapter Assessment and Application

# Project 67—Make It Your Own

## Finalize and Package Bakery Presentations

Whole Grains Bread has asked you to finalize a slide show that can run unattended in a kiosk or as a video on their Web site, as well as a custom show that can be presented to prospective catering clients. In this exercise, you will add the finishing touches, including transitions, animations, links, and custom shows, and then output the presentation in several ways.

## DIRECTIONS

1. Start PowerPoint and open the **PProj67** presentation from the data files for this chapter.

2. Save the presentation as **PProj67_ studentfirstname_studentlastname** in the location where your teacher instructs you to store the files for this chapter.

3. Add a title-only slide between slides 8 and 9 and enter the title, **Catering Bread Pricing**.

4. Embed the data from the **PProj67_Bread Pricing** Word document located in the data files for this chapter. Format the table so that it blends in with the rest of the presentation, as shown in Illustration A.

5. Modify the font and color of the title text on the Slide Master.

6. Apply transitions of your choice to all slides.

7. Display slide 5 and adjust the timing on the animation of the stars so that each one appears at the same time you begin to read that item. (*Hint*: Use the Timing command on the effect's drop-down menu to specify a delay.)

8. Display slide 7 and animate the text box below the picture using an entrance effect of your choice.

9. Insert the following comment on slide 4: **Link these items to custom shows**.

10. Create a custom show with the name **Catering** for slides 8 through 10. Create a second custom show with the name **Rental** for slides 11 through 12.

11. On slide 7, insert an action button or link that will take the viewer back to slide 1. Format the action button as desired.

12. Link the bullet items on slide 4 to the custom shows you created. Specify Show and return for these custom shows.

13. Delete the comment on slide 4.

14. Rehearse the slide show as it will be presented: on slide 4, jump to the first custom show; then, after the custom show ends and slide 4 appears again, jump to the second custom show. After the second show ends, proceed from slide 4 to slide 7 and then use the action button to return to slide 1.

15. Save slide timings, and then save your changes so far.

16. Package this version of the presentation in a folder named **Proj67_Bakery Presenter**. Include TrueType fonts with the package.

17. Remove the action button from slide 7. Then save the current version as a video named **PProj67_ BakeryShow_studentfirstname_studentlastname** that will be played on their Web site.

18. Save the current file as a PowerPoint presentation named **PProj67_BakeryKiosk_ studentfirstname_studentlastname**.

19. Hide slide 4. Set up the show to be browsed at a kiosk using the current slide timings. (Check to make sure all slides have slide timings.)

20. Run the show to make sure it loops properly. Stop after you have seen slide 2 the second time.

21. **With your teacher's permission**, print slide 9.

22. Save your changes, close the presentation, and exit PowerPoint.

## Illustration A

### Catering Bread Pricing

| Item | Per Item | Dozen/Per Item | Two Dozen/Per Item |
| --- | --- | --- | --- |
| Bread | $3.50 | $2.99 | $1.99 |
| Croissants | $2.00 | $1.75 | $1.25 |
| Bagels | $0.90 | $0.60 | $0.45 |
| Baguettes | $2.50 | $2.00 | $1.75 |
| Muffins | $1.50 | $1.25 | $1.00 |

# Project 68—Master It

## Create a Custom Presentation

The facilities manager for the Campus Recreation Center has asked you to update an old presentation to add to a new marketing program. He went through the old presentation materials and added comments throughout, letting you know the changes he expects. In this exercise, you will work with and delete comments, create a custom theme based on an existing presentation, update the text on the presentation, and improve the general appearance of the presentation.

## DIRECTIONS

1. Start PowerPoint and open the **PProj68** presentation from the data files for this chapter.

2. Save the presentation as **PProj68_ studentfirstname_studentlastname** in the location where your teacher instructs you to store the files for this chapter.

3. Read through each of the comments inserted by the facilities manager.

4. Open the file **PProj68_Aquatics Center Presentation** from the data files for this chapter.

5. Using the settings in this file, create a custom theme named **Aquatics** to apply to the new presentation.

6. Apply the new theme to the file **PProj68**.

7. Duplicate slide 2 and split the information over slides 2 and 3. Divide the material as requested by the manager and add additional information to improve the slides.

8. Create separate slides for the world-class facilities and for each of the three sports covered: swimming, diving, and water polo. Add appropriate content as needed.

9. Update slide 8 with the new membership information for the Campus Recreation Center's Aquatics program.

10. Add graphics to 6 of the 8 slides. Modify their color and format to blend with the presentation and with each other, as shown in Illustration B.

11. Add transitions to all slides.

12. Apply an animation to at least one element.

13. Review each comment. When the tasks are completed, delete the comment. Check spelling.

14. Watch the slide show and ensure that everything is working appropriately.

15. Save your changes and send the presentation to your teacher as a PDF file, if requested by your teacher.

16. Exit PowerPoint.

**Illustration B**

## Chapter 5

# Working with Masters, Comments, Handouts, and Pictures

## Lesson 31
## Advanced Slide Master Features
## Projects 69-70

- Inserting a New Slide Master
- Inserting a Picture on the Slide Master
- Inserting a Shape on the Slide Master
- Customizing Placeholders on the Slide Master

## Lesson 32
## Working with Notes and Handouts
## Projects 71-72

- Using Advanced Notes and Handout Master Formats
- Working with Linked Notes (OneNote 2010)

## Lesson 33
## Working with Comments in a Presentation
## Projects 73-74

- Comparing Presentations
- Reviewing Comments
- Deleting Comments

## Lesson 34
## Exporting Slide Handouts to Word
## Projects 75-76

- Exporting Handouts to Word
- Linking Presentations to Word

## Lesson 35
## Working with Presentation Properties
## Projects 77-78

- Viewing Presentation Properties
- Entering or Editing Properties
- Viewing Advanced Properties

## Lesson 36
## Making a Presentation Accessible to Everyone
## Projects 79-80

- Running the Compatibility Checker
- Checking Accessibility
- Saving a Slide or Presentation As a Picture

## End-of-Chapter Assessments
## Projects 81-82

# Lesson 31

# Advanced Slide Master Features

➤ **What You Will Learn**

**Inserting a New Slide Master**
**Inserting a Picture on the Slide Master**
**Inserting a Shape on the Slide Master**
**Customizing Placeholders on the Slide Master**

**Software Skills**   You can add variety to presentations by inserting additional slide masters, which allows you to have additional options within the same theme. For example, you have one slide master in which you've inserted a shape and one without it. You can also customize a slide master by adding a shape or picture or by modifying the placeholder arrangement. Use the Master Layout dialog box to restore master elements that have been removed.

**Application Skills**   You will work on a presentation for Yesterday's Playthings. In this lesson, you add and customize a new slide master and add a graphic element to the slide master.

## What You Can Do

### Inserting a New Slide Master

- You can add themes to a presentation by adding slide masters in Slide Master view.
- Clicking Insert Slide Master in the Edit Master group on the Slide Master tab adds a new slide master in the slide thumbnail pane.
- The new master displays the default Office theme and is designated as 2, indicating it is the second master in the presentation. The new master includes all the standard layouts below the slide master. You can use the Rename command to give the new slide master a more meaningful name.

- A small pushpin symbol appears below the new slide master. This symbol indicates the master is being preserved for use even though no slide currently uses this master. If a slide master that you add does not automatically display this symbol, you can click the Preserve button in the Edit Master group to preserve the master.

- You can also add a new slide master with a theme other than the Office theme using the Themes button in the Edit Themes group.

- You can add as many masters as you want, but keep in mind that using many themes in a presentation will compromise your presentation's visual consistency.

- When adding multiple slide masters to a presentation, you can add completely distinct themes, or you can add another instance of the same theme. Using multiple versions of the same theme allows you to apply different background or color formatting to slides while maintaining the same fonts and layouts for a consistent appearance.

- The Master Layout group of the Slide Master tab contains several commands that help you work more efficiently with slide masters.

---

**Try It!** **Inserting a New Slide Master**

**1** Start PowerPoint and open **PTry31** from the data files for this lesson.

**2** Save the file as **PTry31_studentfirstname_ studentlastname** in the location where your teacher instructs you to store the files for this lesson.

**3** Click View > Slide Master 🖼.

**4** Click the Insert Slide Master button 🖼.

**5** With the new slide master selected, click Slide Master > Themes 🅰.

**6** Right-click on the Tradeshow 🅰 theme and select Apply to Selected Slide Master.

  ✓ *If you do not have Tradeshow available on your PC, you can use the PTry31_Tradeshow.thmx file in the data files for this lesson.*

**OR**

- Click View > Slide Master 🖼.

- Click Slide Master > Themes 🅰.

- Right click on the Tradeshow 🅰 theme and select Add as New Slide Master.

**7** Save changes, and leave the file open to use in the next Try It.

Insert a New Slide Master in a Second Theme

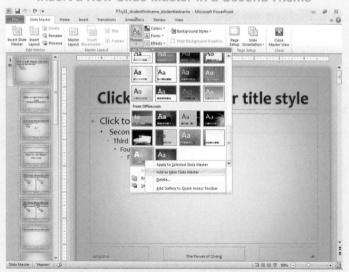

## Inserting a Shape on the Slide Master

■ You can save time by adding a shape to a slide master so that it will appear whenever that slide layout is used.

■ Use the shapes on the Home tab or Insert tab to draw basic objects, such as lines, rectangles, and circles, as well as more complex shapes such as stars, banners, and block arrows on a slide master.

■ You control the size and shape of most shapes as you draw. Some shapes also have a yellow diamond adjustment handle that you can use to modify the appearance of the shape.

---

**Try It!**    **Inserting a Shape on the Slide Master**

**1**   With **PTry31_studentfirstname_ studentlastname** open in Slide Master view, go to the Tradeshow Slide Master.

**2**   Click Insert > Shapes 🔲.

**3**   Select the Rounded Rectangle shape.

**4**   Draw and position the shape to enable text to be entered.

**5**   Right-click the shape and select Edit Text.

**6**   Type **Helping Hands**.

**7**   Save changes, and leave the file open to use in the next Try It.

---

## Inserting a Picture on the Slide Master

■ The easiest way to have a picture appear on multiple slides is to insert it on the slide master.

■ You can use the Insert Picture from File icon in any content placeholder or the Picture button on the Insert tab to place your own picture file on a slide. This command opens the Insert Picture dialog box so you can navigate to and select the picture you want to insert.

■ If you want to insert a picture on a slide master that doesn't contain a content placeholder, use the Insert Picture button on the Insert tab.

---

**Try It!**    **Inserting a Picture on the Slide Master**

**1**   With **PTry31_studentfirstname_ studentlastname** open in Slide Master view, click the Trade Show Slide Master.

**2**   Click Insert > Insert Picture from File 🖻.

**3**   Navigate to the data files for this lesson, select the **PTry31_soup** image, and click Insert

*(continued)*

**Try It!**    **Inserting a Picture on the Slide Master** *(continued)*

**4**   Drag the picture to the position shown in the figure.

**5**   Save changes, and leave the file open to use in the next Try It.

A figure placed in a slide master

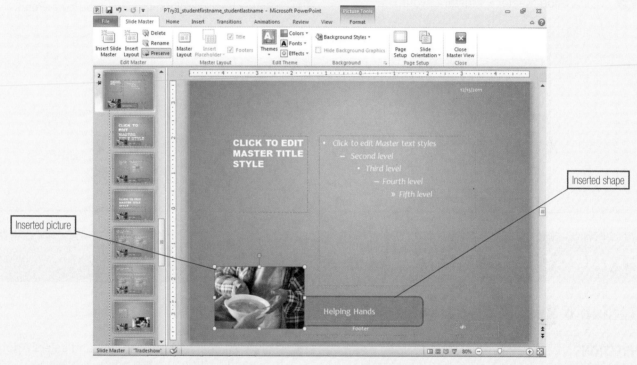

## Customizing Placeholders on the Slide Master

■ When a slide layout master is selected (rather than the slide master), the Title and Footers check boxes are checked. Uncheck either or both to remove the title or the date, footer, and slide number placeholders from the master. Display these placeholders again by checking the appropriate check box.

■ You can also select and delete any default placeholder on a master.

■ You can restore deleted placeholders using the Master Layout dialog box. This command is active when the slide master is selected.

■ By default, the dialog box shows all placeholders selected and unavailable for change. Only deleted placeholders are active in the Master Layout dialog box so that you can select them to restore them.

**Try It!**    **Customizing Placeholders on the Slide Master**

**1**   With **PTry31_studentfirstname_ studentlastname** open in Slide Master view, select the Tradeshow Slide Master, if necessary.

**2**   Click the border of the footer placeholder under the inserted shape.

**3**   Press DEL.

**4**   Save changes, and leave the file open to use in the next Try It.

**Try It!**     **Restoring Master Layout Placeholders**

**1** With **PTry31_studentfirstname_ studentlastname** open in Slide Master view, select the Tradeshow Slide Master, if necessary.

**2** Click Slide Master > Master Layout .

**3** Select check boxes of the footer placeholder to restore.

**4** Click OK.

**5** Save changes, close the file, and PowerPoint.

The Master Layout dialog box

# Project 69—Create It

## Adding a New Slide Master

### DIRECTIONS

1. Start PowerPoint, if necessary, and open **PProj69** from the data files for this lesson.

2. Save the presentation as **PProj69_ studentfirstname_studentlastname** in the location where your teacher instructs you to store the files for this lesson.

3. Click **View** > **Slide Master** .

4. Click the **Insert Slide Master** button .

5. Select the new slide master and click **Slide Master** > **Themes** .

6. Right-click on the **Module** theme and select **Apply to Selected Slide Master**.

7. Click **Slide Master** > **Rename** .

8. Type **Light Module** in the Layout Name box and click **Rename**.

9. Click **Slide Master** > **Close Master View**.

10. Save the changes to the document.

11. Close the document, and exit PowerPoint.

# Project 70—Apply It

## Enhancing a New Slide Master

### DIRECTIONS

1. Start PowerPoint, if necessary, and open **PProj70** from the data files for this lesson.

2. Save the file as **PProj70_studentfirstname_ studentlastname** in the location where your teacher instructs you to store the files for this lesson.

3. Create a footer that includes your full name and today's date.

4. Display the **Light Module** slide master in the Slide Master View.

   a. Click **View** > **Slide Master**.

   b. In the pane that contains the slide masters and layouts, scroll down the thumbnails using ScreenTips to help you locate the Light Module slide master.

   c. Click the **Light Module** slide master thumbnail.

5. Display the Background Styles gallery and select **Style 6**.

6. Apply a shape style to the black bar at the top of the slide.

   a. Select the black shape at the top of the slide behind the title placeholder.

   b. Click **Drawing Tools Format** > **More** to open the Shape Styles gallery.

   c. Select **Subtle Effect – Aqua, Accent 2** Quick Style.

7. Select the thin gray horizontal shape below the shape you just reformatted and apply a fill of **Orange, Accent 5, Darker 25%**.

8. Click the **Title** placeholder. Click **Drawing Tools Format** > **Text Fill** > **Gray 25%, Background 1, Darker 25%**.

9. Change the size of first-level bulleted text to **20** and second-level bulleted text to **25**.

10. Click the title slide layout below the **Light Module** slide master, change the background style to **Style 7**.

11. Select the black shape that takes up the top third of the slide and apply the **Moderate Effect – Aqua, Accent 2** Quick Style shape style to the black shape.

12. Select the thin white horizontal shape below the shape you just reformatted and apply a fill of **Gold, Accent 1**.

13. Change the title font color to **Black, Text 1, Lighter 50%**.

14. Close Slide Master view. Display **Slide 6** and apply the **Light Module Title and Content** layout. Your slide should look similar to Figure 31-1.

15. **With your teacher's permission**, print slide 6. It should look similar to Figure 31-1.

16. Close the document, saving all changes, and exit PowerPoint.

**Figure 31-1**

## Summer Show Specials . . .

| Item | Originally | Sale Price |
|------|-----------|-----------|
| Keepsake marbles | $12.95 | $8.95 |
| Duncan yoyos | $15.50 | $11.50 |
| Vintage golf clubs | $35.00 - $75.00 | $18.50 - $30.00 |

And Much, Much More!

8/20/2011          Student Name

# Lesson 32

# Working with Notes and Handouts

➤ **What You Will Learn**

**Using Advanced Notes and Handout Master Formats**
**Working with Linked Notes (OneNote 2010)**

**Software Skills**   You can customize your notes and handouts by making changes to the notes and handout masters. You can also use the new Linked Notes feature to take notes on a presentation that can be shared when collaborating.

**Application Skills**   You will work on a presentation for Planet Earth, a nonprofit organization. In this lesson, you customize the notes master and apply custom formats to the handout master. You will also work with the new Linked Notes feature.

## What You Can Do

### Using Advanced Notes and Handout Master Formats

- You can customize both the notes and handout masters to improve visual appearance when notes pages or handouts are printed.
- By default, the notes and handout masters use the Office theme colors, fonts, and effects, no matter what theme is applied to the slides in the presentation. Changing fonts and colors to match the current theme can give your notes pages consistency with the slides.
- You can apply graphic formats such as Quick Styles or fills, borders, and effects to any placeholder on the notes or handout master.
- You can also add content to the handout master, such as a new text box or a graphic that will then display on all pages.

- When adding content such as a text box to the handout master, consider that your added content must be positioned so it doesn't interfere with the slide image placeholders for layouts other than the one you are currently working with.

- If you insert a text box above the slide image on the one-slide-per-page layout, for example, it will obscure the slide images for other handout layouts.

- You can, however, use the Colors, Fonts, and Effects buttons to apply theme formatting to your masters.

✓ Note that even though the Themes button appears on the Notes Master tab and the Handout Master tab, you cannot use it to apply a theme.

- Use the Background Styles option in the Background group to apply a background that will fill the entire notes page or handout. Background colors are controlled by the theme colors you have applied to the master.

---

**Try It!** **Applying Notes Master Formats**

**1** Start Word and open **PTry32** file from the data files for this lesson.

**2** Save the file as **PTry32 _studentfirstname_ studentlastname** in the location where your teacher instructs you to store the files for this lesson.

**3** Click View > Notes Master .

**4** Click Theme > Theme Fonts Ⓐ and select the Austin theme font.

**5** Click the Notes placeholder, then click Drawing Tools Format > Colored Outline – Blue Accent 1 Ⓐᵇᶜ in the Shape Styles gallery.

**6** Click Notes Master > Theme > Background Styles and select Style 6.

**7** Save changes, and leave the file open to use in the next Try It.

Applying custom formats to the notes master

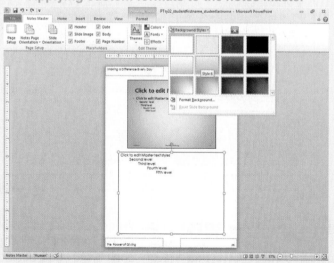

---

**Try It!** **Applying Handout Master Formats**

**1** In **PTry32 _studentfirstname_ studentlastname**, click View > Handout Master .

**2** Click Handout Master > Theme Colors .

*(continued)*

**Try It!**    **Applying Handout Master Formats** *(continued)*

**3** Select the Origin theme color.

**4** Click Insert > Shapes 🔲 > Rectangle.

**5** Draw a rectangle that covers the top of the page, as shown in the figure.

**6** Right click the shape and select Send to Back.

**7** Select the Header and Date placeholders, then click Home > Font Color ▲ ˙ and select White.

**8** Click File > Print and click Full Page Slides and select 1 Slide Handout to see how the new handout will look.

**9** Save changes, and leave the file open to use in the next Try It.

A formatted handout

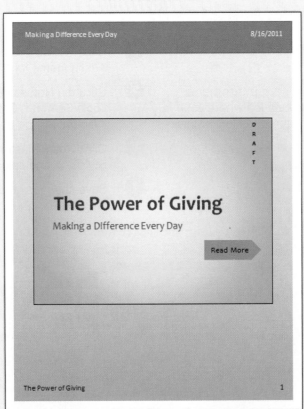

## Working with Linked Notes (OneNote 2010)

- Linked notes allow you to keep a set of notes on a presentation that retain the context of the original slides.

- You can create Linked Notes using the Linked Notes button 🔲 on the Review tab.

- If you have OneNote installed, but don't see the Linked Notes button on your Review tab, you can add it from Backstage View using the Options page.

- OneNote attaches a note-taking dock to the desktop next to the PowerPoint window.

- When you take linked notes in the dock, a PowerPoint icon will appear next to the dock to show what application the notes are linked to.

- To see the subject of the note, hover over the icon. To review the original presentation, just click on the icon.

- You can tag a note as a To Do item using the keyboard shortcut `CTRL` + `1`.

- When you use shared OneNote notebooks to store your Linked Notes, team members can see and respond to each other's notes.

**Try It!**     **Adding the Linked Notes Button to the Ribbon**

**1** In **PTry32 _studentfirstname_ studentlastname**, click File > Options > Customize Ribbon.

✓ *Remember that OneNote 2010 must be installed on your computer in order to use this feature.*

**2** On the Customize Ribbon page, select All Tabs in the Choose commands from: drop-down menu.

**3** Click the ⊞ button next to Review in the Main Tabs list on the left to expand the Review tab options, and select OneNote.

**4** Select the Review tab in the Main Tabs list on the right as the location for the button.

**5** Click the Add button and click OK.

**6** Save changes, and leave the file open to use in the next Try It.

---

**Try It!**     **Working with Linked Notes (OneNote 2010)**

**1** In **PTry32 _studentfirstname_ studentlastname**, select slide 6.

**2** Click Review > Linked Notes 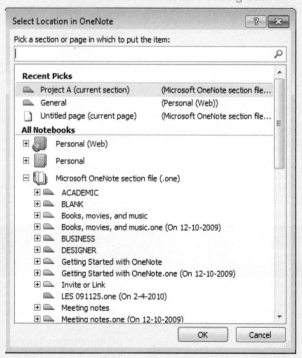.

Select Location in OneNote dialog box

*(continued)*

**Try It!**        **Working with Linked Notes (OneNote 2010)** *(continued)*

**3** Select Academic in the All Notebooks area and click OK.

**4** In the header box, type your full name and press ENTER .

**5** In the note box, type **Find out when the MS Walk and AIDS Awareness Week will take place.**

**6** Switch to slide 8.

**7** Hover your mouse over the PowerPoint icon next to the note box to see the original slide.

**8** Close the OneNote dock and close **PTry32 _studentfirstname_studentlastname**, saving all changes, and exit PowerPoint.

A Linked Note

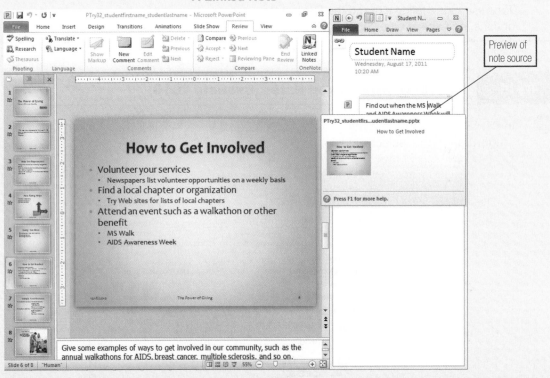

# Project 71—Create It

## Formatting Notes

### DIRECTIONS

1. Start PowerPoint, if necessary, and open **PProj71** from the data files for this lesson.

2. Save the file as **PProj71_studentfirstname_ studentlastname** in the location where your teacher instructs you to store the files for this lesson.

3. Click **View** > **Notes Master** .

4. Click **Notes Master** > **Background Styles** > **Style 6.**

5. Click **Notes Master** > **Colors** .

6. Select **Austin.**

7. Click **Notes Master** > **Fonts** > **Aspect.**

8. Click **Notes Master** > **Close Master View.**

9. Insert a header on the Notes and Handouts that includes your full name and today's date.

10. Save the changes to the document. Your presentation should look similar to Figure 32-1.

11. Close the document, and exit PowerPoint.

**Figure 32-1**

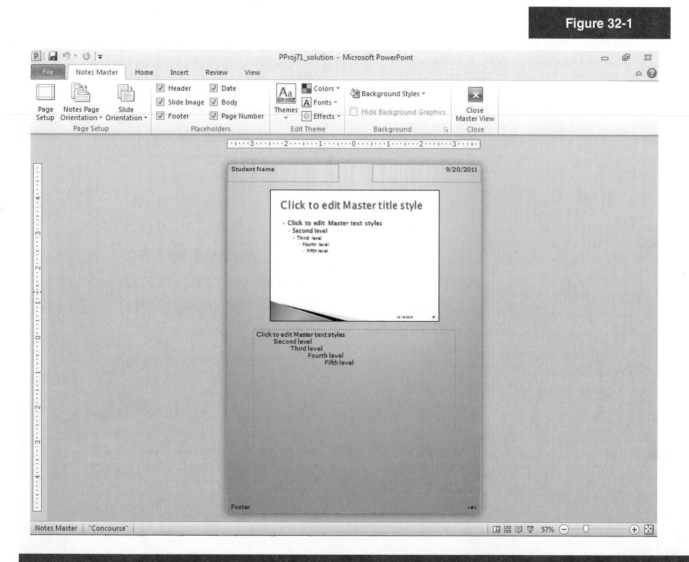

# Project 72—Apply It

## Formatting Notes

### DIRECTIONS

1. Start PowerPoint, if necessary, and open **PProj72** from the data files for this lesson.

2. Save the file as **PProj72_studentfirstname_studentlastname** in the location where your teacher instructs you to store the files for this lesson.

3. Display the presentation in Notes Master View.

4. Insert a **Rectangle** shape at the top of the page the same height as the header and date placeholders.

5. Use the Shape Style gallery to apply a **Moderate Effect – Black, Dark 1** and send it to the back.

6. Change the size of the header and date text to **14 point**, apply **bold**, and change the color if desired to contrast better with the shape behind the text.

7. Select the content placeholder and apply the **Colored Outline – Olive Green, Accent 4** shape style.

8. Close Notes Page Master view and switch to Notes Page view. Figure 32-2 shows a sample of one of the presentation's slides in this view.

9. Type **Going green can help save the planet, but it is also a great way to save you real green in your wallet!** in the content placeholder.

10. Save the changes to the document.

11. **With your teacher's permission**, print the Notes page for slide 1. It should look similar to Figure 32-2.

12. Close the document, saving all changes, and exit PowerPoint.

**Figure 32-2**

# Lesson 33

# Working with Comments in a Presentation

➤ **What You Will Learn**

**Compare Presentations**
**Review Comments**
**Delete Comments**

**Software Skills**   You can use the Compare feature to quickly see any changes made to your presentation after it has been reviewed by others. When you're working with others on a project, comments are a great way to communicate ideas. After a presentation has been reviewed by coworkers, you need to review the presentation to resolve and delete any comments you find.

**Application Skills**   In this lesson, you will work on a presentation you created for Restoration Architecture. The presentation has been reviewed by the marketing department and you need to resolve any comments and review the presentation for changes.

## What You Can Do

### Comparing Presentations

- You can use the Compare feature in PowerPoint 2010 to instantly see any changes to a presentation that you've sent out for review.

- Reviewers often make small changes to a presentation without bothering to add comments. The best way to spot these changes is using the compare feature to merge the presentations.

- When comparing presentations you can choose whether to keep a reviewer's changes.

## Try It!    **Comparing and Merging Presentations**

**1** Start PowerPoint and open the **PTry32_ studentfirstname_studentlastname** file that you worked with in the Try Its for Lesson 32.

**2** Save the file as **PTry33_studentfirstname_ studentlastname** in the location where your teacher instructs you to store the files for this lesson.

**3** Click Review > Compare 🔲.

**4** In the Choose File to Merge with Current Presentation window, select **PTry33** from the data files for this lesson and click Merge.

✓ Note that the presentation skips to slide 2 (the first one with a change) and that a Revisions pane opens along the right of the PowerPoint window showing changes.

**5** Save changes and leave **PTry33_ studentfirstname_studentlastname** open to use in the next Try It.

Merging two presentations

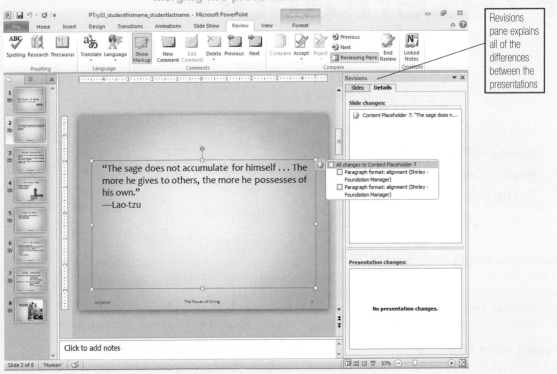

Revisions pane explains all of the differences between the presentations

## Try It!    **Reviewing Changes to a Presentation**

**1** In **PTry33_studentfirstname_ studentlastname**, click the Slides tab in the Revisions pane to see changes to the slides. Notice the difference in the alignment of the content on slide 2.

**2** Click the change indicator 🗒 on the slide to see a description of the changes. Select the third option to see that change on your slide.

*(continued)*

**Try It!**     **Reviewing Changes to a Presentation** *(continued)*

**3**   On the Review tab, click the Reject down arrow. Select Reject All Changes to the current slide.

**4**   Click Next in the Compare group to see the next change.

**5**   Click Review > Accept to keep the color change and click Next.

**6**   Click the change indicator to see the inserted content and click the box to see the change on your slide.

**7**   Click Review > Accept to keep the changes and click Next.

**8**   Click Cancel when PowerPoint asks if you want to start reviewing changes from the beginning.

**9**   Click Review > End Review. When prompted, click Yes.

**10**   Save changes, and leave the file open to use in the next Try It.

Rejecting changes to a slide

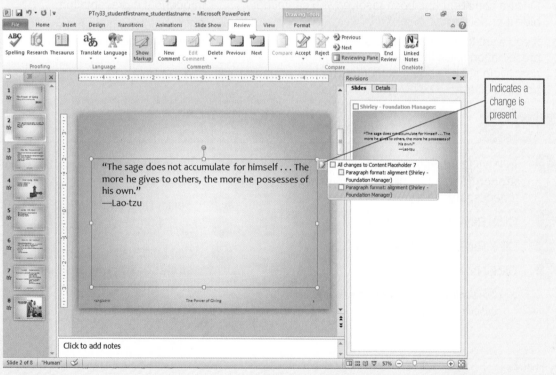

## Reviewing Comments

- You use the Comments group on the Review tab to work with comments and markup.
- When you open a presentation that contains comments, the comment markers display on the slides by default, and the Show Markup button is active on the Review tab.
- The name and initials that display on each comment are those of the current user. The date displayed is the current date.

- To read a comment that is not open, point to the comment marker to open the comment box.
- If you have a number of comments in a presentation, the Previous and Next buttons allow you to move quickly from comment to comment, opening each so you can read it.

**Try It!**     **Reviewing Comments**

**1**   In **PTry33_studentfirstname_ studentlastname**, select slide 6 and click Review > Next Comment 🗐.

**2**   Move to the end of the text in the content placeholder and press [ENTER].

**3**   Type **For the food bank**. Press [TAB]. Type **Pantry staples**.

**4**   Click Review > Next Comment 🗐 twice.

**5**   After you've read the comment on slide 5, press [ENTER] at the end of the first line in the content placeholder.

**6**   Press [TAB] and type **The foundation has an immediate need for a Webmaster**.

**7**   Save changes, and leave the file open to use in the next Try It.

## Deleting Comments

- Once a comment has been resolved you can either hide it or delete it.

- If you want to hide comments as you review a presentation, click the Show Markup button to deactivate it. The comment markers then disappear from the slides.

- The Delete button allows you to remove a single comment, all comments on a slide, or all comments throughout a presentation.

- Before you complete a presentation, you should make sure you've resolved and deleted every comment.

**Try It!**     **Deleting Comments**

**1**   In **PTry33_studentfirstname_ studentlastname**, click the comment on slide 5, if necessary.

**2**   Click Review > Next Comment 🗐.

**3**   Click Review > Delete 🗐.

**4**   Click Next Comment 🗐.

   ✓ *Click Continue when PowerPoint asks whether to continue from the beginning.*

**5**   On the Review tab, click the Delete down arrow 🗐.

**6**   Select Delete All Markup in this Presentation.

**7**   Click Yes to confirm the deletion.

**8**   Close **PTry33_studentfirstname_ studentlastname**, saving all changes, and exit PowerPoint.

Deleting all the comments in a presentation

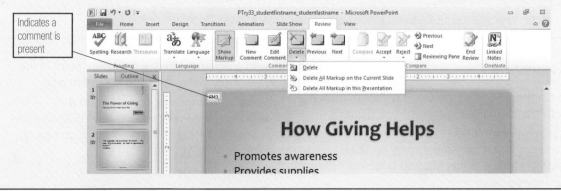

# Project 73—Create It

## Resolving Comments

### DIRECTIONS

1. Start PowerPoint, if necessary, and open **PProj73** from the data files for this lesson.

2. Save the file as **PProj73_studentfirstname_ studentlastname** in the location where your teacher instructs you to store the files for this lesson.

3. Click **Review > Next Comment** 🗂 in the Comments group to see the first change.

4. Read the comment.

5. Click **Design > Colors** ■ and right-click on **Couture**.

6. Select **Apply to Selected Slides**.

7. Select the comment again and click **Review > Delete Comment**.

8. Click **Review > Next Comment** 🗂 and read the comment.

9. Double-click the table on the slide to open the Excel Ribbon commands.

10. Click cell **A8** and type **Total**.

11. Click cell **B8** and click **Home > Sum** and press ENTER.

12. Click cell **C8** and repeat.

13. Select cells **A8:C8** and click **Home > Fill Color** 🎨. Select **Olive Green – Accent 3, Lighter 40%**.

14. Click outside of the table to return to the PowerPoint ribbon.

15. On the Review tab, click the **Delete Comment** down arrow 🗙 and select **Delete All Markup in this Presentation**.

16. Save the changes to the document.

17. **With your teacher's permission**, print slide 7. It should look similar to Figure 33-1.

18. Close the document, saving all changes, and exit PowerPoint.

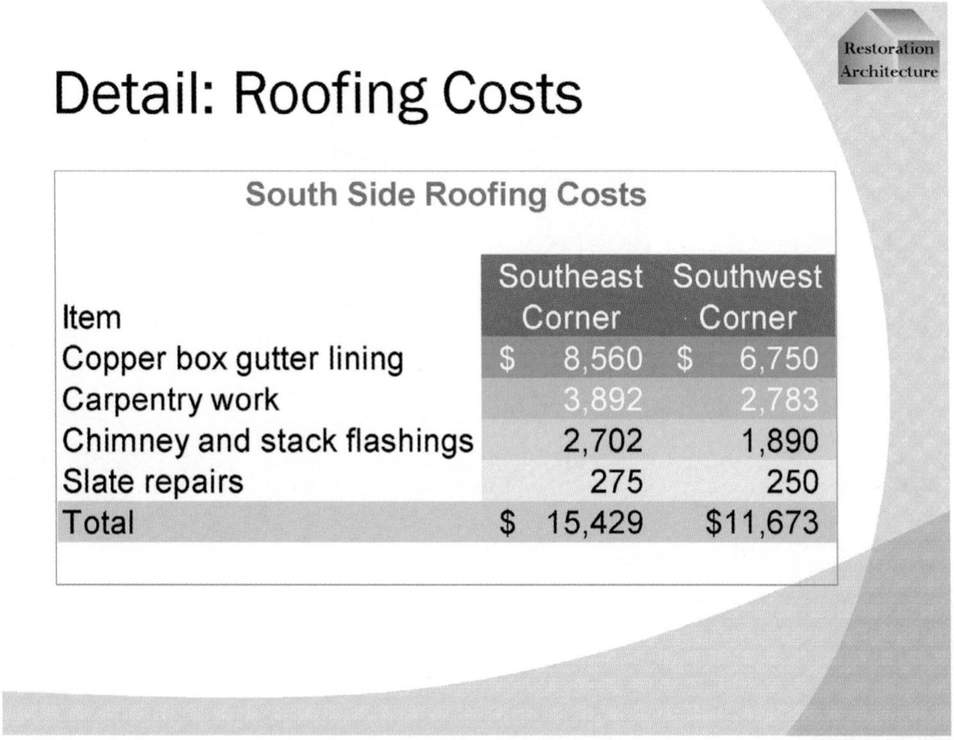

**Figure 33-1**

# Detail: Roofing Costs

| South Side Roofing Costs | | |
|---|---|---|
| Item | Southeast Corner | Southwest Corner |
| Copper box gutter lining | $ 8,560 | $ 6,750 |
| Carpentry work | 3,892 | 2,783 |
| Chimney and stack flashings | 2,702 | 1,890 |
| Slate repairs | 275 | 250 |
| Total | $ 15,429 | $11,673 |

Restoration Architecture

# Project 74—Apply It

## Comparing Presentations

### DIRECTIONS

1. Start PowerPoint, if necessary, and open **PProj74** from the data files for this lesson.

2. Save file as **PProj74_studentfirstname_ studentlastname** in the location where your teacher instructs you to store the files for this lesson.

3. Click **Review** > **Compare** 📄.

4. Select the file **PProj74_Reviewed** from the data files for this lesson.

5. Click **Merge**.

6. Click **Slides** in the Revisions pane.

7. Click **Review** > **Next Change** repeatedly to view each change until you return to slide 2.

8. Reject the change on slide 2.

9. Accept the changes on slides 3 and 4.

10. Reject the changes on slides 6 and 7.

11. Accept the change on slide 8.

12. Click **Review** > **End Review**.

13. Spell check the presentation.

14. **With your teacher's permission**, print slide 4. It should look similar to Figure 33-2.

15. Close the document, saving all changes, and exit PowerPoint.

**Figure 33-2**

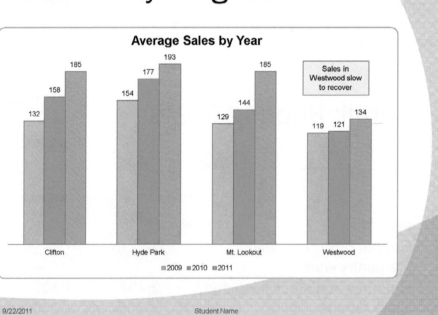

# Lesson 34

# Exporting Slide Handouts to Word

> **What You Will Learn**

**Exporting Handouts to Word**
**Linking Presentations to Word**

**Software Skills**   Send presentation materials to Microsoft Word to take advantage of Word's formatting options. You can also choose to link the presentation materials to a Word document. Handouts linked to a presentation will change automatically when the presentation is updated.

**Application Skills**   You will work with the presentation for Holmes Medical Center. In this lesson, you send the presentation data to Microsoft Word and create linked handouts.

## What You Can Do

### Exporting Handouts to Word

- You can send presentation data to Microsoft Word to create handouts or an outline. Exporting a presentation to Microsoft Word gives you the option of using Word's tools to format the handouts.

- You can modify the size of the slide images, format text, and add new text as desired to customize your handouts.

- Use the Create Handouts command on the Save and Send page in Backstage View to begin the process of sending materials to Word.

- The Send To Microsoft Word dialog box opens to allow you to select an export option.

- You have two options for positioning slide notes relative to the slide pictures and two options for placing blank lines that your audience can use to take their own notes.

- You can also choose to send only the outline. The exported outline retains the font used in the presentation and displays at a large point size.

**Try It!**        **Exporting Handouts to Word**

1. Start PowerPoint and open **PTry34** file from the data files for this lesson.

2. Save the file as **PTry34_studentfirstname_studentlastname** in the location where your teacher instructs you to store the files for this lesson.

3. Click File > Save & Send.

4. Click Create Handouts under File Types, and then click Create Handouts in the right pane.

5. Select Blank lines next to slides and Paste under Add slides to Microsoft Word document.

6. Click OK.

7. View the newly created Microsoft Word document to see how the handouts look. Close Microsoft Word without saving changes.

8. Save **PTry34_studentfirstname_studentlastname**, and leave the file open to use in the next Try It.

The Send To Microsoft Word dialog box

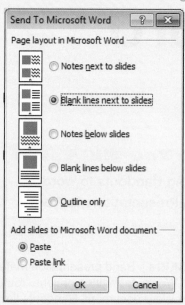

## Linking Presentations to Word

- If the presentation might change over time, the best option is to maintain a link between the handouts in Word and the material displayed on a slide.

- When you choose the Paste link option, you create a link between the Word document and the PowerPoint presentation. Any changes you save to the slides in PowerPoint will appear in the Word document.

✓ You do not have the paste/paste link options when exporting an outline.

- To create a link between your presentation and the handouts choose the Paste Link option in the Send to Microsoft Word dialog box.

**Try It!**        **Linking Presentations to Word**

1. In **PTry34_studentfirstname_studentlastname**, click File > Save & Send.

2. Click Create Handouts under File Types, and then click Create Handouts in the right pane.

*(continued)*

**Try It!**    **Linking Presentations to Word** *(continued)*

**3** Select Notes next to slides and Paste Link under Add slides to Microsoft Word document.

**4** Click OK.

**5** View the newly created Microsoft Word document to see how the handouts look.

**6** Return to **PTry34_studentfirstname_ studentlastname** and click Design > Colors ▇ > Pushpin.

**7** Close **PTry34_studentfirstname_ studentlastname**, saving all changes, and exit PowerPoint.

**8** Return to the Microsoft Word document and click File > Print.

**9** Save the file as **PTry34a_studentfirstname_ studentlastname** in the location where your teacher instructs you to store the files for this lesson.

**10** Close Microsoft Word.

**Updated linked handouts**

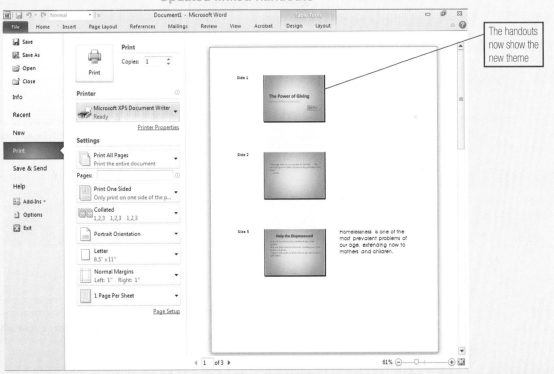

**Project 75—Create It**

## Creating Presentation Handouts in Word

**DIRECTIONS**

1. Start PowerPoint, if necessary, and open **PProj75** from the data files for this lesson.

2. Click **File > Save & Send**.

3. Click **Create Handouts** under File Types, and then click **Create Handouts** in the right pane.

4. Select **Notes next to slides**.

5. Select **Paste Link** under Add slides to Microsoft Word document and click **OK**.

6. Close PowerPoint without saving any changes.

7. View the newly created Microsoft Word document to see how the handouts look and save the file as **PProj75_studentfirstname_studentlastname**.

8. **With your teacher's permission**, print the document. It should look similar to Figure 34-1.

9. Close the document, saving all changes, and exit Word.

---

**Figure 34-1**

Slide 1

Welcome to Holmes Medical Center!

Slide 2

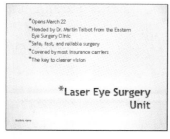

Give a brief summary of Dr. Talbot's experience with laser surgery.

Slide 3

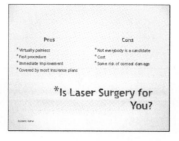

The pros usually outweigh the cons for most candidates.

# Project 76—Apply It

## Modifying Linked Handouts in Word

### DIRECTIONS

1. Start Wo
   studentf
   location
   ✓ *Click Ye*

2. Save the
   studentl
   teacher i
   lesson.

3. Double-
   the linke

4. Click De

5. Click **Home** > **Reset** to ensure the correct
   placement of elements.

*[Handwritten note overlay:]*
*Project 67 - 68*
*PROJ 76 NO Need*
*MOTHER BOARD*
*iphoe 6 screen*
*iphone 5s replan.*
*iphone 5 Screen*
*iphone 6 screen white box.*

6. Save the file as **PProj76a_studentfirstname_
   studentlastname** in the location where your
   teacher instructs you to store the files for this
   lesson and then close PowerPoint.

   Return to the Word document. Notice the updated
   slides.

   Click **Insert** > **Header** and choose **Tiles** from the
   list of built-in header styles.

   Click **[YEAR]** in the header.

   Click the down arrow and click **Today**.

   Click **[TYPE THE DOCUTMENT TITLE]** in the
   header and type your full name.

12. Click **Design** > **Close Header and Footer View**.

13. **With your teacher's permission**, print the
    document. It should look similar to Figure 34-2.

14. Close the document, saving all changes, and exit
    PowerPoint.

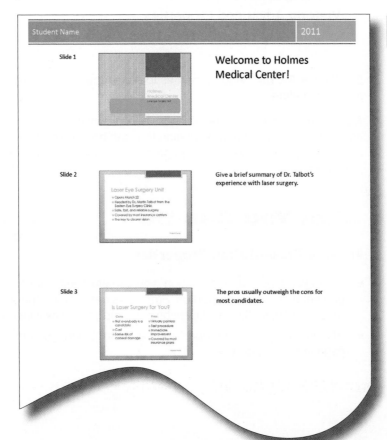

Figure 34-2

# Lesson 35

# Working with Presentation Properties

## ➤ What You Will Learn

**Viewing Presentation Properties**
**Entering or Editing Properties**
**Viewing Advanced Properties**

**Software Skills**   Add properties to a presentation to identify information about the presentation.

**Application Skills**   Planet Earth, a local environmental action group, has asked you to prepare a presentation that can be shown at your civic garden center to encourage city residents to "go green." In this lesson, you will add presentation properties.

## What You Can Do

### Viewing Presentation Properties

- When you create a presentation, you can store information about the presentation called properties. Properties can include the author of the presentation, its title, and keywords to help you quickly identify the presentation.

- After you have added properties to a presentation, you can view them on the Info page in Backstage View.

## Try It!    Viewing Document Properties in Backstage View

**1** Start PowerPoint and open **PTry35** file from the data files for this lesson.

**2** Save the file as **PTry35_studentfirstname_ studentlastname** in the location where your teacher instructs you to store the files for this lesson.

**3** Click File > Info.

**4** View the properties listed on in the Document Information pane on the right of the screen.

**5** Leave the presentation open to use in the next Try It.

Document properties in Backstage View

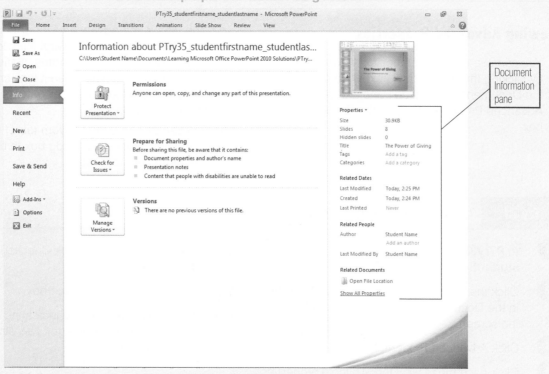

## Try It!    Viewing Document Properties Using the Document Information Panel

**1** In **PTry35_studentfirstname_ studentlastname**, click File > Info.

**2** Click the down arrow next to Properties in the Document Information pane.

**3** Click Show Document Panel.

**4** Leave the presentation open to use in the next Try It.

## Entering or Editing Properties

■ Document properties, which are sometimes referred to as *metadata*, are also an easy way to organize and locate files that have the same kinds of information. When searching for files, for example, you can use document properties as criteria in the search.

■ The Document Information Panel shows information that PowerPoint collects for you, such as the file location, as well as standard properties you supply yourself, such as the author, title, status, and any comments you want to add.

■ You can add properties using either the Document Information pane on the Info page in Backstage View or using the Document Information Panel.

**Try It!**        **Adding Document Properties**

**1** In **PTry35_studentfirstname_ studentlastname**, type your full name in the Author box.

**2** Type **Foundation Fundraiser** in the Subject box and **Draft** in the Status box.

**3** Close the Document Information Panel.

**4** Click File > Info.

**5** Type **Promotions** in the Tags box in the Document Information pane on the right of the screen.

**6** Save changes, and leave the file open to use in the next Try It.

## Viewing Advanced Properties

■ You can see more properties for a document by clicking the down arrow next to Properties in the Document Information Pane and selecting Advanced Properties to open the Properties dialog box.

■ The tabs in the Advanced Properties dialog box allow you to view general file information, a summary of current properties, statistics about the presentation, such as when it was created and how many slides it has, and the contents of all slides in the presentation.

■ You can also use the Custom tab of the Advanced Document Properties dialog box to create your own categories of properties.

**Try It!**        **Viewing Advanced Properties**

**1** In **PTry35_studentfirstname_ studentlastname**, click File > Info, if necessary.

**2** Click the down arrow to the right of Properties in the Document Information pane to the right of the screen.

**3** Click Advanced Properties.

**4** Click each tab to view the available properties.

**5** On the Custom tab, click Checked by in the Name list.

**6** Type **Shirley** in the Value box.

**7** Click Add to add a note indicating that Shirley, the Foundation's manager, has already reviewed the presentation.

*(continued)*

**Try It!**    **Viewing Advanced Properties** *(continued)*

**8** Click OK when finished viewing properties.

**9** Close **PTry35_studentfirstname_studentlastname**, saving all changes, and exit PowerPoint.

Working with Advanced Properties

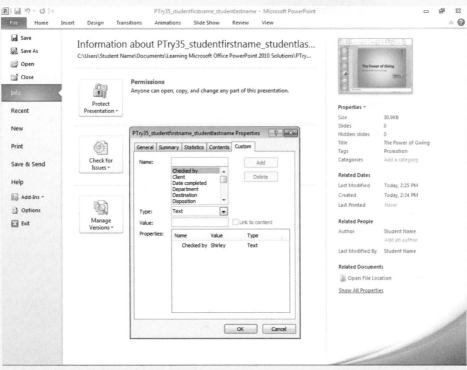

# Project 77—Create It

## Potential Cost Table

### DIRECTIONS

1. Start PowerPoint, if necessary, and open **PProj77** from the data files for this lesson.

2. Save the presentation as **PProj77_studentfirstname_studentlastname** in the location where your teacher instructs you to store the files for this lesson.

3. Click **File** > **Info**.

4. Click **Add an author** in the Document Information pane on the right of the screen.

5. Type your full name.

6. Click **Add a title** in the same pane and type **Going Green**.

7. Click **Add a tag** and type **lawn, organic, composting**. Your presentation should look similar to Figure 35-1.

8. Close the document, saving all changes, and exit PowerPoint.

Figure 35-1

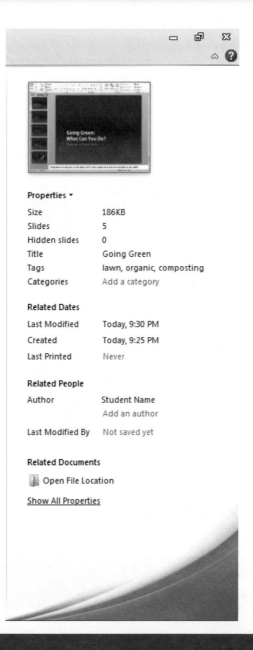

Properties ▾

| | |
|---|---|
| Size | 186KB |
| Slides | 5 |
| Hidden slides | 0 |
| Title | Going Green |
| Tags | lawn, organic, composting |
| Categories | Add a category |

**Related Dates**

| | |
|---|---|
| Last Modified | Today, 9:30 PM |
| Created | Today, 9:25 PM |
| Last Printed | Never |

**Related People**

| | |
|---|---|
| Author | Student Name |
| | Add an author |
| Last Modified By | Not saved yet |

**Related Documents**

Open File Location

Show All Properties

# Project 78—Apply It

## Adding Custom Properties

### DIRECTIONS

1. Start PowerPoint, if necessary, and open **PProj78** from the data files for this lesson.

2. Save the file as **PProj78_studentfirstname_ studentlastname** in the location where your teacher instructs you to store the files for this lesson.

3. Click **File** > **Info**.

4. Click the arrow next to the word **Properties** in the pane and select **Show Document Panel**.

5. Type **Green Strategies** in the Subject box.

6. Type **In progress** in the Status box.

7. Type **Public Presentations** in the Category box.

8. Close the Document Information Panel and click **File** > **Info**.

9. Click the arrow next to the word **Properties** in the pane and select **Advanced Properties**.

10. On the Custom tab, click **Checked by** from the Name list, as shown in Figure 35-2.

11. In the Value box, type your full name.

12. Click **Add** and then **OK**.

13. Close the document, saving all changes, and exit PowerPoint.

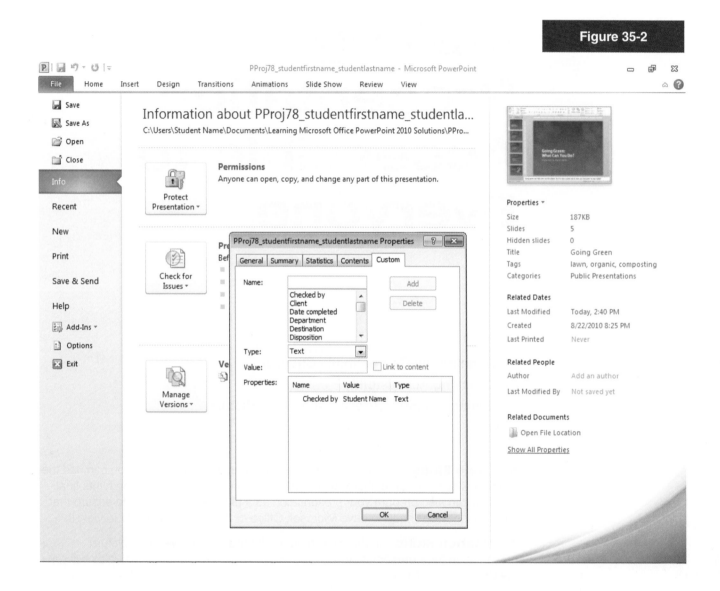

**Figure 35-2**

# Lesson 36

# Making a Presentation Accessible to Everyone

> **What You Will Learn**

**Running the Compatibility Checker**
**Checking Accessibility**
**Saving a Slide or Presentation As a Picture**

**Software Skills**   If you need to share a presentation with others, you can use the Compatibility Checker to check accessibility and prepare a presentation for its final use. You can also prepare your presentation as a picture presentation to ensure that the recipient won't need to have Microsoft Office or the Internet in order to view it.

**Application Skills**   In this lesson, you will prepare a PowerPoint picture presentation for a presentation you created for Thorn Hill Gardens. You also will run the Compatibility Checker.

## What You Can Do

### Running the Compatibility Checker

- The Compatibility Checker is a tool designed to flag features in your current presentation that are not supported in previous PowerPoint versions.
- Always run the Compatibility Checker before saving to an earlier version of PowerPoint, because some of PowerPoint 2010's effects cannot be edited in previous versions of the program.

■ When you click Run Compatibility Checker from the Info page in Backstage View, the Compatibility Checker reviews each slide for compatibility issues and then displays a report.

■ The report tells you any compatibility issues, such as a SmartArt graphic that cannot be edited in earlier versions of PowerPoint, lets you know how many times the issue occurs, and offers a Help link that provides more information about the issue.

■ You'll want to go through each slide listed and look for the compatibility issues.

■ In most cases, nothing needs to be done. The compatibility issues will not compromise the look of the slides when they are shown in other versions of PowerPoint.

✓ *For example, although you will not be able to edit a SmartArt graphic, its components are saved as pictures that will display the same way they do in PowerPoint 2010.*

■ The help files offer advice on how to modify PowerPoint 2010 features to improve compatibility. For example, you can convert a SmartArt graphic to separate shapes so that you can edit them in any version of PowerPoint.

---

**Try It!**     **Running the Compatibility Checker**

**1** Start PowerPoint and open **PTry36** from the data files for this lesson.

**2** Save the file as **PTry36_studentfirstname_studentlastname** in the location where your teacher instructs you to store the files for this lesson.

**3** Click File > Info.

**4** Under Prepare for Sharing, click Check for Issues > Check Compatibility.

**5** Click OK.

**6** Look through the slides listed (1, 2, 3, 4, 5, 6, & 7).

✓ *Note that on some slides (such as 1 and 3) the compatibility issue is obvious. On other slides there is no visible problem.*

**7** Since none of these issues will cause a problem, you decide to leave the presentation as is.

**8** Leave the presentation open to use in the next Try It.

The Compatibility Checker dialog box

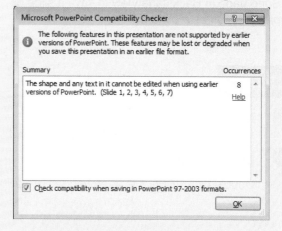

---

## Checking Accessibility

■ The Accessibility Checker looks for places in your presentation that could potentially make it difficult for someone with disabilities to view the entire presentation.

■ When the Accessibility Checker finds problems, it will open a task pane listing each issue and classifying them as Errors, Warnings, or Tips.

● Errors are extremely difficult, if not impossible, for someone with disabilities to understand.

● Warnings are places where the content might be difficult for people with disabilities to understand.

● Tips are suggestions about places that can be modified to make it easier for someone with disabilities to understand.

■ When the Accessibility Checker finds problems, it will provide you with instructions that you can use to eliminate the problems.

■ You can choose whether you want to resolve the issues found or leave the presentation as is.

**Try It!**    **Checking Accessibility**

**1** In **PTry36_studentfirstname_ studentlastname**, click File > Info.

**2** Under Prepare for Sharing, click Check for Issues > Check Accessibility.

**3** Click on each issue located and read the Additional Information box at the bottom of the task pane.

**4** Follow the instructions in the Additional Information box to resolve each issue.

**5** Save changes, and leave the presentation open to use in the next Try It.

## Saving a Slide or Presentation As a Picture

■ You can save a single slide or an entire presentation in a graphic file format that allows you to insert the slides as pictures in other applications, such as Word documents.

■ By saving a slide or presentation as a picture you can ensure that it is viewable by anyone with a computer regardless of whether they have a Mac or PC, or what version of software they are using.

■ Use the Change File Type option on the Save & Send page in Backstage View to save a slide or presentation as a picture.

■ You can choose among four picture file formats. PNG and JPEG are listed on the Change File Type page. If you prefer GIF or TIFF, you can use the Save As button at the bottom of the pane and choose either option in the File as Type box.

■ Once you have provided a name for the new file, selected a format, and PowerPoint displays a dialog box to ask if you want to save only the current slide or every slide in the current presentation.

■ The resulting files can be used just like any other picture file.

**Try It!**    **Saving a Slide As a Picture**

**1** In **PTry36_studentfirstname_ studentlastname**, click File > Save & Send.

**2** Under File Types, click Change file type.

**3** Double click JPEG File Interchange Format.

**4** Save changes to **PTry36_studentfirstname_ studentlastname** in the location where your teacher instructs you to store the files for this lesson.

**5** Select Current Slide Only at the prompt.

**6** Save changes to **PTry36_studentfirstname_ studentlastname**, close the file, and exit PowerPoint.

Save a slide as a picture

# Project 79—Create It

## Checking the Compatibility of a Presentation

### DIRECTIONS

1. Start PowerPoint, if necessary, and open **PProj79** from the data files for this lesson.

2. Save the presentation as **PProj79_ studentfirstname_studentlastname** in the location where your teacher instructs you to store the files for this lesson.

3. Click **File** > **Info**.

4. Under Prepare for Sharing, click **Check for Issues** > **Check Compatibility**.

5. Read the error and click **OK**.

6. Click on slide 4 to view the SmartArt graphic identified by the compatibility checker.

7. Since the organization chart will not need to be modified in a previous version of PowerPoint you decide to leave it as is.

8. Close the document, saving all changes, and exit PowerPoint.

# Project 80—Apply It

## Checking the Accessibility of a Presentation

### DIRECTIONS

1. Start PowerPoint, if necessary, and open **PProj80** from the data files for this lesson.

2. Save the presentation as **PProj80_ studentfirstname_studentlastname** in the location where your teacher instructs you to store the files for this lesson.

3. Create a slide footer with an automatically updating date and your full name.

4. Click **File** > **Info**.

5. Under Prepare for Sharing, click **Check for Issues** > **Check Accessibility**.

6. Click on the first error listed (Picture 3) and right-click the picture on slide 2.

7. Select **Format Picture** and click **Alt Text**.

8. Type **Lily pond in the garden** in the **Title** box and click **Close**.

9. Click on the next error listed and right-click the object on slide 4.

10. Select **Format Object** and click **Alt Text**.

11. Type **Organizational Chart** in the **Title** box and click **Close**.

12. Click on the tip listed in the Accessibility Checker pane and read the Additional Information.

13. Follow the instructions to organize the reading order as shown in Figure 36-1.

14. Click the **✗** button to close the Accessibility Checker pane.

15. Click **File** > **Save & Send** > **Change File Type** > **JPEG File Interchange Format** > **Save As**.

16. Name the file **PProj80_studentfirstname_ studentlastname**. Choose **CurrentSlide Only**.

17. Close the document, saving all changes, and exit PowerPoint.

**Figure 36-1**

**Opportunity Knocks**

- Money is currently available to fund one or more new features
- New feature(s) should enhance visitor experience; for example, visitors might want to:
  - Learn more about horticulture in a library
  - Purchase high-quality merchandise related to the site in a gift shop
  - Relax and enjoy the atmosphere while eating or drinking

Student Name                                                    4/22/2011

# Chapter Assessment and Application

## Project 81—Make It Your Own

### Reviewing Comments and Finalizing a Presentation

You've been working on a presentation for Voyager Travel Adventures about their newest adventure location, Glacier National Park. You sent the draft of the presentation to your boss, Jan Weeks. In this project, you'll review her comments and make any necessary changes to the presentation so that you can submit the final presentation.

### DIRECTIONS

1. Start PowerPoint, if necessary, and open **PProj81** from the data files for this project.

2. Save the presentation as **PProj81a_ studentfirstname_studentlastname** in the location where your teacher instructs you to store the files for this project.

3. Click **Review > Next Comment** and read the remarks.

4. Click **Review > Next Comment** to read the comment on slide 6 of the presentation.

5. On the slide tab, right-click slide 6 and choose **Duplicate Slide**.

6. Select the comment and click **Review > Delete Comment**.

7. Select the slide title and type **Fauna**.

8. Select the first image and click **Picture Tools Format > Change Picture** 🖼.

9. Select one of the **PProj81_fauna** pictures from the data files for this lesson.

10. Repeat this process for each picture on this slide. The order of the images is not important.

11. Click **Review > Next Comment** and read the next comment.

12. To resolve this comment, click **Insert > Picture** and select the **PProj81_glacier** picture from the data files for this lesson.

13. Adjust the size and spacing of the elements on this slide as shown in Illustration A.

14. Click **Review > Delete > Delete All Markup in this Presentation** to remove all remaining comments.

15. Click **File > Save** 🖫 and then click the **File** tab again.

16. Click **Check for Issues** and select **Check Compatibility**. Since these graphics and smart art elements won't need to be changed in 97-2003 format you can just click **OK** to close the box.

17. Click **File > Save & Send**.

18. Click **Create Handouts** under File Types, and then click **Create Handouts** in the right pane.

19. Select **Blank lines** next to slides and **Paste**. Click **OK**.

20. Add a slide footer that includes a date that updates automatically, and your full name. Apply the footer to all slides.

21. In the Word document, change the margins to **Narrow**.

23. Insert an **Austere (Odd Page)** header to the Word document with your full name as the title. Save the Word document as **PProj81b_studentfirstname_ studentlastname**.

23. **With your teacher's permission**, print the handouts. They should look similar to Illustration B.

24. Close Word and PowerPoint, saving all your changes.

**Illustration A**

**Illustration B**

# Project 82—Master It

## Creating a Kiosk Presentation

Peterson Home Health Care has asked you to create a presentation that can be used at local health fairs to give viewers information about the company's home health care options. You will start work on that presentation in this project.

### DIRECTIONS

1. Start PowerPoint, if necessary, and open **PProj82** from the data files for this project.

2. Save the presentation as **PProj82_ studentfirstname_studentlastname** in the location where your teacher instructs you to store the files for this project.

3. Click **View** > **Slide Master** 🖻.

4. On the slide master make the following changes.
   a. Select the title placeholder and change the font to **Corbel**.
   b. Select the content placeholder and change the font to **Calibri**.
   c. Change the color of headings to **Black, Text 1**.

5. On the title slide master, make the following changes.
   a. Move the subtitle placeholder to the right to align at the right side with the title placeholder.
   b. Change the alignment of both the title and subtitle to right alignment.
   c. Click **Drawing Tools Format** > **More** and select a Shape Style of your choice to the title placeholder.
   d. Insert an appropriate figure.

6. Add a complementary slide master.

7. On the new slide master's two content master, insert a narrow rectangle shape along the inside edge of the right hand content placeholder. Adjust the position of the shape to leave room between it and the picture, and to be as tall as the content placeholder. Apply a Quick Style of your choice to the rectangle shape. Your slide should look similar to Illustration A.

8. Display the notes page master and make the following changes to the master.
   a. Apply different theme colors and theme fonts that complement the presentation's appearance.
   b. Change the background style to **Style 10**.
   c. Apply a Quick Style of your choice to the Notes placeholder.
   d. Change the size of the text in the placeholder to **14 point**.

9. Apply the new slide master, two content layout to slides 4 and 5. Make any changes necessary to the size and format of the slide contents to match the new master. Your slides should look similar to Illustration B.

10. Open the Document Information Panel and add the following properties to the presentation.
    **Author: Your full name**
    **Title: Our Reputation**
    **Category: Kiosk presentations**
    **Status: In progress**

11. **With your teacher's permission**, print the presentation.

12. Close and save all files.

**Illustration A**

**Illustration B**

## Chapter 6

# Applying Advanced Graphics and Media Techniques

## Lesson 37
## Advanced Picture Formatting
## Projects 83-84

- Understanding Picture Formats
- Applying Advanced Picture Formatting
- Adding a Border to a Picture

## Lesson 38
## Advanced Multimedia
## Features
## Projects 85-86

- Understanding Multimedia Presentations
- Embedding a Web Video in a Presentation
- Setting Advanced Video Options
- Setting Advanced Sound Options

## Lesson 39
## Working with Advanced
## Photo Album Features
## Projects 87-88

- Editing a Photo Album
- Adding Captions
- Compressing Pictures

## Lesson 40
## Advanced Animation
## Features
## Projects 89-90

- Applying Advanced Animation Effects
- Creating a Motion Path Animation
- Changing the Order of Animation Effects
- Applying Advanced Effect Options
- Adjusting Animation Timing
- Working with the Animation Timeline
- Changing or Removing an Animation

## Lesson 41
## Finalizing Slide Shows
## Projects 91-92

- Creating Presentation Sections
- Adding Narration to a Presentation

## Lesson 42
## Working with Actions
## Projects 93-94

- Using Advanced Hyperlink Settings
- Working with Action Settings

## End-of-Chapter Assessments
## Projects 95-96

# Lesson 37

# Advanced Picture Formatting

## WORDS TO KNOW

**Bitmap image**
Graphic created from arrangements of small squares called *pixels*. Also called raster images.

**Lossless compression**
Compression accomplished without loss of data.

**Lossy compression**
Compression in which part of a file's data is discarded to reduce file size.

**Pixel**
Term that stands for picture element, a single point on a computer monitor screen.

**Vector image**
Drawings made up of lines and curves defined by vectors, which describe an object mathematically according to its geometric characteristics.

## ➤ What You Will Learn

**Understanding Picture Formats**
**Applying Advanced Picture Formatting**
**Adding a Border to a Picture**

**Software Skills**    Understanding picture formats helps you select an appropriate file type for your presentation. Advanced formatting options such as brightness and contrast adjustments and recoloring options allow you to create sophisticated picture effects.

**Application Skills**    Thorn Hill Gardens wants to run a presentation on a kiosk at the main entrance advertising the annual Butterfly Show. In this exercise, you add several pictures to a presentation and format pictures according to file type.

## What You Can Do

### Understanding Picture Formats

- PowerPoint 2010 can accept a number of picture formats, including both **bitmap** and **vector** images.

- Understanding the advantages and disadvantages of these common graphic file formats can help you choose pictures for your presentations.

- The following table lists some of the more common formats that PowerPoint supports, with their file extensions.

- When selecting pictures, consider the following:

  - If you plan on displaying it only on a screen, GIF and JPEG files will provide a good-quality appearance.

**Table 37-1**

| Format | Extension | Characteristics |
|--------|-----------|-----------------|
| WMF | .wmf | Windows Metafile. Contains both bitmap and vector information and is optimized for use in Windows applications. |
| PNG | .png | Portable Network Graphic. A bitmap format that supports lossless compression and allows transparency; no color limitations. |
| BMP | .bmp | Windows Bitmap. Does not support file compression so files may be large; widely compatible with Windows programs. |
| GIF | .gif | Graphics Interchange Format. A widely supported bitmap format that uses lossless compression; maximum of 256 colors; allows transparency. |
| JPEG | .jpg | Joint Photographic Experts Group. A bitmap format that allows a tradeoff of lossy compression and quality; best option for photographs and used by most digital cameras. |
| TIFF | .tif | Tagged Image File Format. Can be compressed or uncompressed; uncompressed file sizes may be very large. Most widely used format for print publishing; not supported by Web browsers. |

- If you plan to print your slide materials, you may want to use TIFF images for better-quality printed appearance.

- For small graphics with a limited number of colors, for example, a picture in GIF or PNG format will be perfectly adequate.

- Photographs, on the other hand, should be saved in JPEG or TIFF format.

  ✓ *Remember the higher the picture quality, the larger the presentation's file size.*

- You can modify file size by compressing pictures you have inserted in the presentation.

## Applying Advanced Picture Formatting

- The Picture Styles gallery on the Picture Tools Format tab is the easiest way to change the shape and appearance of a picture on a slide.

- Other options on this tab allow you to create interesting and unusual picture effects as well as specify a precise size.

- Use the tools in the Adjust group to modify the appearance of the image. Some of these tools provide menus of preset adjustments; you may also have the option of opening a dialog box for more control over the adjustment.

- Use the Corrections options to adjust the brightness and contrast of the image.

- The Color Option allows you to modify the colors in an image using a variety of different tint options.

- You can also select the Set Transparent Color command on the Color gallery to make one of the image's colors transparent.

- When you click this command, a paintbrush icon attaches to the pointer. Click on the color you want to make transparent and all pixels of that color are removed to allow the background to show through.

- The Change Picture option reopens the Insert Picture dialog box so you can replace the currently selected picture with a different one.

- Use the Reset Picture option to restore a picture's original settings. Clicking this button reverses any changes you have made to size, brightness, contrast, or color.

**Try It!**    **Making Part of a Graphic Transparent**

**1** Start PowerPoint and open **PTry37** from the data files for this lesson.

**2** Save the file as **PTry37_studentfirstname_studentlastname** in the location where your teacher instructs you to store the files for this lesson.

*(continued)*

**Try It!**    **Making Part of a Graphic Transparent** *(continued)*

**3** Click on the graphic on slide 2.

**4** Click Picture Tools Format > Color and then click Set Transparent Color.

    ✓ *The cursor will change to a pointing wand. Aim the tip of the wand at the color in the object you want to make transparent.*

**5** Click the white background on the graphic.

**6** Save changes, and leave the file open to use in the next Try It.

Making part of a graphic transparent

# The Pilot Project
ॐ

    ॐ A goal of our organization is grass-roots participation in strategies to save our planet

    ॐ The Eco-Sales Pilot Project was conceived to help our community put green strategies in place

    ॐ A survey was conducted to determine which of a number of fairly simple green strategies our neighbors would support

---

**Try It!**    **Recoloring a Picture**

**1** In **PTry37_studentfirstname_studentlast name**, click the clip art image on slide 2, if necessary.

**2** Click Picture Tools Format > Color.

**3** Click Green, Accent color 1, Light from the Recolor group.

**4** Save changes, and leave the file open to use in the next Try It.

Changing the color of a graphic

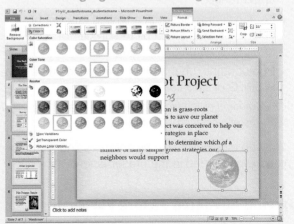

---

**Try It!**    **Adjusting Brightness and Contrast**

**1** In **PTry37_studentfirstname_studentlast name**, click the photo in slide 6.

**2** On the Picture Tools Format tab, click the Corrections button.

**3** Under Brightness and Contrast, select Brightness: +20% Contrast: +40%.

**4** Save changes, and leave the file open to use in the next Try It.

*(continued)*

---

**Try It!** | **Adjusting Brightness and Contrast** (continued)

Correcting the brightness and contrast of a graphic

---

**Try It!** | **Resetting a Graphic to Normal**

1. In **PTry37_studentfirstname_studentlast name**, click the clip art image in slide 6, if necessary.

2. Click Picture Tools Format > Reset Picture.

3. Save changes, and leave the file open to use in the next Try It.

---

**Try It!** | **Applying a Picture Style to a Graphic**

1. In **PTry37_studentfirstname_studentlast name**, click the clip art image in slide 6, if necessary.

2. Click Picture Tools Format > More in the Picture Styles group.

3. Select Drop Shadow Rectangle.

   ✓ *Live Preview enables you to see the effect of a style by hovering over the option.*

4. Save changes, and leave the file open to use in the next Try It.

---

## Adding a Border to a Picture

■ Another way to add emphasis to a graphic is to apply a border to it.

■ Use the Picture Border button on the Picture Tools Format tab to add a border to a graphic.

■ When you use the Picture Border button, a gallery of border colors that coordinate with your theme opens.

■ Alternatively, you can choose More Outline Colors at the bottom of the gallery to open a dialog box that lets you select any possible color.

■ You can also control the weight of the outline and give it a pattern.

---

### Try It!    Adding a Border to a Picture

**1** In **PTry37_studentfirstname_studentlast name**, click the clip art image in slide 6, if necessary.

**2** Click Picture Tools Format > Picture Border in the Picture Styles group.

**3** Select Light Blue in the Standard group.

**4** Click Picture Tools Format > Picture Border > Weight and select 3 pt.

**5** Close the file, saving all changes, and exit PowerPoint.

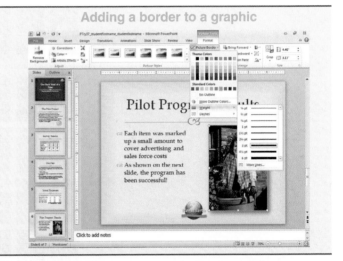

Adding a border to a graphic

---

# Project 83—Create It

## Kiosk Presentation Graphics

### DIRECTIONS

1. Start PowerPoint, if necessary, and open **PProj83** from the data files for this lesson.

2. Save the file as **PProj83_studentfirstname_ studentlastname** in the location where your teacher instructs you to store the files for this lesson.

3. Select slide 1 and click **Insert > Picture** .

4. Open **PProj83a** from the data files for this lesson.

5. With the image selected, click **Picture Tools Format > Crop** .

6. Drag the left center cropping handle to the right **1.5** inches until the width is approximately **4.5** inches.

7. Click **Picture Tools Format > Crop** .

8. Right-click the image and select **Format Picture** to open the Format Picture dialog box.

9. Click **Size** and then in the **Scale** area, type **75%** in the Height box and press ENTER.

10. With the image selected, click **Picture Tools Format > More** in the Picture Styles group. Select **Soft Edge Oval**.

11. Click **Picture Tools Format > Color** and select **Blue-Grey, Accent Color 6, Dark**.

12. Drag the image to position as shown in Figure 37-1.

13. Insert a footer with your full name in it for all slides.

14. **With your teacher's permission**, print the document. It should look similar to Figure 37-1.

15. Close the file, saving all changes, and exit PowerPoint.

Figure 37-1

Thorn Hill Gardens Presents . . . .

Butterflies in the Round!

Student Name

# Project 84—Apply It

## Kiosk Presentation Graphics

### DIRECTIONS

1. Start PowerPoint, if necessary, and open **PProj84** from the data files for this lesson.

2. Save the file as **PProj84_studentfirstname_ studentlastname** in the location where your teacher instructs you to store the files for this lesson.

3. Select slide 3 and insert the JPEG picture file **PProj84a** in the content placeholder.

4. Format the picture as follows.
   a. Adjust the brightness to make the picture **20%** brighter. Adjust the contrast to **+40%**.
   b. Apply a **Drop Shadow Rectangle** picture style. Your slide should look similar to Figure 37-2.

5. Select slide 4, and insert the JPEG picture file **PProj84b** in the content placeholder.

6. Format the picture as follows.
   a. Apply a correction to sharpen the image **50%**.
   b. Apply a **Drop Shadow Rectangle** picture style.
   c. Increase the contrast by **20%**.
   d. Apply a picture border using the color **Teal, Accent 2, Darker 25%.**

7. Select the clip art on slide 2. Recolor it using **Lime, Accent color 1, Light**.

8. The resulting clip isn't very exciting. Reset the picture to its original appearance, then make the background brown color transparent.

9. Apply the **Teal, Accent color 2, Light** color effect.

10. Add a footer with your full name.

11. **With your teacher's permission**, print the document.

12. Close the file, saving all changes, and exit PowerPoint.

**Figure 37-2**

# Lesson 38

# Advanced Multimedia Features

➤ **What You Will Learn**

**Understanding Multimedia Presentations**
**Embedding a Web Video in a Presentation**
**Setting Advanced Video Options**
**Setting Advanced Sound Options**

**WORDS TO KNOW**

**Multimedia**
Presentation of information using a variety of media such as text, still images, animation, video, and audio.

**Software Skills**   To make a presentation "come alive," use multimedia content such as animation, movies, and sounds. Media clips can add considerable impact to a presentation as well as convey information in ways that other graphic objects cannot.

**Application Skills**   Voyager Adventure Travel is beginning the task of adding a new hiking package to its list of adventures. The decision-making process requires consideration of both pros and cons for each suggested venue, and you have been asked to prepare a slide show to present the information. In this lesson, you will begin work on the presentation with pros and cons for Glacier National Park.

## What You Can Do

### Understanding Multimedia Presentations

- **Multimedia** presentations display information in a variety of media, including text, pictures, movies, animations, and sounds.

- Multimedia content not only adds visual and audio interest to slides but also presents information in ways that plain text cannot. A simple picture can convey an image that would take many words to describe; likewise, a movie can show a process or sequence of events that might take many pictures to convey.

- You can choose how much or how little multimedia content to include in a presentation.

- When deciding on multimedia options for a presentation, you must consider the trade-off between multimedia impact and the presentation's file size. Multimedia files such as videos and sounds can be quite large.

- You also need appropriate computer resources, such as speakers and video or sound cards to play media files successfully.

- Use good research standards when locating multimedia content. Always request permission to use materials you may find on the Internet, or follow directives for crediting persons or agencies.

- When creating a presentation for personal use, you can use CD music tracks for background sound, but you should not use such copyrighted materials if you plan to present your presentation to a public audience or publish it on the Web.

- If you decide to include multimedia content in a presentation, you will find that PowerPoint offers a number of options for playing both movies and sounds.

## Embedding a Video from the Web in a Presentation

- You have three options for adding a video to your presentation:
  - Insert an animated clip art graphic.
  - Insert a movie file saved in a format such as AVI or MPEG.
  - Insert a movie from the Web.

- You can embed a video from the Web using the Video button on the Insert tab.

- When you insert a video from the Web, the Video Tools Format and Video Tools Playback tabs open.

- When you insert a video, a small star symbol appears next to the slide's thumbnail in the slide tab. This symbol signifies the file is animated.

- To see the animation in motion, display the slide in Slide Show view or click Video Tools Format > Play.

---

**Try It!**    **Embedding a Web Video in a Presentation**

1. Start PowerPoint and open **PTry38** file from the data files for this lesson.

2. Save the file as **PTry38_studentfirstname_ studentlastname** in the location where your teacher instructs you to store the files for this lesson.

3. Open your Internet browser and navigate to *http://www.youtube.com/watch?v=vdvksW6RAWs*.

   ✓ This video is copyright-free. Be sure to only use videos that are copyright-free. If you are unsure, do an Internet search for "copyright-free videos."

4. Under the video screen, click <Embed> to open a box containing the embed code for this video.

5. Press CTRL + C to copy the embed code.

6. In the presentation, select slide 9 and click Insert > Video down arrow.

7. Select Video from Web site to open the Insert Video From a Web Site dialog box.

8. In the Insert Video From Web Site box, press CTRL + V.

9. Click Insert.

10. Close the browser window, save the changes to the **PTry38_studentfirstname_ studentlastname** file, and leave it open to use in the next Try It.

Using embed code to insert a video from a Web site

## Setting Advanced Video Options

■ You need to understand video formats to determine the quality of video clips you intend to insert. A file in MPEG1 format, for example, is not likely to display with the same quality as an MPEG2 file, but it will be smaller in size.

■ PowerPoint does not support some popular video formats, such as QuickTime or RealMedia files.

**Table 38-1**

| Format | Extension | Characteristics |
|--------|-----------|-----------------|
| ASF | .asf | Advanced Streaming Format. Microsoft's streaming format that can contain video, audio, slide shows, and other synchronized content. |
| AVI | .avi | Audio/Video Interleave. A file format that stores alternating (interleaved) sections of audio and video content; widely used for playing video with sound on Windows systems; AVI is a container (a format that stores different types of data), not a form of compression. |
| MPEG | .mpg, .mpeg | Moving Picture Experts Group. A standard format for lossy audio and visual compression that comes in several formats, such as MPEG1 (CD quality) and MPEG2 (DVD quality). |
| WMV | .wmv | Windows Media Video. Microsoft's lossy compression format for motion video; it results in files that take up little room on a system. |

■ Once you have selected and inserted a video clip, you can use the tools on the Video Tools Playback tab to work with a movie.

■ Use the Play button in the Preview group to preview the movie while in Normal view.

■ The Video Tools Playback options give you more control over how the movie plays during the presentation.

- Change the play setting using the Start list. You can play the movie automatically, when clicked, or set the movie to continue playing as you continue to display later slides.

- You can choose to hide the movie during the show, play it at full screen size, loop it (play it over and over) until you stop it by pressing ESC, or return the movie to its first frame after it has finished playing.

■ Use the Volume button to control the playback of the individual video clip within the overall presentation.

■ The Fade Duration settings allow you to ease into and out of video playback. Depending on the video contents, this can be less jarring to the viewer.

■ Using the Video Tools Playback tab you can trim an inserted video so that only a small portion of the video plays.

**Try It!**    **Setting Advanced Video Options**

1. In **PTry38_studentfirstname_studentlastname**, select the video on slide 5.

2. On the Video Tools Playback tab, add a timed fade to the beginning of your video by clicking the up arrows to increase the Fade In time to 00.50.

3. Click Video Tools Playback > Start
   Start: On Click ▾ down arrow.

4. Select Automatically.

5. Click Video Tools Playback > Play ▶ to watch the video.

6. Save changes, and leave the file open to use in the next Try It.

*(continued)*

**Try It!**    **Setting Advanced Video Options** *(continued)*

The Video Tools Playback tab

**Try It!**    **Trimming a Video**

**1**   In **PTry38_studentfirstname_studentlast name**, select the video on slide 5.

**2**   Click Video Tools Playback > Trim Video.

**3**   In the Trim Video dialog box, drag the green start indicator ▮ to the right until the Start Time indicates approximately 00:02:50.

**OR**

Click in the Start Time box and type **00:02:50**.

**4**   Drag the End Time indicator ▮ to the left until the End Time box shows 00:15:00.

**OR**

Click in the End Time box and type **00:15:00**.

**5**   Click OK.

**6**   Save changes, and leave the file open to use in the next Try It.

Trimming a video

## Setting Advanced Sound Options

- Use the Audio Tools Playback tab to control sound options.

- Many of these options look similar to those on the Video Tools Playback tab and operate in the same way. For example, you can use Play to listen to the sound in Normal view and use the Audio Options group tools to hide the sound icon, loop the sound, or adjust the play setting.

## Try It!  Setting Advanced Sound Options

**1** In **PTry38_studentfirstname_student lastname**, select the audio clip on slide 9.

**2** On the Audio Tools Playback tab, add a timed fade to the beginning of your audio by clicking the up arrows to increase the Fade In time to 00.25.

**3** Click Audio Tools Playback > Volume 🔊 down arrow and select Medium.

**4** Click Audio Tools Playback > Loop until Stopped.

**5** Save changes, and leave the file open to use in the next Try It.

The Audio Tools Playback tab

## Try It!  Setting a Trigger for an Embedded Sound

**1** In **PTry38_studentfirstname_student lastname**, select the audio clip on slide 9, if necessary.

**2** Click Audio Tools Playback > Start 🔊 Start: On Click down arrow.

**3** Select Automatically.

**4** Click Slide Show > From Beginning 🖥 to watch the show.

✓ Note that because the video on slide 9 is embedded, you will need to click the screen once to open the video controls and then click on the video again to start the playback.

**5** Close the file, saving all changes, and exit PowerPoint.

# Project 85—Create It

## Multimedia Presentation

### DIRECTIONS

1. Start PowerPoint, if necessary, and open **PProj85** from the data files for this lesson. Save the file as **PProj85_studentfirstname_studentlastname** in the location where your teacher instructs you to store the files for this lesson.

2. Select slide 5 and click Insert > Video 🎞 > Video from file. The Insert Video dialog box opens.

3. Navigate to the location where the data files for this lesson are stored and select **PProj85a.mpeg**.

4. Click Insert. The video appears in the placeholder.

5. Right-click the video and select **Format Video** to open the Format Video dialog box.

6. Click **Size** and then in the **Scale** area type **75%** in the Height box and press [ENTER]. Click **Close**.

7. Click the **Start** down arrow on the **Video Tools Playback** tab and select **Automatically**.

8. Select slide 6 and click the **Audio** down arrow on the **Insert** tab.

9. Select **Clip Art Audio** to open the Clip Art task pane.

10. Type **helicopter** in the Search for box and click **Go**.

11. Locate a clip that sounds like a helicopter flyover. Rest the mouse pointer on each thumbnail to see file sizes. Click on one that is larger than 100 KB.

12. Close the file, saving all changes, and exit PowerPoint.

# Project 86—Apply It

## Multimedia Presentation

### DIRECTIONS

1. Start PowerPoint, if necessary, and open **PProj86** from, the data files for this lesson.

2. Save the file as **PProj86_studentfirstname_ studentlastname** in the location where your teacher instructs you to store the files for this lesson.

3. Display slide 5, select the video, and click **Video Tools Playback** > **Play Full Screen**.

4. Click **Video Tools Playback** > **Trim Video** 🎞 .

5. Trim the beginning of the video clip so that the start time is **00:01**.

6. Apply the **Glow Rounded Rectangle** picture style to the video on slide 5.

7. Display slide 6 and drag the sound icon off the slide so that it won't show during a slide show.

8. Set the sound to play across slides so that it will play from slide 6 to slide 7 and have it play across slides:

   a. Select the audio clip icon.
   b. Click **Audio Tools Playback** > **Start** 🎞 drop-down list.
   c. Select **Play across slides**.

9. Display slide 7 and insert the JPEG file **PProj86a** from the data files for this lesson.

10. Format the picture to match the picture on slide 6.

11. View the slide show, see the movie, and hear the sound. Your presentation should look similar to Figure 38-1.

12. Close the file, saving all changes, and exit PowerPoint.

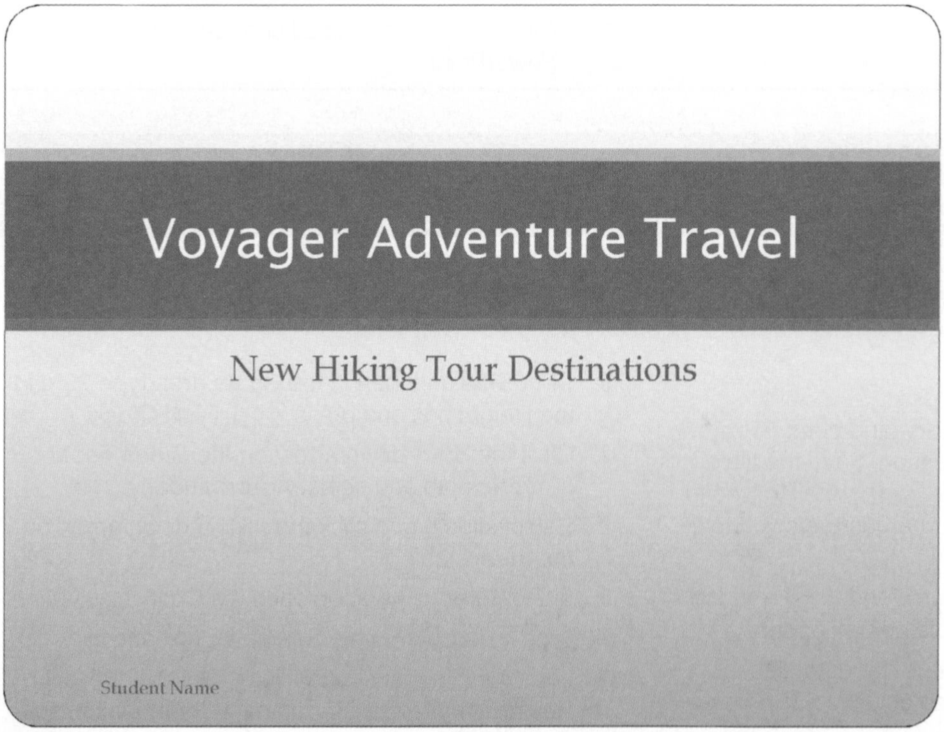

**Figure 38-1**

Voyager Adventure Travel

New Hiking Tour Destinations

Student Name

# Lesson 39

# Working with Advanced Photo Album Features

> **What You Will Learn**

**Editing a Photo Album**

**Adding Text and Captions**

**Compressing Pictures**

**Software Skills**   Working with PowerPoint's advanced photo album features makes it easy to modify and enhance a photo album. You can arrange the photos in a number of layouts and apply enhancements such as frames, captions, and other effects. To reduce the file size of a presentation, you can also compress the pictures.

**Application Skills**   Voyager Adventure Travel has decided to approve the Glacier National Park hiking adventure and wants you to create a photo album of Glacier Park images to present at a travel show.

## What You Can Do

### Editing a Photo Album

- You can edit an existing photo album by displaying it in Normal view and then clicking the down arrow on the Photo Album button. Choosing Edit Photo Album opens the Photo Album dialog box.

- The Photo Album dialog box is where you rearrange pictures in the album and select settings for the way the pictures will display.

- Selected picture file names display in the Pictures in album list in the center of the dialog box. The currently selected picture displays in the Preview area.

- You can adjust the order of pictures or remove a selected picture. Use the buttons below the preview to flip the picture horizontally or vertically, adjust its contrast, or adjust its brightness.

- After you make changes, click the Update button to apply your changes to the album.

**WORDS TO KNOW**

**Resolution**
The number of dots or pixels per linear unit of output. For example, a computer monitor's resolution is usually 72 pixels per inch.

**Try It!**    **Removing a Picture from a Photo Album**

1. Start PowerPoint and open **PTry39** file from the data files for this lesson.

2. Save the file as **PTry39_studentfirstname_ studentlastname** in the location where your teacher instructs you to store the files for this lesson.

3. Click View > Normal , if necessary to show the presentation in Normal view.

4. Right click slide 7 and select Delete Slide from the content menu.

5. Click Insert > Photo Album  down arrow.

6. Click Edit Photo Album.

7. Select Summer River Sun from the Pictures in album list.

8. Click Remove.

9. Leave the dialog box open to use in the next Try It.

---

**Try It!**    **Changing the Layout Options in a Photo Album**

1. In the Edit Photo Album dialog box for presentation **PTry39_studentfirstname_ studentlastname**, click the Frame shape down arrow.

2. Select Center Shadow Rectangle from the list.

3. Leave the dialog box open to use in the next Try It.

---

**Try It!**    **Changing the Order of Pictures in a Photo Album**

1. In the Edit Photo Album dialog box for presentation **PTry39_studentfirstname_ studentlastname**, click Raccoon Wave in the Pictures in album list.

2. Click the reorder Down  button three times.

3. Leave the dialog box open to use in the next Try It.

Quickly change the order of pictures in an album

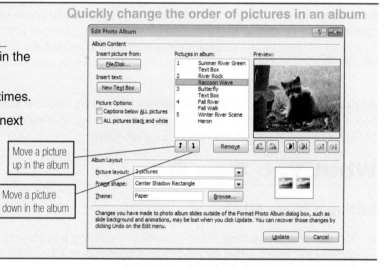

Move a picture up in the album

Move a picture down in the album

---

## Adding Text and Captions

- A PowerPoint photo album is just like a physical photo album in that it is designed primarily to showcase images, but you also can add text in the form of captions or text boxes.

- The Picture Options check boxes allow you to add a caption to each picture or transform all pictures to black and white.

- By default, PowerPoint uses a picture's file name as its caption, but you can replace these captions with more descriptive ones on the slides.

- You can choose to add a text box to the list of pictures. Text boxes display according to the current picture layout, at the same size as the pictures.

- PowerPoint might insert a text box placeholder for you, if you choose a layout that requires more images on a slide than you've included in your album. To turn on this text box placeholder, select the text box in the Edit Photo Album dialog box and click Update.

---

**Try It!**    **Inserting a Text Box in a Photo Album**

1. In the Edit Photo Album dialog box for presentation **PTry39_studentfirstname_ studentlastname**, select Winter River Scene in the Pictures in album list.

2. Click the New Text Box button in the Album Content area.

3. Click Update and select slide 6.

4. Select the words *Text Box* on slide 6 and type **Thanks for all your hard work!**

5. Save the file, and leave it open to use in the next Try It.

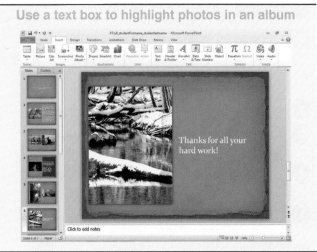
Use a text box to highlight photos in an album

---

**Try It!**    **Adding Captions to a Photo Album**

1. In **PTry39_studentfirstname_studentlast name**.

2. Click Insert > Photo Album 🖼 > Edit Photo Album.

3. Select Captions below ALL pictures.

4. Click Update.

5. Select the caption below the raccoon picture on slide 3.

6. Type **Wildlife is returning to the park.**

7. Save the file, and leave it open to use in the next Try It.

You can add custom captions to every picture in an album

---

## Compressing Pictures

- A photo album—or any presentation that contains pictures, movies, or sounds—can turn into a large file that may be a challenge to store, or may take extra time to open.

- To streamline a presentation's file size, use the Compress Pictures option on the Picture Tools Format tab to open the Compress Pictures dialog box.

- By default, PowerPoint will compress all pictures in the presentation. If you want to compress only a selected picture or pictures, click the Apply to selected pictures only check box.

- The Target output settings allow you to choose a resolution appropriate for the way the pictures will be viewed. Measurements for the resolution are given in ppi, pixels per inch.

- Choose the compression resolution based on how the presentation will be viewed (print, screen, or e-mail).

- If you have cropped pictures to hide areas you don't want to see, you can also choose to delete the cropped portions of the pictures. Keep in mind, of course, you cannot go back and uncrop a picture once you have cropped portions.

## Try It!    Compressing Pictures

**1** In **PTry39_studentfirstname_studentlast name**, click File > Info and note the size of the file in the Document Information pane on the right of the window.

**2** Click Home and select the picture on slide 2.

**3** Click Picture Tools Format > Compress Pictures 🖾.

**4** Deselect Apply only to this picture in the Compression options area.

**5** Select Screen (150 ppi); good for Web pages and projectors in the Target output area.

**6** Click OK.

**7** Click File > Save 🖫 and then click Info. Note that the file size in the Document Information pane on the right of the window has gone down significantly.

**8** Close **PTry39_studentfirstname_studentlast name** and exit PowerPoint.

The Compress Pictures dialog box

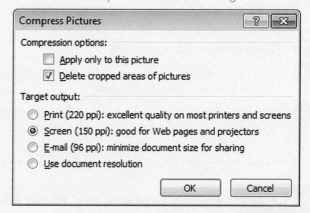

---

# Project 87—Create It

## Enhanced Photo Album

### DIRECTIONS

1. Start PowerPoint, if neccesary and click **Insert > Photo Album** 🖾.

2. Click **File/Disk**, select the JPEG files **PProj87a -PProj87e** in the location where the data files are stored for this lesson, and click **Create**.

3. Save the new album as **PProj87_ studentfirstname_studentlastname** in the location where your teacher instructs you to store the files for this lesson.

4. Click **Insert > Photo Album** 🖾 **> Edit Photo Album**.

5. In the Album Layout area, click the **Picture Layout** down arrow and select **1 picture**.

6. In the Album Layout area, click the **Frame Shape** down arrow and select **Compound Frame, Black**.

7. In the Album Content area, select **Captions below ALL pictures**.

8. Click **Update**.

9. **With your teacher's permission**, print the document. It should look similar to Figure 39-1.

10. Close the file, saving all changes, and exit PowerPoint.

Figure 39-1

PProj87a

# Project 88—Apply It

## Enhanced Photo Album

### DIRECTIONS

1. Start PowerPoint, if necessary, and open **PProj88** from the data files for this lesson.
2. Save the file as **PProj88_studentfirstname_studentlastname** in the location where your teacher instructs you to store the files for this lesson.
3. View the album as a slide show.
4. Change the title to **Voyager Travel Adventures Presents**.
5. Place your cursor at the beginning of the subtitle text, type **Glacier National Park**, then press ENTER. On the second subtitle line, replace Student Name with your full name.
6. Click **Insert** > **Photo Album** > **Edit Photo Album**.
7. In the Pictures in album box, move **PProj88b** below figure **PProj88c**.
8. Delete figure **PProj88e** from the album.
9. Turn off the captions since they don't add much to this album.
10. In the Album Layout area, change the frame shape to **Simple Frame, White**.
11. In the Album Layout area, add the **Elemental** theme to the album and click **Update**.
12. Use the **Picture Tools Format** tab to compress all the pictures in the album.
13. Use the Header & Footer dialog box to add a footer that includes your name and a date that updates automatically.
14. Click **Slide Show** > **From Beginning** and view the entire slide show to see your changes.
15. **With your teacher's permission**, print slide 4. It should look similar to Figure 39-2.
16. Close the file, saving all changes, and exit PowerPoint.

**Figure 39-2**

# Lesson 40

# Advanced Animation Features

➤ **What You Will Learn**

**Applying Advanced Animation Effects**
**Creating a Motion Path Animation**
**Changing the Order of Animation Effects**
**Applying Advanced Effect Options**
**Adjusting Animation Timing**
**Working with the Animation Timeline**
**Changing or Removing an Animation**

**WORDS TO KNOW**

Path
A line or shape on a slide that an object will follow when a Motion Path animation is applied to the object.

**Software Skills**   Animating slides is another way to add multimedia interest to a presentation. Using custom animation options, you can add entrance, emphasis, and exit effects, as well as move an object along a path. Use advanced features to trigger animations and delay effects. Change or remove an animation at any time.

**Application Skills**   Natural Light has asked you to add animations to a presentation that will be available in the showroom for visitors to browse. In this lesson, you work with a number of custom animation options.

## What You Can Do

### Applying Advanced Animation Effects

■  There are many additional animation features available on the Advanced Animation group of the Animation tab.

- Options in the Advanced Animation group allow you to select individual parts of an object to animate, to apply special effects, to adjust timing so that an effect occurs just when you want it to, and to set an animation so that it occurs when you click on another object on the slide.

## Try It!    Applying Advanced Exit Effects

1. Start PowerPoint and open **PTry40** file from the data files for this lesson.

2. Save the file as **PTry40_studentfirstname_ studentlastname** in the location where your teacher instructs you to store the files for this lesson.

3. Click the title and subtitle placeholders on slide 9.

4. Click Animations > Add Animation ★.

5. Select More Exit Effects from the list.

6. Select Preview Effect in the Add Exit Effects dialog box and scroll down to the bottom of the list.

7. Select Contract and watch the preview. Click OK.

8. Save changes, and leave the file open to use in the next Try It.

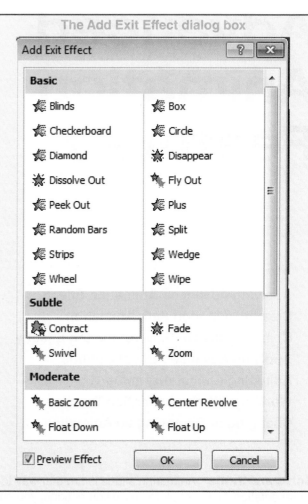

The Add Exit Effect dialog box

## Try It!    Applying More Than One Animation Effect to the Same Object

1. In **PTry40_studentfirstname_studentlast name**, select the profit text box on slide 7.

2. Click Animations > Preview ★.

3. Click Animations > Add Animation ★.

4. Select Pulse from the list.

5. Click Animations > Preview ★.

6. Save changes, and leave the file open to use in the next Try It.

## Try It! — Animating Separate Parts of an Object

**1** In **PTry40_studentfirstname_studentlastname**, select the chart on slide 8.

**2** Click Animation > Add Animation ⭐.

**3** Click Shape ⭐ from the Animation list.

**4** Click Animation > Effect Options 🔅.

**5** Select By Category 📊.

**6** Save changes, and leave the file open to use in the next Try It.

Use the Effect Options button to animate separate parts of an object

---

## Creating a Motion Path Animation

- You can also set a motion path that an object will follow on the slide.

- The path may be one of a number of straight lines, such as Diagonal Down Right, Left, or Up, or you can draw a custom path using the Line, Freeform, Curve, or Scribble tool.

- You can also click More Motion Paths on the Motion Paths submenu to open a dialog box where you can select from many shape options, such as stars, arcs, loops, and spirals.

- After you choose the motion path, a dotted line represents the path, and the red arrow and line represent the end of the path, the point at which animation stops.

- You can adjust the motion path if it is not in the right position or the right duration by dragging the red arrow on the display. It will maintain its direction or shape as you move it.

- To move one end of the path, or to change its length, click on one of the handles at the end of the path.

---

## Try It! — Applying Motion Paths

**1** In **PTry40_studentfirstname_studentlastname**, click the earth logo on slide 9.

**2** Click Animations > Add Animation ⭐ > Arcs ⌒.

**3** Save changes, and leave the file open to use in the next Try It.

Motion path options

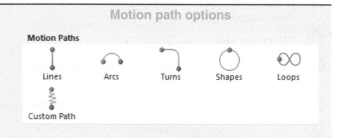

## Try It!        Adjusting a Motion Path

**1**  In **PTry40_studentfirstname_studentlast name**, click the motion path on slide 1, if necessary to select it.

**2**  Click Animations > Effect Options > Up.

**3**  Click Animations > Effect Options > Reverse Path Directions.

**4**  Select the path indicator and drag it to the left so that that green end indicator is placed on the globe.

**5**  Drag the red end point left to extend the line.

**6**  Use the rotate handle to adjust the angle of the arc.

**7**  Make any further modifications to ensure that the end point is centered above the green line.

**8**  Save changes, and leave the file open to use in the next Try It.

Use the Motion Path lines to adjust the path of the animation

## Changing the Order of Animation Effects

- Each type of animation effect has its own symbol, such as the green star for entrance effects and the red star for exit effects.

- These symbols help you identify items in the animation pane. The symbols make it easy to check that the effects are in the correct order.

- If the object you are animating has more than one line or part, such as a text content placeholder or a chart or diagram, a bar displays below the effect with a Click to expand contents arrow. Clicking the arrow displays all the parts of the object.

- When you have finished animating the parts, use the Click to hide contents arrow to collapse the effect and save room in the animation list.

## Try It!        Changing the Order of Animation Effects

**1**  In **PTry40_studentfirstname_studentlast name**, select slide 6.

**2**  Click Animations > Preview ⭐.

**3**  Click Animations > Animation Pane 🔲 Animation Pane.

**4**  Click on the entrance effect ⭐ item in the Animation Pane.

**5**  Click the Re-Order Up button 🔼.

**6**  Click on the exit effect ⭐ item in the Animation Pane.

**7**  Click the Re-Order Down button 🔽 two times.

**8**  Save changes, and leave the file open to use in the next Try It.

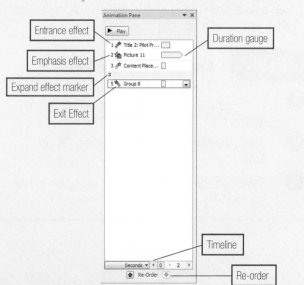

Use the Animation Pane to control your animation effects

## Applying Advanced Effect Options

- When you select an animation in the Animation Pane, a down arrow appears containing a number of options that you can use to modify an effect.

- Selecting Effect Options from the content list opens a dialog box. The Effect tab offers a number of special effects that you can apply to an object, depending on the type of object being animated.

- You can adjust the direction of the animation and choose Smooth start and Smooth end to control how the object starts and stops during the animation.

- All animation types allow you to select a sound effect from the Sound list to accompany the effect.

✓ Use sound effects sparingly; it can be distracting to hear the same sound effect over and over when multiple parts of an object are animated.

- The After animation palette gives you a number of options for emphasizing or deemphasizing an object after the animation ends. You can hide the object after the animation, hide it the next time you click the mouse, or change its color.

- If the animated object contains text, the Animate text settings become active, allowing you to animate the text all at once, by word, or by letter, and set the delay between words or letters.

### Try It! Applying Advanced Effect Options

1. In **PTry40_studentfirstname_studentlast name**, select slide 7.

2. Click on the Entrance animation in the animation pane and then on the down arrow and select Effect Options.

3. On the Effect tab, select Applause in the Sound box.

4. Click OK.

5. Click the first animation in the animation pane and press CTRL. Then select the second animation in the animation pane.

6. Click the down arrow that appears and select Effect Options.

7. Select Hide After Animation in the After animation box.

8. Click OK.

9. Save changes, and leave the file open to use in the next Try It.

**Set advanced animation effects**

Fly In — Effect | Timing | Text Animation

Settings
- Direction: From Right
- Smooth start: 0 sec
- Smooth end: 0 sec
- Bounce end: 0 sec

Enhancements
- Sound: Applause
- After animation: Don't Dim
- Animate text: All at once
- % delay between letters

OK  Cancel

### Try It! Animating Text on a Slide

1. In **PTry40_studentfirstname_studentlast name**, select slide 1.

2. Click the down arrow on the animation in the Animation Pane and select Effect Options.

3. On the Effect tab, select By word in the Animate text box.

4. Type **20** in the % delay between words box.

5. Click OK.

6. Save changes, and leave the file open to use in the next Try It.

*(continued)*

**Try It!**   **Animating Text on a Slide** *(continued)*

The Fade dialog box

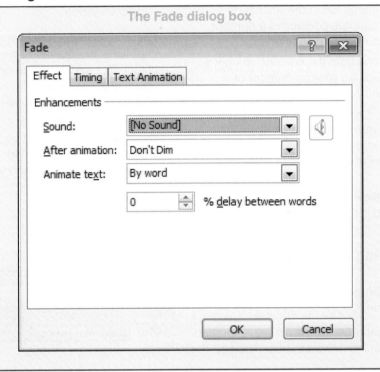

## Adjusting Animation Timing

- The Animations tab contains duration, delay, and trigger tools for controlling the timing on your animations.
  - Use the Delay setting to control exactly when an animation takes place by specifying the amount of time that must elapse before the animation begins.
  - Use the Duration setting to adjust the speed of the animation.
  - Use the Trigger setting to control what starts an animation.

- Using triggers is one way to make a slide show interactive by controlling which object on the slide to click to start the animation.

- You can also control animation timing using controls on the Timing tab in the Effect Options dialog boxes, such as Repeat and Rewind.
  - Use the Repeat setting to replay the animation a specific number of times or until the next click or the next slide displays.
  - Use the Rewind when done playing option to return the object to its original position or state. If you have a picture fade into view, for example, the Rewind setting will remove it from the slide after the animation finishes.

**Try It!**   **Adjusting Timing Using the Animations Tab**

**1** In PTry40_studentfirstname_studentlast name, select the animation on slide 1, if necessary.

**2** Type 02.00 in the Duration box.

**3** Type 00.75 in the Delay box.

**4** Save changes, and leave the file open to use in the next Try It.

**Try It!** **Adjusting Timing Using the Effect Options Dialog Box**

**1** In **PTry40_studentfirstname_studentlast name**, select the first two text boxes on slide 7.

**2** Click the down arrow on the animation in the Animation Pane and select Effect Options.

**3** On the Timing tab, select 1 seconds (Fast) in the Duration box.

**4** Select Rewind when done playing.

**5** Select 0.5 in the Delay box.

**6** Click OK.

**7** Save changes, and leave the file open to use in the next Try It.

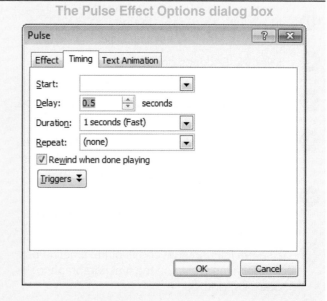
The Pulse Effect Options dialog box

**Try It!** **Setting the Start for an Animation**

**1** In **PTry40_studentfirstname_student lastname**, select the Profit text box on slide 7.

**2** Select After Previous in the Start box on the Animations tab.

**3** Save changes, and leave the file open to use in the next Try It.

**Try It!** **Setting an Animation Trigger**

**1** In **PTry40_studentfirstname_ studentlastname**, select the chart and the three text boxes at the bottom of slide 7.

✓ *Hint: Press and hold* CTRL *to select multiple objects.*

**2** Click Animations > Float In.

**3** Click Animations > Trigger ⚡ > On Click Of > Textbox 7.

**4** Save changes, and leave the file open to use in the next Try It.

## Working with the Animation Timeline

- The easiest way to fine-tune animation timing is to use the timeline feature in the Animation pane.

- The bars next to the individual effects in the Animation pane indicate the duration of each effect and when it starts relative to other effects.

- The timeline includes a seconds gauge at the bottom of the task pane. You can use this gauge to see the duration of each effect as well as the overall duration of all animations on the slide.

- You can use the timeline to set a delay or adjust the length of an effect or double-click an orange bar to open the Timing dialog box for further adjustments.

## Try It!   Adjusting the Duration of an Effect in the Timeline

**1** In **PTry40_studentfirstname_ studentlastname**, select slide 6.

**2** Click the Seconds box at the bottom of the Animation Pane and select Zoom Out.

**3** Click the timeline box for the second animation effect in the Animation Pane.

**4** Click the right edge of the box until the mouse indicator changes, and drag the line to the left until the screen tip indicates 2.5s.

**5** Click the expand contents arrow below the Content Placeholder effect in the Animation Pane.

**6** Use the left and right edges of the timeline box to adjust the timing on the first paragraph to Start: 2s, End: 3s.

**7** Adjust the timing of the second paragraph to Start: 3s, End: 4s.

**8** Save changes, and leave the file open to use in the next Try It.

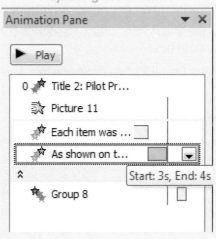

Adjusting the timeline

## Try It!   Setting a Delay Using the Timeline

**1** In **PTry40_studentfirstname_studentlast name**, click the Seconds box at the bottom of the Animation Pane and select Zoom In.

**2** Select the exit effect and drag the entire timeline box to the right until the indicator shows Start: 4.5s.

**3** Save changes, and leave the file open to use in the next Try It.

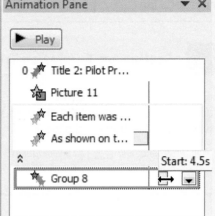

Set a Delay in the Animation Pane

## Changing or Removing an Animation

■ If you find that a particular animation option isn't giving you the effect you want, you can easily change the animation effect using the Animation Pane.

■ You can also click the Remove button to delete the effect entirely.

## Try It! Removing an Animation Effect

1. In **PTry40_studentfirstname_student lastname**, click the globe logo on slide 6.

2. Click the effect down arrow in the Animation Pane.

3. Click Remove.

4. Save changes, and leave the file open to use in the next Try It.

Remove an effect in the Animation Pane

## Try It! Change an Animation

1. In **PTry40_studentfirstname_studentlast name**, click the effect for the picture in the Animation Pane.

2. Click Animation > More ⌄ to open the Animation Gallery.

3. Select the Pulse ☆ emphasis effect.

4. Click Play ▶ Play in the Animation Pane to see the changes to the slide.

5. Close the file, saving all changes, and exit PowerPoint.

# Project 89—Create It

## Animating a Kiosk Presentation

### DIRECTIONS

1. Start PowerPoint, if necessary, and open **PProj89** from the data files for this lesson.

2. Save the file as **PProj89_studentfirstname_ studentlastname** in the location where your teacher instructs you to store the files for this lesson.

3. On slide 1, select the **Star** object.

4. Click **Animations** > **Add Animation** 🌟 > **Color Pulse** ☆.

5. Click **Animations** > **Effect Options** and select the last color on the top row.

6. Click **Animations** > **Start** ▶ > **After Previous**.

7. Click **Animations** > **Animation Pane** 🎞 and then click the emphasis animation down arrow in the Animation Pane.

8. Select **Timing** from the menu and click the **Repeat** down arrow.

9. Select **Until Next Click** and then click **OK**.

10. Select the title and subtitle placeholders on slide 1 and click **Animations** > **Add Animation** ★ > **More Entrance Effects**.

11. Select **Dissolve In** and click **OK.**

12. Select the subtitle placeholder and click **Animations** > **Start** 🖫 > **After Previous**.

13. Select the title placeholder and click **Animations** > **Animation Pane** 🗱 .

14. Click the title animation down arrow and select **Effect Options**.

15. On the Effect tab, click the **After animation** down arrow and select the black square.

16. Click the Animate text box, and select **By word.**

17. On the Timing tab, click the **Start** down arrow and select **With Previous**.

18. Click **OK**.

19. Close the Animation Pane and click **Animations** > **Preview** 🌟 to see your changes.

20. Close the file, saving all changes, and exit PowerPoint.

# Project 90—Apply It

## Animating a Kiosk Presentation

### DIRECTIONS

1. Start PowerPoint, if necessary, and open **PProj90** from the data files for this lesson.

2. Save the file as **PProj90_studentfirstname_ studentlastname** in the location where your teacher instructs you to store the files for this lesson.

3. Display slide 4 and apply animation effects as follows:

   a. Set the **Sales** placeholder to **Fly In** from the left, **After Previous, Fast**.

   b. Select the **Sales** animation in the Animation pane and then change the effect to a **Fade** entrance effect.

   c. Select the content placeholder below the Sales object and fade the text into view **After Previous**.

   d. Animate the **Service** placeholder to **Fly In** from the right, **After Previous**.

   e. Select the **Sales** content placeholder and then click **Animations** > **Animation Painter**.

   f. Click the **Service** content placeholder to apply the same settings to the Service content placeholder that you applied to the Sales content placeholder.

   g. Delay the start of the Service placeholder by **1.5** seconds.

4. Display slide 5 and apply a **Fly In** entrance animation to the SmartArt graphic, **After Previous, Fast From Left**. Then modify the animation effects as follows:

   a. Change the SmartArt Animation option in the Effect Options dialog box to **One by one**, then expand the effect to see all the shapes that make up the diagram.

   b. Using the timeline, adjust the duration and delay of each shape so that a viewer has time to read the Step 1 shape before the first bulleted shape appears, read the text in this shape before the Step 2 shape appears, and so on.

   c. Use the **Play** button and the **Slide Show** button to test your delays until you are satisfied with the results.

5. On slide 6, set a trigger to animate the picture with a **Wipe** entrance effect, **From Top, Fast**, when the slide title is clicked. Then animate the picture description with a **Fade** effect so it displays after the picture.

   ✓ Hint: You might need to reorder the effects to get the animation right.

6. On slide 7, apply to the WordArt object the **Fade** entrance effect, the **Grow/Shrink** emphasis effect, and the **Fade** exit effect. Apply the following settings.

   a. **After Previous** to all of the effects.

   b. Change the timing of the entrance effect to **Slow**.

   c. Change the timing of the emphasis effect to **Medium**.

   d. Change the timing of the exit effect to **Slow**.

7. On slide 7, add a motion path to the **Star** object so that it moves to the center of the slide after the WordArt object exits. Then apply a **Grow/Shrink** emphasis effect and use the Effect Options dialog box to increase the size of the object **200%**. Apply **After Previous** to both. The motion path should look similar to Figure 40-1.

8. View the slide show to see the effects. Make any adjustments necessary.

9. After viewing the slide show, you decide that the title animation on the first slide is unnecessary. Remove the animation from the title and subtitle.

10. Close the file, saving all changes, and exit PowerPoint.

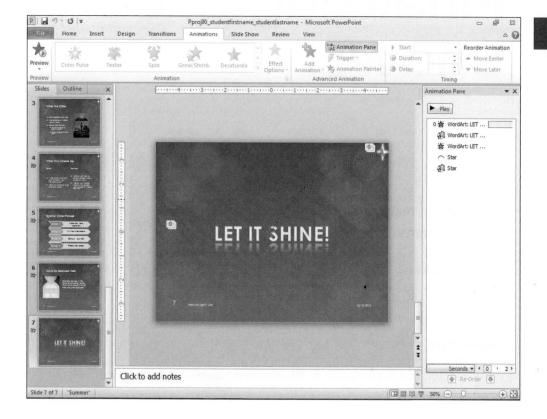

**Figure 40-1**

# Lesson 41

# Finalizing Slide Shows

**WORDS TO KNOW**

Narration
A recording of your
voice that describes or
enhances the message in
each slide.

## ➤ What You Will Learn

**Creating Presentation Sections**
**Adding Narration to a Presentation**

**Software Skills**   You can use sections in order to organize a large presentation.
You can add narration to a presentation so that you don't have to be present to get
your main points across.

**Application Skills**   In this lesson, you will add narration to a presentation
designed to convince Peterson Home Healthcare to update their IT equipment.
You'll then add that presentation to the Peterson Healthcare Annual Board Meeting
presentation and use sections to organize the slide show.

## What You Can Do

### Creating Presentation Sections

- Sections are used to organize large presentations into more manageable
  groups.
- You can also use presentation sections to assist in collaborating on projects. For
  example, each colleague can be responsible for preparing slides for a separate
  section.
- You can apply unique names and effects to different sections.
- You can also choose to print by section.

### Try It!    Creating Presentation Sections

Creating a presentation section

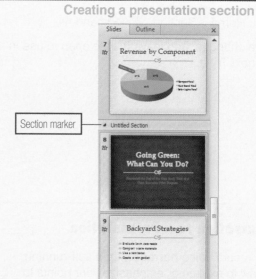

1. Start PowerPoint and open **PTry41** file from the data files for this lesson.

2. Save the file as **PTry41_studentfirstname_ studentlastname** in the location where your teacher instructs you to store the files for this lesson.

3. Switch to Normal view, if necessary.

4. Click between slides 3 and 4.

5. Click Home > Section.

6. Click Add Section.

7. Right-click between slides 7 and 8. Select Add Section.

8. Save changes, and leave the file open to use in the next Try It.

### Try It!    Renaming Presentation Sections

1. In **PTry41_studentfirstname_studentlast name**, right-click the presentation section bar between slides 7 and 8.

2. Select Rename Section from the content menu.

   **OR**

   Click Home > Section > Rename Section.

3. In the Rename Section dialog box, type **Going Green** in the Section Name box.

4. Click Rename.

5. Save changes, and leave the file open to use in the next Try It.

Rename Section dialog box

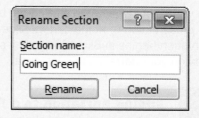

### Try It!    Working with Presentation Sections

1. In **PTry41_studentfirstname_studentlast name**, right-click the presentation section bar between slides 7 and 8.

2. Select Collapse All.

   **OR**

   Click Home > Section > Collapse All.

3. Right-click the Going Green section bar and select Move Section Up.

   **OR**

   Click the Going Green section bar and drag it up above the Default section bar.

4. Right-click the Untitled section bar and select Remove Section & Slides.

5. At the confirmation box, click yes.

*(continued)*

**Try It!**    **Working with Presentation Sections** (continued)

**6** Click Home > Section 🗒 > Expand All.

**7** Save changes, and leave the file open to use in the next Try It.

Collapsed Presentation Section

| Slides | Outline | ✕ |
|---|---|---|
| ▷ Default Section (8) | | |
| ▷ Going Green (6) | | |

Rename Section
Remove Section
Remove Section & Slides
Remove All Sections
▲ Move Section Up
▾ Move Section Down
Collapse All
Expand All

## Adding Narration to a Presentation

■ You can record voice **narration** for a self-running slide show to explain or emphasize your points to the audience. Narration takes precedence over all other sounds on a slide.

  ✓ *To do so, your computer must have a microphone, speakers, or headphones and sound card.*

■ Before you begin adding narration to slides, make sure your microphone is working correctly.

■ To record narration, use the Record Slide Show button on the Slide Show tab.

  ● When you select whether to start at the beginning of the presentation or at the current slide, the presentation begins in Slide Show view so you can match your narration to each slide.

● You also have the option to record timings and narration or just narration.

■ You will see that each slide to which you added narration has a sound icon displayed in the lower right corner. Viewers can click the icons to hear your narration, or you can use the Audio Tools Playback tab to specify that the narration will play automatically.

■ Before you begin, remember these tips:

  ● Click through the entire presentation at least once, reading each slide's content.

  ● Don't begin reading until the timing indicates 00:01.

  ● If you make a mistake, keep reading (especially if you're also recording timings). Remember, you can always go back and redo a single slide.

**Try It!**    **Adding Narration to a Presentation**

**1** In **PTry41_studentfirstname_student lastname**, select slide 1, if necessary.

**2** On the Slide Show tab, click the Record Slide Show 🕓 down arrow.

**3** Click Start Recording from Beginning.

**4** If you have a microphone attached to your computer, select both options in the Record Slide Show box. If you don't have a microphone set up, deselect the option for Narrations and laser pointer. Click Start Recording.

**5** When the slide show opens, read the text on the slide as clearly as possible. Be sure to time your reading with the way the text appears on screen.

**6** When you've finished with slide 1, click the screen to move to the next slide.

**7** Continue recording the slide text until the end of the presentation.

**8** Save changes, and leave the file open to use in the next Try It.

Record Slide Show dialog box

**Try It!**    **Correcting the Narration on a Slide within a Presentation**

**1** In **PTry41_studentfirstname_studentlast name**, select slide 8.

**2** Click Slide Show > Record Slide Show ⏱.

**3** Click Start Recording from Current Slide.

**4** Select only the Narration and laser pointer options and click Start Recording.

**5** When the slide show opens, read the text on the slide as clearly as possible. Be sure to time your reading with the way the text appears on screen.

✓ *If you need to start over, click the Undo button* ↺ *to restart the slide narration recording.*

**6** When you've finished correcting the narration, click the Close button ✖.

**7** Close the file, saving all changes, and exit PowerPoint.

Recording dialog box    Restarts recording narration of the slide

---

# Project 91—Create It

## Adding Narration

### DIRECTIONS

1. Start PowerPoint, if necessary, and open **PProj91** from the data files for this lesson.

2. Save the file as **PProj91_studentfirstname_studentlastname** in the location where your teacher instructs you to store the files for this lesson.

3. Create a footer with your full name in it.

4. Click **Design** > **Fonts** Ⓐ > **Apothecary**.

5. Click **Design** > **Background Styles** 🎨 > **Style 6**.

6. Click **Slide Show** > **Record Slide Show** ⏱ > **Start Recording from Beginning**.

7. If you have a microphone attached to your computer, select both options in the Record Slide Show box. If you don't have a microphone set up, deselect the option for Narrations and laser pointer.

8. Click **OK** to begin.

9. Read through the contents of each slide. When you are finished, click the ✖ to close the Recording dialog box.

10. Click **Slide Show** > **From Beginning** 🖥 to view your changes.

11. Select slide 4 and in the Stage 2 box, place the insertion point at the beginning of the bullet point. Type **Hire a contractor** and press ENTER.

12. Click **Slide Show** > **Record Slide Show** ⏱ > **Start Recording from Current Slide**.

13. Select the same options in the Record Slide Show box that you chose for the initial recording and click **OK**.

14. Read the entire slide and then close the recording box.

15. **With your teacher's permission**, print slide 4. It should look similar to Figure 41-1.

16. Close the file, saving all changes, and exit PowerPoint.

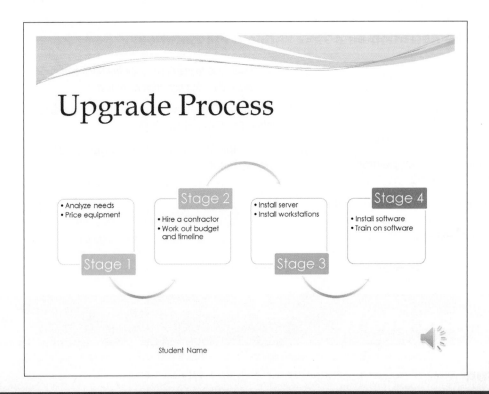

**Figure 41-1**

# Project 92—Apply It

## Organizing with Sections

### DIRECTIONS

1. Start PowerPoint, if necessary, and open **PProj92** from the data files for this lesson.

2. Save the file as **PProj92_studentfirstname_ studentlastname** in the location where your teacher instructs you to store the files for this lesson.

3. Right-click slide 2 and choose **Duplicate Slide**.

4. Click between slides 2 and 3 and click **Home** > **New Slide** > **Reuse Slides** to open the reuse slides pane.

5. Click **Browse** > **Browse File** and select the file **PProj91_studentfirstname_studentlastname** that you created in the previous project.

6. Click **Keep source formatting** and click each of the four slides to add them to the large presentation. Close the task pane.

7. Click between slides 1 and 2 and add a section.

8. Add a section marker between slides 6 and 7, 16 and 17, and 25 and 26.

9. Right-click the first untitled section marker and select **Rename Section**. Type **Upgrading Peterson's IT Equipment** and click **Rename**. When you are finished, click the arrow on the section marker to collapse the section.

10. Repeat the process to name each section according to the headings on the Agenda.

11. You've just been informed that the new patient education portion of the presentation is going to be moved to another meeting. Remove that section and all of its slides.

12. Expand all the sections to see if this will cause any conflicts. You'll need to go through and remove the first line item from each of the three remaining agenda slides (2, 7, and 16).

13. Collapse all the sections.

14. **With your teacher's permission**, print slide 2. It should look similar to Figure 41-2.

15. Close the file, saving all changes, and exit PowerPoint.

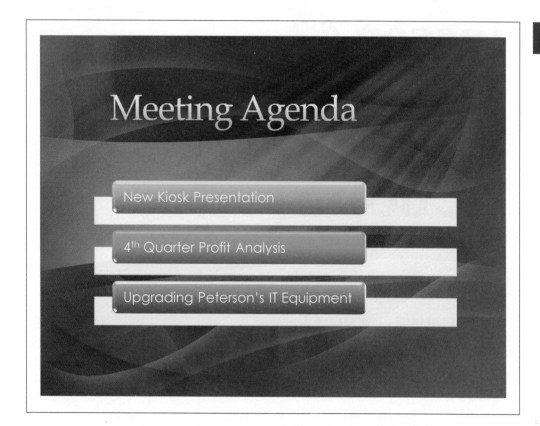

**Figure 41-2**

# Lesson 42

# Working with Actions

**WORDS TO KNOW**

**Action**
A setting that performs a specific action, such as running an application or jumping to a specific slide.

**Target**
The slide, show, file, or page that will display when you click a link on a slide.

> **What You Will Learn**

**Using Advanced Hyperlink Settings**
**Working with Action Settings**

**Software Skills**   Hyperlinks and action settings can be used to create interactive presentations that allow viewers to jump to different locations in the presentation, open other presentations or Web sites, send an e-mail message, run programs, or interact with objects on the slide.

**Application Skills**   Peterson Home Healthcare is starting the process of training employees on Microsoft Office 2010 after the installation of the new network and workstations. In this lesson, you will begin work on a presentation that employees can access from their own computers to learn more about Microsoft Office 2010. You will create links and action items to make it easy for employees to interact with the training materials.

## What You Can Do

### Using Advanced Hyperlink Settings

- You can use links to move from a presentation to another application to view data in that application. For example, you could link to Microsoft Excel data during a presentation.
- If the computer on which you are presenting the slides has an active Internet connection, you can also use a link to jump from a slide to any site on the Web.
- You can set up a link using text from a text placeholder or any object on the slide, such as a shape or picture.
- You have four target options to choose from.
  - Existing File or Web Page lets you locate a file on your system or network.

- Browse the Web button opens your browser to allow you to locate the page you want to use as a target.
- Place in This Document lets you select a slide or custom show from the current presentation. As you click a slide for the target, it displays in the Slide preview area.
- Create New Document allows you to specify the name of a new document and link to it at the same time. If you create a file with the name Results.xlsx, for example, Excel opens so you can enter data in the Results workbook.
- The E-mail Address option lets you link to an e-mail address. You might use this option when setting up a presentation to be viewed by an individual on his or her own computer so that they can follow the link to send a message to the specified e-mail address.

■ If you want to provide a little extra help to a viewer about what will happen when a link is clicked, you can provide a ScreenTip.

---

### Try It!    Inserting a Link to an External Document

**1** Start PowerPoint and open **PTry42** file from the data files for this lesson.

**2** Save the file as **PTry42_studentfirstname_studentlastname** in the location where your teacher instructs you to store the files for this lesson.

**3** Select the Discussion object on slide 10.

**4** Click Insert > Hyperlink.

**5** Click Existing File or Web Document.

**6** Locate file **PTry42a** from the data files for this lesson.

**7** Click OK.

**8** Save changes to **PTry42_studentfirstname_studentlastname** and keep the file open to use in the next Try It.

The Insert Hyperlink dialog box

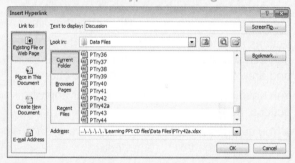

---

### Try It!    Inserting a Link to an E-mail Address

**1** In **PTry42_studentfirstname_studentlastname**, select the information object on slide 17.

**2** Click Insert > Hyperlink.

**3** In the E-mail address box, type **info@planet_earth.com**.

**4** In the Subject box, type **Request for more information**.

**5** Click OK.

**6** Save changes, and leave the file open to use in the next Try It.

---

### Try It!    Creating a ScreenTip for a Hyperlink

**1** In **PTry42_studentfirstname_studentlastname**, right-click the information object on slide 17.

**2** Click Edit Hyperlink.

**3** Click ScreenTip.

**4** Type **E-mail us for more information**.

**5** Click OK two times.

**6** Save changes, and leave the file open to use in the next Try It.

*(continued)*

## Try It!    Creating a ScreenTip for a Hyperlink *(continued)*

Editing a hyperlink to add a ScreenTip

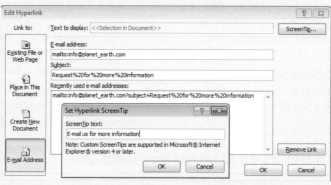

## Working with Action Settings

- Like links, actions allow you to link to a slide in the current presentation, a custom show, another presentation, a Web page URL, or another file.

- Actions are most commonly associated with action buttons: shapes you select from the Shapes gallery and draw on a slide to perform specific chores.

- You have a number of other options for applying actions; however:
  - You can use an action to run a program, such as Excel, or a macro.
    - ✓ *You may have to respond to a security warning the first time you run a program.*
  - You can also use an action to control an object you have inserted on the slide; the object must be inserted using the Insert Object dialog box.

- ✓ *If you use an existing file, you can choose Insert Object dialog box to display the object as an icon on the slide.*

- You can use an action setting to play a sound effect or sound file.

- Use the action options, such as Hyperlink, to Run program, or Play sound, on the Action Settings dialog box to set the target for the action.

- Note the Highlight check box in the Action Settings dialog box. When this option is checked, the shape or text to which you are applying the action setting will change size as you click it.

- By default, you set actions on the Mouse Click tab, which means that the action takes place when you click on the action object during the presentation.

- The Mouse Over tab contains the same options as the Mouse Click tab. Actions you set on this tab will take place when you hover the mouse pointer over the action object.

## Try It!    Working with Advanced Action Settings

**1** In **PTry42_studentfirstname_studentlast name**, click the action button on slide 9.

**2** Click Insert > Action.

**3** Click Run program.

**4** Click Browse.

**5** Click Desktop in the left pane and select one of the shortcuts on the Desktop.

**6** Click OK twice.

**7** Click the first action button on slide 2.

**8** Click Insert > Action.

**9** Click Play Sound.

**10** Select Chime.

**11** Click OK.

**12** Repeat for the remaining two action buttons.

*(continued)*

## Try It!    **Working with Advanced Action Settings** *(continued)*

**13** Click Slide Show > From Beginning 🖳 and watch the slide show, clicking all the action buttons as they appear.

**14** Close the file, saving all changes, and exit PowerPoint.

**Edit Action Button dialog box**

# Project 93—Create It

## Making an Interactive Presentation

### DIRECTIONS

1. Start PowerPoint, if necessary, and open **PProj93** from the data files for this lesson.

2. Save the file as **PProj93_studentfirstname_studentlastname** in the location where your teacher instructs you to store the files for this lesson.

3. Start Word, if necessary, and open **PProj93a** from the data files for this lesson.

4. Save the file as **PProj93a_studentfirstname_studentlastname** in the location where your teacher instructs you to store the files for this lesson.

5. Display slide 2 and select the first bullet item.

6. Click **Insert > Hyperlink** 🌐 **> Place in this document** and select the Introduction slide. Click **OK**.

7. Repeat this process for each of the other bullet items on slide 2, linking them to the corresponding slide.

8. Select the object on slide 6. Click **Insert > Hyperlink** 🌐 **> Existing File or Web Page**.

9. Select the file **PProj93a_studentfirstname_studentlastname** from the data files for this lesson. Click **OK**.

10. **With your teacher's permission**, print slide 2. It should look similar to Figure 42-1

11. Close the file, saving all changes, and exit PowerPoint.

**Figure 42-1**

# Project 94—Apply It

## Running an Interactive Presentation

### DIRECTIONS

1. Start PowerPoint, if necessary, and open **PProj94** from the data files for this lesson. Save the file as **PProj94_studentfirstname_studentlastname** in the location where your teacher instructs you to store the files for this lesson.

2. Open **PProj94a** from the data files for this lesson and save it as **PProj94a_studentfirstname_studentlastname** in the location where your teacher instructs you to store the files for this lesson.

3. Select the shape at the top of the first slide in **PProj94a_studentfirstname_studentlastname** and create a hyperlink to **PProj94_studentfirstname_studentlastname**.

4. Close **PProj94a_studentfirstname_studentlastname.**

5. Select the word *here* in the last bullet item on slide 8 and link it to **PProj94a_studentfirstname_studentlastname.**

6. Open Slide Master view. On the Title and Content layout (not the slide master), select the Questions text box and create a link to an e-mail address. Use the address **jpeterson@petersonhomehealth.com.**

   ✓ *This e-mail address is or setup purposes only.*

7. Select the More info box and create a link to the Office Online home page at **http://office.microsoft.com/en-us.**

8. Add the following ScreenTip to the More info link: **Visit Microsoft Office Online.**

9. Insert a Custom action button from the Shapes gallery to the right of the More info box and link the button to slide 2. Type **Contents** on the action button, and format the button with the same Quick Style as the text boxes but using a different color, as shown in Figure 42-2.

10. Make sure all three boxes are the same height. Align top and distribute the three boxes horizontally. Then select the boxes, copy them, and paste them on all slide layouts except the title and section header layout and the picture layouts. Exit Slide Master view.

11. Display slide 4 and select the *Open Word* shape. Apply an action setting that will run Microsoft Word: Browse to **C:\Program Files\Microsoft Office\Office14\WINWORD**.

    ✓ *You may need to display hidden files to have access to the program files directory; consult your instructor if necessary.*

12. Select the *Open Excel* shape and browse to the same location, but select **EXCEL** in the Office14 folder.

13. You are ready to test your interactive presentation. Follow these steps in Slide Show view:

    a. On slide 2, test each of the links to slides, using the **Contents** action button to return each time to slide 2.

    b. Test the **Questions** and **More info** buttons. Close the e-mail message window without creating a message, and close the Web page after you are done viewing it.

    c. On slide 4, click the **Open Word** shape, and then click **Enable** when alerted to the potential security risk. Close Word, then click the **Open Excel** shape, Enable if necessary, and close Excel.

    d. On slide 6, click the **Test Your Knowledge** object to open a Word document with three questions. For extra credit, answer the questions and then save the document with a new name such as **PProj94b_studentfirstname_studentlastname**. Close the document to return to the presentation.

    e. On slide 8, click the link that takes you to **PProj94a_studentfirstname_studentlastname**. Use the link to navigate to the information on customizing the Quick Access Toolbar, then use the action button to return to the first slide and the button to return to **PProj94_studentfirstname_studentlastname**.

14. **With your teacher's permission**, print the document. It should look similar to Figure 42-2.

15. Close the file, saving all changes, and exit PowerPoint.

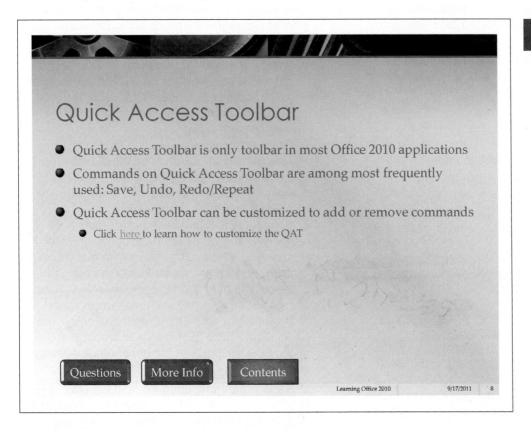

**Figure 42-2**

## Quick Access Toolbar

- Quick Access Toolbar is only toolbar in most Office 2010 applications
- Commands on Quick Access Toolbar are among most frequently used: Save, Undo, Redo/Repeat
- Quick Access Toolbar can be customized to add or remove commands
  - Click here to learn how to customize the QAT

Questions    More Info    Contents

Learning Office 2010     9/17/2011   8

# Chapter Assessment and Application

## Project 95—Make It Your Own

### Glacier National Park

Voyager Travel Adventures is preparing a presentation on their newest adventure location, Glacier National Park. In this project, you complete some final tasks on the presentation, including creating animations, inserting links, and adding action buttons.

### DIRECTIONS

1. Start Word and open **PProj95a** from the data files for this project. Save the document as **PProj95a_ studentfirstname_studentlastname** in the location where your teacher instructs you to store the files for this project. Close Word.

2. Start PowerPoint, if necessary, and open your solution file **PProj88_studentfirstname_ studentlastname** from the location where your teacher instructs you to store the files for this project. If you did not complete project 88, you can open file **PProj95b** from the data files for this project.

3. Edit the photo album. Add the JPEG figure **PProj95c** and make it the third picture in the album. Update the album.

4. Save the presentation as **PProj95b_ studentfirstname_studentlastname** in the location where your teacher instructs you to store the files for this project. Close the file.

5. Open **PProj95** from the data files for this lesson. Save the presentation as **PProj95_ studentfirstname_studentlastname** in the location where your teacher instructs you to store the files for this project.

6. On slide 6 of **PProj95_studentfirstname_student lastname**, select one of the images and apply the following formatting:
   a. Apply the **Reflected Bevel, White** picture format.
   b. Use the **Picture Borders** button to change the border color to **Ice Blue, Accent 1, Lighter 40%**.
   c. Use the **Corrections** button to increase the sharpness by **25%** and the contrast by **20%**.

7. With the picture still selected, click **Home** > **Format Painter** twice.

8. Then click on each of the other pictures on the slide to transfer the formatting to each.

9. Animate the images using the **Zoom** effect, **From Center, After Previous** and with a **1.50** duration and a **00.25** delay. Use the Animation Painter to apply the same effect settings to each image in whatever order you wish.

10. Display slide 2 and create a link from the phrase Web cams in the last bullet item to **http://www. nps.gov/glac/photosmultimedia/webcams.htm**

11. Still on slide 2, insert actions as follows:
   a. Create a text box in the lower-right corner with the text **A brief look at . . .** Add an action setting to the text box that links to the **PProj95a_ studentfirstname_studentlastname** file in your solution folder.
   b. Draw a Custom action button about the same size as the text box and use the Mouse Over tab in the Action Settings dialog box to link to the first slide in the **PProj95b_studentfirstname_ studentlastname** presentation.
   c. Format the text button and action button as desired, and position the action button behind and slightly below the text box, so that you can easily rest the mouse pointer on it during the presentation.

12. On slide 3, apply the **Float In** animation effect to the SmartArt diagram, using the **One by One** Effect Option. Use the timeline to create **2.5** second delays to adjust the appearance of each element.

13. On slide 4, insert a sound file from the Clip Organizer of a train. Set the sound to play across slides if it is fairly long and move it off the slide and set the volume to medium.

14. On slide 7, make the following changes.

   a. Apply one of the soft edge picture formats to each image and change the size of each shape to approximately 3.0 wide.

   b. Stack the images so they are centered on each other in the middle of the slide.

   c. Use motion path settings to move each picture to a new location on the slide. Make sure each animation uses the After Previous trigger.

15. On slide 8, apply emphasis or exit animation to the text.

16. Change *Student Name* in the Footer to your full name.

17. Run the presentation to test your animations and links. Close the browser after testing the Web cams link; close Word after viewing the packages document; play the album slide show all the way through and then end it to return to your main presentation. Save your changes.

18. **With your teacher's permission**, print the presentation handouts, 4 slides horizontal in landscape orientation.

19. Compress the images in the presentation and save the presentation as a PowerPoint Show. Exit PowerPoint.

**Illustration A**

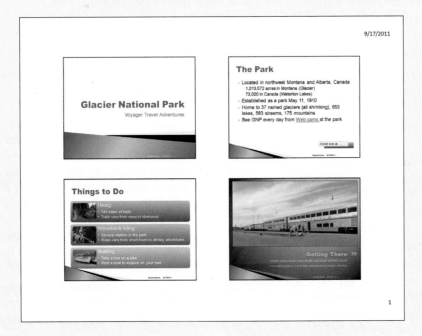

**Illustration B**

# Project 96—Master It

## Getting to Know Shakespeare

Your English Literature class is about to begin a unit on Shakespeare's plays. To get the class in the mood, your instructor has asked you to prepare a presentation that lists some famous quotes and common sayings that can be found in Shakespeare's plays.

To add interest, you will create the presentation in the form of a quiz to challenge students to guess which plays the quotes come from. Before you begin, locate:

- A picture of Shakespeare that you can download and save to your computer.
- A good dictionary of quotations (you can also use an online quotation dictionary).
- Information on Shakespeare's contributions to the English language.

## DIRECTIONS

1. Start PowerPoint and begin a new presentation. You may use a blank presentation or use one of PowerPoint's online presentation templates.
2. Save the file as **PProj96a_studentfirstname_ studentlastname** in the location where your teacher instructs you to store the files for this project.
3. Insert an appropriate title and subtitle on the first slide. Place the picture of Shakespeare on this page and format as desired. (If you don't have access to the Internet, you can use the JPEG **PProj96** as the picture.)
4. Create an introductory slide that gives some information on Shakespeare's contributions to English language and literature.
5. Modify the slide masters to set up a main frame that will contain the quote, allowing room on the right for the names of plays and on the left for buttons you will use as triggers to identify the correct play.
6. Use the dictionary of quotations to identify a number of quotes that are familiar to you, or familiar sayings.
   a. Divide the quotations by the type of play: histories, comedies, and tragedies. If necessary, look up how Shakespeare's plays are assigned to these categories online or in a volume of Shakespeare's plays.
   b. Place the quotes on three slides, one each for history, comedy, and tragedy.
   c. Add answer buttons for each quote and text boxes that contain the names of the plays from which the quotes are taken, arranged in alphabetical order.
   d. Align and distribute the quotes, buttons, and text boxes to space them evenly on the slides. Illustration A shows one arrangement.
7. Set up animations so that when a viewer clicks the answer button to the left of the quote, the text box containing the correct play title blinks three times.
8. If you have the capability to add narration, use narration to explain on slide 3 how to use the answer buttons to trigger the correct answer. Test the presentation to check your triggers.
9. **With your teacher's permission**, print the presentation.
10. Set up the presentation to be browsed by an individual. Then save the changes to your presentation as **PProj96_ studentfirstname_ studentlastname.**
11. Save it as a PowerPoint Show, **PProj96b_ studentfirstname_studentlastname**.
12. Close the file, saving all changes, and exit PowerPoint.

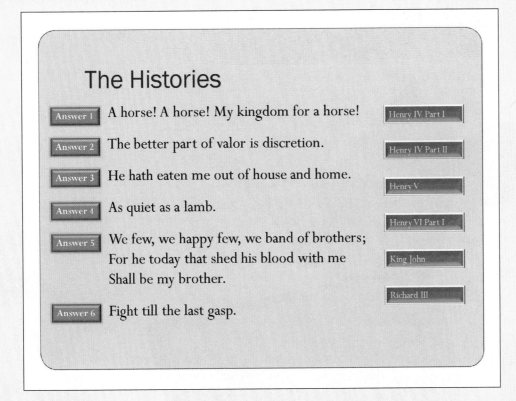

## Chapter 7

# Creating Presentations Using Tables and Charts

## Lesson 43
## Drawing and Adjusting Tables
## Projects 97-98

- Drawing a Table
- Using the Eraser to Merge Cells
- Adjusting Column Width and Row Height
- Adjusting Cell and Table Size
- Changing Text Alignment and Direction

## Lesson 44
## Formatting Tables
## Projects 99-100

- Applying a Table Style
- Modifying Cell Fill, Borders, and Effects
- Adding an Image to a Table

## Lesson 45
## Formatting Charts
## Projects 101-102

- Applying Advanced Chart Formatting

## Lesson 46
## Adding Objects to Your Presentation
## Projects 103-104

- Adding Existing Objects to Slides
- Using Paste Special to Embed or Link Object Data
- Copying Objects from Slide to Slide

## End-of-Chapter Assessments
## Projects 105-106

## WORDS TO KNOW

**Cell**

A cell is the intersection of a table row and column.

**Column**

A column is a vertical segment of a table, and may include one or many rows.

**Distribute rows and columns**

Distributing table content means to evenly space the data or cells across the selected area.

**Merge**

To merge cells means to combine their space into one larger cell or section.

**Row**

A row is one horizontal segment of a table, consisting of a single or multiple columns.

**Table**

A table is a container that displays data divided into rows and columns. You can use tables to organize information so the readers can understand it easily.

**Table handles**

When you select a table, table handles appear in the corners and in the middle of each side so that you can drag the table border to move it or change its size.

**Text alignment**

Text alignment refers to the way in which the text in the cell is arranged. Text can be aligned with the left margin, the right margin, or centered, and you can also choose to align the text vertically at the top, center, or bottom of the table cell.

# Lesson 43

# Drawing and Adjusting Tables

## ➤ What You Will Learn

**Drawing a Table**
**Using the Eraser to Merge Cells**
**Adjusting Column Width and Row Height**
**Adjusting Cell and Table Size**
**Changing Text Alignment and Direction**

**Software Skills**   One of the secrets to presenting information effectively on your PowerPoint slides is to keep the text brief and easy to understand. When you are presenting new concepts, comparing products, or designing a slide that needs to show contrasting items, it is tempting to try to cram a lot of information on the slide. Tables can help you present information clearly and succinctly by displaying information in a column-and-row format. Viewers will be able to understand your key points without reading through paragraphs of text.

**Application Skills**   Your local college is offering a series of summer classes that give students a range of experiences in different fields. One of the professors asks you to create a PowerPoint presentation that tells a little bit about each class. At the end of the presentation, you want to include a table that shows the different features in each class so that students can easily decide among the course offerings. The table will include different column sizes, merged cells (for the title), and vertical text direction for the column labels.

## What You Can Do

### Drawing a Table

- Add a **table** to your PowerPoint 2010 slide when you want to present information in a clear, easy-to-understand format.

- PowerPoint 2010 includes an Insert Table tool in the content placeholder of any slide, but when you want to draw your own custom table, use Draw Table.

- You find Draw Table by clicking the Insert tab and clicking Table in the Tables group. The Draw Table option is on the list that appears.

- After you click Draw Table, the pointer changes to a pencil, indicating that you can draw the table you want on the screen. Click and drag to draw the table.

- Add **rows** to the table by clicking the Draw Table tool in the Draw Borders group of the Table Tools Design tab. At the point in the left edge of the table where you want to begin a row, click and drag the pencil to the right edge of the table.

- Click Draw Table again and create **columns** by clicking along the top or bottom of the table and drawing a vertical line to create a column divider.

- Draw as many rows and columns as you like by drawing horizontal and vertical lines.

- You can change the color, style, and thickness of the lines you use to draw the table by using the Pen Style, Pen Weight, and Pen Color tools, also in the Draw Borders group.

  ✓ *If you click outside the table accidentally, the Table Tools contextual tab disappears. Click the table and then click the Table Tools Design tab to display the Draw Borders group again so that you can click Draw Table.*

## Try It!    Drawing a Table

**1** Start PowerPoint, and open **PTry43** from the data files for this lesson.

**2** Save the file as **PTry43_studentfirstname_ studentlastname** in the location where your teacher instructs you to store the files for this lesson.

**3** Click Insert > Table.

**4** Click Draw Table.

**5** Draw a new table in the center of the slide area. Save changes and leave the presentation open to use in the next Try It.

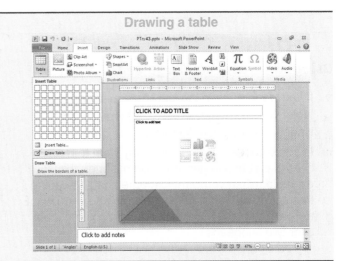

Drawing a table

## Try It!    Adding Rows and Columns

**1** In **PTry43_studentfirstname_studentlast name**, click Table Tools Design > Draw Table.

**2** Click on the left side of the new table and drag the pencil to the right border.

  ✓ *Be sure that you click directly on the border of the table; otherwise, PowerPoint may create a table within a table. If you accidentally insert a new table by clicking in the wrong place, simply press* CTRL *+* Z *to undo the error and try again.*

**3** Repeat until you have created four rows.

**4** Click the top border of the table and drag the pencil down to the bottom border.

**5** Repeat to create a third column.

**6** Save changes and leave the file open on to use in the next Try It.

## Try It!    Changing the Look of Table Lines

**1** In **PTry43_studentfirstname_studentlast name**, click Table Tools Design > Pen Style drop-down list. Select one of the dotted line styles.

**2** Click Table Tools Design > Pen Weight drop-down list and choose 3 pt.

**3** Click Table Tools Design > Pen Color ✎ and select a red pen color.

**4** Click at the top of the table to the right of the existing column lines, and draw a new line in the new style, weight, and color that extends to the bottom table border.

**5** Choose a new Pen Style, Weight, and Color and draw a fourth line, similar to the third.

**6** Save changes and leave the file open on to use in the next Try It.

Drawing new table lines with various styles

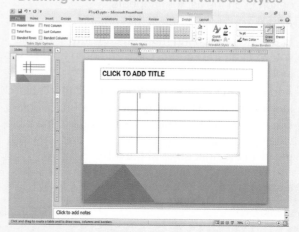

## Using the Eraser to Merge Cells

■ If you want to erase the last line you added to your table, you can simply press `CTRL` + `Z` or click Undo to reverse your last action.

■ In some cases, however, you may want to **merge** cells to create a larger area. You might do this, for example, when you want to create a table heading that spans the width of the table, or when you want to combine a cell that will serve as a column label over two subheads.

■ The Eraser tool is available in the Draw Borders group of the Table Tools Design tab.

■ To erase a line using the Eraser, click the tool and then click the line segment you want to erase. You can also drag the eraser over the line to erase several segments.

■ When you erase a row or column line, the cells in the affected row or column merge to make a larger cell.

■ The Eraser tool remains selected until you click Eraser again or click a different tool.

## Try It!    Using the Eraser to Merge Table Cells

**1** In **PTry43_studentfirstname_studentlast name**, click the table.

**2** Click Table Tools Design > Eraser 🖺 .

**3** Click the first vertical segment in column 1 of your table.

**4** Click the remaining vertical segments in row 1.

**5** Click Table Tools Design > Eraser again to turn off the tool.

✓ *You can also merge cells in the table by selecting the cells you want to merge, clicking the Table Tools Layout tab, and clicking Merge Cells in the Merge group.*

**6** Click in the new large cell and type **New Courses**.

**7** Click outside the table and save your work. Leave the file open to use in the next Try It.

## Adjusting Column Width and Row Height

■ PowerPoint 2010 makes it simple for you to adjust the column widths in your table. Simply position the mouse pointer over the column you want to change. When the pointer changes to a double-arrow, click and drag the column to increase or decrease the width.

■ Similarly, to adjust the row height, hover the mouse over the row you want to change. The mouse pointer changes to a double arrow; then click and drag the row to increase or reduce the height.

---

### Try It!    Adjusting Column Width and Row Height

**1** In **PTry43_studentfirstname_studentlast name**, position the mouse over the rightmost column divider.

**2** When the pointer changes, click and drag the column divider to the left, enlarging the column.

**3** Release the mouse button and save your file.

**4** Adjust the three columns on the right by dragging the column dividers until they look as though they are of equal width.

**5** Position the mouse over the row divider in the bottom row of the table.

**6** When the pointer changes, drag the row divider downward, enlarging the height of the bottom row and making the table a little bigger.

**7** Release the mouse button and save changes. Leave the file open to use in the next Try It.

Drag column dividers to make columns of equal width

CLICK TO ADD TITLE

New Courses

---

## Adjusting Cell and Table Size

■ The tools in the Table Tools Layout tab give you what you need to adjust cell and table size.

■ If you want to control the size of the table or cell so that it fits a precise measurement, you can enter the precise width and heights in the Table Column Width and Table Row Height fields in the Cell Size group.

■ If you want to space the columns or rows evenly throughout the table, click the **Distribute Rows** or **Distribute Columns** tools.

■ In the Table Size group, you can enter size values for the Height and Width of the table.

■ Click the Lock Aspect Ratio check box if you want to preserve the shape of the current table no matter how you resize it.

■ You can also drag a **table handle** or **border** to change the size of the table on the slide. If the Lock Aspect Ratio check box is selected, the table will be resized while still preserving its original shape if you enter new values in the measurement boxes.

---

### Try It!    Changing Cell Size

**1** In **PTry43_studentfirstname_studentlast name**, click in the second row in the table.

**2** Click Table Tools Layout, click in the Row Height box, and type **.75**.

**3** Click Table Tools Layout, click in the Column Width box, and type **1.5**. Press Enter.

**4** Save changes and leave the file open to use in the next Try It.

✓ *Notice that the new column or row value is applied only to the current selection. To apply the new value to more than one column or row, select the additional columns or rows before entering the new value.*

---

## Try It!    **Distributing Columns and Rows**

**1** In **PTry43_studentfirstname_studentlastname**, click in column 2 in the table.

**2** Click Table Tools Layout > Distribute Rows ⊞ .

**3** Click Table Tools Layout > Distribute Columns ⊞ .

**4** Save changes and leave the file open to use in the next Try It.

---

## Try It!    **Resizing the Table**

**1** In **PTry43_studentfirstname_studentlastname**, select the table.

**2** Click the Lock Aspect Ratio check box on the Table Tools Layout tab.

**3** Click in the Height text box and type **4**.

**4** To create more room for the table, drag the table to the left side of the slide.

**5** Click the lower left corner of the table and enlarge the size of the table by dragging down and to the right until the Width shows 8.5.

**6** Release the mouse button.

**7** Save changes and leave the file open to use in the next Try It.

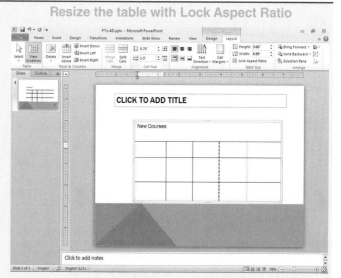

Resize the table with Lock Aspect Ratio

---

## Changing Text Alignment and Direction

- The way you align your text can help readers make sense of the information you're presenting.

- PowerPoint 2010 enables you to align text along the left margin, center it between cell margins, or align it along the right cell margin.

- You can also change text direction so that text extends vertically in a cell. This is sometimes helpful when you have long column titles but don't want to use wide columns.

- PowerPoint gives you a number of options for changing text direction. You can choose Horizontal, Rotate All Text 90˚, Rotate All Text 270˚, or Stacked.

- You can also choose More Options in the Text Direction list to further control cell margins, alignment, and spacing options.

---

## Try It!    **Aligning Text**

**1** In **PTry43_studentfirstname_studentlastname**, click in the second row of the table, and type the following in each of the cells:

No.

Course Title

Instructor

Days Offered

Features

✓ *You may need to reduce the size of the font for the new column headings you have just added. To do this, highlight the cell text you want to change and click 16 in the Font Size list when the Mini Toolbar appears.*

**2** Select the row of text you just entered and click Table Tools Layout > Center ▤ .

**3** Click Table Tools Layout > Center Vertically ▤ .

**4** Save changes and leave the file open to use in the next Try It.

## Try It!  Changing Text Direction

**1** In **PTry43_studentfirstname_studentlast name**, select the column labels if necessary.

**2** Click Table Tools Layout > Text Direction ⫼ᴬ .

**3** Click Rotate All Text 270˚.

**4** Click Table Tools Layout > Text Direction ⫼ᴬ , then click More Options.

**5** Click the Horizontal alignment drop-list arrow and choose Center.

**6** Click Close.

**7** Adjust the row height as needed to accommodate the text.

**8** Close the file, saving all changes, and exit PowerPoint.

✓ You can format the text labels as you would format any text in your presentation, by changing the font, style, size, or effect of the text. You may also want to click to position the insertion point between the word "Days" and "Offered" and press Enter to format the label on two lines.

**New text alignment**

| CLICK TO ADD TITLE |
| --- |

New Courses

| No. | Course Title | Instructor | Days Offered | Features |
| --- | --- | --- | --- | --- |
| | | | | |
| | | | | |

# Project 97—Create It

## Course Listing

### DIRECTIONS

1. Start PowerPoint 2010 if necessary, and open the file **PProj97** from the data files for this lesson.

2. Save the file as **PProj97_studentfirstname_ studentlastname** in the location where your teacher instructs you to store the files for this lesson.

3. Select **slide 2** and click in the title placeholder. Type **Course Offerings** and click outside the box.

4. Click the **Insert** tab and click **Table** ⊞ .

5. Choose **Draw Table** and move the pointer to the slide area.

6. Click and drag to draw a table that covers all but a small margin along the edges of the slide.

   ✓ Notice that the table is given a border using the same pen style, color, and weight you selected in the previous Try It. You will learn how to change border settings later in this chapter.

7. Click the **Table Tools Design** tab, click the **Pen Style** drop-down list, and choose the solid line.

8. Click **Table Tools Design** > **Pen Weight** drop-down list and click **2¼ pt**.

9. Click **Table Tools Design** > **Pen Color** ✎ and choose a dark orange color.

10. Move the pointer to the table.

11. Click at the top of the table and drag the mouse down to the bottom to create a column divider.

12. Repeat this step three times so that you create five columns.

13. Click at the left side of the table and draw a line to the right side of the table.

14. Repeat this step four times so that you have a total of six rows in your table.

15. Click **Table Tools Design** > **Eraser** ⊟ and erase all the column segments in **row 1**. Click the **Eraser** ⊟ button a second time to turn off the tool.

16. To merge the last two columns, highlight all cells in the last two columns of the table and click **Table Tools Layout** > **Merge Cells** ⊞ .

17. Resize the column on the right by dragging the column divider to the right.

18. Add the table title and column labels as shown in the following figure.

19. Select the column labels and click **Table Tools Layout > Center** ≣.

20. With the labels still selected, click **Table Tools Layout > Center Vertically** ≣.

21. **With your teacher's permission**, print the changed slide in the presentation. It should look similar to Figure 43-1.

22. Close the file, saving all changes, and exit PowerPoint.

**Figure 43-1**

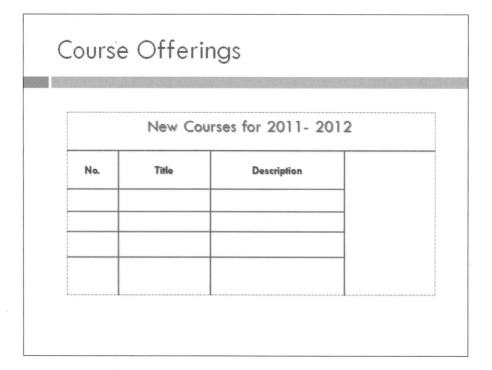

## Project 98—Apply It

## Course Listing

### DIRECTIONS

1. Start PowerPoint 2010 if necessary, and open the file **PProj98** from the data files for this lesson.

2. Save the file as **PProj98_studentfirstname_studentlastname** in the location where your teacher instructs you to store the files for this lesson.

3. Select a slide where you want to create a table and click in the title placeholder. Type the title **Courses New This Year** for the slide and click in the main area of the slide.

4. Draw a new large table on the slide.

5. Select a pen style, weight, and color.

6. Draw four columns and six rows.

7. Use the **Eraser** to merge the bottom two cells in each row so that you have a total of four columns and five rows.

8. Add the following column labels:

   Course name
   Instructor
   Days Offered
   Prerequisites

9. Change the text direction of the labels in columns 2-4 so that they rotate **270°**.

10. Adjust the row height to accommodate the labels.

11. Change the column width so **Course Name** has the majority of the room and the other three columns are narrower.

12. Align the column labels so that the text appears centered in the cells.

13. Select the **Course Name**, center it horizontally in the cell, and align it at the bottom.

14. **With your teacher's permission**, print the changed slide. It should look similar to Figure 43-2.

15. Close the file, saving all changes, and exit PowerPoint.

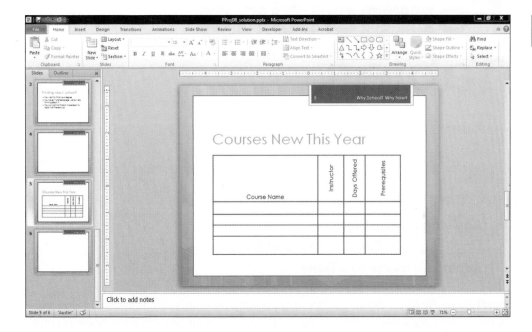

**Figure 43-2**

## WORDS TO KNOW

**Cell fill**
To fill an individual cell or selected cells with color.

**Gradient fill**
To add color with a particular gradient to selected cells.

**Table effects**
You can add table effects to selected cells, sections, or the entire table by using shadows, reflections, or a beveled appearance.

**Table shading**
You can add shading to individual cells, table sections, or your entire table by adding a color, pattern, texture, or picture as shading in your table.

**Table style**
A table style is a set of formatting choices you can apply automatically to your table.

**Texture fill**
Adding a textured visual effect (for example, Sand or Granite), to selected cells.

# Lesson 44

# Formatting Tables

## ➤ What You Will Learn

**Applying a Table Style**
**Modifying Cell Fill, Borders, and Effects**
**Adding an Image to a Table**

**Software Skills**   When you first draw a table on your slide, PowerPoint assigns a basic table style that reflects the overall theme of your presentation. Knowing how to choose a different table style, create your own custom styles, or change the look of individual cells, rows, and columns are all important skills, giving you the ability to tailor your tables and add that designer touch. Depending on the type of information you're displaying, you may want to add an image to the table as a background. This special effect can add "wow" to your presentation but you need to make sure you format the text carefully so the information in the table is still readable.

**Application Skills**   Your local wildlife organization is hosting a Habitat Stewards training, and you have been asked to create a presentation to help them spread the word. You want to create a table that showcases the training and lists the age groups, leaders, and locations. You want to create a table style that matches the organization's logo, and add a photo to the background of the table.

## What You Can Do

### Applying a Table Style

- A **table style** applies a particular color scheme, font selection, and background style to your table.
- You can use PowerPoint's built-in table styles and customize the look by adding Table Style Options.
- **Table shading** enables you to apply a **cell fill**, **gradient fill**, picture, or **texture fill** to selected cells or the entire table.

■ Click on the check boxes in the Table Style Options group to add specific elements to your table— Header Row, Table Row, Banded Rows, First Column, Last Column, Banded Column. These options control how shading is used in your table style.

■ Click the More button in the lower right corner of the Table Style gallery to display a large palette of table style choices. The table styles match the theme you have selected for your presentation; choose the one that best fits your content and audience.

## Try It!　Adding a Table Style

**1** Start PowerPoint, and open **PTry44** from the data files for this lesson.

**2** Save the file as **PTry44_studentfirstname_ studentlastname** in the location where your teacher instructs you to store the files for this lesson.

**3** Click in the table to select it.

**4** Click the Table Tools Design tab.

**5** In the Table Styles group, click the More button to display the gallery of choices.

**6** Click Themed Style 1, Accent 2.

**7** Click the Banded Rows check box in the Table Style Options group.

**8** Save changes and leave the file open to use in the next Try It.

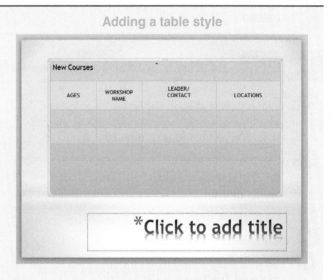

Adding a table style

## Modifying Cell Fill, Borders, and Effects

■ You can easily change the look and style of cells within the table by changing the **table effects**, or modifying the colors, borders, and effects of cells.

■ After you apply the table style to your table, you can fine-tune the look by changing the appearance of selected cells, rows, or columns.

■ One way to make a segment of a table stand out is to change the background color of the section.

■ You can also use borders to give a section of cells a special look.

■ PowerPoint 2010 also enables you to apply special effects to the table as a whole, adding a bevel effect, creating a reflection, or adding shadows.

■ The tools you need for fine-tuning the format of the table are on the Table Tools Design tab, which appears when you select the table.

■ The Shading, Border, and Effects tools are found in the right side of the Table Styles group.

✓ *You can change the background of the table as a whole by choosing the Effects tool and clicking the Table Background option at the bottom of the list.*

■ Each tool gives you a range of additional options from which to choose. Shading, for example, lets you select whether you want to add a cell fill color, a gradient, texture, or picture to the cell.

■ When you choose the Border tool, you can select from a list of 12 border options. You can customize the look of the border by changing the pen color, style, and weight in the Pen Color group.

■ Choosing Effects displays a list of three effects choices: Cell Bevel, Shadow, or Reflection. Cell Bevel changes the look of the individual cell, while Shadow and Reflection apply to the entire table.

**Try It!**    **Changing Cell Shading**

**1** In PTry44_studentfirstname_studentlast name, click the table and select the cells under Workshop Name.

**2** Click Table Tools Design > Shading 🪣.

**3** Click Turquoise, Accent 2 in the Theme Colors palette.

**4** Click Table Tools Design > Shading 🪣 > Gradient.

**5** In the Light Variations palette, click the first gradient in the upper left.

**6** Save your file and leave it open to use in the next Try It.

---

**Try It!**    **Adding a Border to Selected Cells**

**1** In PTry44_studentfirstname_ studentlastname, select the cells in the left column (below the column labels).

**2** Set the color of the border you want to create by choosing the Pen Style, Pen Weight, and Pen Color settings before you add the border.

**3** Click Table Tools Design > Borders ▦.

**4** Click All Borders.

**5** Save changes and leave the file open to use in the next Try It.

Adding a border to cells

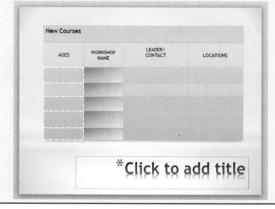

---

**Try It!**    **Adding Table Effects**

**1** In PTry44_studentfirstname_ studentlastname, select all the cells in the row containing the column labels.

**2** Press CTRL + B to bold the labels.

**3** Click Table Tools Design > Effects 🔲.

**4** Click Cell Bevel and click the Cool Slant bevel style.

**5** Click outside the table to see the effect of the beveling.

**6** Save changes and leave the file open to use in the next Try It.

✓ *If you want the text of the column labels to stand out a bit more, you may want to change the color of the column labels, or click the Home tab and in the Font group, click Text Shadow. This gives the text a 3-D effect on top of the beveling.*

---

## Adding an Image to a Table

■ You can add a special touch to your tables by including pictures.

■ You might add pictures of products you're introducing, company logos, or images that represent particular programs or people.

■ Add images by using the Shading tool in the table Styles group of the Table Tools Design tab.

■ If you choose an image that is not large enough to fill the selected area, PowerPoint will tile the image so the amount of space you selected is covered.

■ You can add an image to an individual cell or apply the image to the entire table background.

■ If you add an image to the table background, be sure to preview your slides to ensure that the text shows up against the image you have added.

## Try It! Adding a Picture to a Cell

1. In **PTry44_studentfirstname_studentlast name**, click the top cell in column 4, just beneath the column label.

2. Click Table Tools Design > Shading ◢ > Picture.

3. Navigate to the data files for this lesson, click **rick.jpg**, and click Open.

4. Resize the row height and column width if necessary to allow for the clear display of the photo.

5. Repeat with **kara.jpg**, **tuan.jpg**, and **etienne.jpg**.

6. Remove the unused table row by right-clicking in the last row of the table and choosing Delete Rows.

7. Save changes and leave the file open to use in the next Try It.

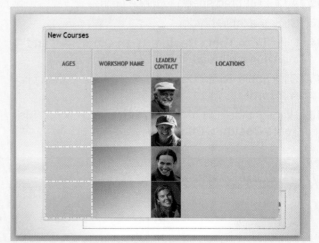
Adding pictures to cells

## Try It! Adding a Picture to the Table Background

1. In **PTry44_studentfirstname_studentlast name**, click Table Tools Design > Shading ◢ > Table Background.

2. Click Picture.

3. Navigate to the data files for this lesson and choose **background.jpg**.

4. Click Open.

5. Make text changes as necessary to ensure the text is readable against the picture background.

6. Close the files, saving all changes, and exit PowerPoint

# Project 99—Create It

## Program Spotlight

### DIRECTIONS

1. Start PowerPoint 2010 if necessary, and open the file **PProj99** from the data files for this lesson.

2. Save the file as **PProj99_studentfirstname_studentlastname** in the location where your teacher instructs you to store the files for this lesson.

3. Click **slide 2** and enter the slide title **Our Most Popular Programs**.

4. Draw a table in the center of the slide area. Add four columns and five rows.

5. Merge the cells in row 1. Enter the title **Join Us!**.

6. Click the **Table Tools Design** tab and click the **More** button in the **Table Styles** gallery.

7. Click the **Themed Style 2, Accent 6** style to apply it to the table.

8. Click **Table Tools Design** > **Banded Rows**.

9. Click in the column labels row and type **Program, For Ages, Leaders,** and **Locations**.

10. Click **Home** > **Text Shadow** Ⓢ to make the characters stand out.

11. Highlight the last column on the right (from the column labels down) and click **Table Tools Design** > **Shading** 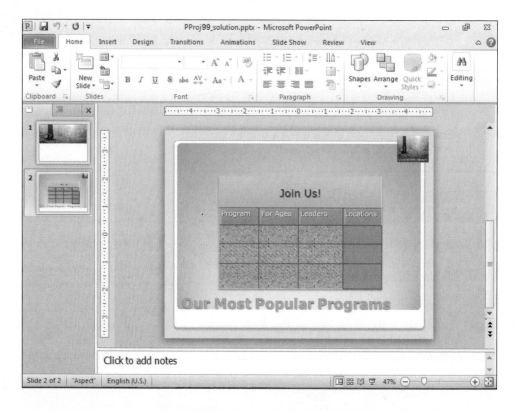.

12. Add a light red shade to these cells.

13. Click the table border.

14. Click Table **Tools Design** > **Pen Color**, and then choose a dark tan.

15. Click Table **Tools Design** > **Borders**, then click **All Borders**.

16. Highlight the row of column labels and click **Table Tools Design** > **Effects**.

17. Point to **Cell Bevel** and click the first item in the gallery.

18. Highlight all cells below the column labels in **columns 1** through **3**.

19. Click **Table Tools Design** > **Shading**, and then click **Texture**.

20. Click the **Woven Mat** texture.

21. **With your teacher's permission**, print slide 2. It should look similar to Figure 44-1.

22. Close the file, saving all changes, and exit PowerPoint.

**Figure 44-1**

# Project 100—Apply It

## Program Spotlight

### DIRECTIONS

1. Start PowerPoint 2010 if necessary, and open the file **PProj100** from the data files for this lesson.

2. Save the file as **PProj100_studentfirstname_ studentlastname** in the location where your teacher instructs you to store the files for this lesson.

3. Choose a slide where you want to add the table.

4. Type a title of your choosing for the slide.

5. Create a new table by clicking the Insert Table icon in the center of the slide and add columns for each of the following items:

    **Program name**
    **Year started**
    **# of campers then**
    **# of campers now**

6. Enter the data shown in Figure 44-2.

7. Apply a table style that complements the design.

8. Add any Table Options you feel fit what you want to show in this table.

9. Change the background color of the column that shows the number of campers in the various programs today.

10. Bevel the column label cells.

11. Right-click the column on the left and choose **Insert Column to the Right**.

12. Adjust the new column so that its width is **1 inch**.

13. Add a column label for the new column, select the text, and change the Text Direction.

14. Add the following photos from the data files to the background of the cells in column 2, then adjust the column width or row height as needed:

    **Swimming – swimming.jpg**
    **Hiking – hiking.jpg**
    **Camping – camping.jpg**
    **Gardening – garden.jpg**

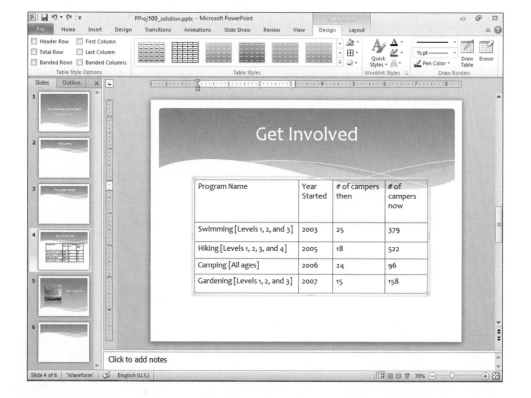

**Figure 44-2**

**15.** Format the slide text as needed to ensure that the program names stand out against the table background.

✓ *You may need to change the text font, size, or color to increase the contrast so the text is readable.*

**16.** Click the table border and add a shadow effect to the entire table.

**17.** **With your teacher's permission**, print the slide. It should look similar to Figure 44-3.

**18.** Close the file, saving all changes, and exit PowerPoint.

**Figure 44-3**

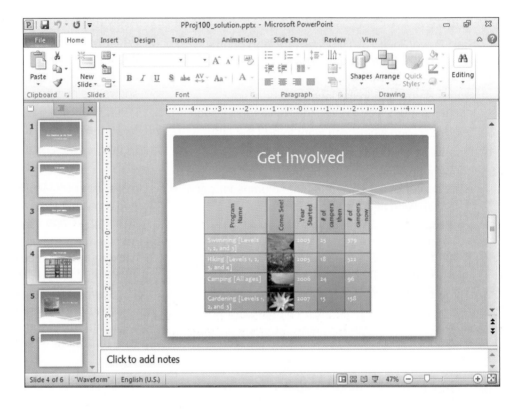

# Lesson 45

# Formatting Charts

## ➤ What You Will Learn

**Applying Advanced Chart Formatting**

**Software Skills**　Being able to present information in different ways is an important part of really connecting with your audience. Some people understand concepts best when they see them diagrammed; others like text; others like numbers and charts. PowerPoint includes an easy-to-use but fairly sophisticated charting tool that uses Excel 2010 as the basis for charts you create in PowerPoint.

**Application Skills**　In this lesson, you will explore PowerPoint's advanced charting tools.

**WORDS TO KNOW**

**Error bars**
A chart feature available for some chart types that enables you to show a range of possible values.

**Trendlines**
A chart feature that displays a line showing the progression of value change over time.

## What You Can Do

### Applying Advanced Chart Formatting

- PowerPoint 2010 includes a number of features you can use to add advanced formatting to your **chart elements**.

- Two advanced tools that help you in analyzing and presenting your data are **trendlines** and **error bars. Trendlines** show the progression of your data over time, and **error bars** show the high and low range of values that are possible for the given data item.

- You'll find the tools you need in the Chart Tools Layout tab.

- The advanced options that are available will depend on the type of chart you have created and selected. For example, you cannot add trendlines to 3-D, radar, pie, doughnut, or surface charts.

- You can customize advanced formatting—such as trendlines and error bars—by changing the line color, style, regression type, and format.

## Try It!    Adding Trendlines

1. Start PowerPoint, and open **PTry45** from the data files for this lesson.

2. Save the file as **PTry45_studentfirstname_studentlastname** in the location where your teacher instructs you to store the files for this lesson.

3. Click slide 3 and click in the chart on that slide.

4. Click Chart Tools Layout > Trendline.

5. Choose Linear Trendline.

6. Save your changes and leave the file open to use in the next Try It.

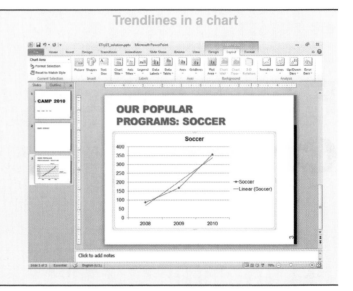

Trendlines in a chart

## Try It!    Modifying Trendlines

1. In **PTry45_studentfirstname_studentlast name**, click the chart, then click Chart Tools Layout > Trendline > More Trendline Options.

2. In the Format Trendline dialog box, click Moving Average.

3. Click Line Color and select Solid Line.

4. Click the Color arrow and choose Red.

5. Click Line Style, and set Begin Type and End Type to Diamond Arrow.

6. Click Close.

7. Save changes and leave the file open to use in the next Try It.

## Try It!    Adding Error Bars

1. In **PTry45_studentfirstname_studentlast name**, click slide 4 and select the chart.

2. Click Chart Tools Layout > Error Bars > Error Bars with Standard Error.

3. Click Chart Tools Layout > Error Bars > More Error Bar Options.

4. In the Add Error Bars dialog box, click the 2010 data series.

5. Click Line Color and choose Gradient Line.

*(continued)*

### Try It!    Adding Error Bars *(continued)*

**6** Click the Preset Colors arrow and choose Ocean.

**7** Drag the Gradient Stops to set the color gradient as you'd like it to appear.

**8** Click Close.

**9** Close the file, saving all changes, and exit PowerPoint

> ✓ *Note that the changes are applied only to the data series currently selected. To modify another set of error bars, choose the data series in the Chart Elements setting in the Current Selection group of the Chart Tools Layout tab.*

The chart with error bars

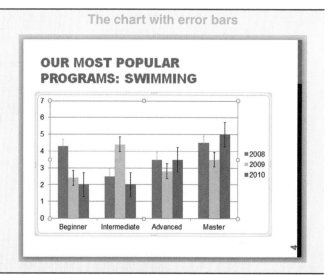

---

# Project 101—Create It

## Growth Chart

### DIRECTIONS

1. Start PowerPoint 2010 if necessary, and open the file **PProj101** from the data files for this lesson.

2. Save the file as **PProj101_studentfirstname_ studentlastname** in the location where your teacher instructs you to store the files for this lesson.

3. Click **slide 3** and select the chart.

4. Click the **Chart Tools Layout** tab, then click the **Chart Elements** drop-down list in the Current Selection group.

5. Click Series **"Program 1"**.

6. Click **Chart Tools Layout** > **Error Bars** 📊 > **Error Bars with Standard Error**.

7. Change the look of the bars by clicking **Chart Tools Layout** > **Error Bars** 📊 > **More Error Bars Options**.

8. Click the **Line Color** setting and click **Solid Line**.

9. Click the **Color** arrow and choose a dark aqua color.

10. Drag the **Transparency** slider to **30%**.

11. Click **Close**.

12. **With your teacher's permission**, print slide 3. It should look similar to Figure 45-1.

13. Close the file, saving all changes, and exit PowerPoint.

**Figure 45-1**

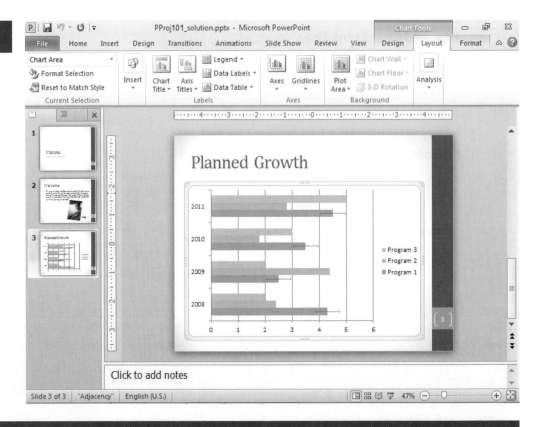

# Project 102—Apply It

## Growth Chart

### DIRECTIONS

1. Start PowerPoint 2010 if necessary, and open the file **PProj102** from the data files for this lesson.

2. Save the file as **PProj102_studentfirstname_studentlastname** in the location where your teacher instructs you to store the files for this lesson.

3. Click **slide 4** and select the **Program Changes** chart.

4. On the **Chart Tools Layout** tab, click **Series "Waste Management"** in the **Chart Elements** drop-down list, found in the Current Selection group.

5. Add trendlines to the "**Waste Management**" series.

6. Change the look of the trendline by choosing a different color, line style, and weight.

7. Customize the color, style, and weight of those trendlines to contrast against "**Waste Management**".

8. Click the **Glow and Soft Edges** option in the **Format Trendline** dialog box, and add a **Glow** setting to one of the trendlines.

9. **With your teacher's permission**, print the presentation. It should look similar to Figure 45-2.

10. Close the file, saving all changes, and exit PowerPoint.

Figure 45-2

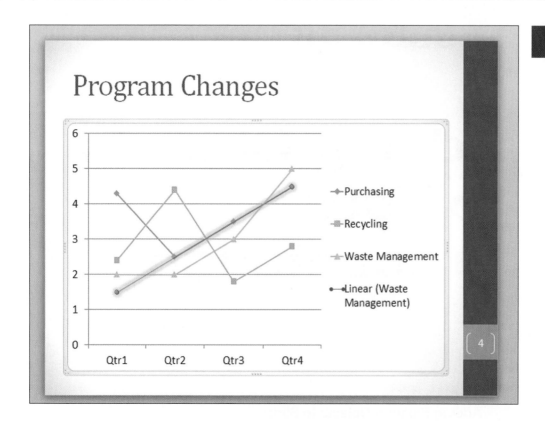

# Lesson 46

## Adding Objects to Your Presentation

> **What You Will Learn**

**Adding Existing Objects to Slides**
**Using Paste Special to Embed or Link Object Data**
**Copying Objects from Slide to Slide**

**Software Skills**   One of the great things about PowerPoint is that if you've created items in other programs that you'd like to show in your presentation, you can easily add the item as an object on your PowerPoint slide. PowerPoint enables you to create new objects or add existing objects to your presentation, and you can link the object or embed it, depending on how you plan to work with the object in the future.

**Application Skills**   You are working on two presentations for a volunteer organization. You have previously created a worksheet in Excel that you'd like to include in the presentation, but you want to link the file so that if you make changes in the original worksheet later, the presentation will update automatically.

## What You Can Do

### Adding Existing Objects to Slides

- If you've created other presentations, video clips, tutorials, interviews, graphic designs, or other items you'd like to add to your slides, you can add the elements as objects in your PowerPoint presentation.

- When you add an object to a slide, you have the option of linking the object or embedding it.

■ Linking an object enables you to maintain a link to the original file so that if you update the file later, the changes are reflected in the PowerPoint presentation.

■ If you choose to embed an object in the file, the information is included as part of the PowerPoint file. In some cases this can make the size of the PowerPoint file very large.

## Try It! Adding an Object to a Slide

**1** Start PowerPoint, and open **PTry46** from the data files for this lesson.

**2** Save the file as **PTry46_studentfirstname_ studentlastname** in the location where your teacher instructs you to store the files for this lesson.

**3** Display slide 5 of the presentation.

**4** Click Insert > Object 📄.

**5** In the Insert Object dialog box, click the Create From File button.

**6** Click Browse and navigate to the data files for this lesson. Click **energy_current.xlsx** and click OK.

**7** Click the Link check box and click OK again to add the object to the slide.

**8** Add a second object, **energy_green.xlsx**, on the right side of the slide, also linking to the source file.

**9** Save your changes and leave the file open to use in the next Try It.

✓ *If you want to create a link to the object you have added so that any changes that are made to the original file appear in your PowerPoint presentation, click the Link check box before clicking OK.*

Inserting an object

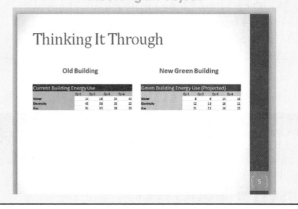

## Using Paste Special to Embed or Link Object Data

■ You can also copy and paste an object from one application to another by copying the item in the original application and using Paste Special in PowerPoint.

■ You have the option of either linking or embedding the pasted file, just as you do when you insert the object on the slide.

■ The Paste Special tool is available when you click the Paste tool in the Clipboard group of the Home tab.

## Try It! Adding an Object Using Paste Special

**1** With **PTry46_studentfirstname_studentlast name** open, navigate to open the Excel worksheet **PTry46_worksheet** from your data folder.

**2** Select the chart in **PTry46_worksheet** and copy it by pressing `CTRL` + `C`.

**3** Click on **PTry46_studentfirstname_ studentlastname**, then click slide 6.

**4** Click Home > Paste 📋 > Paste Special.

**5** In the Paste Special dialog box, click Paste Link.

**6** Click OK.

**7** Close **PTry46_worksheet**. Save changes in **PTry46_studentfirstname_studentlastname** and leave it open to use in the next Try It.

✓ *This process maintains a link to the original file so that when that file is changed the object on the slide will reflect the changes.*

✓ *If you want to include the data in the file instead of creating a link, select Paste and click OK.*

## Copying Objects from Slide to Slide

■ Copying an object from slide to slide in PowerPoint is a simple copy and paste operation.

■ Click the object you want to copy and press `CTRL` + `C` or choose Copy from the Clipboard group of the Home tab.

■ Click the slide where you want to paste the object and press `CTRL` + `V` or choose Paste from the Clipboard group of the Home tab.

---

**Try It!** **Copying and Pasting Objects from Slide to Slide**

1. In **PTry46_studentfirstname_studentlast name**, click slide 2, then click the photo.

2. Press `CTRL` + `C` to copy it.

3. Display the Clipboard by clicking the dialog box launcher in the lower right corner of the Clipboard group.

4. Click slide 5 so that you can paste the object.

5. Click the photo in the Clipboard.

6. Click Paste.

7. Close the file, saving all changes, and exit PowerPoint

---

# Project 103—Create It

## Insert a Worksheet

1. Start PowerPoint 2010 if necessary, and open the file **PProj103** from the data files for this lesson.

2. Save the file as **PProj103_studentfirstname_ studentlastname** in the location where your teacher instructs you to store the files for this lesson.

3. Click **Home** > **New Slide** to add a slide to the presentation. Choose the **Title and Content** layout.

4. Click in the title area and type **Operating Expenses**.

5. Click **Insert** > **Object**.

6. In the Insert Object dialog box, click **Create From File**.

7. Click **Browse** and navigate to the data folder for this lesson.

8. Click the **PProj103_worksheet** file, click **Open**, and then click **OK**.

9. Click the added object and press `CTRL` + `C`.

10. Add a new slide.

11. Click **Home** > **Paste**.

   ✓ If you want to see which objects are currently stored on the Clipboard, click the Clipboard dialog box launcher in the lower right corner of the Clipboard group.

12. Resize the object by clicking the border and dragging in the direction you want to resize.

13. Add a gradient behind the worksheet to see which version you want to keep.

14. Delete the slide you don't want to use by right-clicking it and clicking **Delete Slide**.

15. **With your teacher's permission**, print the changed slide, which should look similar to Figure 46-1.

16. Close the file, saving all changes, and exit PowerPoint.

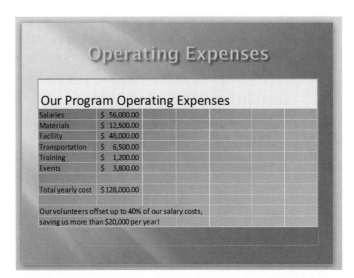

Figure 46-1

# Project 104—Apply It

## Link a Worksheet

### DIRECTIONS

1. Start PowerPoint 2010 if necessary, and open the file **PProj104** from the data files for this lesson.

2. Save the file as **PProj104_studentfirstname_ studentlastname** in the location where your teacher instructs you to store the files for this lesson.

3. Create a new slide that will store the worksheet object.

4. Add a title for the slide.

5. Insert the object **wildlife_worksheet.xlsx** from the data files for this lesson.

6. Create a link from the file to the object on the slide.

7. Open **PProj104b** from your lesson data files.

8. Click the logo on slide 1.

9. Copy the logo (be sure to click both parts) and close the file.

10. In the original file, use Paste Special to add the logo to the slide.

11. Copy the new logo, and paste it in the lower right corner of the slide.

   ✓ *Alternately, you can add the logo to the slide master so that it will appear on every slide. Click the View tab and click Slide Master in the Master Views group. Paste the object at the place on the slide where you want it to appear and click Close Master View.*

12. **With your teacher's permission**, print the changed slide in the presentation. It should look similar to Figure 46-2.

13. Close the file, saving all changes, and exit PowerPoint.

**Figure 46-2**

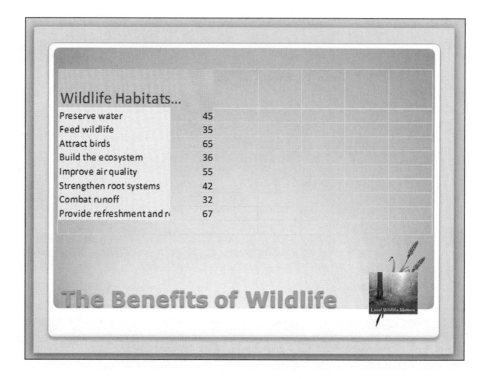

# Chapter Assessment and Application

# Project 105—Make It Your Own

## Children's Book Table

A local literacy organization is hosting a panel discussion for teachers on great children's literature. You have been asked to help them prepare a presentation they will introduce at the beginning of the session.

You will create a table to spotlight four favorite children's books for different ages, listing the title, author, showing a cover image (and attributing the copyright holder), and suggesting the appropriate age level. You will also create a chart to showcase the contribution children's literature makes to reading scores in the primary grades and incorporate a worksheet showing national reading averages.

### DIRECTIONS

1. Start PowerPoint 2010 if necessary, and open the file **PProj105** from the data files for this project.

2. Save the file as **PProj105_studentfirstname_ studentlastname** in the location where your teacher instructs you to store the files for this project.

3. Create a new title and content slide and add a slide title.

4. Create a table on the new slide.

5. Choose the pen color, weight, and style you want to use and add four columns and six rows.

6. Add column labels (**Title**, **Author**, **Cover**, and **Age**) and format the labels as you'd like.

7. Increase the width of the **Title** column.

8. Increase the row height to make room for the cover images you will place later in this project.

9. Resize the table to maximize the amount of room it uses on the slide.

10. Enter the text shown in Illustration A.

**Illustration A**

## BOOKS YOU HAVE TO READ

| Title | Author | Cover | Age |
|---|---|---|---|
| *Pat the Bunny* | Dorothy Kunhardt | | Toddler |
| *The Very Hungry Caterpillar* | Eric Carle | | Preschool |
| *Where the Wild Things Are* | Maurice Sendak | | Kindergarten-Grade 2 |
| *Eloise* | Kay Thompson | | Grade 2-Grade 4 |

9/7/2010                                                                 2

11. Center the column labels.

12. Left-align the table text.

13. Select the cells beneath the **Age** column label, and change their shade to a color that complements the table style you selected.

14. Click **Table Tools Design** > **Border** and choose **All Borders** for those cells.

15. Right-click in the top cell of the table and choose **Delete Row**.

16. Highlight the column labels, click **Table Tools Design** > **Effects** , and click **Cell Bevel**. Click the second item in the gallery.

17. Click in the cell just beneath the **Cover** column label, and click **Picture Tools Design** > **Shading** .

18. From the data files for this project, add the cover for **Pat the Bunny** to this cell.

19. Continue adding the other cover images to the table.

20. Save the file and create **slide 3** using the title and content format.

21. Add the title **Our Research Shows**.

22. Insert a column style chart.

23. In the datasheet that appears, enter the information shown in Illustration B.

24. Add trendlines to show the progression of the **Read To** data series.

25. Customize the trendlines so they stand out in contrast to the chart.

26. Add a new slide with the title **National Statistics**.

27. Open the **PProj105b** file, click the table image, and press CTRL + C.

28. Return to **PProj105_studentfirstname_ studentlast name**, click **Home** > **Paste** > **Paste Special**.

29. Click **Bitmap** and click **OK**. The image is added to your slide.

30. Resize the image as needed and add a picture effect, shadow, or other style if you'd like.

31. **With your teacher's permission**, print the changed slide in the presentation. It should look similar to Illustration C.

32. Close the file, saving all changes, and exit PowerPoint.

**Illustration B**

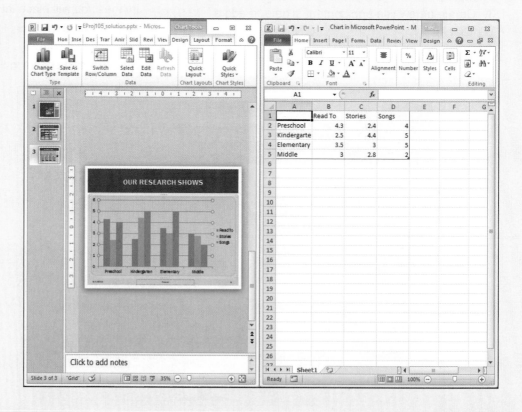

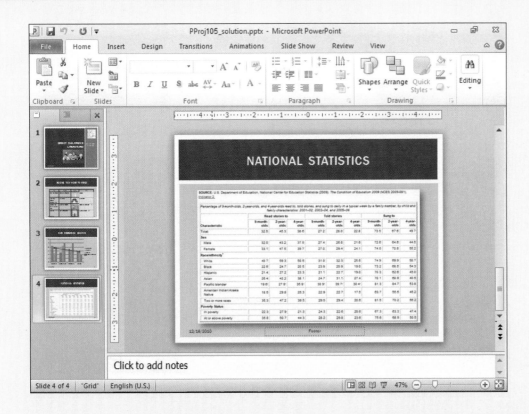

Illustration C

# Project 106—Master It

## Jazz Showcase

A local jazz ensemble is putting out a presentation that will share what they've done over the past year and invite jazz lovers to contribute to their upcoming event. They've asked you to help prepare the presentation they will use in their fundraising. One part of the presentation involves creating a table of jazz samples from their various performances.

In this project, you create and format the table, adding links to the sound clips and activating the object so that listeners will be able to hear the clips during the presentation.

### DIRECTIONS

1. Start PowerPoint 2010 if necessary, and open the file **PProj106** from the data files for this lesson.

2. Save the file as **PProj106_studentfirstname_ studentlastname** in the location where your teacher instructs you to store the files for this lesson.

3. Click **slide 2** and title it **Jazz Samples**.

4. Create a table with three columns and six rows.

5. Choose the pen color, weight, and style you want to use.

6. Merge the top row into one cell and add a table title.

7. Add column labels (**Date**, **Event**, and **Sound Clip**) and center them.

8. Increase the size of the **Event** column.

9. Enter the text shown in Illustration A, left-aligning the table text and centering it vertically.

**Illustration A**

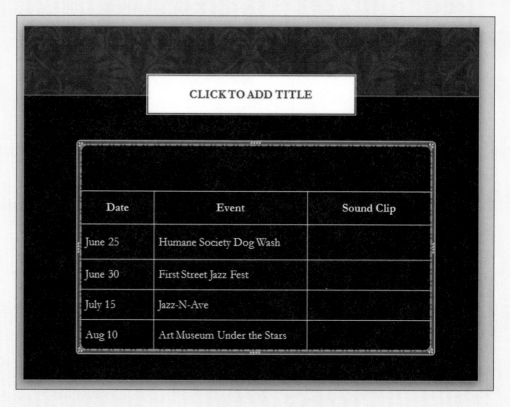

CLICK TO ADD TITLE

| Date | Event | Sound Clip |
|------|-------|------------|
| June 25 | Humane Society Dog Wash | |
| June 30 | First Street Jazz Fest | |
| July 15 | Jazz-N-Ave | |
| Aug 10 | Art Museum Under the Stars | |

10. Lock the aspect ratio of the table and enter new values in the measurement boxes to enlarge it as much as possible.

11. Apply a table style that fits the overall theme of the presentation. Adjust the text and border colors as needed to complement the table style.

12. Select the table cells in the **Sound Clip** column and apply a lighter shade of background color.

13. Insert the sound objects (**jazz01.mid**, **jazz02.mid**, **jazz03.mid**, and **jazz04.wav**), one in each cell in that column.

14. Activate the sound objects by clicking each one and clicking the **Animations** tab, choosing **Add Animation**, **OLE Action Verbs**, and **Activate Contents**. Click **OK**.

15. Create slides 3 through 6 using the **Title and Content** layout for each.

16. Copy the first sound clip on **slide 2** and paste it in the brown box on **slide 3**.

17. Copy the second sound clip on **slide 2** and paste it on **slide 4**.

18. Repeat this copy and paste operation for the remaining two slides.

19. Save your work and press F5 to view the presentation.

20. On **slide 2**, click the first sound clip in the table to ensure that it plays correctly.

21. **With your teacher's permission**, print the changed slides in the presentation.

22. Close the file, saving all changes, and exit PowerPoint.

## Chapter 8

# Publishing a
# Presentation

## Lesson 47
## Customizing Your Presentation
## Projects 107-108

- Using the Outline Tab to Create Slide Content
- Applying More Than One Theme
- Replacing Fonts Throughout a Presentation

## Lesson 48
## Fine-Tuning Content Placement
## Projects 109-110

- Adjusting Paragraph Indents
- Setting Tab Stops
- Working with Placeholders and Text Boxes
- Using Text Alignment and Direction Options

## Lesson 49
## Searching for and Researching Content
## Projects 111-112

- Finding and Replacing Text
- Using the Research Tools
- Viewing Slides in Grayscale or Black and White

## Lesson 50
## Sharing a Presentation
## Projects 113-114

- Preparing to Share a Presentation
- Using the PowerPoint Web App
- Working with Co-Authors

## Lesson 51
## Presenting on the Web
## Projects 115-116

- Preparing to Broadcast
- Broadcasting and Viewing a Web Presentation

## Lesson 52
## Protecting and Finalizing a Presentation
## Projects 117-118

- Applying Passwords to a Presentation
- Marking a Presentation as Final
- Adding a Digital Signature

## End-of-Chapter Assessment
## Projects 119-120

# Lesson 47

# Customizing Your Presentation

**WORDS TO KNOW**

**Collapse**
When you collapse a level in the Outline tab, you hide text levels in the outline beneath the one you're collapsing.

**Demote**
To change selected text to a lower level (for example, to turn a bullet entry into a secondary bullet).

**Expand**
Expanding text levels in the Outline tab displays the text levels beneath the selected level in the outline.

**Outline tab**
The Outline tab in PowerPoint appears as a tab in the Slides pane that appears along the left side of Normal view. You can use the Outline tab to enter or paste text in your presentation quickly.

**Promote**
To move selected text up one text level (for example, to move text from a bullet entry to a title).

## ➤ What You Will Learn

**Using the Outline Tab to Create Slide Content**
**Applying More Than One Theme**
**Replacing Fonts Throughout a Presentation**

**Software Skills**   In some situations you may be creating presentations that are based on content you already have. Maybe you're using text from a Web page, an annual report, or a product catalog. Or perhaps you think best by writing all the content first and then formatting it on the slides as you go. In both these cases, you can use the Outline tab to enter the content quickly and then apply the formats you want afterwards. You can also apply multiple themes to different parts of your presentation and even change all the fonts with a simple search and replace operation.

**Application Skills**   You are working with a local recycling center to produce an informational presentation that shows visitors how to use the new recycling bins. You will be copying some of the content from an existing training manual, and you'll be typing the rest. You want to apply a different theme to different sections in the presentation, and then replace the font used for slide content throughout the presentation.

## What You Can Do

### Using the Outline Tab to Create Slide Content

- The **Outline** tab is located behind the Slides tab on the left side of Normal view.
- You can use the Outline tab to add or delete slide text, change the order of slides, or change the text level of slide content.
- You can also **expand** and **collapse** the display of text in the Outline tab. For example, you might collapse text on slides so that only the slide title shows, or you might expand all text so you can see all slide content.

- In the Outline tab you can also **promote** and **demote** selected text to move it among text levels on your slide.

- You can select and edit text in Outline view just as you can edit text on a slide.

- You can copy and paste text into the Outline tab to add text quickly, and then assign the necessary text levels to the various text items on the slide.

- You can close the Outline tab by clicking the close box in the upper-right corner of the panel. To display the Slide and Outline tab again, position the pointer over the edge of the vertical splitter bar and drag the pane to the right.

---

**Try It!**    **Adding and Changing Text in the Outline Tab**

**1** Start PowerPoint, and open **PTry47** from the data files for this lesson.

**2** Save the file as **PTry47_studentfirstname_studentlastname** in the location where your teacher instructs you to store the files for this lesson.

**3** Click the Outline tab.

**4** Click in Slide 2 and type the following: **Introduction**.

**5** Press `ENTER`, and then press `TAB`.

**6** Type **Our agenda today**, press `ENTER`; type **What you'll learn**, and press `ENTER`; **Why it matters**, press `ENTER`; and type **What you can do next**.

**7** Right-click *What you can do next* and click Promote.

**8** Save changes and leave the presentation open to use in the next Try It.

Adding text in the Outline Tab

---

**Try It!**    **Rearranging Slides in the Outline Tab**

**1** In **PTry47_studentfirstname_studentlastname**, click to select the text in Slide 3 in the Outline tab.

**2** Drag the slide text up to precede slide 2.

**3** Release the mouse button.

*(continued)*

**Try It!**    **Rearranging Slides in the Outline Tab** *(continued)*

④ Click at the end of *Why it matters* and press `ENTER` .

⑤ Type **Meet our staff**.

⑥ Highlight *Meet our staff* and drag the text item so that it follows *Our agenda today*.

⑦ Save and close your file.

## Applying More Than One Theme

■ PowerPoint themes enable you to apply a consistent look and feel—in the form of a color scheme, font selections, and special effects for objects and boxes—for your presentation. You can include more than one theme, creating a kind of presentation within a presentation, by using more than one slide master.

■ PowerPoint 2010 also enables you to create sections for your presentation so that you can easily navigate through your slides and organize headers and footers, designs and more.

■ You can create a new section by clicking the Slides tab and then choosing Section in the Slides group of the Home tab. You can right-click the new section and rename it.

■ You can then add a slide master to the section to ensure that the new theme is used for all the slides you specify.

■ Adding a second theme involves adding the additional design to the Slide Master so that all designs are available for you to include in your presentation.

**Try It!**    **Creating a PowerPoint Section**

① Open **PTry47b** from the data files for this lesson.

② Save the file as **PTry47b_studentfirstname_studentlastname** in the location where your teacher instructs you to store the files for this lesson.

③ Click the Slides tab and click Slide 4.

④ Click Home > Section 📋.

⑤ Click Add Section.

⑥ Right-click the new section in the Slides tab and click Rename Section.

⑦ Enter the name **Green Techniques** in the Rename Section dialog box, and click Rename.

⑧ Save changes and leave the file open to use in the next Try It.

Creating a new section

## Try It!    Adding a Second Theme to Your Presentation

1. In **PTry47b_studentfirstname_ studentlastname**, click View > Slide Master 🗔.

2. Scroll all the way down to the bottom of the Slides tab, and click the space beneath the last slide example. The black insert bar appears.

3. Click Slide Master > Themes 🅰.

4. Click the Concourse theme. The slide masters for this theme are added below the slide masters for the current theme in the Slides tab.

5. Click Slide Master > Close Master View 🗙.

6. Save changes and leave the file open to use in the next Try It.

Adding a second theme to a section

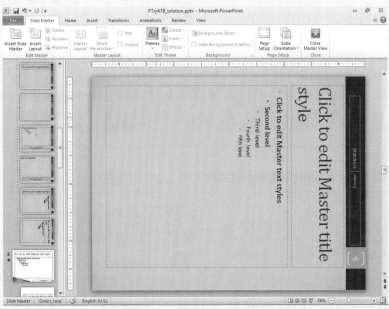

## Try It!    Applying the Second Presentation Theme

1. In **PTry47b_studentfirstname_ studentlastname**, click Slide 4 (the first slide in the second section).

2. Click Home > Layout 🗔.

3. Click the Title and Content slide in the Concourse theme at the bottom of the Layout gallery.

4. Select Slides 5 through 8 and apply the same theme and layout style to those slides.

5. Save changes and leave the file open to use in the next Try It.

## Replacing Fonts Throughout a Presentation

■ The font you choose for the text and titles in your presentation do a lot to convey the tone of the materials. For example, Times New Roman has a business-like feel; Comic Sans is more light-hearted; and Bradley Hand ITC is casual but may be difficult for an audience to read.

■ If you use one specific font throughout your presentation and then decide you want to change it later, you can have PowerPoint replace the font everywhere it is used in your presentation.

- You can change the fonts in your presentation by applying a new theme, selecting a different font using the Fonts selection in the Themes group, or using the Replace tool in the Editing group of the Home tab to search and replace fonts.

- Each theme in PowerPoint defines one font for headings and one font for body text.

- If you use the Font tool to choose a font that is outside the font selection for your current theme, you won't be able to change the font automatically in the future by simply selecting a different theme.

---

**Try It!**    **Replacing Fonts in a Theme**

1. In **PTry47b_studentfirstname_ studentlastname**, click Slide 1.

2. Select the title on the slide and click Home > Font drop-down list.

3. Notice the fonts listed in the Theme Fonts area at the top of the fonts drop-down list.

4. Change the font to Calibri.

5. Click Slide 4 and click in the slide title text.

6. Click Home > Font drop-down list.

7. Notice the fonts in the Theme Fonts area.

8. Save changes and leave the file open to use in the next Try It.

   ✓ *If you add more than one theme to your presentation, all fonts available in the added themes will also appear in your Theme Fonts area. This increases the range of fonts you can choose and still enable PowerPoint to change the fonts automatically if you choose a different theme.*

---

**Try It!**    **Searching and Replacing Fonts**

1. In **PTry47b_studentfirstname_ studentlastname**, click Slide 1.

2. Click the Home > Replace drop-down list.

3. Click Replace Fonts.

4. Click the Replace arrow and choose Calibri.

5. Click the With arrow and choose Georgia.

6. Click Replace to make the change.

7. Save your changes and close the file.

---

# Project 107—Create It

## Adding Content and Applying Themes

### DIRECTIONS

1. Start PowerPoint 2010 if necessary, and open **PProj107** from the data files for this lesson.

2. Save the file as **PProj107_studentfirstname_ studentlastname** in the location where your teacher instructs you to save files for this lesson.

3. Click **Slide 2** and click the **Outline** tab.

4. Type the following information, pressing ENTER after each entry:

   **Introduction**

   **Our Recycling Program**

   **New Additions**

   **Dropping Off Your Recycling**

   **Ordering New Bins**

5. Open **PProj107_recycling.doc** and copy the two paragraphs and list from pages 8 and 9.

6. Click at the end of the title of Slide 3 in the Outline tab.

7. Press ENTER and press TAB .

8. Paste the information from the document.

9. Click **Slide 1** and click the **Design** tab.

10. Apply the theme **Flow** to the presentation.

11. Click Slide 5 in the Slides tab and click **Home** > **Section** . Click **Add Section**.

12. Right-click **Untitled Section** and name the section **How-To Guidelines**.

13. Click **View > Slide Master** 🖽.

14. Scroll to the bottom of the Slides tab, and click the space beneath the last slide.

15. Click **Slide Master > Themes** 🅰.

16. Click the **Austin** theme and click **Slide Master > Close Master View** ☒.

17. Click **Slide 5** again and apply the **Austin** theme to that slide and **Slide 6** by clicking **Home > Layout** 🖽, and then clicking the **Title and Content** layout.

18. Click **Home > Replace** 🔤 to replace the **Century Gothic** font with **Calibri**, so all headings in the presentation are the same.

19. **With your teacher's permission**, print the changed slide in the presentation.

20. Close the file, saving all changes, and exit PowerPoint.

    ✓ *Note that once you search and replace fonts in the file, the fonts will be changed even on new slides you add to the presentation after you make the change.*

# Project 108—Apply It

## Training Presentation

### DIRECTIONS

1. Start PowerPoint if necessary, and open **PProj108** from the data files for this lesson.

2. Save the file as **PProj108_studentfirstname_ studentlastname** in the location where your teacher instructs you to save files for this lesson.

3. Apply a theme to the training presentation.

4. In the **Outline** tab, add the following titles to slides 2 through 5:

   **Welcome!**

   **Introductions**

   **Our Agenda Today**

   **Why Training Matters**

5. Click **Slide 1** and choose a new theme for the presentation.

       ✓ *Customize the theme if you like by using the Colors, Fonts, or Effects tools in the Themes group of the Design tab.*

6. Create a new section beginning with **Slide 5** and name it a name of your own choosing.

7. Add another theme to the presentation and apply that theme to the second section.

8. Use Replace Fonts to ensure that all the headings in your presentation are displayed in the same font.

9. **With your teacher's permission**, print the presentation. Figure 47-1 shows slide 5 in the presentation.

10. Close the file, saving all changes, and exit PowerPoint.

**Figure 47-1**

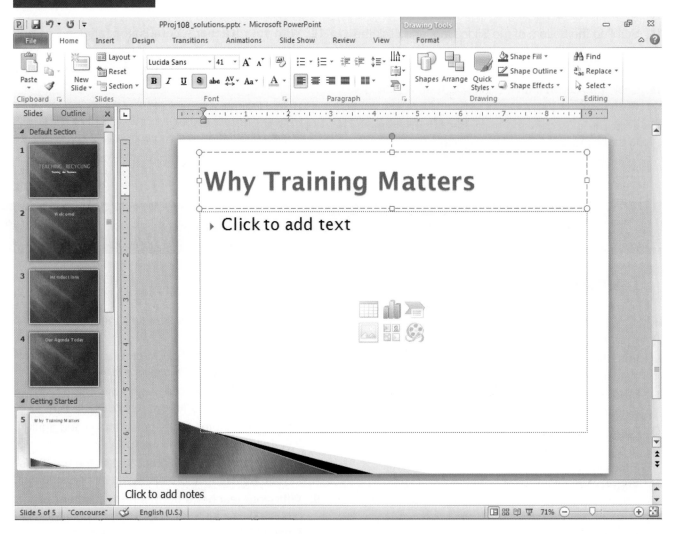

# Lesson 48

# Fine-Tuning Content Placement

➤ **What You Will Learn**

**Adjusting Paragraph Indents**
**Setting Tab Stops**
**Working with Placeholders and Text Boxes**
**Using Text Alignment and Direction Options**

**Software Skills**    Sometimes formatting content in PowerPoint can be a little tricky. You need to know how to control the spacing in your text boxes, add tab stops, and set up the alignment and direction of text just the way you want it. Using the Paragraph settings and the Drawing tools (which give you what you need for formatting text box content), you can make sure the text on your slides appears the way you want it to.

**Application Skills**    To Your Door Donuts is starting a new delivery service and they have asked you to create a presentation that will introduce the service to customers. You will create slides that show the different types of baked goods available for delivery and format all content using indents, tabs, and text alignment settings.

## What You Can Do

### Adjusting Paragraph Indents

- **Indents** can help you format your text so that your audience will be able to read it easily.
- In PowerPoint, different indents are used to show the text level of an item on a slide. A main heading or title may be centered on the slide or aligned with the left margin, depending on the theme you've selected.

### WORDS TO KNOW

**AutoFit**
A feature that adjusts the spacing of text automatically depending on how much space there is in a given area and how large the text is set to be.

**First-line indent**
A first-line indent controls the space you add at the beginning of a text paragraph or line.

**Hanging indent**
A hanging indent enables you to align text items in a bullet list so that the bullet itself is indented and the text aligns throughout the list.

**Indents**
Indents enable you to control the amount of space between the text and the edges of the text box or placeholder.

**Ruler**
The ruler appears along the top and left side of the slide area so that you can indent text and work with tabs on the slide.

**Special indents**
Hanging indents, such as those used with bullet lists, and first-line indents, such as those used at the beginning of paragraphs in some formats, are considered special indents.

**Tab stops**
Tab stops, also called tabs, enable you to align text and numbers according to settings you specify. You can choose to create left, center, right, or decimal tabs.

- The first level of text is aligned with the left margin; the second level of text is indented half an inch. Each level of text beyond that point is indented another half inch.

- You can easily indent your slide text by clicking and dragging the indent markers in the PowerPoint **ruler** or by displaying the Paragraph dialog box and choosing an indent setting there.

- In addition to setting new indents using the ruler, you can use the Indents and Spacing tab in the Paragraph dialog box to set left indents as well as **special indents**, like **first-line indents** or **hanging indents**.

---

**Try It!**    **Adjusting an Indent on the Ruler**

**1** Start PowerPoint, and open **PTry48** from the data files for this lesson.

**2** Save the file as **PTry48_studentfirstname_ studentlastname** in the location where your teacher instructs you to store the files for this lesson.

**3** Create and click Slide 2. Type the title **Why We Do It**.

**4** Type the paragraph, **At To Your Door Donuts, we care about you and we care about the environment. We think we can reduce fuel costs and CO2 emissions, and make you a lot happier, by bringing our donuts right to your door.**

**5** Click in the paragraph text.

**6** Click the top indent marker on the left side of the horizontal ruler.

✓ *If the rulers do not appear along the top and left side of the work area when you click in the paragraph text, click the View tab and click the Ruler check box in the Show group.*

**7** Drag it to the 1˝ mark. Your paragraph indents.

**8** Click the box at the bottom of the lower indent marker and drag it to the 1˝ mark. Both markers move, and the text is indented further.

**9** Save changes and leave the file open to use in the next Try It.

---

**Try It!**    **Setting a Special Indent**

**1** In **PTry48_studentfirstname_ studentlastname**, with the insertion point still in the same paragraph, click the Paragraph dialog launcher on the Home tab.

**2** In the Indentation area of the Paragraph dialog box, click the arrow in the Special box.

**3** Click Hanging.

**4** In the By: text box, type .7.

**5** Click OK.

**6** Save changes and leave the file open to use in the next Try It.

---

## Setting Tab Stops

- **Tab stops** enable you to control how the text lines up on your PowerPoint slides. You can choose to create four different types of tabs: Left, Right, Center, and Decimal tabs.

- You can set tabs by clicking the tab stop style you want to create and clicking the PowerPoint ruler, or you can display the Paragraph dialog box, click the Tabs button, and enter the settings for the tab.

- You can also set your own defaults for the tabs that are created when you press Tab while working on the slide.

- Removing a tab is simple—just drag it off the ruler.

- You can also clear all tabs at once by clicking the Clear All button in the Tabs dialog box.

## Try It! Adding a Tab on the Ruler

**1** In **PTry48_studentfirstname_studentlastname**, create and click Slide 3. Give the slide the title **What We Offer**.

**2** Click in the text placeholder.

**3** Click at the 0.5″ mark in the bottom half of the ruler.

**4** Click the tab selector to the left of the horizontal ruler so that the center tab is displayed.

**5** Click at the 3″ mark on the ruler to add a center tab.

**6** Click the tab selector again to display a right tab, and at the 5″ mark, click the mouse.

**7** Click the tab selector one more time to display a decimal tab, and click at 6 on the ruler.

**8** Now type the following, pressing ⊞TAB after each word: **Left, Center, Right, 100.00**. Each of the entries lines up according to the tab type you specified.

**9** Save changes and leave the file open to use in the next Try It.

Adding tabs to the ruler

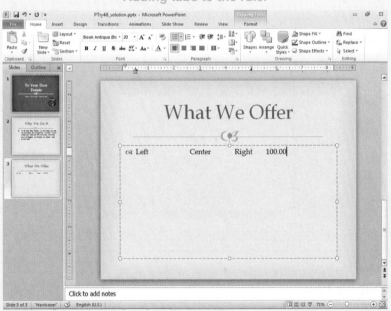

## Try It! Adding Tabs in the Tabs Dialog Box

**1** In **PTry48_studentfirstname_studentlastname**, create and click Slide 4. Add the title **Ordering Online**.

**2** Click in the text placeholder.

**3** Click the dialog launcher in the Paragraph group of the Home tab.

**4** Click the Tabs button.

**5** Click in the Tab stop position box and type **1**.

**6** In the Alignment area, click Center.

**7** Click Set.

**8** Repeat steps 5, 6, and 7 to add a Decimal tab at the tab stop position 4.

**9** Click OK twice.

**10** Press ⊞TAB and type **Cake donuts**.

**11** Press ⊞TAB again and type **.10**. Press ⊞ENTER.

*(continued)*

**Try It!**        **Adding Tabs in the Tabs Dialog Box** *(continued)*

**12** Repeat steps 10 and 11, entering the following information:

| Glazed donuts | .08 |
| Iced donuts | .12 |
| Persians | .15 |
| Blueberry | .15 |
| Cherry | .15 |
| Maple | .12 |

**13** Save changes and leave the file open to use in the next Try It.

Adding tabs from the Tabs dialog box

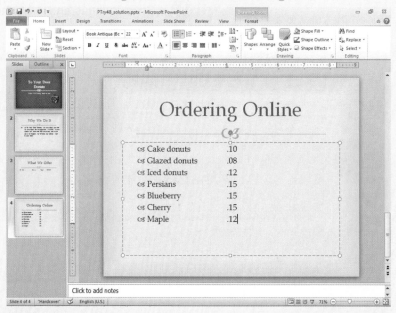

**Try It!**        **Clearing All Tabs**

**1** In **PTry48_studentfirstname_ studentlastname**, click Slide3 and then click the dialog launcher in the Paragraph group of the Home tab.

**2** Click the Tabs button.

**3** Click Clear All.

**4** Click OK twice.

**5** Save changes and leave the file open to use in the next Try It.

## Working with Placeholders and Text Boxes

- Placeholders in PowerPoint provide boxes where you add the content for your slides.

- Depending on the type of slide layout you create, you might add text, a table, a worksheet, chart, diagram, or video clip to a placeholder.

- If you do not use a placeholder on the slide you're creating, you can still see the placeholder border and content prompts while you're working on the slide, but the placeholder information won't appear on the slide during the presentation.

- You can change the placeholders that appear on the page by choosing a different slide layout. For example, you might click a Blank or a Title Only slide layout.

■ You can resize placeholders as needed by clicking and dragging the placeholder border.

■ You can draw a text box anywhere on the slide by clicking the Insert tab and clicking the Text box tool in the Text group. Then click and drag to add the text box to the slide.

■ You can customize a text box by clicking it and using the tools in the Drawing Tools Format contextual tab. You can change the color or shape of the box, modify the line style, layer or rotate the box, or apply a WordArt style to the text.

---

**Try It!**  **Choosing a Different Layout**

**1** In **PTry48_studentfirstname_ studentlastname**, create and click Slide 5. Add the title **Service Areas**.

**2** Click Home > Layout 🖳.

**3** Click the Comparison slide layout. The slide changes to include several text areas.

**4** Click in the top text box on the left and type **Northeast**.

**5** Click in the top text box on the right and type **West**.

**6** Save changes and leave the file open to use in the next Try It.

Changing the slide layout

---

**Try It!**  **Drawing, Formatting, and Resizing a Text Box**

**1** In **PTry48_studentfirstname_ studentlastname**, create and click Slide 6. Choose the Title and Content layout. Add the title **Our Customers Say…**

**2** Click Insert > Text Box 🅰.

**3** Click in the slide and draw a text box.

**4** Click Drawing Tools Format > Shape Fill 🖢.

**5** Click Gradient and choose Linear Left from the gallery.

*(continued)*

**Try It!**     **Drawing, Formatting, and Resizing a Text Box** *(continued)*

**6** Type "We order every week so we have fresh donuts every Sunday morning! Wonderful!" and choose the Text Fill – Gold, Accent 3 style for the text.

**7** Save changes and leave the file open to use in the next Try It.

Formatting a text box

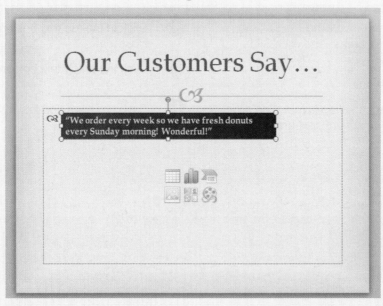

## Using Text Alignment and Direction Options

■ By default, PowerPoint sizes the text you enter in text boxes and placeholders. As you add more text, PowerPoint uses **AutoFit** to resize the text so that it all fits in the amount of space provided.

■ You can resize the text and turn off AutoFit if you don't want PowerPoint to change the sizing of your text.

■ PowerPoint enables you to align text vertically and control whether the text appears in the top, center, or bottom of a text box.

■ You can change the text direction and rotate text 90 or 270 degrees on the slide. You can also stack the characters so they display vertically on the slide.

■ You can also align the text by choosing left, center, right, or justified alignment. You can also change the line spacing and format text in columns if you like.

■ The tools for aligning text are found in the Paragraph group of the Home tab. You can also right-click the text box you want to format and choose Align Text Left, Center, or Align Text Right from the Mini toolbar that appears.

**Try It!**     **Setting Text Alignment and Changing Text Direction**

**1** In **PTry48_studentfirstname_studentlastname**, click in Slide 5.

**2** In the text placeholder on the left, type the following, pressing ENTER after each entry:
**Downtown**
**Orange Heights**

**Restfield**
**Littleton**

**3** In the placeholder on the right, type the following (pressing ENTER after each):
**Westfield**
**Blueville**
**Mantino Division**

*(continued)*

**Try It!**    **Setting Text Alignment and Changing Text Direction** *(continued)*

**4** Highlight the text list on the left and click Home > Center ☰.

**5** Click Home > Align Text ▤, and click Middle.

**6** Select the text in the list on the right, click Home > Align Text ▤, and click Middle.

**7** Click Home > Text Direction ᶣ > Rotate All Text 90.

**8** Save your changes, close the presentation, and exit PowerPoint.

# Project 109—Create It

## Product Presentation

### DIRECTIONS

1. Start PowerPoint if necessary, and open **PProj109** from the data files for this lesson.

2. Save the file as **PProj109_studentfirstname_ studentlastname** in the location where your teacher instructs you to save files for this lesson.

3. Create and click **Slide 2**. Add the title **Our Story**.

4. Add the paragraph, **In 2009, Bob had an epiphany. Instead of encouraging hundreds of customers to get in their cars, drive to our bakery, buy donuts, and take them home, how much greener would it be to take all the donuts to them?**

5. Drag the bottom indent marker to the 1″ mark.

6. Click the **Paragraph** dialog launcher and add a **Hanging** special indent. Set the By value to **0.8** and click **OK**.

7. Press ⏎ and add **This little genius of an idea saves fuel costs for you (so you can buy more donuts) saves trouble, time, and best of all, CO2 emissions.**

8. Press ⏎ and add **Which, as you know, is better for our planet.**

9. Click **Home** > **Layout** ▤, and click the Two Content layout.

10. Click **Insert** > **Text Box** ▣. Click and drag to draw a text box in the placeholder area on the right.

11. Add the following text:

   **Here's how to order:**

   **Order online or call our toll-free number.**

   **Order the night before for fresh donuts in the morning!**

   **Repeat orders welcome!**

12. Format the last three items as bullets.

13. Apply a Shape Fill and Shape Effect to the text box.

14. Click in the text placeholder behind the added text box and type **Donuts! Donuts! Donuts!**

15. Remove the bullet and align the text at the bottom of the text box. Format the text as you'd like to make it stand out.

16. **With your teacher's permission**, print Slide 2. It should look similar to Figure 48-1.

17. Close the file, saving all changes, and exit PowerPoint.

**Figure 48-1**

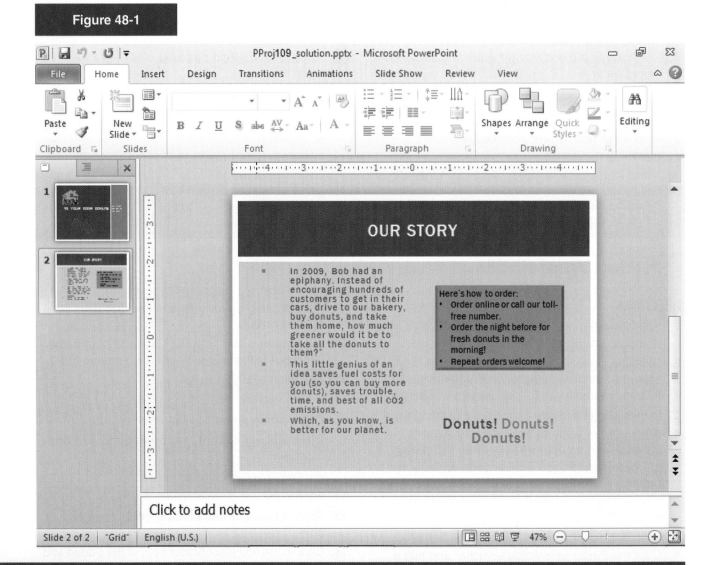

# Project 110—Apply It

## Product Presentation

### DIRECTIONS

1. Start PowerPoint if necessary, and open **PProj110** from the data files for this lesson.

2. Save the file as **PProj110_studentfirstname_ studentlastname** in the location where your teacher instructs you to save files for this lesson.

3. Create and click **Slide 2**. Add the title **You Know You're Hungry**.

4. Add the following text:

   **How about a nice fresh donut?**

   **Made this morning?**

   **At your house in, oh, say, 15 minutes?**

5. Indent the list to the **1 inch** mark.

6. Add the following text after the last bullet:

   **In 2009, Bob had an epiphany. Instead of encouraging hundreds of customers to get in their cars, drive to our bakery, buy donuts, and take them home, how much greener would it be to take all the donuts to them? This little genius of an idea saves fuel costs for you (so you can buy more donuts), saves trouble, time, and best of all CO2 emissions. Which, as you know, is better for our planet.**

7. Format the paragraph text in **22 point** type, and indent it to the **1.5″** mark.

8. Add a text box that matches the theme and style of the presentation, and cut and paste the text into the new box.

9. Add a background fill and an effect to the text box.

10. Change the indent to align with the left margin and center the text in the box.

11. **With your teacher's permission**, print Slide 2. It should look similar to Figure 48-2.

12. Close the file, saving all changes, and exit PowerPoint.

**Figure 48-2**

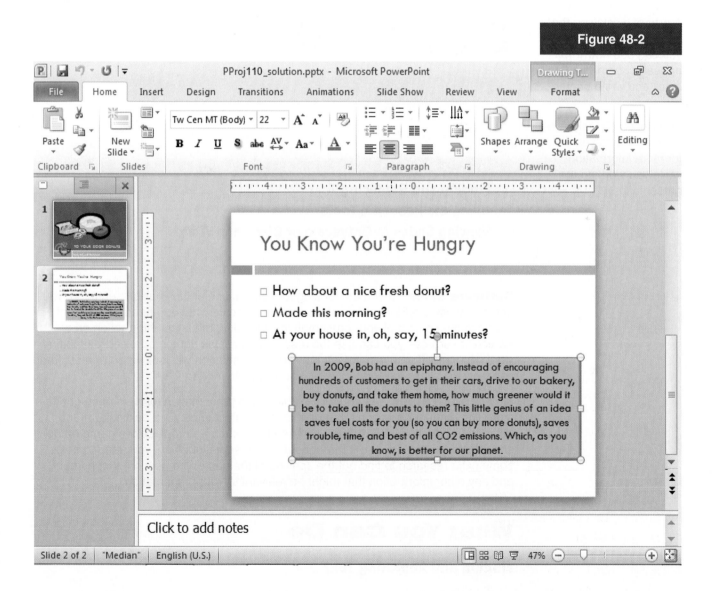

# Lesson 49

# Searching for and Researching Content

**WORDS TO KNOW**

Grayscale
A way of displaying the current slide so that you can see how it will appear when printed on a black and white printer.

Research pane
The Research task pane enables you to search for more information while you work on the presentation.

> ## What You Will Learn

**Finding and Replacing Text**
**Using the Research Tools**
**Viewing Slides in Grayscale or Black and White**

**Software Skills**   If you are looking for specific content in your presentation, you can easily use the Find and Replace feature to locate what you need. If you want to add to the content of your presentation—including the latest information on a particular subject—you can use the research tools built right into PowerPoint to find what you need. If you want to see how your presentation will look when printed, you can view the slides in black and white or grayscale mode.

**Application Skills**   As you are finishing up a presentation for a sporting goods store, the manager mentions that he thinks the latest shoes in a particular brand have been renamed. If that's true, you need to search and replace the name of the shoe, because you've used it throughout the presentation. Also, you need to do some extra research to find out the spelling of the name, the new product number, and any other information that might be relevant to your presentation.

## What You Can Do

### Finding and Replacing Text

- PowerPoint makes it easy for you to find and replace words or phrases on your slides.

- You can choose to replace every occurrence of the text or replace only one (or one at a time).

- Additionally, you can search for words or phrases in a particular case (for example, a sentence that begins with a certain capitalized word).
- You can search for partial words and whole words as well.

- PowerPoint keeps track of your most recent find and replace operations, and you can choose those searches by clicking the arrows in the Find or Replace boxes in the Replace dialog box.

## Try It!    Finding and Replacing Text

**1** Start PowerPoint, and open **PTry49** from the data files for this lesson.

**2** Save the file as **PTry49_studentfirstname_ studentlastname** in the location where your teacher instructs you to store the files for this lesson.

**3** Click Home > Replace ⁱ.

**4** Type **Woodland Lodge** in the Find what box.

**5** Type **Woodlake Inn** in the Replace with box.

**6** Click Replace All and click OK.

**7** Save your changes and leave the file open to use in the next Try It.

## Using the Research Tools

- You can research more about your topic from within PowerPoint.
- Click the Review tab and click Research in the Proofing group.
- The Research task pane appears along the right side of the window, and you can choose the reference books or sites you want to use.

- Click the result in the Research list to find out more about the selection.
- You can update the research services that are set up to work with PowerPoint or purchase additional services online.

## Try It!    Using the Research Tools

**1** In **PTry49_studentfirstname_ studentlastname**, click Review > Research ⁱ.

**2** Type **group training techniques** in the Search for box and click the green button.

**3** Click the arrow to the left of an entry to expand the description.

**4** Click the link of any entry you want to view.

*(continued)*

**Try It!**    **Find Out More about Your Topic with Research Tools** (continued)

**5** Save your changes and leave the file open to use in the next Try It.

✓ By default PowerPoint 2010 uses the Bing search engine to search the web for links related to the search text you entered. You can change the sources PowerPoint uses by clicking the arrow beneath the green button and choosing another source from the list.

Use the Research pane to find information

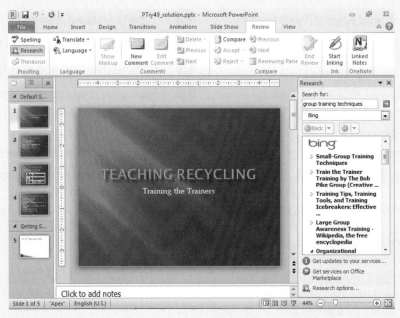

## Viewing Slides in Grayscale or Black and White

- If you plan on printing your presentation, you may want to view the slides in a **grayscale** or black and white mode.

- PowerPoint offers a number of controls you can use to set specific qualities for different objects on your slide.

- If you click the View tab and click Grayscale, a Grayscale tab appears to the left of the Home tab. This tab contains a variety of settings you can use to customize the look of the selected object on your slide.

- Similarly, the Black And White tab offers settings you can apply to the object on the slide. You can change the settings of different elements on the slide using these settings. You can redisplay the presentation in color by clicking the Back To Color View button in either the Grayscale or the Black And White tabs.

**Try It!**    **Viewing Slides in Grayscale or Black and White**

**1** In PTry49_studentfirstname_ studentlastname, click View > Grayscale ▬.

**2** Click in the title of Slide 1.

**3** Click Grayscale > Grayscale ▬.

**4** Click Grayscale > Light Grayscale ▬.

**5** Click Grayscale > White ☐.

**6** Click Grayscale > Back To Color View ▪.

**7** Save your file and close the document, and exit PowerPoint.

# Project 111—Create It

## Research Presentation

### DIRECTIONS

1. Start PowerPoint if necessary, and open **PProj111** from the data files for this lesson.

2. Save the file as **PProj111_studentfirstname_ studentlastname** in the location where your teacher instructs you to save files for this lesson.

3. Click **Home > Replace** .

4. Type **Maxx** in the Find what box.

5. Type **Max** in the Replace with box, and click **Replace All**. Click **OK** after replacements are made.

6. Click **Close**.

7. Click **Review > Research** .

8. Type **basketball shoes** in the Search for box and click the green button.

9. Click the source arrow and click **HighBeam Research**.

10. Click a link that looks interesting to you.

11. Review the information and then close your browser window. Click **Close** on the Research task pane.

12. Click View > Grayscale .

13. Click in the text of **Slide 6**.

14. In the **Grayscale** tab, click **Don't Show** .

15. Click **Grayscale > Gray with White Fill** .

16. Click **Back To Color View** .

17. **With your teacher's permission**, print the presentation. It should look similar to Figure 49-1.

18. Close the file, saving all changes, and exit PowerPoint.

**Figure 49-1**

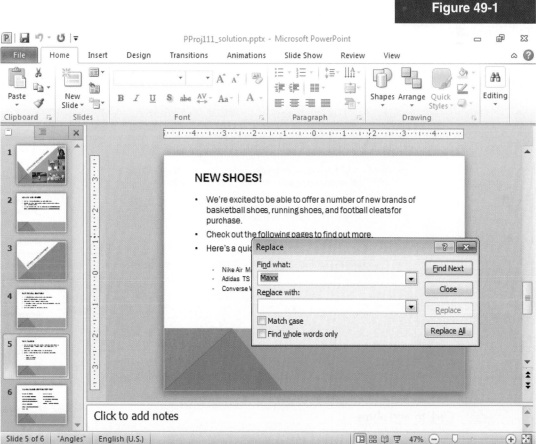

# Project 112—Apply It

## Historical Research Presentation

### DIRECTIONS

1. Start PowerPoint if necessary, and open **PProj112** from the data files for this lesson.

2. Save the file as **PProj112_studentfirstname_ studentlastname** in the location where your teacher instructs you to save files for this lesson.

3. Replace **Physiolgy** with **Physiology** in all occurrences in the presentation.

4. Click **Close**.

5. Use the Research tools to search for information about the history of running.

6. Copy the information from your source (and copy the URL) and paste the data on **Slide 3**.

7. Display the presentation in **Grayscale** and **Black and White** view.

8. Click different settings in the Grayscale or Black And White tabs to get a good balance for the presentation.

9. **With your teacher's permission**, print the presentation. It should look similar to Figure 49-2.

10. Close the file, saving all changes, and exit PowerPoint.

### Figure 49-2

# Lesson 50

# Sharing a Presentation

## ➤ What You Will Learn

**Preparing to Share a Presentation**
**Using the PowerPoint Web App**
**Working with Co-Authors**

**Software Skills**   Teamwork really is the name of the game for many people who work on presentations today. Often more than one person is responsible for content, another works on the design, another prepares the photos, and someone else gathers the video and audio clips.

**Application Skills**   You are working with your local humane society to put together a great presentation that showcases some of the animals currently available for adoption. Several of the other people working on the presentation are volunteers and they will be working from home, so you need to post the presentation to Windows Live SkyDrive so that you can all work on it using the PowerPoint Web App.

## What You Can Do

### Preparing to Share a Presentation

- Getting your presentation ready to share involves some last-minute checks. PowerPoint gives you a set of three tools that help you make sure you're sharing only the information you want to share, that your presentation is accessible for all users, and that others using earlier versions of PowerPoint will be able to view it.
- The Inspect Document tool is available in the Info tab of Backstage view. This tool does a check of all presentation content, looking for hidden or personal information, and alerts you if the search produces any results.
- The Check Accessibility tool checks your presentation to make sure that people of differing ability levels will be able to understand your presentation. The tool will display found issues in the Accessibility Checker task pane and give you tips as well as the opportunity to correct the problems.
- The Compatibility Checker searches for issues in the presentation that viewers using previous versions of PowerPoint will be unable to view.

## Try It! Inspecting Your Presentation

1. Start PowerPoint, and open **PTry50** from the data files for this lesson.

2. Save the file as **PTry50_studentfirstname_ studentlastname** in the location where your teacher instructs you to store the files for this lesson.

3. Click File > Check for Issues 📄 .

4. Click Inspect Document.

5. Click the Off-Slide Content check box, and click Inspect.

6. In the Document Inspector dialog box, click Remove All to erase the extra information.

7. Click Reinspect to ensure there are no additional problems.

8. Click Close.

9. Save your changes and leave the file open to use in the next Try It.

## Try It! Checking Presentation Accessibility

1. In **PTry50_studentfirstname_ studentlastname**, click File > Check for Issues 📄 . Click Check Accessibility.

2. In the Accessibility Checker task pane, review the errors.

3. Correct the errors using the information in the Additional Information panel.

4. Click the Close box to close the Accessibility Checker task pane.

5. Save your changes and leave the file open to use in the next Try It.

## Try It! Running the Compatibility Checker

1. In **PTry50_studentfirstname_ studentlastname**, click File > Check for Issues 📄 .

2. This time, click Check Compatibility.

3. Review the results, and click OK.

4. Save your changes and leave the file open to use in the next Try It.

## Using the PowerPoint Web App

- PowerPoint 2010 offers you the ability to work with your presentation on your desktop, in your Web browser, and even on your Windows-based smartphone.

- Using the **PowerPoint Web App**, you can view, edit, and share your presentation from any point you have Web access.

- You can post your PowerPoint presentation on a **SharePoint** workspace or in your **Windows Live SkyDrive** account.

- If you don't have a Windows Live SkyDrive account, PowerPoint 2010 will prompt you to create one when you choose Save & Send in Backstage view.

- After you save the presentation file to your Windows Live SkyDrive account, you can access the file using the PowerPoint Web App.

- You can log in to your Windows Live account from any point you have Web access. You can then use the PowerPoint Web App to open, review, and edit your presentation online.

- When you are working with the PowerPoint Web App, you can share the presentation and work in the same file with other editors at the same time. This feature is known as **co-authoring**.

## Try It!    Adding a Presentation to Windows Live SkyDrive

**1** In **PTry50_studentfirstname_ studentlastname**, click File > Save & Send.

**2** Click Save to Web.

**3** If you don't have a Windows Live SkyDrive account, click the Sign Up for Windows Live SkyDrive link and sign up.

**OR**

If you already have an account, you will first need to click the Sign In button to connect to Windows Live.

**4** Click the SkyDrive folder in which you want to save the file, then click Save As.

**5** In the Save As dialog box, enter a file name for the file and click Save.

**6** Save your changes and close the file.

## Try It!    Working in the PowerPoint Web App

**1** Open your Web browser and go to www.windowslive.com.

**2** Log in with your Windows Live ID.

**3** Click the Office link at the top of the Windows Live page.

**4** Click Your documents.

**5** Click the folder in which you saved **PTry50_ studentfirstname_studentlastname**.

**6** Click **PTry50_studentfirstname_ studentlastname** to display the presentation in the PowerPoint Web App.

**7** Click Edit in Browser to display the Ribbon with the tools you need to review, edit, and save the file.

**8** When you're finished reviewing the presentation, click File > Close.

✓ *Note that the presentation file won't open unless the file has been closed by other users.*

**Presentation displayed in the Web App**

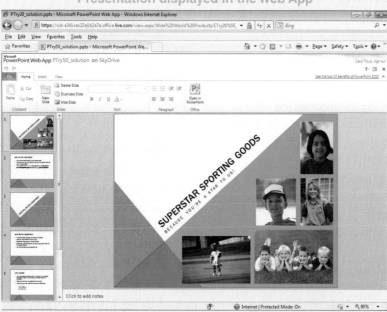

## Working with Co-Authors

- When you're working in the PowerPoint Web App, you can work with co-authors in the same file at the same time.

- You can share the file while viewing the file in the PowerPoint Web App or when you're editing the file in the browser.

- While you're working in the file, your co-authors have the option of opening a read-only copy or editing the file and then synchronizing the file with the presentation on the Windows Live server.

- If a co-author makes a change to the presentation, the changes will be added to the presentation when you close the file.

- You can contact co-authors directly if you are using Office Communicator or SharePoint Workspace.

### Try It!    Sharing and Co-Authoring a Presentation

1. Log in to Windows Live and display your Office files.

2. Click **PTry50_studentfirstname_ studentlastname** to open it in the PowerPoint Web App.

3. Click File > Share.

4. Click the highlighted folder name you used to store the file.

5. On the right side of the screen, click the link following the text Shared with:

6. Click Edit permissions and add the e-mail address of your co-author in the box. Click Save.

7. Click Send.

8. Continue editing the file as normal.

9. Save and close the file, then exit PowerPoint.

# Project 113—Create It

## Sharing a Presentation on the Web

### DIRECTIONS

1. Start PowerPoint if necessary, and open **PProj113** from the data files for this lesson.

2. Save the file as **PProj113_studentfirstname_ studentlastname** in the location where your teacher instructs you to save files for this lesson.

3. Click **File** > **Check for Issues** 🗐 , then click **Inspect Document**. Click **Inspect**.

4. Correct any problems and click **Reinspect**.

5. Click **File** > **Check for Issues** 🗐 , then click **Check Accessibility**.

6. In the Accessibility Checker task pane, review the errors.

7. Correct the errors as needed, and close the Accessibility Checker.

8. Click **File** > **Check for Issues** 🗐 , then click **Check Compatibility**.

9. Review the results, and click **OK**.

10. Click **File** > **Save & Send**, then click **Save to Web**.

11. Click the **SkyDrive** folder in which you want to save the file, and click **Save As**. Enter a name for the file and click **Save**. Choose to replace the file if prompted.

12. Open your Web browser and go to www.windowslive.com. Log in with your Windows Live ID.

13. Click **Office** and click **Your documents**.

14. Open **PProj113_studentfirstname_ studentlastname** and click **Edit in Browser**.

15. Review the presentation and make changes if needed.

16. Click **File** > **Share**.

17. Click the highlighted folder name, and then click the link following the **Shared with:** text on the right side of the window.

18. Add a co-author's e-mail address to your permissions. An invitation is sent and the co-author will be able to access your file.

19. Close the file, saving all changes, and exit PowerPoint.

## Project 114—Apply It

### Sharing a Training Presentation

**DIRECTIONS**

1. Start PowerPoint if necessary, and open **PProj114** from the data files for this lesson.

2. Save the file as **PProj114_studentfirstname_ studentlastname** in the location where your teacher instructs you to save files for this lesson.

3. Use the Check for Issues tool to inspect the document, check accessibility, and check file compatibility.

4. Correct any problems.

5. Save the file to your Windows Live SkyDrive account.

6. Display the presentation in PowerPoint Web App.

7. Change permissions in the site so that others you specify can access the file.

8. Make any necessary changes to the file.

9. Close the file, saving all changes, and exit PowerPoint.

# Lesson 51

# Presenting on the Web

**WORDS TO KNOW**

Broadcast service
A broadcast service enables you to invite others and share the presentation you create in real time over the Web.

> **What You Will Learn**

**Preparing to Broadcast**
**Broadcasting and Viewing a Web Presentation**

**Software Skills**   Sometimes it's cost prohibitive—or at least impractical—to get all your customers in one place in order to share your presentation with them. PowerPoint 2010 includes a new feature that enables you to save your presentation as a video or broadcast it over the Web, using a free broadcast service from Microsoft or one of your own choosing.

**Application Skills**   The presentation you are working on is designed to help managers at your company learn how to use the new blogging tool you've added. You will be creating a presentation you can broadcast online to ten managers all across the country.

## What You Can Do

### Preparing to Broadcast

- PowerPoint 2010 enables you to present your presentation live on the Web in real time.

- Using an online **broadcast service** (provided free by Microsoft), you can send links to participants so that they can join in your presentation as you present it online.

- Setting up for a live broadcast simply involves creating and saving your presentation and then clicking File to display Backstage view.

- In the Broadcast Slide Show dialog box, you can begin the broadcast  by clicking Start Broadcast or choose a different service by clicking Change Broadcast Service.

- A link in the Broadcast Slide Show dialog box enables you to get more information about the service to view Microsoft's service agreement for the service offered.

## Try It!    Preparing to Broadcast Your Presentation

**1** Start PowerPoint, and open **PTry51** from the data files for this lesson.

**2** Save the file as **PTry51_studentfirstname_ studentlastname** in the location where your teacher instructs you to store the files for this lesson.

**3** Click File > Save & Send.

**4** Click Broadcast Slide Show.

**5** Click the Broadcast Slide Show button.

**6** In the Broadcast Slide Show dialog box, click Start Broadcast.

**7** Leave the file open to use in the next Try It.

Getting ready to broadcast a presentation

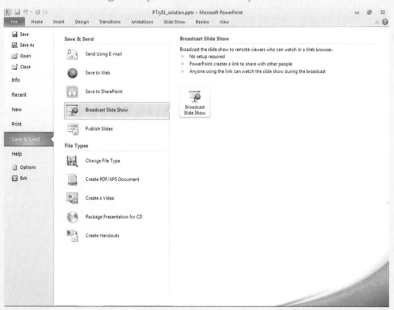

## Broadcasting and Viewing a Web Presentation

- In the Broadcast Slide Show dialog box, click Start Broadcast to begin the process.

- PowerPoint prepares the presentation in broadcast form. You are then given a link you can use to send to those who will be viewing the presentation online.

- You can send the link by instant message or other means. You can also open a new message window so you can send the link in an e-mail message to participants.

- When the participant clicks the link, a Web page opens with the message *Waiting for broadcast to begin*.

✓ *You can also prepare handouts or send slide notes by e-mail before broadcasting the presentation if you want your viewers to have additional information about your presentation.*

- When you click Start Slide Show, the first slide appears in your participants' Web browsers.

- The presentation provides display only. If you want to be able to talk to your participants during the presentation, set up a call with Windows Live Messenger or another communications service.

- Present your slide show as normal, and when you're finished, click End Broadcast to stop the connection. Participants see a message in their Web browser that says *Broadcast is over.*

## Try It!　Inviting Participants and Broadcasting Your Presentation

**1** In **PTry51_studentfirstname_ studentlastname**, if you have not already done so, in the Broadcast Slide Show dialog box, click Start Broadcast.

**2** Click Copy Link.

**3** Click Send in Email.

　✓ *Note that this step and steps 4–5 works only if you are using Microsoft Outlook 2010 on your computer.*

**4** In the View My PowerPoint Presentation window, add the e-mail addresses of the people you want to view the presentation.

**5** Add a note to the body of the message, and click Send.

**6** Click Start Slide Show to begin the presentation.

**7** Present the presentation normally; your viewers will be able to see the presentation by clicking the link they received via e-mail.

**8** Click the blank screen at the close of the presentation.

**9** Save and close your presentation, then exit PowerPoint.

Sharing the broadcast link with viewers online

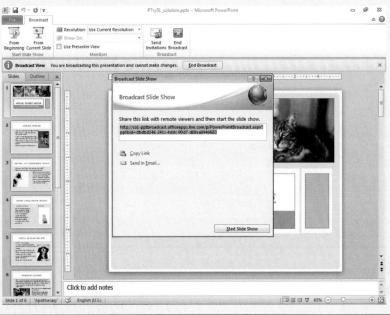

# Project 115—Create It

## Blogging and Branding

### DIRECTIONS

1. Start PowerPoint if necessary, and open **PProj115** from the data files for this lesson.
2. Save the file as **PProj115_studentfirstname_ studentlastname** in the location where your teacher instructs you to save files for this lesson.
3. Click **File > Save & Send**.
4. Click **Broadcast Slide Show**.
5. Click the **Broadcast Slide Show** button.
6. In the Broadcast Slide Show dialog box, click **Start Broadcast**.
7. Click **Copy Link**.
8. Click **Send in Email.**

   ✓ Note that this step and steps 9–10 works only if you have Microsoft Outlook 2010 installed and configured on your computer.

9. In the View My PowerPoint Presentation window, add the e-mail addresses of the people you want to view the presentation.
10. Add a note to the body of the message, and click **Send**.
11. Click **Start Slide Show** to begin the presentation.
12. Present the presentation normally. Your viewers will be able to see the presentation by clicking the link they received via e-mail.
13. Click the blank screen at the close of the presentation.
14. Save and close the file, then exit PowerPoint.

# Project 116—Apply It

## Blogging and Branding

### DIRECTIONS

1. Start PowerPoint if necessary, and open **PProj116** from the data files for this lesson.
2. Save the file as **PProj116_studentfirstname_ studentlastname** in the location where your teacher instructs you to save files for this lesson.
3. Start a broadcast for the presentation.
4. Invite others by e-mail to view the presentation.
5. Present the presentation normally.
6. Click the blank slide to end the presentation.
7. Save changes, close the presentation, and exit PowerPoint.

# Lesson 52

# Protecting and Finalizing a Presentation

## ➤ What You Will Learn

**Applying Passwords to a Presentation**
**Marking a Presentation as Final**
**Adding a Digital Signature**

**Software Skills**   PowerPoint 2010 offers a number of features you can use to secure the presentations you create. From the simple technique involved in protecting your presentation with a password to the more complex task of adding a digital signature or assigning permissions with Information Rights Management, PowerPoint's security features can be tailored to fit your needs.

**Application Skills**   You are working with a group trying to raise funds to renovate a classic movie theatre in the town square. You are working with several different people as you prepare the organization, and you need to set permissions and assign a password to the presentation. Also, before you finalize your work, you add a digital signature to the file so that those who receive it know they are getting the most recent copy directly from you.

## What You Can Do

### Applying Passwords to a Presentation

- Adding a password to a presentation is one of the simplest ways to protect your content.

- You can add a password to your presentation by clicking the File tab and clicking Protect Presentation. Choose Encrypt with Password to display the Encrypt Document dialog box.

- Enter a password for the file. To create a secure password, use a combination of upper- and lower-case letters and numbers.
- Be sure to write your password in a safe location, because PowerPoint does not save the password in a place you can access it if you forget it later.

- PowerPoint will prompt you to enter the password a second time, and after the password is set, the Info tab displays a Permissions setting in the Protect Presentation area of Backstage view.
- When others open your presentation, the Password dialog box appears first, prompting users for the necessary password before opening the file.

**Try It!**  **Applying Passwords to a Presentation**

1 Start PowerPoint, and open **PTry52** from the data files for this lesson.

2 Save the file as **PTry52_studentfirstname_ studentlastname** in the location where your teacher instructs you to store the files for this lesson.

3 Click File > Protect Presentation 🔒 .

4 Click Encrypt with Password.

5 In the Encrypt Document dialog box, enter a password for the file.

6 Click OK.

7 Save changes and leave the file open to use in the next Try It.

## Marking a Presentation as Final

- When you mark your presentation as final, others viewing the presentation see that it is marked as read-only so no further changes can be made.
- For many general purposes, this level of protection may be fine, but it is possible for viewers to save the presentation under another name and then edit the presentation as desired.

- If you need true presentation security, add a password or restrict others' editing privileges before sharing the file.
- When a file is marked as final, the Mark as Final icon appears in the status bar when others are viewing the presentation.
- The message bar at the top of the PowerPoint window also lets users know that the file has been marked as final. The Edit Anyway button gives others the option of continuing to work with the file.

**Try It!**  **Marking a Presentation as Final**

1 In **PTry52_studentfirstname_ studentlastname**, click File > Protect Presentation 🔒 .

2 Click Mark as Final.

3 Click OK twice.

4 Save changes and leave the file open to use in the next Try It.

✓ The Permissions area of the Info tab shows that the presentation has been marked as final.

## Adding a Digital Signature

- A **digital signature** helps others receiving your presentation know that the file is authentically from you.
- You can assign a digital signature to your PowerPoint presentation by clicking in the Info tab of Backstage view.

✓ Be sure to follow your instructor's direction on how—or whether—to use digital signatures with Microsoft PowerPoint.

- The digital signature remains valid as long as the presentation is not changed. If you change the presentation at a later time, you will need to sign the presentation again to make the signature valid.

## Try It!     Adding a Digital Signature

**1** In **PTry52_studentfirstname_ studentlastname**, click File > Protect Presentation , and then click Add a Digital Signature.

**2** Click the option for creating a digital ID and click OK.

**3** In the Create a Digital ID dialog box, enter your name, e-mail address, organization, and location. Click Create.

**4** In the Sign box, type **Validate authenticity of presentation**.

**5** Click Sign.

**6** Click OK.

**7** Click View Signatures to view, edit, or remove the signature in your document.

**8** Save and close your file, then exit PowerPoint.

Creating a digital signature

---

# Project 117—Create It

## Retro Cinema Presentation

### DIRECTIONS

1. Start PowerPoint if necessary, and open **PProj117** from the data files for this lesson.

2. Save the file as **PProj117_studentfirstname_ studentlastname** in the location where your teacher instructs you to save files for this lesson.

3. Click **File > Protect Presentation** ⚐.

4. Click **Encrypt with Password**, enter a password for the file, and click **OK**.

5. Click **Protect Presentation**, then click **Mark as Final**.

6. Click **OK** twice.

7. Click **Protect Presentation**, then click **Add a Digital Signature**.

8. Click **OK**. In the Sign box, type **Most recent version of file**.

9. Click **Sign**, then click **OK**.

10. Click **View Signatures** to view, edit, or remove the signature in your document.

11. Save and close your file, then exit PowerPoint.

## Project 118—Apply It

### NewLine Cinema Presentation

**DIRECTIONS**

1. Start PowerPoint if necessary, and open **PProj118** from the data files for this lesson.

2. Save the file as **PProj118_studentfirstname_studentlastname** in the location where your teacher instructs you to save files for this lesson.

3. Add a password to the file.

4. Mark the file as final.

5. Add a digital signature to the file, adding a purpose that lets other users know this is the most recent version of the file. Your file should look similar to Figure 52-1.

6. View the new signature.

7. Save and close your file, then exit PowerPoint.

**Figure 52-1**

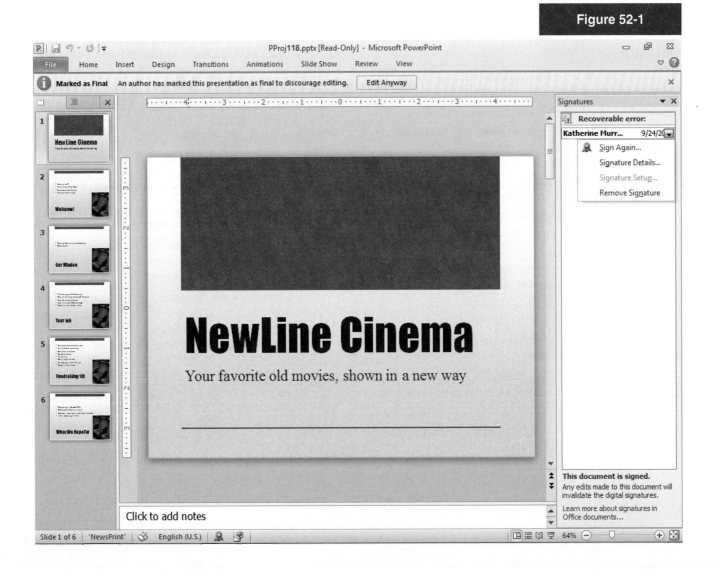

# Chapter Assessment and Application

# Project 119—Make It Your Own

## Urban Farmers Tell the Story

A small nonprofit organization in your area offers ideas, education, and vegetables to city families who don't have access to garden plots of their own. Started with a small grant from the city, Urban Farmers has asked you to help them develop a presentation they can give at area churches, synagogues, and mosques.

This presentation will tell the story of Urban Farmers and show how others can get involved, support the cause, or begin a garden of their own. In addition to the in-person presentations, the group wants to be able to update and work on the presentation collaboratively and ultimately broadcast it on the Web to save time and fuel costs. You will prepare the presentation for broadcast, view the presentation in the PowerPoint Web App, set permissions and protection features, and broadcast the presentation over the Web.

### DIRECTIONS

1. Start PowerPoint if necessary, and open **PProj119** from the data files for this chapter.

2. Save the file as **PProj119_studentfirstname_ studentlastname** in the location where your teacher instructs you to save files for this lesson.

3. Open **PProj119_content.doc** from the data files for this chapter, and copy and paste the content into the Outline tab in PowerPoint.

4. Format the content as needed to create slides and bullets. Apply your own choice for slide and bullet formatting.

5. Click **Slide 5** and add a second theme to the presentation (for example, **Thatch**).

6. Click **Slide 4**, and indent the content by an additional half inch.

7. Click **Slide 1** and search for the word *corps* and replace it with **group**.

8. Research **urban farms** using PowerPoint's research tools and locate two examples of thriving urban farms.

9. View your presentation in black and white view and fine-tune the display using the various tools in the Grayscale and Black and White tabs.

10. Save your presentation normally, then save it to the PowerPoint Web App, using the **Save & Send, Save to Web** option in Backstage view.

11. Log in to your Windows Live SkyDrive account and invite a co-author to share the presentation by setting the necessary permissions for the file.

12. Add a password to the file that you will share with co-authors who want to work on the file with you.

13. Broadcast your presentation online by sending the generated e-mail link to one or two friends you want to view the presentation.

    ✓ *Be sure to check with your instructor before you access the Web or make plans to broadcast your presentation. Depending on the security settings for your computer lab, you may be limited in the types of sites you can access and use.*

14. Save the presentation, close it, and exit PowerPoint.

# Project 120—Master It

## Presenting Belize Vacation Homes

A local travel agency is offering a special sales incentive for time-share condominiums in Belize. You have been asked to help the agency prepare a presentation that it will broadcast to prospective customers all over the United States.

As part of creating the presentation, you will work with the owner of the travel agency by using the PowerPoint Web App. When the presentation is finished, you will mark it as final and add a digital signature, before broadcasting it to customers the owner has identified.

### DIRECTIONS

1. Start PowerPoint if necessary, and open **PProj120** from the data files for this lesson.

2. Save the file as **PProj120_studentfirstname_ studentlastname** in the location where your teacher instructs you to save files for this chapter.

3. Open **PProj120_content.doc** from the data files for this chapter, and copy and paste the content into the Outline tab in PowerPoint.

4. Format the content as needed to create slides and bullets as shown in Illustration A.

5. Change the color of the text (headings and paragraph text) to create a contrast with the background image.

6. Click **Slide 6** and add a second theme to the presentation (for example, **Waveform**).

7. Click **Slide 4**, remove the bullets, and center the content.

8. Click **Slide 1** and search for the word *amenities* and replace it with **utilities**.

9. Research **Belize condos** using PowerPoint's research tools and locate two competitors you can mention in contrasting the benefits of this condo development.

10. Save your presentation normally, then save it to the PowerPoint Web App, using the **Save & Send, Save to Web** option in Backstage view.

11. Log in to your Windows Live SkyDrive account and, with your teacher's permission, invite a co-author to share the presentation by setting the necessary permissions for the file.

12. Mark the presentation as final.

13. Broadcast your presentation online by sending the generated e-mail link to one or two friends you want to view the presentation.

14. Save the presentation, close it, and exit PowerPoint.

**Illustration A**

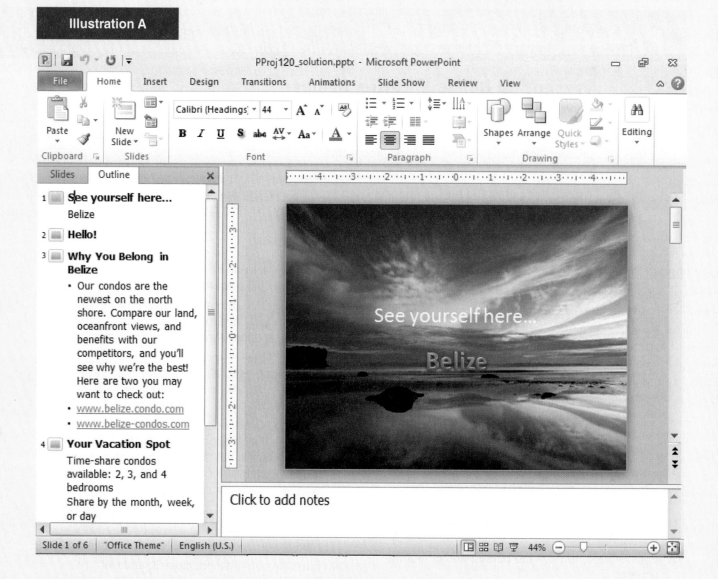

# Index

## A

**accessibility of presentations, 242–247, 356**
**Action buttons, 180, 183**
**actions, 290, 292–293**
**active slides, 12**
**adding**
    backgrounds, 313
    borders, 258, 312
    captions, 268–269
    columns, 303
    comments, 193, 194
    content, 338
    digital signatures, 365–366
    error bars, 318–319
    narration, 284, 286–287
    objects, 322–327
    pictures
        cells, 313
        table backgrounds, 313
    rows, 303
    shapes to diagrams, 102–103
    speaker notes, 21
    styles, 310–311
    tables, 302–303
    text, 85, 268–269, 335
    themes, 337
    transitions, 51–53
    trendlines, 318
**advanced properties, viewing, 238–239**
**advance slide timing, 51, 53, 128**
**albums, editing, 267–268**
**aligning, 302**
    Clip Art, 68–69
    first-time indents, 341
    objects, 91
    text, 36–37, 306–307, 346–347

**analyzing the effectiveness of multimedia presentations, 134**
**animation, 128**
    applying, 273–283
    charts, 150
    deleting, 280–281
    modifying, 280–281
    reordering, 276
    timelines, 279–280
    timing, 278–279
**Animation Painter, applying, 130**
**annotating slides, 188**
**applying**
    animation, 273–283
    Animation Painter, 130
    backgrounds with fill colors, 124–125
    charts, 147–152
    Clip Art, 67
    entrance effects, 128–129
    fills, 83
    gridlines, 80–81
    guides, 80–81
    Linked Note button, 220–222
    multimedia, 261–267
    multiple columns in text boxes, 76–77
    outlines, 83
    Outline tabs, 334–336
    passwords to presentations, 364–365
    placeholders, 344–346
    Redo, 33
    Research task pane, 351–352
    rulers, 80–81
    shapes
        effects, 84
        styles, 84–85
    Slide Masters, 158–165

styles
  tables, 310–311
  videos, 136
  WordArt, 95–96
templates, 176
text boxes, 344–346
themes, 8–9, 176, 336–337
Undo, 33
**arranging slides, 47–50**
**artistic effects, formatting pictures, 26–27**
**aspect ratios, 79**
**AutoFit, 36, 39, 341**
**automatically running presentations, 190–191**

**B**

**backgrounds**
  adding, 313
  fill colors, applying, 124–125
  graphics, hiding, 124
  modifying, 121–127
  pictures
    deleting from, 70
    formatting, 125
  slides, resetting, 125–126
  styles, modifying, 116–117
**bitmap images, 254**
**black and white, viewing, 352**
**blogs, 363**
**borders**
  adding, 258, 312
  modifying, 311–312
**brightness, 255–256**
**broadcasting, 360**
  preparing, 360–361
  slide shows, 201–202
**Broadcast Slide Show dialog box, 361–362**
**bulleted lists, 60–61**
  numbered lists, modifying, 61
  styles, 61–63
**bullets**
  deleting, 60–61
  modifying, 63–64
  pictures, 60

**C**

**captions, adding, 268–269**
**CDs, Package Presentation for CD feature, 200–201**

**cells, 302**
  filling, 310, 311–312
  merging, 302, 304
  pictures, adding, 313
  shading, 312
  sizing, 305–306
**charts**
  animations, 150
  applying, 147–152
  elements, 317
  formatting, 148–150, 317–321
  inserting, 147–148
  modifying, 148–150
**checking**
  accessibility, 243–244
  spelling, 9
**clearing**
  formatting, 33
  tabs, 344
**Clip Art, 67**
  inserting, 67–68
  positioning, 68–69
  resizing, 68–69
  task panes, inserting pictures from, 70
**closing presentations, 9**
**co-authoring content, 355, 358**
**collapsing levels, 334**
**colors**
  diagrams, modifying, 104
  filling, applying to backgrounds, 124–125
  modifying, 32
  themes, modifying, 117–118
  videos, modifying, 136
**columns, 302**
  adding, 303
  distributing, 302
  multiple, applying in text boxes, 76–77
  width, modifying, 305
**comments, 193, 225–230**
  adding, 194
  deleting, 228
  reviewing, 227–228
**comparing presentations, 225–227**
**Compatibility Checker, 242–243**
  running, 356
**compression**
  lossless, 254

lossy, 254
pictures, 269–270
**content**
adding, 338
co-authoring, 355, 358
diagrams, reordering, 103
slides, creating, 334–336
**contrast, 255–256**
**controlling**
slides, 187
video in presentations, 136–137
**copying**
objects from slide to slide, 324
slides, 47–48
text, 32–33, 38
**cropping**
images, 25
pictures, 26–27
**customizing**
actions, 292–293
animation, 273–283
links, 290–292
placeholders, 215–216
presentations, 334–340
Slide Masters, 160–161
slide shows, 189–190
sounds, 264–265
templates, 173–179
themes, 173–179
videos, 263–264
**custom shows, 180.** *See also* **slide shows**

**D**
**deleting**
animation, 280–281
backgrounds from pictures, 70
bullets, 60–61
comments, 228
shapes from diagrams, 102–103
slides, 47–48
**demoting text, 334, 335**
**diagrams**
colors, modifying, 104
content, reordering, 103
modifying, 104
shapes
adding, 102–103

deleting, 102–103
resizing, 102–103
SmartArt, formatting, 100–102
**dialog boxes, Broadcast Slide Show, 361–362**
**digital signatures, 364, 365–366**
**direction, text, 346–347**
**distributing**
columns, 302
objects, 91
presentations, 199–207
rows, 302
**documents**
handouts, exporting, 231–235
linking, 291
**drawing**
shapes, 81
tables, 302–309
text boxes, 346–347
**duplicating**
objects, 90
slides, 47–48

**E**
**editing**
albums, 267–268
checking spelling, 9
presentation properties, 237–238
videos, 135
**effects**
animation, 273–283
Animation Painter, applying, 130
entrance, applying, 128–129
guidelines, 51–52
modifying, 311–312
options, formatting, 129
reordering, 276
shapes, applying, 84
tables, adding, 312
**elements**
charts, 317
Slide Masters, customizing, 160–161
**e-mail addresses, inserting links into, 291**
**embedding, 166**
objects, 322, 323
videos, 262
**entering text, 7–8**
**entrance effects, applying, 128–129**

**Eraser tool, merging cells, 304**
**error bars, 317, 318–319**
**Excel data, presentations**
    inserting, 168–169
    linking, 169–170
**existing objects, adding to slides, 322–323**
**existing presentations, opening, 6**
**existing text, applying WordArt to, 95–96**
**expanding text, 334**
**exporting handouts, 231–235**

**F**

**files. *See also* presentations**
    formats, 255
    handouts, exporting, 231–235
    pictures, inserting from, 25–26, 69
**filling**
    applying, 83
    cells, 310, 311–312
    colors, applying to backgrounds, 124–125
    gradients, 310
**finalizing presentations, 196, 365**
**finding text, 30–31**
**first-time indents, 341**
**fonts, 116**
    guidelines, 51–52
    replacing, 337–338
    searching, 338
    sizing, 32
    themes, formatting, 118
**footers, 19, 21, 22**
**Format Painter, 30**
**formatting. *See also* layouts**
    actions, 292–293
    animation, 273–283
    AutoFit, 341
    backgrounds with pictures, 125
    charts, 148–150, 317–321
    clearing, 33
    effect options, 129
    first-time indents, 341
    handouts, 218–220
    indenting, 341–342
    multimedia, 133–140, 261–267
    notes, 218–220
    pictures, 26–27, 254–260
    placeholders, 39–40

presentations
    accessibility, 242–247
    sections, 284–286
    templates, 167
resolution, 267
sections, 336
slides, 12
    content, 334–336
    from outlines, 121–123
SmartArt, 100–102, 105
sounds, 264–265
tables, 142–144, 310–317
templates, 175
text, 30–35, 32–33
text boxes, 75–76, 346–347
themes, 4, 118, 173, 174–175
videos, 203
WordArt, 94–95, 96–97

**G**

**gradients, fills, 310**
**graphics**
    backgrounds, hiding, 124
    guidelines, 51–52
    SmartArt, applying to, 130
    transparencies, 255–256
**grayscale**
    printing, 350
    viewing, 352
**gridlines, 79, 80–81**
**groups, 88, 90**
**growth charts, 319. *See also* charts**
**guidelines, 51–52**
**guides, 79, 80–81**

**H**

**handles, tables, 302**
**handouts, 19, 21, 218–225**
    exporting, 231–235
    Slide Masters, 163
**hanging indents, 341**
**headers, 19, 21, 22**
**height, modifying rows, 305**
**hiding**
    backgrounds, graphics, 124
    slides, 186
**hyperlinks, customizing, 290–292**

# I

**images**
albums, editing, 267–268
bitmap, 254
compressing, 269–270
cropping, 25
file formats, 255
formatting, 26–27
inserting, 25–26, 214–215
vector, 254
**indenting, 341**
first-time indents, 341
hanging indents, 341
modifying, 341–342
special indents, 341
**information sources, selecting, 52**
**inserting.** *See also* **adding**
Action buttons, 183
charts, 147–148
Clip Art, 67–68
Excel data, 168–169
footers, 22
headers, 22
links on slides, 182
music, 137–138
pictures, 25–26, 69, 70, 214–215
shapes, 214
Slide Masters, 212–213
slides, 12–13
sounds, 137–138
symbols, 73–74
tables, 141–142
text boxes, 75–76
videos, 134–135
WordArt, 96–97
**inspecting presentations, 356**

# K

**keywords, 67**

# L

**landscape orientation, 19, 21–22**
**Layout Master, 60**
**layouts**
selecting, 345
Slide Masters, 162
slides, 4, 13

**levels**
collapsing, 334
lists, modifying, 14–15
**lines, modifying spacing, 37**
**Linked Note button, 220–222**
**linking, 166**
customizing, 290–292
Excel data, 169–170
objects, 322
presentations to Word, 232–233
slides, 182
templates, 166–173
**lists**
bulleted, 60–61
levels, modifying, 14–15
numbered lists, 61
**looping presentations, 190–191**
**lossless compression, 254**
**lossy compression, 254**

# M

**managing slides, 47–50, 53**
**merging cells, 302, 304**
**modifying**
animation, 276, 280–281
backgrounds, 121–127
borders, 311–312
bulleted lists to numbered lists, 61
bullets, 63–64
charts, 148–150
checking spelling, 9
colors, 32, 104
column width, 305
diagrams, 104
effects, 311–312
indenting, 341–342
lines, spacing, 37
list levels, 14–15
orientation, 21–22
paragraphs, 38, 341–342
placeholders, 39–40
row height, 305
styles, 32, 116–117
tables, 142–144, 302–309
text, 32, 335, 346–347
themes, 116
colors, 117–118

styles, 118
timing, 278–279
trendlines, 318
video colors, 136
**motion path animation, 275–276**
**moving**
animation, 276
Clip Art, 68–69
shapes, 82
slides, 336
from slide to slide, 14
text, 38
**multimedia, 133–140, 261–267**
**multiple columns, applying to text boxes, 76–77**
**multiple themes, 336–337.** *See also* themes
**music, inserting, 137–138**

# N

**naming presentation sections, 285**
**narration, adding, 284, 286–287**
**navigating**
Normal view, 4, 6–7
presentations, 4–5
Slide Masters, 159
slides, 14
**Normal view, 4, 6–7**
**notes, 218–225**
Linked Note button, 220–222
Slide Masters, 163
**numbered lists, 61**

# O

**objects, 322**
adding, 322–327
aligning, 91
animations, applying to, 130
distributing, 91
duplicating, 90
embedding, 322, 323
groups, 90
linking, 322
scaling, 25, 26–27
slides, copying, 324
stacks, 88–89
**online presentations, viewing, 43–46**
**opening existing presentations, 6.** *See also* starting

**options**
actions, 292–293
animation, 273–283
effects, formatting, 129
placeholders, 215–216
slide shows, 189–190
sounds, 264–265
videos, 263–264
**orientation**
landscape, 19
modifying, 21–22
portrait, 19
**outlines**
applying, 83
slides, creating from, 121–123
**Outline tab, 334–336**

# P

**Package Presentation for CD feature, 200–201**
**paragraphs**
first-time indents, 341
modifying, 38, 341–342
**passwords, applying, 364–365**
**Paste Special, 322, 323**
**paths, 273, 275–276**
**photo albums.** *See* albums
**pictures**
albums, editing, 267–268
backgrounds
deleting from, 70
formatting, 125
bullets, 60
cells, adding, 313
compressing, 269–270
cropping, 25
files formats, 255
formatting, 26–27, 254–260
inserting, 25–26, 69, 70, 214–215
slides, saving as, 244–245
SmartArt, formatting, 105
**pixels, 254**
**placeholders, 4, 7–8**
applying, 344–346
AutoFit, 36, 39
customizing, 215–216
formatting, 39–40

modifying, 39–40
selecting, 31
**points, deleting bullets, 60–61**
**portrait orientation, 19, 21–22**
**positioning Clip Art, 68–69**
**PowerPoint Web App, 355, 356–357**
**preparing**
  broadcast services, 360–361
  slide shows, 185–192
**presentations, 4**
  accessibility, 242–247, 356
  Broadcast Slide Show dialog box, 361–362
  checking spelling, 9
  closing, 9
  comments, 225–230
  comparing, 225–227
  customizing, 334–340
  distributing, 199–207
  Excel data
    inserting, 168–169
    linking, 169–170
  finalizing, 196, 365
  fonts, replacing, 337–338
  guidelines, 51–52
  inspecting, 356
  looping, 190–191
  multimedia, 133–140, 261–267
  navigating, 4–5
  online, viewing, 43–46
  opening, 6
  passwords, applying, 364–365
  printing, 16
  properties, 236–241
    editing, 237–238
    viewing, 236–237
  publishing, 333–370
  reviewing, 193–198
  saving, 5–6
  sections, formatting, 284–286
  security, 364–367
  sharing, 355–356
  slides. *See also* slides
    annotating, 188
    controlling, 187
  starting, 5
  templates, formatting, 167

videos
  controlling, 136–137
  embedding, 262
**printing presentations, 16**
**promoting text, 334, 335**
**properties, presentations, 236–241**
  editing, 237–238
  viewing, 236–237
**protecting presentations, 364–367**
**publishing**
  presentations, 333–370
  slides, 204–205

**R**
**Reading view, 44**
**rearranging slides, 48**
**recoloring pictures, 255**
**Redo, applying, 33**
**rehearsing timings, 188–189**
**removing.** *See* **deleting**
**renaming presentation sections, 285**
**reordering**
  animation, 276
  diagram content, 103
**replacing**
  fonts, 337–338
  text, 30–31, 350–351
**Research task pane, 350, 351–352**
**resetting slide backgrounds, 125–126**
**resizing**
  Clip Art, 68–69
  shapes in diagrams, 102–103
  tables, 306
  text boxes, 346–347
**resolution, 267**
**reusing slides, 20, 123–124**
**reviewing**
  comments, 227–228
  presentations, 193–198
**rows, 302**
  adding, 303
  distributing, 302
  height, modifying, 305
**rulers, 80–81, 341**
**running**
  Compatibility Checkers, 242–243, 356

Package Presentation for CD feature, 200–201
presentations, looping, 190–191
slide shows, 180–184

## S

**saving**
  presentations, 5–6
  slides as pictures, 244–245
**scaling objects, 25, 26–27**
**ScreenTips, creating, 291**
**searching**
  fonts, 338
  text, 350–351
**sections, formatting, 284–286, 336**
**security, presentations, 364–367**
**selecting**
  information sources, 52
  layouts, 345
  placeholders, 31
  slides, 13
  text, 31
**sending presentations for review, 194**
**servers, SharePoint, 355**
**services, broadcast, 360**
**shading**
  cells, 312
  tables, 310
**Shape Effects, 79**
**shapes**
  diagrams
    adding, 102–103
    deleting, 102–103
    resizing, 102–103
  drawing, 81
  effects, applying, 84
  inserting, 214
  moving, 82
  sizing, 82
  styles, applying, 84–85
  text, adding to, 85
**Shape Styles, 79**
**SharePoint, 355**
**sharing presentations, 355–356**
**signatures, digital, 364, 365–366**
**sizing**
  AutoFit, 36, 39

  cells, 305–306
  fonts, 32
  shapes, 82
  slides, 21–22
  tables, 305–306
  text boxes, 346–347
**Slide Masters, 60**
  advanced features, 212–217
  applying, 158–165
  bullets, modifying, 63–64
  customizing, 160–161
  handouts, 163
  inserting, 212–213
  layouts, 162
  navigating, 159
  notes, 163
**slides.** *See also* **presentations**
  active, 12
  advance timing, 51, 128
  annotating, 188
  arranging, 47–50
  backgrounds, resetting, 125–126
  content, creating, 334–336
  controlling, 187
  copying, 47–48
  deleting, 47–48
  duplicating, 47–48
  existing objects, adding to, 322–323
  formatting, 12
  hiding, 186
  inserting, 12–13
  layouts, 4, 13
  linking, 182
  moving, 336
  navigating, 14
  objects, copying, 324
  outlines, creating from, 121–123
  pictures, saving as, 244–245
  publishing, 204–205
  rearranging, 48
  reusing, 20, 123–124
  sizing, 21–22
  tables, adding, 302–303
  text, animating, 277–278
  timing, 53
  transitions, adding, 51–53

viewing, 352

**slide shows**
broadcasting, 201–202
Broadcast Slide Show dialog box, 361–362
customizing, 189–190
preparing, 185–192
running, 180–184

**Slide Sorter view, 48**

**SmartArt, 100**
animations, applying to, 130
diagrams, formatting, 100–102

**snapping, 79**

**sounds**
formatting, 264–265
inserting, 137–138

**spacing**
lines, modifying, 37
paragraphs, modifying, 38

**speaker notes, adding, 21**

**special effect guidelines, 51–52**

**special indents, 341**

**spelling, checking, 9**

**stacks, objects, 88–89**

**starting presentations, 5**

**stops, tabs, 341, 342–344**

**styles**
backgrounds, modifying, 116–117
bulleted lists, 61–63
diagrams, modifying, 104
images, 257
modifying, 32
pictures, formatting, 26–27
shapes, applying, 84–85
SmartArt, 100
tables, 310–311
themes, modifying, 118
videos, applying, 136
WordArt, applying, 95–96

**symbols, 73**
bullets, deleting, 60–61
inserting, 73–74

**T**

**tables**
adding, 302–303
drawing, 302–309

formatting, 142–144, 310–317
handles, 302
inserting, 141–142
modifying, 142–144, 302–309
resizing, 306
shading, 310
sizing, 305–306
styles, 310–311

**tabs**
clearing, 344
Outline, 334–336
stops, 341, 342–344

**targets, 290**

**task panes, Clip Art, 70**

**templates**
customizing, 173–179
formatting, 175
linking, 166–173
presentations, formatting, 167
Slide Master, 60, 63–64

**text**
adding, 268–269, 335
aligning, 36–37, 302, 306–307, 346–347
animating, 277–278
AutoFit, 36, 39, 341
copying, 38
demoting, 334, 335
direction, 346–347
entering, 7–8
expanding, 334
finding, 30–31
first-time indents, 341
fonts, replacing, 337–338
formatting, 30–35, 32–33
modifying, 32, 335
moving, 38
promoting, 334, 335
replacing, 30–31, 350–351
searching, 350–351
selecting, 31
shapes, adding to, 85
WordArt, applying, 95–96

**text boxes, 73**
applying, 344–346
formatting, 75–76
inserting, 75–76

multiple columns, applying, 76–77
**themes, 4**
   adding, 337
   applying, 8–9, 336–337
   colors, modifying, 117–118
   customizing, 173–179
   fonts, formatting, 118
   formatting, 173, 174–175
   modifying, 116
   styles, modifying, 118
**timelines, animation, 279–280**
**timing**
   advance slide, 53
   animation, 278–279
   rehearsing, 188–189
   slides, 51, 128
**tools, Eraser, 304**
**transitions, 51–53, 128**
**transparencies, graphics, 255–256**
**trendlines, 317**
   adding, 318
   modifying, 318
**triggering embedded sounds, 265**
**trimming videos, 264**
**types of diagrams, 104**

**U**
**Undo, applying, 33**

**V**
**vector images, 254**
**videos**
   colors, modifying, 136

customizing, 263–264
   editing, 135
   embedding, 262
   formatting, 203
   inserting, 134–135
   presentations, controlling, 136–137
   styles, applying, 136
**viewing**
   advanced properties, 238–239
   black and white, 352
   grayscale, 352
   presentations
      online, 43–46
      properties, 236–237
   slides, 352
   Web presentations, 361–362
**views**
   Normal, 4, 6–7
   Reading, 44
   Slide Sorter, 48

**W**
**Web presentations, viewing, 361–362**
**Web videos, embedding, 262**
**width, modifying columns, 305**
**Windows Live SkyDrive, 355**
**WordArt**
   formatting, 94–95, 96–97
   inserting, 96–97
   styles, applying, 95–96
**Word handouts, exporting, 231–235**
**worksheets, 169–170.** *See also* Excel data